CW01117852

MAKING THE LAW EXPLICIT

Legal argumentation consists in the interpretation of texts. Therefore, it has a natural connection to the philosophy of language. Central issues of this connection, however, lack a clear answer. For instance, how much freedom do judges have in applying the law? How are the literal and the purposive approaches related to one another? How can we distinguish between applying the law and making the law?

This book provides answers by means of a complex and detailed theory of literal meaning. A new legal method is introduced, namely the further development of the law. It is so far unknown in Anglo-American jurisprudence, but it is shown that this new method helps in solving some of the most crucial puzzles in jurisprudence.

At its centre the book addresses legal indeterminism and refutes linguistic-philosophical reasons for indeterminacy. It spells out the normative character of interpretation as emphasised by Raz and, with the help of Robert Brandom's normative pragmatics, it is shown that the relativism of interpretation from a normative perspective does not at all justify scepticism. On the contrary, it supports the claim that legal argumentation can be objective, and maintains that statements on the meaning of a statute can be right or wrong, and take on inter-subjective validity accordingly.

This book breaks new ground in transferring Brandom's philosophy to legal theoretical problems and presents an original and exciting analysis of the semantic argument in legal argumentation. It was the recipient of the European Award for Legal Theory in 2002.

European Academy of Legal Theory Series: Volume 7

EUROPEAN ACADEMY OF LEGAL THEORY
MONOGRAPH SERIES

General Editors
Professor Mark Van Hoecke
Professor François Ost
Professor Luc Wintgens

Titles in this Series
Moral Conflict and Legal Reasoning
Scott Veitch

The Harmonisation of European Private Law
edited by Mark Van Hoecke & Francois Ost

On Law and Legal Reasoning
Fernando Atria

Law as Communication
Mark Van Hoecke

Legisprudence
edited by Luc Wintgens

Epistemology and Methodology of Comparative Law
edited by Mark van Hoecke

The Policy of Law
A Legal Theoretical Framework
Mauro Zamboni

Making the Law Explicit

The Normativity of Legal Argumentation

Matthias Klatt

HART
PUBLISHING

OXFORD AND PORTLAND, OREGON
2008

Published in North America (US and Canada) by
Hart Publishing
c/o International Specialized Book Services
920 NE 58th Avenue, Suite 300
Portland, OR 97213–3786
USA
Tel: +1 503 287 3093 or toll-free: (1) 800 944 6190
Fax: +1 503 280 8832
E-mail: orders@isbs.com
Website: www.isbs.com

© Matthias Klatt 2008

Matthias Klatt has asserted his right under the Copyright, Designs and Patents Act 1988, to be identified as the author of this work.

All rights reserved. No part of this publication may be reproduced, stored in a retrieval system, or transmitted, in any form or by any mean, without the prior permission of Hart Publishing, or as expressly permitted by law or under the terms agreed with the appropriate reprographic rights organisation. Enquiries concerning reproduction which may not be covered by the above should be addressed to Hart Publishing at the address below.

Hart Publishing, 16C Worcester Place, Oxford, OX1 2JW
Telephone: +44 (0)1865 517530 Fax: +44 (0)1865 510710
E-mail: mail@hartpub.co.uk
Website: http://www.hartpub.co.uk

British Library Cataloguing in Publication Data
Data Available

ISBN-13: 978-1-84113-491-8

Typeset by Columns Design Ltd, Reading
Printed and bound in Great Britain by
CPI Antony Rowe, Chippenham

The sense of a sentence—one would like to say—may, of course, leave this or that open, but the sentence must nevertheless have a definite sense. An indefinite sense—that would really not be a sense at all. Here one thinks perhaps: if I say 'I have locked the man up fast in the room—there is only one door left open'—then I simply haven't locked him in at all; his being locked in is a sham. One would be inclined to say here: 'You haven't done anything at all'. An enclosure with a hole in it is as good as none.—But is that true?

(Wittgenstein, Philosophical Investigations, § 99)

Preface

This book is the English translation of a German monograph (Matthias Klatt (2004), *Theorie der Wortlautgrenze. Semantische Normativität in der juristischen Argumentation*, Baden-Baden, Nomos). For the purposes of this edition, the introduction was added and the first and third chapters were slightly shortened. The German book had benefited from the inspiring advice of Professor Dr. Dr. h. c. Robert Alexy (University of Kiel) and Professor Dr. Ralf Dreier (University of Göttingen) as well as from the long lasting support by the German National Academic Foundation. It received the European Award for Legal Theory 2002.

This edition was made possible by generous support from the Warden and Fellows of New College, the Young Academy and Hart Publishing. The translation was provided with great care and skill by Jörg Rampacher and Neil Mussett. It further profited from most valuable advice by Professor Dr. Dres. h. c. Stanley L. Paulson (Washington University, St. Louis).

To all these people and institutions I owe my profound thanks.

New College, Oxford
July 2008
Matthias Klatt

Table of Contents

Preface — vii

Introduction — 1

I. The Doctrine of the Limits of the Wording — 4
   A. Interpretation as a Legal Method — 4
   B. Judicial Development of the Law — 5
   C. Why the Differentiation Matters — 6

II. Interpretation and Invention in English Legal Reasoning — 7
   A. Statutory Interpretation and Democracy — 7
      (i) The Purposive Versus the Literal Approach — 7
      (ii) Law-Applying Versus Law-Making — 9
      (iii) The Missing Method: Judicial Development of the Law — 12
   B. Human Rights Act: What Is Possible? — 13
   C. Result — 14

III. Towards a Common European Approach — 15

IV. The Possibility of the Rule of Law Defended — 18

V. The Sceptical Challenge: Indeterminacy and Vagueness — 19
   A. The Concept of Indeterminacy — 20
   B. Vagueness as Boundarylessness — 20
      (i) Higher-order Vagueness — 21
      (ii) The Significance of Interpretation in the Law — 22
   C. Scepticism in Law — 22

VI. The Rationality and Objectivity of Legal Reasoning — 23
   A. Justification, Rationality and Legitimacy — 24
   B. The Dworkin–Fish Controversy — 25
   C. 'B' Semantics versus 'KP' Semantics — 26
   D. The Objectivity of Law Defended — 27

VII. At a Glance — 27
   A. General Approach — 27
   B. Chapter 1 — 28
   C. Chapter 2 — 29
   D. Chapter 3 — 31

x *Table of Contents*

Chapter 1: The Doctrine of the Limits of the Wording　　33

I. The Limits of the Wording in Hermeneutic Legal Theory　　33
　A. The Reception of Ontological Hermeneutics in Legal Theory　　33
　　(i) The Limits of the Wording and Pre-Judgements　　35
　　　(a) Ontological Prerequisites for the Understanding of Normative Texts　　35
　　　(b) Significance for the Application of Law in General　　36
　　　(c) Significance for the Limits of the Wording　　37
　　(ii) Limits of the Wording and Typology　　40
　　(iii) The Limits of the Wording and the Analogicity of Language　　42
　B. Hermeneutics and Legal Interpretation　　43

II. The Limits of the Wording in Analytic Legal Theory　　44
　A. The Clarification of the Limits of the Wording by Koch, Rüßmann, and Herberger　　44
　　(i) Establishing and Assigning Meaning　　45
　　(ii) Classification of Unclear Usage Rules　　46
　　　(a) Ambiguity　　47
　　　(b) Inconsistency　　47
　　　(c) Vagueness　　48
　　(iii) The Limits of the Wording According to Koch, Rüßmann, and Herberger　　48
　B. The Role of the Limits of the Wording in Alexy's Theory of Legal Argumentation　　50
　　(i) The Discursive Character of Interpretation　　50
　　(ii) Main Features of the Theory of Legal Argumentation　　51
　　　(a) Internal Justification and the Word Usage Rule　　51
　　　(b) External Justification and Semantic Arguments　　52

III. The Deconstructivistic Challenge of the Structuring Legal Theory　　54
　A. Basic Premises of Structuring Legal Theory　　54
　B. Criticism of New Hermeneutics　　56
　C. Criticism of the Theory of Legal Reasoning According to Koch and Rüßmann　　56
　D. Criticism of Alexy's Theory of Legal Argumentation　　58
　E. Structuring Legal Theory and the Limits of the Wording　　59
　　(i) The Limits of the Wording as a Result of the Concretisation of Rules　　59
　　(ii) Binding Effects of Legal Culture　　60
　　(iii) The Limits of the Wording as the Limits of the Normative Program　　62
　　(iv) The Role of the Limits of the Normative Program　　63

	F.	Structuring Legal Theory—Summary	63
IV.	The Results of the First Chapter		64
	A.	State of Research	64
		(i) The Hermeneutic Position	65
		(a) Pre-Judgements and Typology	65
		(b) Arguments in Support of the Hermeneutic Position	65
		(1) Argument of Ontological Hermeneutics	65
		(2) Argument of Analogicity	66
		(3) Argument of Procedural Correctness	66
		(4) Argument of Normative Necessity	66
		(ii) The Analytic Position	66
		(a) Establishing and Assigning Meaning	66
		(b) Arguments for the Analytic Viewpoint	67
		(1) Argument of Clear Cases	67
		(2) Argument of the Empirical Discernibility of Meaning	67
		(3) Argument of Possible Corrections	68
		(iii) The Structuring Legal Theory Position	68
		(a) Putting Rules in Specific Terms and the Limits of the Normative Program	68
		(b) Arguments in Support of Structuring Legal Theory	68
		(1) Argument of the Indefiniteness of the Legal Text	68
		(2) Argument of Legal Culture	68
		(iv) Arguments Against the Limits of the Wording	69
		(a) Argument of Practical Ineffectiveness	69
		(b) Argument of Necessary Failure	69
		(c) Argument of the Lacking Normative Necessity	69
		(d) Argument of Reversal	69
		(e) The Language Game Argument	70
		(1) Argument of Openness	70
		(2) Argument of Innovation	70
		(3) Argument of Context Dependency	70
		(4) Argument of Circularity	70
		(f) Argument that Meaning Remains Unclarified	71
		(1) Argument of Objectivism	71
		(2) Argument of Features Semantics	71
		(3) Argument of the Incorrect Reception of the Speech Act Theory	71
		(4) Argument of Excessive Commitment	71
		(5) Argument of the Impossibility of the Empirical Determination of Meaning	71
	B.	Criticism	72
		(i) Analytic Versus Post-Positivistic Legal Theory	72

xii *Table of Contents*

(ii) A Critical Look at Structuring Legal Theory		73
(a) The Basic Norm		74
(b) Circularity		75
(c) Normal and Exceptional Cases		76
(d) Commitment to the Majority Opinion		77
(e) Inconsistency		78
(f) Concluding Remarks		79
(iii) Controversial Issues		81

Chapter 2: Normativity and Objectivity of Linguistic Meaning 87

I. Introduction 87
   A. Meaning Scepticism and the Indeterminacy Thesis 87
   B. Meaning as a Problem of the Philosophy of Language 89
   C. Language-Philosophical Theories of Meaning 90
      (i) Classification in Categories 91
         (a) Referent, Idea, and Behaviour 91
         (b) Realism and Anti-Realism 93
         (c) Functions of Language 94
      (ii) Significance for the Limits of the Wording 94
   D. An Integrative Theory of Meaning 94

II. The Normativity of Linguistic Meaning 96
   A. The Concept of Semantic Normativity 96
      (i) The General Thesis of Normativity 96
      (ii) The Three Conditions for Normativity Theories 98
         (a) The Condition of Anti-Reductionist Supervenience 98
         (b) The Condition of Internality 99
         (c) The Condition of Possible Semantic Mistakes 100
      (iii) Four Strategies of Arguing Semantic Normativity 100
         (a) Normativity and Truth 101
         (b) Normativity and Internal Relation 103
         (c) Normativity and Rationality 104
         (d) Normativity and Regularity 106
            (1) Semantic Normativity According to the Rule Model 106
            (2) Objection of the Analytic Priority of Individualism 107
            (3) Objection of the Incoherence of Prescriptivity and Constitutivity 109
      (iv) Normativity and Connection Thesis 114
   B. Brandom's Linguistic Normativity 115
      (i) Normative Pragmatics 117
         (a) Anthropologic Basis and Implicit Normativity 117

			(b) Normative Attitudes and Sanctions	119
			(c) Result: Principle of Instituting Norms through Social Practice	122
		(ii)	Inferential Semantics	122
			(a) The Pragmatic Priority of Propositional Meaning	122
			(b) Meaning and Material Inference	123
			(c) Result: The Principle of the Normative Significance of Conceptual Systems	125
		(iii)	Interlocking Normative Pragmatics and Inferential Semantics in a Discursive Practice Model	126
			(a) Commitment and Entitlement as Deontic Statuses	127
			(b) Three Types and Three Dimensions of Inferential Structure	129
			(c) The Deontic Score-keeping Model	131
			(d) Propositional Meaning in Discursive Practice	133
		(iv)	Theory of the Meaning of Subsentential Expressions	134
			(a) Substitution	135
			(b) Anaphora	139
			(c) Results of the Theory of the Meaning of Subsentential Expressions	140
	C.	Objections against the Theory of Normativity		141
		(i)	Kripke's Theory of Rule-Following	142
			(a) Kripke's Sceptical Paradox	142
			(b) Kripke's Sceptical Solution	145
			(c) Criticism	145
			(1) Normativity and Agreement	146
			(2) Naturalism, Reductionism, and Regress	147
		(ii)	The Objection of Semantic Holism	151
			(a) The Doctrine of Semantic Holism	151
			(b) WVO Quine's Two Dogmas of Empiricism	152
			(c) Criticism	156
			(1) The Central Chains of Argument	157
			(2) Reversibility and the Status of Logical Laws	158
			(3) Dummett's Argument of the Possibility of Communication	165
			(4) Canonical Standards in Moderate Holism	166
		(iii)	The Objection of the Impossibility of Analyticity	167
			(a) Analyticity, Aprioricity, Modality	168
			(b) WVO Quine's *Word and Object*	169
			(c) Criticism	173
			(1) Relativity and Normativity	174
			(2) Analyticity's Triadic Relativity	175
			(3) OLOL Analyticity	179
	D.	Result for the Normativity of Linguistic Meaning		180

xiv *Table of Contents*

III. The Objectivity of Linguistic Meaning	181
A. The Concept of Objectivity	181
B. Objectivity as Reference	183
(i) Reference and Inference	184
(ii) Frege's Analysis of Picking out Objects	185
(iii) Reference and *de re* Ascriptions	187
(iv) Doxastic Gap and Objectivity	189
(v) Reference and Interpersonal Anaphora	191
C. Objectivity as Intersubjectivity	192
(i) The Social Perspectival Character of Conceptual Content	193
(ii) The Paradox of Relative Objectivity	193
D. Objections to the Objectivity Theory	196
(i) Quine's Objection of the Indeterminism of Reference	197
(ii) The Objection of the Special Role Played by Theoretical Terms	197
(iii) Wright's Objection of the Impossibility of a Conventional Objectivity Theory	198
(a) Subjective Attitude and Objective Status	199
(b) The Possibility of Communal Errors	200
(iv) The Objection of Incompatibility	201
(v) The Objection that There Is No Objective World	203
E. Conclusion on the Objectivity of Linguistic Meaning	205
IV. The Results of the Second Chapter	207
A. The Three Dimensions of Linguistic Meaning	207
B. The Universality Challenge	208
C. Scope and Role of Language-Analytical Discourse	208
Chapter 3: Semantic Normativity in the Law	**211**
I. Addressing the Three Central Issues	211
A. Clear and Unclear Cases	212
(i) The Relevance in Legal Theory of the Distinction Between Clear and Unclear Cases	212
(ii) The Concept of the Clear Case	212
(a) Semantic Clarity and Juridical Clarity	212
(b) Constitutive Clarity and Epistemic Clarity	213
(iii) Semantic Clarity in Accordance with the Model of Deontic Scorekeeping	213
(a) Semantic Clarity in the First Inferential Dimension	214
(b) Semantic Clarity in the Second Inferential Dimension	215
(c) Semantic Clarity in the Third Inferential Dimension	215
(d) Result	215
(iv) The Existence of Semantically-Clear Cases	216

		(v) Limitations in Hard Cases	218
		(vi) Result on the First Issue	218
	B.	The Epistemic Openness of the Meaning of Norms	219
		(i) Rejection of the Critical Arguments	220
		(ii) Confirmation of the Argument of Epistemic Openness	222
		(a) Semantic Normativity and Rules for the Use of Words	222
		(b) Semantic Object-Relatedness and the Theory of Meaning of Koch and of Rüßmann	224
		(c) The Objection of the Reification of the Law	226
		(iii) Result on the Second Issue	227
	C.	The Objectivity of the Meaning of Norms	229
	D.	Result Regarding the Three Central Issues	229
II.	The Theory of the Limits of the Wording		230
	A.	The Relationship Between Semantic Clarity and Semantically-Unclear Meaning	230
	B.	The Limits of the Wording with Constitutive Semantic Clarity	231
		(i) The Function of Rules for the Use of Words in the Internal Justification	231
		(ii) Semantic Limits in the First Linguistic Dimension	233
		(a) The Four Limits of Inferential Relations	233
		(1) Conditional Commitment Limit	233
		(2) Conditional Entitlement Limit	236
		(3) Consequential Commitment Limit	238
		(4) Consequential Entitlement Limit	242
		(5) The System and Function of the Inferential Limits	243
		(b) The Inferential Limits at Subsentential Level	248
		(iii) Semantic Limits in the Second Linguistic Dimension	250
		(iv) Semantic Limits in the Third Linguistic Dimension	252
		(v) The System of Semantic Limits	254
	C.	The Limits of the Wording with Constitutive Semantically-Unclear Meaning	255
		(i) The Classification of Semantically-Unclear Cases in Inferential Semantics	256
		(a) The Concept of Vagueness	256
		(b) The Concept of Ambiguity	262
		(c) The Concept of Inconsistency	263
		(d) The Concept of Evaluative Openness	263
		(e) Result on the Classification of Unclear Cases	264
		(ii) Semantic Limits in the Case of Vagueness	265

	(a) Connection Between the Three-Candidate Model and the Model of Rules for the Use of Words	265
	(1) Preliminary Considerations	265
	(2) The Scheme of the Positive Limits of the Wording	267
	(3) The Scheme of the Negative Limits of the Wording	268
	(4) Summary	269
	(b) The System of Semantic Limits with Vagueness	270
	(iii) Semantic Limits with Ambiguity	270
	(iv) Semantic Limits with Evaluatively-Open Concepts	272
D.	Result on the Theory of the Limits of the Wording	273
III. The Results of the Third Chapter		274
A.	Results	274
B.	The Rehabilitation of Semantic Argumentation in the Law	276
C.	The Objectivity of Legal Rulings	278
Bibliography		283
Index		301

Introduction

If the assignment of legislative power to parliament is to be otherwise than fictional, the process of interpretation must be divorced so far as may be from that of legislation.[1]

ANGLO-AMERICAN LEGAL philosophy has long struggled with how to differentiate legislation and adjudication. Traditionally, the judiciary is supposed to interpret and to apply the law rather than invent and make new law, the latter task being exclusively reserved for the legislature. This old ideal of the judges as *'bouche de la loi'* was rigidly adhered to in England, for example, during the 'age of strict literalism', that is, between 1830 and 1950.[2] The judiciary was seen as merely the enforcing agent for decisions already made by the legislature. According to this view, adjudication did not involve any creativity. Rather, it consisted of mere retrieval of the 'fixed' meaning of a norm. This can be called the discovery model of judicial interpretation, in which the accompanying literalist method of legal reasoning exercises near-absolute predominance.

This old ideal, however, was abandoned long ago, and the relevance of literalism has diminished along with it. Nowadays, the inevitability of judicial law-making is widely accepted. This modern understanding of adjudication stems from insights into the indeterminacy of law and the vagueness of language. There is no 'heaven of concepts' from which judges can derive the meaning of norms for particular cases.[3] As interpretation is dependent on reasons, it is necessarily relative to a normative perspective, and therefore entails the possibility of change. These characteristics undermine the notion of interpretation as retrieval.[4]

So far, so good. The problems start when we move beyond this point, and they are alarmingly far-reaching and challenging. Once judicial law-making is accepted, the very foundations of our constitutional order come under attack. Nothing less than the possibility of the rule of law is at stake.

---

[1] ER Hopkins, 'The Literal Canon and the Golden Rule' (1937) 15 *Canadian Bar Review* 689.

[2] EA Driedger, *Driedger on the Construction of Statutes*, 3rd edn (Toronto, 1994) 80; A Lester, 'English Judges as Law Makers' (1993) *Public Law* 269 at 273 fn 22. For a lucid and comprehensive analysis of the age of strict literalism, see S Vogenauer, *Die Auslegung von Gesetzen in England und auf dem Kontinent. Eine vergleichende Untersuchung der Rechtsprechung und ihrer historischen Grundlagen* (Tübingen, 2001) 780–962.

[3] *Cf* HLA Hart, 'Jhering's Heaven of Concepts and Modern Analytical Jurisprudence' in HLA Hart (ed), *Essays in Juriprudence and Philosophy* (Oxford, 1983).

[4] J Raz, 'Interpretation without Retrieval' in A Marmor (ed), *Law and Interpretation. Essays in Legal Philosophy* (Oxford, 1995) 174 f.

2   *Introduction*

Legal indeterminacy needs to be constrained if 'rule of law' values such as stability, predictability and certainty are to amount to more than mere words. Yet it is wholly unclear where such constraints are to be found.

Moreover, the vagueness of language directly affects the claim to correctness which is of necessity inherent in legal reasoning.[5] If propositions on meaning in general are not inter-subjectively valid, how could propositions on the meaning of a norm be so? And if propositions on the meaning of a norm cannot be objective, how then can legal reasoning be so? If propositions in legal reasoning cannot be objective, the latter loses its claim to correctness.

Whenever adjudication fills in the indeterminate contours of legal provisions—especially, but not only, in the context of a constitutional interpretation—it answers questions that in a democracy should be answered by the people or their representatives, not by a judicial elite.[6] So, while on the one hand, the general features of language and reasoning seem to make judicial legislation unavoidable, on the other hand it is vital that democracy provides for limits on this legislative role if one is to avoid reaching highly sceptical conclusions about the law's rationality. Jurisprudence has yet to provide adequate or convincing limits.

This book sets out to tackle this problem. It provides answers to the question of how the indeterminacy of law can be accepted without drawing far-reaching sceptical conclusions about the objectivity and rationality of legal reasoning. It addresses the legitimacy of adjudication.

In evaluating the adequacy of a theory of legal reasoning, two criteria have been suggested as arguably the most important.[7] The first is whether the theory offers an account of how interpretation can be constrained which would amount to an answer to the question of indeterminacy. The second criterion is whether the constraints imposed by a theory of legal reasoning provide a plausible answer to the question of authority.

This book acknowledges the overriding importance of these two criteria, and aims to do justice to them by defending limited or moderate indeterminism. Legal indeterminism can stem from many causes, but among the most prominent is the vagueness of language. This is labelled 'semantic indeterminism' here, indicating that the source of indeterminism is meaning. Thus, linguistic-philosophical reasons for indeterminacy are at the heart of the book. The entire second chapter is devoted to the philosophy of language, and spells out the normative character of interpretation as

---

[5] See R Alexy, 'Law and Correctness' in MDA Freeman (ed), *Current Legal Problems* (Oxford, 1998) 205.

[6] *Cf* F Schauer, 'Judicial Supremacy and the Modest Constitution' (2004) 92 *California Law Review* 1061 f.

[7] N Stoljar, 'Survey Article: Interpretation, Indeterminacy and Authority. Some Recent Controversies in the Philosophy of Law' (2003) 11 *Journal of Political Philosophy* 470 at 494 f.

emphasised by Joseph Raz.[8] With the help of Robert Brandom's normative pragmatics, it is shown that the relativism of interpretation from a normative perspective does not at all justify scepticism. On the contrary, it supports the claim that legal reasoning can be objective. It is maintained here that statements on the meaning of a statute can be right or wrong, and take on inter-subjective validity accordingly. In that respect, this book breaks new ground in applying Brandom's philosophy squarely to theoretical legal problems.

The central constraint on legal interpretation developed in this book relies on a specific doctrine in German legal reasoning, namely the doctrine of the limits of the wording. This book therefore provides a detailed account of, in Lord Steyn's words, 'what meanings the language is capable of letting in'.[9] English readers should be careful to note that this doctrine does *not* maintain that the judge's task ends with the limits of the wording. Rather, the limits of the wording separate two distinct kinds of application of the law, namely interpretation and development of the law. The latter is, as a technical term, unknown in Anglo-American jurisprudence, and it will be argued that this is a serious disadvantage because it generates the inability to solve some of the crucial puzzles in jurisprudence. This book therefore introduces a new and important judicial method to Anglo-American jurisprudence.

The remainder of this introduction explores in some detail the issues mentioned so far. First, it introduces the German concept of the limits of the wording, which plays a predominant role in the book (I). Secondly, the English law-making process is analysed (II). Particular attention is paid to the lack of a clear distinction between interpretation and invention and, most importantly, to the new function of the judiciary under the Human Rights Act 1998. Thus, it will become clear that the German doctrine is much clearer and more precise as to the distinction between interpretation and invention than the English doctrine, and in this respect is superior to it.

The third part anchors the doctrine of the limits of the wording in European legal methodology (III), while the fourth spells out how this doctrine amounts to a significant defence of the possibility of the rule of law (IV). Next, the sceptical challenge of indeterminism and vagueness is addressed, and it is argued that the doctrine of the limits of the wording reduces indeterminism to a negligible level, so that far-reaching sceptical consequences can be avoided (V). Overall, the doctrine of the limits of the wording has important implications for the rationality and objectivity of legal reasoning, as debated by Dworkin, Fish, Stavropoulos and others,

---

[8] *Cf* Raz, 'Interpretation without Retrieval' (n 4 above) 174 f.
[9] J Steyn, 'Does Legal Formalism Hold Sway in England?' (1996) 49 *Current Legal Problems* 42. See also LH Hoffmann, 'The Intolerable Wrestling with Words and Meanings' (1997) 114 *South African Law Journal* 656.

and some of these implications are discussed in a preliminary way (VI). The introduction ends with an overview of the three main chapters of the book (VII).

I. THE DOCTRINE OF THE LIMITS OF THE WORDING

Based on the doctrine of the limits of the wording, the German theory of legal 'argumentation' distinguishes sharply between two sets of methods, namely interpretation (A) and judicial development of the law (B).

A. Interpretation as a Legal Method

Every application of law requires some act of interpretation. In its wide sense 'interpretation', which refers to the simple necessity of some form of understanding, is a ubiquitous and unavoidable feature of every law-applying activity.[10]

Interpretation as a legal method is concerned with 'interpretation in the strict sense', which can be defined as the understanding of a legal text that allows for some doubt with regard to its meaning or proper application. 'Interpretation in the strict sense' begins with a question and ends with a choice between different possible constructions.[11] This choice is made by means of argument, and this establishes a close connection between interpretation and argumentation. This connection has been formulated by Robert Alexy in the shortest possible form: 'Interpretation is argumentation'.[12]

Legal interpretation is distinguished from other types of interpretation by its normative and institutional character.[13] Its normative character stems from the claim to correctness inherent in every proposed interpretation.[14] Its institutional character is rooted in both the authoritative objects of interpretation (statutes, sub-statutory enactments, etc) and the subjects who interpret—most prominently the judiciary.

Methods of interpretation are arguments. Interpretive arguments can be classified in many different ways.[15] German theory of legal argumentation

---

[10] N MacCormick, 'Arguing About Interpretation' in N MacCormick (ed), *Rhetoric and the Rule of Law. A Theory of Legal Reasoning* (Oxford, 2005) 121.
[11] R Alexy, 'Juristische Interpretation' in R Alexy (ed), *Recht, Vernunft, Diskurs. Studien zur Rechtsphilosophie* (Frankfurt am Main, 1995) 73.
[12] *Ibid*, 78.
[13] *Ibid*, 73 f.
[14] R Alexy, *Theorie der juristischen Argumentation. Die Theorie des rationalen Diskurses als Theorie der juristischen Begründung* (Frankfurt am Main, 1978) 264 ff, 428 f; Alexy, 'Law and Correctness' (n 5 above) 205.
[15] *Cf* MacCormick, 'Arguing About Interpretation' (n 10 above) 124 f.

has discussed the so-called canons of interpretation ever since the time of Savigny.[16] Alexy distinguishes between six canons: The semantic argument concerns the linguistic usage of a term; the genetic argument refers to the intention of the legislator; the historical argument uses facts concerning the history of the legal problems under discussion; the comparative argument looks at different legal systems; the systematic argument examines the position of a norm or single term in a legal text; and the teleological argument considers the purpose, aims and goals of a legal norm.[17]

B. Judicial Development of the Law

The defining characteristic of judicial interpretation is that all canons can be considered only within the outer boundaries of 'the limits of the wording'. As soon as an application of a legal norm cannot be reconciled with its wording, this application is not an interpretation but rather a further development of the law. Therefore, semantic limits enable the separation between the interpretation of the law and the further development of the law.[18] Every application of a statute within the scope of the possible meaning of its wording is interpretation. Every application beyond this is a development of the law. Such developments of the law are either analogies, which extend application beyond the scope of the possible meaning, or teleological reductions, which constrict the application to a smaller scope than the meaning allows.[19] This is known as 'reading in' and 'reading down', respectively, in English legal methodology.

Every interpretation changes the law and, in that sense, develops it.[20] This is development in the broad sense, from which we have to distinguish development in the narrow sense.[21] The latter's characteristic is that the decision is not within the semantic limits of the wording of a statute.

---

[16] FK von Savigny, *System des heutigen römischen Rechts. Band 1* (Berlin, 1840) 212 ff.
[17] R Alexy, *A Theory of Legal Argumentation. The Theory of Rational Discourse as Theory of Legal Justification* (Oxford, 1989) 234–44.
[18] See K Engisch and T Würtenberger, *Einführung in das juristische Denken*, 9th edn (Stuttgart, 1997) 100 n 47; H-J Koch and H Rüßmann, *Juristische Begründungslehre. Eine Einführung in die Grundprobleme der Rechtswissenschaft* (München, 1982) 182; K Larenz and C-W Canaris, *Methodenlehre der Rechtswissenschaft*, 3rd edn (Berlin, 1995) 143. Most unclear is BVerfGE 35, 263 (278 f): 'The judges do not have to stop at the wording of a norm. Their binding to the statute (Art 20 III, Art 97 I Basic Law) does not mean a binding to its letter, implying a strict literal rule, but a binding to the spirit and the purpose of the law. Interpretation is a means by which judges explore the content of a legal norm with regard to its place in the whole legal system, without being restricted by the formal wording of the statute'. (Translated by MK) Equally unclear is BVerwGE 40, 78 (81).
[19] For these and two additional subdivisions (extinction and creation of a norm), see Alexy, 'Juristische Interpretation' (n 11 above) 91.
[20] *Cf* TAO Endicott, *Vagueness in Law* (Oxford, 2000) 179 f on a similar distinction.
[21] Alexy, 'Juristische Interpretation' (n 11 above) 91.

It is important to note that the doctrine of the limits of the wording does not mean sticking to strict textualism. Textualism equates the literal meaning of a statute with its only significant meaning.[22] In stark contrast, the German doctrine, although arguing for a rehabilitation of the semantic argument in legal interpretation, introduces development as a distinct legal method, which allows for far-reaching activity on the part of the judges. It has long been established that the limits of the wording do not constitute the limits of judicial activity.[23] The German Federal Constitutional Court accepted development as a distinct method of legal argumentation in its famous 'Princess Soraya' case.

> Justice is not identical with the aggregate of the written laws. Under certain circumstances law can exist beyond the positive norms which the state enacts ... The judge's task is not confined to ascertaining and implementing legislative decisions. He/she may have to make a value judgement (an act which necessarily has volitional elements); that is, bring to light and implement in his/her decisions those value concepts which are inherent in the constitutional legal order, but which are not, or not adequately, expressed in the language of the written laws ... Where the written law fails, the judge's decision fills the existing gap by using common sense and general concepts of justice established by the community.[24]

All this means that in German doctrine, interpretations that are impossible on the basis of the wording are not necessarily ruled out. Rather, they may be admissible as 'further development of the law'.

C. Why the Differentiation Matters

One could assume, then, that the distinction between interpretation and development was merely a matter of labelling and categorising different judicial activities. In fact, many legal systems do not sharply distinguish judicial development from interpretation. However, this differentiation is extremely important, for both constitutional and methodological reasons.[25]

Apart from these reasons, there is one important link to the limits of the judiciary that should be spelled out here. The limits of the judiciary (regardless of how its activities might be labelled) matter for obvious

---

[22] On textualism, see Stoljar, 'Survey Article: Interpretation, Indeterminacy and Authority' (n 7 above) 480.
[23] BVerfGE 34, 269; 35, 263; 49, 304; 65, 182; 71, 354; 82, 6.
[24] BVerfGE 34, 269 (Soraya) at 287. Cf DP Kommers, *The Constitutional Jurisprudence of the Federal Republic of Germany*, 2nd edn (Durham NC, 1997) 125.
[25] See p 18 below. Zimmermann is therefore mistaken in maintaining that the distinction was a 'disputed though practically irrelevant question'; see R Zimmermann, 'Statuta Sunt Stricte Interpretanda? Statutes and the Common Law: A Continental Perspective' (1997) 56 *Cambridge Law Journal* 321.

reasons. These limits are indirectly addressed when judicial development is defined, and it is precisely this indirect connection that makes it so important to distinguish development from mere interpretation. Directly, the doctrine of the limits of the wording does not concern the *limits* of development, but the *concept* of it. The doctrine clarifies by means of conceptual arguments when legal reasoning leaves the realm of interpretation and must be classified as a distinct form of legal reasoning, namely 'development'. However, clarifying the *concept* of development has significant implications for clarifying its *limits*. Defining the entry into development as a legal method enables us to clarify the exit as well. The limits of development, and thus the limits of the judiciary, are dependent on a clear concept of development. Thus, the limits of the wording indirectly help us to analyse the limits of the judiciary more clearly.

II. INTERPRETATION AND INVENTION IN ENGLISH LEGAL REASONING

A. Statutory Interpretation and Democracy

Two central issues lack a clear answer in English theory of legal reasoning. First, the relation between the literal and the purposive approaches in statutory interpretation (i); secondly, the relation between applying the law and making the law (ii). The solutions which have been proposed so far are imprecise. A clearer and more satisfactory answer to both problems can be found in the doctrine of the limits of the wording (iii).

(i) The Purposive Versus the Literal Approach

Statutory interpretation consists of the construction and application of provisions adopted by legislatures.[26] One of the most crucial issues related to this activity is how much weight to attach to the purposes as opposed to the wording of particular provisions. This issue is closely related to the rule of law. For American textualists, for example, statements of purpose tend to be vague and encourage judges to follow their own policy views under the guise of 'discovering' the legislator's 'intent'.[27] These scholars, then, emphasise the priority of the text in order to delimit judicial discretion.

---

[26] Cf K Greenawalt, 'Constitutional and Statutory interpretation' in JL Coleman, S Shapiro and KE Himma (eds), *The Oxford Handbook of Jurisprudence and Philosophy of Law* (Oxford, 2002) 271.
[27] A Scalia, *A Matter of Interpretation. Federal Courts and the Law. An Essay* (Princeton NJ, 1997) 18–23.

8 *Introduction*

Contrary to the conventional view,[28] English law is not based on extreme textualism. This view applies only to the age of strict literalism (1830–50).[29] The leading idea of this age is expressed in Lord Halsbury's statement that the draftsman of a statute was the worst person in the world to interpret a statute because he was likely to be unconsciously influenced by what he meant rather than by what he had said.[30] Nowadays, English judges are no longer prepared to follow plain meanings if they lead to a manifest injustice.[31] The purposive approach has been on the rise since the mid-twentieth century:

> The days have long passed when the courts adopted a strict constructionist view of interpretation which required them to adopt the literal meaning of the language. The court now adopts a purposive approach.[32]

Under this regime of *telos*, the words of the statute have only prima facie primacy, which is relatively weak. The following quotation from Lord Clyde illustrates how, according to the purposive approach, although the words of the statute are taken as a starting point, they are subject to amendments, extensions or restrictions:

> My Lords, it is an elementary rule in the interpretation and the application of statutory provisions that it is to the words of the legislation that attention must primarily be directed. Generally it will be the ordinary meaning of the words which will require to be adopted. On appropriate occasion it may be proper as a matter of interpretation to adopt extended meanings to words or phrases, particularly if thereby the purpose of the legislation can be best effected or the validity of the legislation preserved. On other occasions it may be appropriate to adopt a strict or narrow meaning of the language used.[33]

---

[28] See Vogenauer, *Die Auslegung von Gesetzen in England und auf dem Kontinent* (n 2 above) 5–11 with many further references.
[29] Even in this period, the literal rule was applied in a differentiated manner rather than mechanically, *cf ibid* 798–844.
[30] *Hilder v Dexter* [1902] AC 474 (HL) 477.
[31] 'If the precise words used are plain and unambiguous, in our judgment, we are bound to them in their ordinary sense, even though it do [sic] lead, in our view of the case, to an absurdity or manifest injustice'. *Abley v Dale* (1851) 11 CB 378, 391.
[32] *Pepper v Hart* [1993] AC 593 (HL) 617.
[33] *Murray v Foyle Meats Ltd* [1993] 3 WLR 356 (HL) 360. *Cf Re British Concrete Pipe Association* [1983] 1 All ER 203 at 205 (Donaldson MR): 'Our task ... is to construe the 1969 Act, and in so doing, the prima facie rule is that words have their ordinary meaning. But that is subject to the qualification that if, giving words their ordinary meaning, we are faced with extraordinary results which cannot have been intended by Parliament, we then have to move on to a second stage in which we re-examine the words and see whether they must in all the circumstances have been intended by Parliament to have a different meaning or a more restricted meaning'.

The main problem with these considerations is that the issue is totally unresolved as to which criteria determine whether there is 'appropriate occasion' to depart from the words, and, if so, in what direction the departure should take place.

Moreover, the predominance of the literal rule has not yet waned as much as one would infer from the above statement by Lord Clyde. Although the courts have extended statutory provisions explicitly beyond the wording since the 1980s,[34] numerous cases show that the literal approach is 'still alive and flourishing'.[35] Most remarkably, the House of Lords is still reluctant to extend statutory provisions beyond their wording, as the following example from 1998 demonstrates:

> It may be perfectly proper to adopt even a strained construction to enable the object and purpose of legislation to be fulfilled. But it cannot be taken to the length of applying unnatural meanings to familiar words or of so stretching the language that its former shape is transformed into something which is not only significantly different but has a name of its own. This must particularly be so where the language has no evident ambiguity or uncertainty about it.[36]

What matters here is that English legal reasoning theory has no criteria that determine where an admissible 'strained construction' ends and where a transformation into a 'significantly different shape' begins. Overall, the inconsistent practice of the courts nowadays shows a serious lack of both orientation and legal certainty. English legal doctrine and the courts oscillate unpredictably between the literal and the purposive approaches.

(ii) Law-Applying Versus Law-Making

The literal approach usually rests on the honourable, yet most unconvincing, attempt to completely separate law-applying and law-making, as the following quotation from Lord Brougham illustrates:

> If we depart from the plain and obvious meaning on account of such views, we in truth do not construe the Act but alter it ... are really making the law and not interpreting it.[37]

This view of a complete separation is based on the discovery model of judicial interpretation, which restricts the judiciary to retrieving the law

---

[34] Vogenauer, *Die Auslegung von Gesetzen in England und auf dem Kontinent* (n 2 above) 1014, with further reference in n 366.

[35] M Zander, *The Law-Making Process*, 6th edn (Cambridge, 2004) 146 f with regard to *Shah v Barnet London Borough Council* [1983] 1 All ER 226; *Griffith v Secretary of State for the Environment* [1983] 2 WLR 172; *Reynolds* [1981] 3 All ER 849, *Lees v Secretary of State for Social Services* [1985] 2 All ER 203; *R v Broadcast Complaints Commission, ex p Owen* [1985] 2 All ER 522.

[36] *Clarke v Kato* [1998] 1 WLR 1647 (HL) 1655 (Lord Clyde).

[37] *Gwynne v Burnell* (1840) 6 Bing NC 453 at 561.

10 Introduction

and denies it the authority to change it, since that authority lies exclusively with the legislature. As was shown earlier, both the discovery model and the complete separation thesis have now become part of the history of ideas. It is widely acknowledged today that judges *make* law. Yet scholars still stick to the old ideal:

> When judges *interpret* the law, they often have to rely on considerations about that which the law is there to settle, yet—within certain *limits*—they can still be said to be following the law, not *inventing* it.[38]

> The question whether there is scope for substantive disagreement in law runs parallel to the question of the *limits of law*, once put in terms of fidelity (to the law) versus repair (of it), and more recently in terms of *interpretation versus invention*.[39]

Throughout jurisprudence, there is a desperate search for the 'limits of interpretation'.[40] Even the classical acknowledgement of the inseparability of law-making and law-applying is immediately followed by, and indeed more noted for, a statement of limitation:

> I recognise without hesitation that judges do and must legislate, but they can do so only interstitially; they are confined from molar to molecular motions.[41]

On the basis that judges do 'legislate', viz change and develop the law, the problem of separation is still vital. When does a judgment belong to the category of 'molecular motion', and when does it become a 'molar motion'? When does a judgment fill the interstices of the existing fabric of the law, and when does it change that fabric itself? Anglo-American jurisprudence does not provide satisfactory answers to these questions. This is alarming, as any sensible adherence to the distinction between law-applying and law-making indeed requires an answer to these questions; otherwise it must be abandoned.

Symptomatic of this worrying lack of clarity in Anglo-American jurisprudence is its unsound position on the analogy. While English courts are increasingly prepared to extend statutory provisions beyond their wordings,[42] the classical view that the filling of gaps amounts to a naked

---

[38] A Marmor, *Interpretation and Legal Theory*, 2nd edn (Oxford, 2005) 122.
[39] N Stavropoulos, *Objectivity in Law* (Oxford, 1996) 127.
[40] M Stone, 'Focusing the Law: What Legal Interpretation Is Not' in A Marmor (ed), *Law and Interpretation. Essays in Legal Philosophy* (Oxford 1995) 34–43. See, however, Hart's postscript: 'It will not matter for any practical purpose whether in so deciding cases [ie by making the best moral judgement, MK] the judge is making law in accordance with morality ... or alternatively is guided by his moral judgements as to what already existing law is revealed by a moral test for law'. HLA Hart, *The Concept of Law*, 2nd edn (Oxford, 1994) 254.
[41] *Southern Pacific Company v Jenson* (1917) 244 US 205 at 221.
[42] See Vogenauer, *Die Auslegung von Gesetzen in England und auf dem Kontinent* (n 2 above) 1014 fn 366.

usurpation of the function of the legislature 'under the thin disguise of interpretation'[43] is still alive. In *Clarke v Kato*, the House of Lords dismissed the analogy because such an extension was the task of the legislature.[44]

These contradictory statements illustrate that it is still an unsettled issue whether judges should be authorised to fill gaps by means of analogies. Moreover, Anglo-American jurisprudence does not provide precise criteria for distinguishing extensive interpretation from judicial law-making.[45] Gummow, for example, dedicates a separate section to 'analogy', yet does not separate it clearly from interpretation, as his phrase 'analogical interpretation' indicates.[46] Lücke maintains that the distinction between analogy and extension is 'useful and indeed necessary', but at the same time claims that extensions beyond the letter amount to interpretation rather than analogy.[47] English judges frequently label extensions beyond the letter as 'construction'.[48]

Raz notes that the courts do not take much trouble to identify the exact borderline between application and innovation, and often move imperceptibly from one function to another.[49] Yet he is more precise in his analysis when arguing that applying law and making law form a 'strong continuity' because very similar types of argument are relevant to both purposes. In spite of this 'intricate interconnection', Raz does not conclude that this distinction should be abandoned. Rather, he maintains that law-making and law-applying are 'conceptually distinct'. Therefore, Raz also adopts a somewhat unstable position because he maintains a distinction whose possibility is not sufficiently defended.[50]

---

[43] *Magor and St Mellons v Newport Corpn* [1951] 2 All ER 839 (Lord Simonds).
[44] *Clarke v Kato* [1998] 1 WLR 1647 (HL) 1655, 1660 (Lord Clyde).
[45] Cf Vogenauer, *Die Auslegung von Gesetzen in England und auf dem Kontinent* (n 2 above) 1134.
[46] WMC Gummow, *Change and Continuity. Statute, Equity, and Federalism* (Oxford, 1999) 11 ff, 16.
[47] HK Lücke, 'Statutory Interpretation: New Comparative Dimensions' (2005) 54 *International & Comparative Law Quarterly* 1023 at 1030 and fn 41.
[48] See, for example, *Jones v Wrotham Park Estates* [1980] AC 74 (HL) 105 (Lord Diplock): 'I am not reluctant to adopt a purposive construction where to apply the literal meaning of the legislative language used would lead to results which would clearly defeat the purposes of the Act. But in doing so the task on which a court of justice is engaged remains one of construction; even where this involves reading into the Act words which are not expressly included in it'.
[49] J Raz, *The Authority of Law. Essays on Law and Morality* (Oxford, 1979) 207–9.
[50] For an analysis of judicial discretion, explaining the law-making power of judges, see M Klatt, 'Taking Rights Less Seriously. A Structural Analysis of Judicial Discretion' (2007) 20 *Ratio Juris* 506.

(iii) The Missing Method: Judicial Development of the Law

It is suggested here that Anglo-American jurisprudence can come to terms with the aforementioned two problems in a uniform manner. Both the relation between the purposive approach and the literal approach, and the relation between law-making and law-applying, can be clarified by introducing a method that is absent in Anglo-American jurisprudence, namely the judicial development of the law. To recapitulate: the judicial development of the law is defined as the application of a norm that goes beyond its wording.

The notion that judges develop the law is of course familiar to Anglo-American jurisprudence, yet judicial development has not been analysed sufficiently as a legal method distinct from interpretation. Not long ago, the responsibility of judges to further develop common law was acknowledged while simultaneously being denied with regard to statute law.[51] Later, it was discussed whether the common law could carry policies inherent in statutes beyond the words of statutes.[52] Nowadays, as Vogenauer has shown, the courts will develop the law further within certain limits even in areas of the law which are exclusively of statutory origin.[53]

Judicial development remains nebulous in Anglo-American jurisprudence. It does not yet have the status of a separate legal method. Anglo-American jurisprudence pursues an all-or-nothing approach: either application or legislation, either strict literalism or freedom due to purposive considerations. To draw sharp distinctions between extensive interpretation and analogy and between restrictive interpretation and purposive reduction, and thus between interpretation and judicial development of the law, would provide a much clearer, more complex and more subtle account. Such clearness matters, as the two problems discussed above illustrate.

Judicial development, then, is the missing middle term between interpretation and judicial legislation that would enable Anglo-American jurisprudence to solve these problems by supplying formal rules about how courts may extend or restrict rules contrary to their wording. Introducing the

---

[51] 'Judges ... have a responsibility for the common law, but in my opinion they have none for statute law; their duty is simply to apply it and not to obstruct'. P Devlin, 'Judges and Lawmakers' (1976) 39 *Modern Law Review* 1 at 13.

[52] Lücke, 'Statutory Interpretation: New Comparative Dimensions' (n 48 above) 1031.

[53] Vogenauer, *Die Auslegung von Gesetzen in England und auf dem Kontinent* (n 2 above) 1134–47. Cf *Corocraft Ltd v Pan American Airways Inc* [1969] 1 QB 616 (QBD) 638 (Donaldson J): The courts 'are not legislators, but finishers, refiners and polishers of legislation which comes to them in a state requiring varying degrees of further processing'.

judicial development of the law as a distinct legal method depends on introducing its defining feature, namely the doctrine of 'the limits of the wording'.

B. Human Rights Act: What is Possible?

The doctrine of the limits of the wording is even more important to English law if we look not at the general theory of statutory interpretation, but at a specific provision recently incorporated into English law, namely section 3(1) of the Human Rights Act 1998 (HRA). It provides that

> '[s]o far as it is possible to do so, primary legislation and subordinate legislation must be read and given effect in a way which is compatible with the Convention rights.'

It has been noted that this provision requires construing the enactments in question according to the wider European system of purposive construction, and thus 'drastically alters existing methods' in English law.[54] It is a novelty within the English legal tradition and establishes a 'far reaching new approach to the construction of statutes'.[55] It is no wonder that it has spawned an extensive literature.[56]

What matters here is that it brings about a need to clarify the distinction between law-making and law-applying. Lord Hope considered that 'the rule is only a rule of interpretation. It does not entitle the judges to act as legislators'.[57] Lord Woolf was engaged in 'finding the boundary between re-interpretation and legislation'.[58] Kavanagh pointed out that reliance on this distinction has been the most prominent way of separating legitimate from illegitimate adjudication in the emerging case law under the HRA.[59]

Even more important, the search for a distinctive criterion has so far ended up with the limits of the wording.[60] This return to issues of language in statutory interpretation is most remarkable, given that the literal

---

[54] F Bennion, 'What Interpretation Is "Possible" Under Section 3(1) of the Human Rights Act 1998?' (2000) *Public Law* at 91.

[55] *R v Lambert* [2002] 2 AC 545 (HL) para 78 (Lord Hope).

[56] R Clayton, 'The Limits of "What's Possible": Statutory Construction under the Human Rights Act' (2002) *European Human Rights Law Review* 559 at 560 with bibliography in fn 4.

[57] *R v A (No 2)* [2002] 1 AC 45 (HL) para 108 (Lord Hope).

[58] *Poplar Housing and Regeneration Community Association Ltd v Secretary of State for the Environment, Transport and the Regions* [2002] QB 48 (HL) 76 f.

[59] A Kavanagh, 'The Elusive Divide between Interpretation and Legislation under the Human Rights Act 1998' (2004) 24 *Oxford Journal of Legal Studies* 259 at 260, with references in fn 14.

[60] Note the following statement from the former president of the German Federal Constitutional Court: British courts have applied 'a kind of implicit constitution-conformable interpretation. This means that *if the wording of the statute so allows*, the court will interpret

approach was about to vanish into thin air not long ago. The limits of the wording mark the limits of 'so far as it is possible' in section 3(1) of the HRA.[61] Section 3(1) is not applicable where the suggested interpretation is 'contrary to expressed statutory words'.[62] It has been underlined in this context that judges are bound by the wording.[63] In determining the limits of the 'possible', case law has found the outer boundary in an outright contradiction between statutory wording and its proposed interpretation.[64]

> Going against the express words of the statute would go beyond judicial interpretation and enter the realm of judicial legislation.[65]

The details, however, are still unsettled:

> Does 'possible' refer to the literal meaning, or does it also allow for a strained meaning, and if so to what extent?[66]

And this is precisely the point on which this book purports to shed light.

C. Result

All in all, it is submitted here that the German doctrine of the limits of the wording is extremely helpful in clarifying not only the relationship between interpretation and invention (above A), but also the exact boundaries of what is 'possible' under section 3(1) of the HRA (above B). It helps in establishing both the scope and the limits of judicial creativity in statutory interpretation.

Thus, the intensive and heated discussion in German legal theory about whether it is at all possible to state 'boundaries of meaning' very much matters to English legal theory. In fact, this contested doctrine is even more important to English than to German law, since the new English approach

---

parliamentary legislation in such a way as to avoid a violation of fundamental principles' (emphasis added). J Limbach, 'The Concept of the Supremacy of the Constitution' (2001) 64 *Modern Law Review* 1 at 6.

[61] TR Arden, 'The Interpretation of UK Domestic Legislation in the Light of European Convention on Human Rights Jurisprudence' (2004) 25 *Statute Law Review* 165 at 168.

[62] *In Re S (Minors) (Care Order: Implementation of Care Plan)* [2002] 2 AC 291 (HL) 313–14, para 41 (Lord Nicholls of Birkenhead); *R (Anderson) v Secretary of State for the Home Department* [2003] 1 AC 837 (HL) para 59 (Lord Steyn).

[63] Kavanagh, 'The Elusive Divide between Interpretation and Legislation under the Human Rights Act 1998' (n 59 above) 271.

[64] *R v A (No 2)* [2002] 1 AC 45 (HL) para 108 (Lord Hope); *R (H) v London North and East Region Mental Health Review Tribunal* [2000] QB 1 (HL) 10 (Lord Phillips of Worth Matravers); *R v Lambert* [2001] 3 WLR 206 (HL) paras 79–81 (Lord Hope).

[65] Kavanagh, 'The Elusive Divide between Interpretation and Legislation under the Human Rights Act 1998' (n 59 above) 276.

[66] Bennion, 'What Interpretation Is "Possible" Under Section 3(1) of the Human Rights Act 1998?' (n 54 above) 77.

under section 3(1) of the HRA treats the wording as an absolute limit whereas the limits of the wording are not absolute in German doctrine.[67]

III. TOWARDS A COMMON EUROPEAN APPROACH

The legitimacy and limits of judicial development of the law are important issues at European level as well.[68] Roman legal systems do not recognise a doctrine of the limits of the wording.[69] In particular, French[70] and Dutch[71] legal theories speak of a 'floating crossover' between interpretation and analogy, or even consider them a unity. European legal systems take quite different views on the existence of limits of the wording. This fact leads to problems with regard to the jurisdiction of the European Court of Justice. Therefore, the doctrine of the limits of the wording can be seen as a touchstone for any unification of national doctrines of interpretation that would amount to a common European approach.[72] This is even truer in

---

[67] It should be noted, however, that English doctrine labels the German 'judicial development of the law' as 'interpretation'; the reading in and reading down of statutory wording is not separated from interpretation in England. See Arden, 'The Interpretation of UK Domestic Legislation in the Light of European Convention on Human Rights Jurisprudence' (n 61 above) 171; Kavanagh, 'The Elusive Divide between Interpretation and Legislation under the Human Rights Act 1998' (n 59 above) 279.

[68] Concerning the competence of the ECJ to further develop the law, see K-D Borchardt, 'Richterrecht durch den Gerichtshof der Europäischen Gemeinschaften' in A Randelzhofer, R Scholz and D Wilke (eds), *Gedächtnisschrift für Eberhard Grabitz* (München, 1995) 29; W Dänzer-Vanotti, 'Unzulässige Rechtsfortbildung des Europäischen Gerichtshofs' (1992) *Recht der Internationalen Wirtschaft* 733; U Everling, 'Richterliche Rechtsfortbildung in der Europäischen Gemeinschaft' (2000) *Juristenzeitung* 217; J Ukrow, *Richterliche Rechtsfortbildung durch den EuGH. Dargestellt am Beispiel der Erweiterung des Rechtsschutzes des Marktbürgers im Bereich des vorläufigen Rechtsschutzes und der Staatshaftung* (Baden-Baden, 1995).

[69] Cf W Fikentscher, *Methoden des Rechts in vergleichender Darstellung. Band III: Mitteleuropäischer Rechtskreis* (Tübingen, 1976) 690.

[70] French courts label their method 'interpretation' even when they clearly decide *contra legem*, see F Ferrand, *Cassation française et révision allemande. Essai sur le contrôle exercé en matière civile par la Cour de cassation française et par la Cour fédérale de Justice de la République Fédérale d'Allemagne* (Paris, 1993) 318. Accordingly, French legal theory does not apply the criterion of the limits of the wording, nor does it acknowledge any difference between interpretation and analogy or reduction, see ÉEH Perreau, *Technique de la jurisprudence en droit privé* (Paris, 1923) 260. For an exception, however, see Gény, who distinguishes *interprétation de la loi* from *création de droit*: F Geny, *Méthode d'interprétation et sources en droit privé positif. Essai critique*, 2nd edn (Paris 1919) 304, 314 f. See also L-J Constantinesco, *Das Recht der Europäischen Gemeinschaften* (Baden-Baden, 1977) 807; H Rabault, *L'interprétation des normes. L'objectivité de la méthode herméneutique* (Paris, 1997); Vogenauer, *Die Auslegung von Gesetzen in England und auf dem Kontinent* (n 2 above) 289–91.

[71] W Fikentscher, *Methoden des Rechts in vergleichender Darstellung. Band I: Frühe und religiöse Rechte, Romanischer Rechtskreis* (Tübingen, 1975) 564–72.

[72] For an account of the problems of such unification arising from divergent legal traditions, see Everling, 'Richterliche Rechtsfortbildung in der Europäischen Gemeinschaft' (n 68 above) 222; P Legrand, 'European Legal Systems Are Not Converging' (1996) 45

view of recent research that undermines the traditional view of fundamentally different European approaches to statutory interpretation, and posits a fundamental unity instead.[73]

The European Court of Justice (ECJ) follows the French doctrine and does not distinguish between interpretation and development; *interprétation* and *justification* embrace both.[74] The Court is reluctant to go beyond the wording when simply applying norms that allow for an encroachment or a sanction.[75] In general, the Court assumes that even in cases of clear law-making it is only constructing and interpreting.[76]

In view of this practice, it has been suggested that the doctrine of the limits of the wording does not matter in Community law. Herbert finds his doubts about semantic arguments empirically confirmed by the jurisdiction of the ECJ.[77] Herberger analyses the example of a vertical direct effect of

---

International & Comparative Law Quarterly 74. More optimistic is K Langenbucher, 'Vorüberlegungen zu einer europarechtlichen Methodenlehre' in T Ackermann and A Arnold (eds), *Jahrbuch junger Zivilrechtswissenschaftler 1999. Tradition und Fortschritt im Recht* (Stuttgart, 2000) 67, 70; Vogenauer, *Die Auslegung von Gesetzen in England und auf dem Kontinent* (n 2 above) 1295–1308.

[73] *Cf* Vogenauer, *Die Auslegung von Gesetzen in England und auf dem Kontinent* (n 2 above) 1295–1308.

[74] *Cf* ECJ 23 March 2000, Case C-208/98 *Berliner Kindl v Siepert*, *Neue Juristische Wochenschrift* 2000, 1323, paras 17 f; ECJ 23 April 1986, Case 294/83 *Les Verts v Parlament*, Slg 1986, 1339, paras 23–5. See also J Anweiler, *Die Auslegungsmethoden des Gerichtshofs der Europäischen Gemeinschaften* (Frankfurt am Main, 1997); J Bengoetxea, *The Legal Reasoning of the European Court of Justice. Towards a European Jurisprudence* (Oxford, 1993) 112 ff, 141 ff; A von Bogdandy, 'Beobachtungen zur Wissenschaft vom Europarecht. Strukturen, Debatten und Entwicklungsperspektiven der Grundlagenforschung zum Recht der Europäischen Union' (2001) *Der Staat* 3 at 19; Borchardt, 'Richterrecht durch den Gerichtshof der Europäischen Gemeinschaften' (n 68 above) 37; Dänzer-Vanotti, 'Unzulässige Rechtsfortbildung des Europäischen Gerichtshofs' (n 68 above) 743; H Kutscher, 'Thesen zu den Methoden der Auslegung des Gemeinschaftsrechts aus der Sicht eines Richters ' in Gerichtshof der Europäischen Gemeinschaften (ed), *Begegnung von Justiz und Hochschule am 27. und 28. September 1976. Berichte* (Luxemburg, 1976) I-7 ff; T Millett, 'Rules of Interpretation of E.E.C. Legislation' (1989) *Statute Law Review* 163 at 172 f; Vogenauer, *Die Auslegung von Gesetzen in England und auf dem Kontinent* (n 2 above) 366 fnn 169–72.

[75] ECJ Case 16/70 *Nemocout*, Slg 1970, 921 (932); Case 169/80 *Gondrand Frères*, Slg 1981, 1931 (1942); Case C-314/91 *Weber*, Slg 1993, I-1093 (1111). *Cf* Anweiler, *Die Auslegungsmethoden des Gerichtshofs der Europäischen Gemeinschaften* (n 74 above) 402–7.

[76] *Cf* Dänzer-Vanotti, 'Unzulässige Rechtsfortbildung des Europäischen Gerichtshofs' (n 68 above) 734 n 4.

[77] M Herbert, 'Buchbesprechung "Bruha/Seeler, Die Europäische Union und ihre Sprachen"' (2001) *Der Staat* 637 f.

directives, and maintains that it is not the distinction between interpretation and development that matters, but arguments based on principles.[78] And Everling insists that the distinction is merely one of terminology.[79]

Against these arguments, it is maintained here that the doctrine of the wording is important at European level for four reasons. First of all, even the ECJ begins nearly every judgment with a consideration of semantic arguments.[80] Secondly, Community law does entail norms prohibiting analogies[81]; but such norms would make no sense if analogies could not be distinguished from extensive interpretations. Thirdly, all reasons that support the doctrine of the limits of the wording at national level are valid at European level as well. And finally, the important boundary of competence between the Member States and the Community can be drawn with the help of the limits of the wording.[82]

All in all, the limits of the wording have the same importance and relevance in European law that they have in domestic law.[83] Therefore, the ECJ's tendency not to distinguish between interpretation and development has to be countered.[84]

---

[78] M Herberger, 'Eine Frage des Prinzips. Auslegung, Rechtsfortbildung und die Wirksamkeit nicht umgesetzter Richtlinien' in P Forstmoser (ed), *Rechtsanwendung in Theorie und Praxis. Symposion zum 70. Geburtstag von Arthur Meyer-Hayoz* (Basel, 1993) 42 f.

[79] Everling, 'Richterliche Rechtsfortbildung in der Europäischen Gemeinschaft' (n 68 above) 218. See also Borchardt, 'Richterrecht durch den Gerichtshof der Europäischen Gemeinschaften' (n 68 above) 37.

[80] Case 23 March 1982, Rs. 55/81 *Levin*, Slg 1982, 1035, para 9; ECJ 11 November 1997, Case C-251/95 *Sabèl v Puma*, Slg 1997, I-6191 para 18.

[81] The doctrine *nulla poena sine lege* is part of European law, see Art 7 of the ECHR and ECJ Case C-63/83 *Regina v Kent Kirk*, Slg 1984, 2689. The relation between the Community and the Member States is also guided by a prohibition of analogy, Art 5 of the EC Treaty. *Cf* K Langenbucher, 'Vorüberlegungen zu einer europarechtlichen Methodenlehre' in T Ackermann and A Arnold (eds), *Jahrbuch junger Zivilrechtswissenschaftler 1999. Tradition und Fortschritt im Recht* (Stuttgart, 2000) 76 f.

[82] S Grundmann and K Riesenhuber, 'Die Auslegung des Europäischen Privat- und Schuldvertragsrechts' (2001) *Juristische Schulung* 529 at 535.

[83] Ibid, 530. A specific problem stems from the multilingualism of the Community. The number of interpretative variants is augmented by the number of official languages, *Cf* Anweiler, *Die Auslegungsmethoden des Gerichtshofs der Europäischen Gemeinschaften* (n 74 above) 146–72. Grundmann and Riesenhuber suggested that the limits of the wording are transgressed if an alleged interpretation is incompatible with all text variants, see Grundmann and Riesenhuber, 'Die Auslegung des Europäischen Privat- und Schuldvertragsrechts' (n 82 above) 535.

[84] Dänzer-Vanotti, 'Unzulässige Rechtsfortbildung des Europäischen Gerichtshofs' (n 68 above) 734; Grundmann and Riesenhuber, 'Die Auslegung des Europäischen Privat- und Schuldvertragsrechts' (n 82 above) 535. *Cf*, however, ECJ 11 July 1985, Case 107/84 *Commission v Germany*, Slg 1985, 2655 para 12.

IV. THE POSSIBILITY OF THE RULE OF LAW DEFENDED

The aim of this section is to underline the great constitutional importance of the doctrine of the limits of the wording. This doctrine is the very touchstone of nothing less than the possibility of the rule of law.

'Methodological questions are constitutional questions'.[85] This is particularly true for the doctrine of the limits of the wording. The realisation of both democracy and the rule of law are dependent on the existence of semantic limits. The principle of democracy entails the separation of powers. Any application of a norm beyond its wording is problematic as far as the separation of powers is concerned. The German Federal Finance Court reported the following legal opinion:

> The judgment of the Court of lower instance had infringed the principle of the separation of powers. The judiciary was bound to the clear wording of the statute and was not authorised to realise their own political opinions by means of an exchange of concepts.[86]

Also, the limits of the wording secure the prohibition of an analogy *in malem partem* in criminal law, as the German Federal Constitutional Court emphasises:

> The prohibition of an analogy reserves the creation of criminal offences strictly to the legislature. It rests not only upon the value of predictability as required by the rule of law, but also on the principle of democracy and the consequential responsibility of the legislator, moreover on the principle of the separation of powers and its aim to mitigate all state authorities, and lastly on the idea that criminal law has by necessity to remain fragmentary in order to protect the freedom of the individual.[87]

Rüßmann distinguishes three different ways of understanding how judges are bound by the law. He concludes that the only correct way is that which identifies the binding of the judges to the limits of the wording.[88] The doctrine of the limits of the wording is among the most important embodiments of the binding of judges. It activates stricter justification requirements for legal judgments. For example, analogies are admitted only if there is a gap in the law which contradicts the overall plan of the statute and if the *ratio legis* is applicable to the case under consideration.[89]

---

[85] B Rüthers, *Rechtstheorie. Begriff, Geltung und Anwendung des Rechts* (München, 1999) 401.
[86] BFHE 192, 316 (320), translated by MK.
[87] BVerfGE 73, 206 (247), translated by MK.
[88] H Rüßmann, 'Sprache und Recht. Sprachtheoretische Überlegungen zum Gesetzesbindungspostulat' in J Zimmermann (ed), *Sprache und Welterfahrung* (München, 1978) 229.
[89] Koch and Rüßmann, *Juristische Begründungslehre* (n 18 above) 260. For an example see BFHE 192, 316.

The doctrine of the limits of the wording functions as a means of limiting the interpretive power of the judiciary, and regulates the allocation of the legislative power in a state.

Moreover, rule of law values such as stability, predictability and certainty depend upon the limits of the wording.[90] A legal judgment can be evaluated properly only if the application of the law is categorised either as interpretation or as development. Based on the prohibition of state authorities acting arbitrarily, the German Federal Constitutional Court recognises a general necessity for especially justifying any transgression of the limits of the wording:

> The prohibition of state authorities acting arbitrarily demands with regard to the constitutional binding of the judges to law and justice a justification even of a judgment in the last instance insofar as the judgment departs from the clear wording of a statute, unless the reason for this departure is already known by the parties or otherwise readily identifiable.[91]

It is also important that the limits of the wording restrict not only the extension of a norm, but also the 'reading down' of a norm to a narrower scope.[92] It also limits the adjustment of legal concepts to general changes in society. The wording of a norm demarcates the boundary of any interpretation that aims at reconciling the norm with constitutional requirements.[93] The realisation of fundamental constitutional principles is contingent on the existence of semantic limits. Thus, the doctrine of the limits of wording is one of the most important interfaces between the constitution and legal methodology.

V. THE SCEPTICAL CHALLENGE: INDETERMINACY AND VAGUENESS

The doctrine of the limits of the wording is closely linked to the more fundamental problem of legal indeterminism (A). One main source of legal indeterminism is vagueness of meaning (B). All in all, linguistic-philosophical arguments loom large in legal scepticism (C).

---

[90] MacCormick, 'Arguing About Interpretation' (n 10 above) 126 f; N Stoljar, 'Survey Article: Interpretation, Indeterminacy and Authority. Some Recent Controversies in the Philosophy of Law' (2003) 11 *Journal of Political Philosophy* 482. *Cf* JL Coleman and B Leiter, 'Determinacy, Objectivity, and Authority' in A Marmor (ed), *Law and Interpretation. Essays in Legal Philosophy* (Oxford, 1995) 229–33.
[91] BVerfG NJW 1993, 1909, translated by MK.
[92] BGHSt 43, 237 (238).
[93] BVerfGE 101, 312 (329); 95, 64 (93); dissenting vote in BVerfGE 85, 69 (78).

A. The Concept of Indeterminacy

There are several types of legal indeterminacy, and these differ in terms of their justification and scope. As for the concept of indeterminacy, three distinctions are decisive.[94]

First, we need to distinguish between special and general indeterminism. Special indeterminism looks at special features of the law, and focuses on alleged inconsistencies and gaps. General indeterminism stems from the indeterminism of meaning and semantic scepticism. The doctrine of the limits of the wording is concerned with semantic scepticism, and thus with general indeterminism. For this reason, special indeterminism is excluded here.

Secondly, causal indeterminism has to be distinguished from indeterminism of justification. Causal indeterminism investigates the indeterminism between *causes* and judgments and denies the possibility of explaining judgments by reference to causes. Indeterminism of justification analyses the *reasons* for judgments and denies the possibility of justifying judgments by reference to reasons. The doctrine of the limits of the wording concerns the significance of semantic arguments in the external justification of judgments.[95] Therefore, indeterminism of justification is analysed here.

Thirdly, indeterminism of compliance can be distinguished from indeterminism of content. Indeterminism of compliance arises when a norm leaves latitude for more than one possible method of compliance. Indeterminism of content means that the content of the norm is unclear. Here, we are concerned with the indeterminism of content.

B. Vagueness as Boundarylessness

Among the most popular arguments supporting legal indeterminism is the argument of vagueness. This argument is a very complex one, and it stretches across many areas of philosophy. This book addresses only *semantic* grounds for the vagueness of a legal norm.

Based on semantic vagueness, legal scholars have advanced highly sceptical claims about the possibility of rational justification in the law in general and about the doctrine of the limits of the wording in particular. These debates are essentially linguistic and philosophical in nature, and hence the entire second chapter of this book addresses linguistic-philosophical questions that borrow from Wittgenstein, Kripke, Quine,

---

[94] *Cf* Coleman and Leiter, 'Determinacy, Objectivity, and Authority' (n 90 above) 212–19.

[95] On internal and external justification, see Alexy, *A Theory of Legal Argumentation* (n 17 above) 221–86.

and Brandom. In this introduction we look briefly at only two issues, as they highlight both some of the main points of this book and the relevance of vagueness to the doctrine of the limits of the wording. These are the problem of higher-order vagueness (i) and the problem of the significance of interpretation in the law (ii).

(i) Higher-order Vagueness

Vagueness is a major challenge to the assertion that the philosophy of meaning can provide the means to defend the doctrine of the limits of the wording. Analytical legal methodology in Germany has developed the so-called 'three-candidates' model to cope with semantic vagueness. According to this model, the objects to which a legal term refers can be categorised into *positive* candidates to which the term undoubtedly refers, *negative* candidates to which the term undoubtedly does not refer, and *neutral* candidates where there is doubt whether the term refers to them.[96] On the basis of this categorisation, the model can defend certain limits of the wording, even for vague terms.[97]

However, such a model faces the problem of higher-order vagueness—the borderlines between the three categories may be vague themselves. It is exactly this point that Raz objected to in Dworkin: the claim that vagueness is 'continuous' and 'boundary-less',[98] such that it would be impossible to draw sharp distinctions between any number of categories in the same way as the doctrine of the limits of the wording.

The problem of higher-order vagueness has attracted considerable attention, and it is in fact the most worrying problem of vagueness for any theory of legal argumentation, as Endicott underlines: 'The feature of vague language that is most difficult for legal theories to accommodate is higher-order vagueness'.[99]

If the problem of higher-order vagueness could be solved, vagueness as a whole would no longer be a serious challenge to legal theory. And it is a central aim of this book to defend exactly this solution. It will be argued that, on the basis of Robert Brandom's philosophy of meaning, it is indeed possible to break the circle of higher-order vagueness.[100] With the aid of

---

[96] Koch and Rüßmann, *Juristische Begründungslehre* (n 18 above) 195.
[97] M Herberger and H-J Koch, 'Zur Einführung: Juristische Methodenlehre und Sprachphilosophie' (1978) *Juristische Schulung* 813.
[98] *Cf* J Raz, *The Authority of Law. Essays on Law and Morality* (Oxford, 1979) 73 f; M Sainsbury, 'Concepts without Boundaries' in R Keefe and P Smith (eds), *Vagueness. A Reader* (Cambridge MA, 1997) 251.
[99] Endicott, *Vagueness in Law* (n 20 above) 74.
[100] See p 259 ff below.

22 Introduction

Brandom's default and challenge structure of normative commitments, the doctrine of the limits of the wording can be maintained even for vague concepts.[101]

(ii) The Significance of Interpretation in the Law

In analysing and defending vagueness as a central challenge to legal theory, Endicott aims to defend a so-called 'simple account' of interpretation in the law as an alternative to more ambitious accounts of interpretation. With his 'simple account', he maintains that interpretation has a minor but significant role in adjudication; in fact, Endicott denies that identifying the law is generally an interpretive task at all.[102]

In defending the doctrine of the limits of the wording, this book acknowledges the great significance of interpretation in law, and thus supports Dworkin's rather than Endicott's view. When Endicott argues that the law can be often be understood 'without any creative activity', he disregards even the insights of legal hermeneutics, most notably Gadamer's works on the hermeneutic conditions of understanding.[103] The omnipresence of interpretation is inevitable, and any denial of this fact is not only illusory but misses the potential of rationality that lies in a profound analysis of the process of interpretation.

C. Scepticism in Law

Legal sceptics have argued on a variety of linguistic and non-linguistic grounds against the possibility of the rule of law. The determinacy of language is defended here with the doctrine of the limits of the wording. Thus, only linguistic grounds for legal scepticism are considered and rebutted in this book.

Legal sceptics hold not only that meaning is not fixed on enactment of a statute, but that it evolves in the process of understanding and applying the law.[104] What is more, they take this process to be extremely dynamic and influenced, if not entirely determined, by subjective and emotional factors.

---

[101] See p 270 below.
[102] Endicott, *Vagueness in Law* (n 20 above) 159, 167.
[103] HG Gadamer, *Truth and Method*, 2nd edn (London, 2004). See p 33 ff below.
[104] Sunstein and Eskridge have argued for a dynamic theory of legal interpretation, see WN Eskridge, *Dynamic Statutory Interpretation* (Cambridge MA, 1994); CR Sunstein, 'Interpreting Statutes in the Regulatory State' (1989) 103 *Harvard Law Review* 405. For a discussion of evolutionary versus fixed meaning, see Greenawalt, 'Constitutional and Statutory Interpretation' (n 26 above) 275–7.

Kennedy, for example, claims that judges are ideological players, and that adjudication is based on ideological, strategic preferences.[105]

Hart and Sacks conceive of interpretation as the 'creative elaboration of meaning by judges'.[106] Similarly, Structuring Legal Theory (SLT) in Germany makes far-reaching claims about the influence of the interpreter on the meaning of a text. It claims that the meaning of a norm is not a pre-interpretive standard, and therefore cannot restrict interpretation. As Müller says,

> '[t]here is no magical language with an objective meaning-content or any unquestionable propositions ... An interpretation always just substitutes new text for preceding text'.[107]

This deconstruction of the theory of the limits of the wording has significant consequences. If the meaning of a norm is not only not fixed but also not even able to determine the application of the norm in some way, several constitutional principles, such as democracy, the rule of law and the separation of powers, would have to be abandoned.

If SLT and legal scepticism were sound, then any assertion about the meaning of a statute would dissolve into a multitude of relativistic interpretations. For purely semantic reasons, we would have to admit that our attempts at justifying legal verdicts are, at best, monumental feats of self-deception and, at worst, deliberate ploys of judges to mask their usurpation of legislative power. Thus, any notion of a doctrine of limits of the wording would be illusory. In defending this doctrine, this book also refutes semantic indeterminacy grounds for far-reaching legal scepticism and thereby defends the possibility of the rule of law.

VI. THE RATIONALITY AND OBJECTIVITY OF LEGAL REASONING

The legitimacy of legal judgments depends upon the rationality and objectivity of legal reasoning and the social reality of which it forms a part (A). Legal objectivity was a central issue in the famous debate between Dworkin and Fish (B). As far as semantic grounds for objectivity are concerned, we argue here that Brandomian semantics are superior to Stavropoulos 'KP' semantics (C).

---

[105] D Kennedy, 'Strategizing Strategic Behaviour in Legal Interpretation' (1996) *Utah Law Review* 785.

[106] HM Hart and AM Sacks, *The Legal Process. Basic Problems in the Making and Application of Law* (Westbury NY, 1994) 1415.

[107] F Müller, 'Observations on the Role of Precedent in Modern Continental European Law from the Perspective of "Structuring Legal Theory"' (2000) 11 *Stellenbosch Law Review* 426 at 435. SLT suggests a different concept, namely the limits of the norm-programme. See F Müller, *Juristische Methodik*, 7th edn (Berlin, 1997) 183, 201. For a critical discussion of this view as well as the overall approach of SLT, see p 73 ff below.

24 *Introduction*

A. Justification, Rationality and Legitimacy

Many of those who doubt the objectivity of law[108] and the rationality of adjudication are motivated by scepticism about the objectivity of language in general. However, the problem of the objectivity of law is not only linguistic-philosophical in character, but touches on one of the most fundamental questions in general philosophy: Is there objective truth? The problem of the limits of the wording is closely related to the problems of the existence of legal truths and of the possibility of legal mistakes. Thus, it is related to the objectivity of social reality and of the possibilities and limits of rationality. To what extent is objective social reality possible solely because humans *think* that it is and *act* accordingly?[109] Can judges make mistakes about the law? Are there correct answers in the law?

The problem of the limits of the wording is related to the debate on Habermas's new concept of truth[110] and to the renaissance of American pragmatism.[111] What is at stake is how the speakers of a language make up a common reference to reality. The problem of the limits of the wording concerns the possibility of a common language in the context of a factual plurality of world pictures, language games, forms of life and cultures.

This book raises the issue of the existence and cognition of objective, universal, timeless and mind-independent features of language. Postmodern scepticism, subjectivism, emotivism and projectivism deny the possibility that propositions about the law can be rational. This debate is part of the wider debate on the objectivity of evaluative propositions, be they ethical, interpretive or aesthetic in nature.[112] Insights into the interpretive power challenge the possibility of rational legal argumentation that contrasts with open-ended ideological disputes about the fundamental values and terms of social life. Koch and Rüßmann highlight that

> the explosiveness of this confession lies in the fact that the legitimacy of legal judgments becomes increasingly problematic if the judgment cannot be justified by reference to the content of a legal norm.[113]

---

[108] For a bibliography of the abundant writing on this topic see B Leiter, *Objectivity in Law and Morals* (Cambridge, 2001) 331–49.

[109] JR Searle, *Mind, Language and Society. Philosophy in the Real World* (London, 2000) 111–34.

[110] J Habermas, 'Richtigkeit vs. Wahrheit. Zum Sinn der Sollgeltung moralischer Urteile und Normen' (1998) 46 *Deutsche Zeitschrift für Philosophie* 179.

[111] W Egginton and M Sandbothe, *The Pragmatic Turn in Philosophy. Contemporary Engagements between Analytic and Continental Thought* (Albany, 2004).

[112] *Cf* R Dworkin, 'Objectivity and Truth: You'd Better Believe It' (1996) 25 *Philosophy & Public Affairs* 87 f.

[113] Koch and Rüßmann, *Juristische Begründungslehre* (n 18 above) 23.

B. The Dworkin–Fish Controversy

Dworkin and Fish have been engaged in a long debate on the objectivity of legal interpretation.[114] Fish's criticism focuses on Dworkin's idea of the chain novel and on the constraints on the different participants in this shared enterprise.[115] Fish claims that Dworkin fails to warrant the objectivity of judgements about how the novel is to be continued. Fish challenges Dworkin with the choice of either abandoning the claim of objectivity or adopting a kind of semantic realism.[116] A similar objection has been made by Raz, who claims that there were only two options: to demonstrate the absolute certainty of an alleged interpretation, and to admit that everything is open to endless re-interpretation.[117]

Stavropoulos has shown that these choices fail to recognise an 'objective conception of the practice' as a third option and therefore do not represent an exhaustive set of alternatives.[118] The semantic theory developed in this book elaborates such an objective conception of the practice, based on Brandom's normative pragmatics. It therefore supports Dworkin's position in the debate.

The semantic theory developed in this book dovetails with Dworkin's theory, as it spells out in detail how judgements of interpreters may impose obligations upon other judgements. The notion of 'internal objectivity' defended by Dworkin is analysed here in greater depth by reference to Brandom's philosophy. 'Internal objectivity' claims that an agent's propositions can function as criteria to evaluate the correctness of further propositions of the same and other agents.[119] It will be shown that within a given conceptual scheme objective restrictions can indeed control interpretations.

---

[114] R Dworkin, 'Law as Interpretation' (1982) 60 *Texas Law Review* 527; R Dworkin, 'My Reply to Stanley Fish (and Walter Benn Michaels): Please Don't Talk About Objectivity Any More' in WJT Mitchell (ed), *The Politics of Interpretation* (Chicago, 1983) 287; R Dworkin, 'Pragmatism, Right Answers and True Banality' in M Brint and W Weaver (eds), *Pragmatism in Law and Society* (Boulder CO, 1991) 359; S Fish, 'Working on the Chain Gang. Interpretation in Law and Literature' (1982) 60 *Texas Law Review* 551; S Fish, 'Wrong Again' (1983) 62 *Texas Law Review* 299; S Fish, 'Still Wrong after All These Years' (1987) 6 *Law and Philosophy* 401; S Fish, 'Almost Pragmatism. The Jurisprudence of Richard Posner, Richard Rorty and Ronald Dworkin' in Brint and Weaver (eds), *Pragmatism in Law and Society* at 47.

[115] Dworkin, 'My Reply to Stanley Fish (and Walter Benn Michaels): Please Don't Talk About Objectivity Any More' (n 114 above) 288–97; R Dworkin, *Law's Empire* (London, 1986) 234 f; R Dworkin, *A Matter of Principle* (Oxford, 1986) 151 f, 167–77; Dworkin, 'Pragmatism, Right Answers and True Banality' (n 114 above) 376 f.

[116] Fish, 'Still Wrong after All These Years' (n 114 above) 408.

[117] See J Raz, 'Dworkin: A New Link in the Chain' (1986) 74 *California Law Review* 1103 at 1110 f; Stavropoulos, *Objectivity in Law* (n 39 above) 136 f, 159.

[118] Stavropoulos, *Objectivity in Law* (n 39 above) 159.

[119] On this concept of internal objectivity see M Iglesias Vila, *Facing Judicial Discretion. Legal Knowledge and Right Answers Revisited* (Dordrecht, 2001) 120.

Dworkin's turn towards constructive interpretation is taken by many scholars to demolish the dichotomy between creating and discovering the law.[120] Raz objects that the augmented interpretive attitude does not take seriously the context of the law as an authoritative mode of communication between law-makers and citizens.[121] Yet Dworkin simultaneously claims to defend the idea of objectivity in judicial decision-making.

If his critics were right, then this latter claim would be illusory. It is, however, maintained here that it is indeed possible to have it all: to maintain both the idea of objectivity *and* the dichotomy between interpretation and invention *within* Dworkin's theory of interpretation. Thus, in this respect also, the semantic theory defended here supports Dworkin's triumphal escape from false choices.

C. B Semantics versus KP Semantics

In the context of defending claims for the objectivity of legal reasoning, Stavropoulos has suggested supplementing Dworkin's theory with a certain semantic theory, called Kripke-Putnam semantics or KP semantics. Brandomian semantics, by contrast, are proposed in this book with the same aim, namely of supplementing Dworkin, but they are richer and more powerful than KP semantics.

KP semantics and Stavropoulos's defence of Dworkin's view on substantive disagreement in legal discourse both rest on legal things being real-world properties rather than mere conventional facts.[122] There is, however, no reality of legal propositions apart from legal practice itself.

> Meaning in law does not reflect or directly relate to anything but the meaning others have given to legal propositions or legal concepts.[123]

It is the central weakness of Stavropoulos's book that, in his search for greater objectivity, he completely abandons the conventional and pragmatic basis of meaning. Therefore, it focuses on one aspect of meaning only: It is a theory of *content* only, while a full theory of meaning must also explain *application*.[124]

It is precisely these weaknesses that are avoided by Brandomian semantics. The latter spell out how the legal concepts that underlie our practices

---

[120] M Powers, 'Truth, Interpretation, and Judicial Method in Recent Anglo-American Jurisprudence' (1992) 46 *Zeitschrift für philosophische Forschung* 120.
[121] Raz, 'Dworkin: A New Link in the Chain' (n 117 above) 1103.
[122] *Cf* JE Penner, 'Nicos Stavropoulos: Objectivity in Law' (1997) 60 *Modern Law Review* 747 at 748.
[123] A De Moor, 'Nothing Else to Think? On Meaning, Truth and Objectivity in Law' (1998) 18 *Oxford Journal of Legal Studies* 345 at 360.
[124] Penner, 'Nicos Stavropoulos: Objectivity in Law' (n 122 above) 749.

are to be understood, and elaborate with great analytical power the 'joint commitments'[125] in an interpretive community that allows for legal propositions being correct or false.

In addition to their pragmatic analysis, they accommodate the main points of KP semantics. Brandomian semantics incorporate an explanation of the reference to objects as a necessary condition of any theory of meaning. While KP semantics oppose conventional or pragmatic theories and look at reference as a sufficient condition for explaining meaning, Brandomian semantics are both pragmatic and reference-based, and therefore a much richer and more potent theory than KP semantics.

D. The Objectivity of Law Defended

Brandomian semantics support the epistemic conception of interpretation, which holds that interpretation is linked to knowledge and understanding, and can produce correct answers and true judgements.[126] Most importantly, Brandomian semantics are able to explain and defend the paradox of Dworkin's theory that the restrictions controlling interpretation are internal to conceptual schemes and thus agent-dependent, but still objective in the sense of restricting the agents.[127]

The doctrine of the limits of the wording is looked at here as a touchstone for the possibility of objectivity and rationality in legal discourse. The Brandomian theory of meaning supports the view that legal propositions can indeed be objective and rational.

VII. AT A GLANCE

This section provides an overview on the contents of this book. This includes some remarks on the general scientific approach (A) and an overview of the three main chapters (B–D).

A. General Approach

A theory of legal argumentation can be called 'specific' if it investigates the structures and conditions of the interpretation of specific kinds of norm.

---

[125] *Cf* De Moor, 'Nothing Else to Think? (n 123 above) 362.
[126] On the epistemic conception of interpretation, see M Iglesias Vila, *Facing Judicial Discretion. Legal Knowledge and Right Answers Revisited* (Dordrecht, 2001) 112.
[127] Dworkin, *Law's Empire* (n 115 above) 234–6; Dworkin, *A Matter of Principle* (n 115 above) 152–4, 168; R Dworkin, 'Law, Philosophy and Interpretation' (1994) 80 *Archiv für Rechts- und Sozialphilosophie* 468.

An example is the theory of *constitutional* interpretation.[128] This book analyses the structure and conditions of legal argumentation in general. The doctrine of the limits of the wording is examined in the framework of a general theory of legal argumentation.

The problem of the limits of the wording can be investigated in three basic ways: empirically, normatively and analytically. Empirical-sociological approaches analyse the social processes in order to obtain indications of the reconstruction of the cognitive and normative components of the belief systems of agents.[129] Their aim is to find the mechanisms of selection operating on the concretisation of legal norms.[130]

The issue of investigation here is not the actual effectiveness of the limits of the wording in the practice of the court.[131] This book does not undertake socio-legal or linguistic analyses of the behaviour of judges.[132] Rather, its objective is a clarification of the *normative* premises and an *analytical* reconstruction of the *theory* of the limits of the wording. Whether, and under which conditions, judgments follow from legal norms, or are at least compatible with them, are questions that can be answered separately from the factors that influence judgments in reality; what matters here are the rules of language and logic.[133]

B. Chapter 1

The first chapter focuses on the intense debate on the limits of wording in German legal theory. It provides a precise formulation of the problem and

---

[128] *Cf* E-W Böckenförde, 'Die Methoden der Verfassungsinterpretation—Bestandsaufnahme und Kritik' (1976) 29 *Neue Juristische Wochenschrift* 2089; R Dreier and F Schwegmann (eds), *Probleme der Verfassungsinterpretation. Dokumentation einer Kontroverse* (Baden-Baden, 1976); C Starck, '§ 164: Die Verfassungsauslegung' in J Isensee and P Kirchhof (eds), *Handbuch des Staatsrechts der Bundesrepublik Deutschland. Band VII* (1992) 189; M Vocke, *Verfassungsinterpretation und Normbegründung. Grundlegung zu einer prozeduralen Theorie der Verfassungsgerichtsbarkeit* (Frankfurt am Main, 1995).

[129] *Cf* H Albert, *Kritik der reinen Hermeneutik. Der Antirealismus und das Problem des Verstehens* (Tübingen, 1994) 180.

[130] G Teubner, 'Generalklauseln als sozionormative Modelle' in W Hassemer, W Hoffmann-Riem and M Weiß (eds), *Generalklauseln als Gegenstand der Sozialwissenschaften* (Baden-Baden, 1978) 13.

[131] For an empirical analysis see U Neumann, 'Der "mögliche Wortsinn" als Auslegungsgrenze in der Rechtsprechung der Strafsenate des BGH' in E von Savigny (ed), *Juristische Dogmatik und Wissenschaftstheorie* (München, 1976) 50–52.

[132] L Solan, *The Language of Judges* (Chicago, 1993).

[133] H Rüßmann, 'Sprache und Recht. Sprachtheoretische Überlegungen zum Gesetzesbindungspostulat' in J Zimmermann (ed), *Sprache und Welterfahrung* (München, 1978) 212.

develops the state of the art. The existing theories are systematised. Their historical sources and their development have been described in detail elsewhere.[134]

The four most important theories addressing the limits of the wording are discussed in chronological order. Finally, the three crucial issues of debates and their respective arguments are explicated, namely the distinction between easy and hard cases of semantic interpretation, the empirical establishment of meaning, and the objectivity of the meaning of legal norms. The linguistic-philosophical questions as to the structure and the cognition of meaning are identified as the core problem of the doctrine of the limits of the wording.

C. Chapter 2

The second chapter is entirely linguistic-philosophical in nature. It develops the central point that meaning is normative and objective both in the sense of being reference-related and in the sense of inter-subjective validity. This thesis is defended against meaning-sceptical criticism by Quine and Kripke.

Every philosophy of language has to clarify the conceptual structures of the practice of language. The central aspect of this practice is the attribution of meaning. This practice of attribution is dependent upon the meaning *limiting* the application of concepts and propositions. The concept of semantic limits is a *normative* concept. Thus, the concept of meaning itself has to be normative, and its analysis has to identify the conditions for a correct application of concepts and propositions.[135]

There are two main currents in contemporary analytical philosophy: naturalism and normativism.[136] The fundamental debate between naturalism and normativism takes place both in semantics and in legal theory.[137] Meaning sceptics like Quine maintain that there is only a gradual, not a categorical, distinction between empirical and non-empirical, and between analytical and non-analytical, propositions.

Normativism has been strongly supported by Robert Brandom's *Making It Explicit*. Its reception is the central task of the second chapter. However, Brandom's book is by no means the only recent publication which defends

---

[134] Cf M Klatt, *Theorie der Wortlautgrenze. Semantische Normativität in der juristischen Argumentation* (Baden-Baden, 2004) 40–95; Vogenauer, *Die Auslegung von Gesetzen in England und auf dem Kontinent* (n 2 above) 606–8.
[135] Coleman and Leiter, 'Determinacy, Objectivity, and Authority' (n 90 above) 208.
[136] WVO Quine, *Word and Object* (Cambridge MA, 1960) 161, 228 f, 275 f.
[137] Cf JL Coleman, *The Practice of Principle. In Defence of a Pragmatist Approach to Legal Theory* (Oxford, 2001) 175 on 'Normativity and naturalism'.

normativism in general philosophy.[138] Thus, we could speak of a *renaissance of normative theories* in analytical philosophy.

The second chapter focuses on three issues: first, Kripke's problem of how to explain the normativity of meaning; secondly, how theory of meaning can come to terms with the intuition that world knowledge is also a criterion of the correct application of concepts; and thirdly, how to explicate the relationship between meaning and inter-subjectively shared forms of life. How can the idea of context-transcendental objectivity be reconciled with the existing plurality of word pictures and language games? How can we allow for the view that meaning grounds conventional practices in a language community without at the same time reducing the meaning of Quine's *common-sense platitudes*?[139] How can we acknowledge the background dependence of argumentation while maintaining a claim for objectivity?

The central paradox of meaning is how it is possible that a language practice is bound by semantic norms developed by that same practice, an aspect portrayed by the image of Ulysses tying himself to the mast. Some argue that the very existence of debates on the meaning of many concepts disproves that semantic norms could be inter-subjectively, let alone inter-culturally, valid. As Brandom remarks, the practice of language lives

> in this tension between practical agreement that the same norms are binding for all of us, on the formal side, and the disagreement about which these norms are, on the material side.[140]

Some argue that theories of meaning post-Wittgenstein cannot assume objectivity and normativity of meaning at the same time. Meaning was determined *either* by rule of a community *or* by reference to the world. Since rules were not fixed, but elaborated in practices, these very rules could not restrict and limit *this practice*.[141] This paradox of the possibility of limits of meaning is used by Structuring Legal Theory (SLT) in order to deconstruct the doctrine of the limits of the wording. In opposition to SLT, an integrative theory of meaning is maintained here that incorporates both a usage theory of meaning, and normativity and objectivity of meaning.

---

[138] *Cf* L BonJour, *In Defense of Pure Reason. A Rationalist Account of A Priori Justification* (Cambridge 1998); MN Lance and J Hawthorne, *The Grammar of Meaning. Normativy and Semantic Discourse* (Cambridge, 1997).

[139] WVO Quine, *Pursuit of Truth* (Cambridge MA, 1990) 13.

[140] RB Brandom, 'Von der Begriffsanalyse zu einer systematischen Metaphysik. Interview von Susanna Schellenberg' (1999) 6 *Deutsche Zeitschrift für Philosophie* 1005 at 1019.

[141] *Cf* Ayer: 'The acceptance of a rule does not put us into a strait jacket. We are left free to decide at any given point what the rule enjoins or forbids.' AJ Ayer, *Philosophy in the Twentieth Century* (London, 1984) 147 f.

The second chapter is grounded in a pragmatic theory of meaning. This, however, does not mean the sort of pragmatism which demotes argumentation to mere conversation and concludes that substantial disagreements are impossible since discourses are but language games. On the contrary, the pragmatic theory defended here takes up the problem of the relationship between truth and justification, and understands the role of the concept of truth in our discursive practices.

D. Chapter 3

The third chapter brings together the results of the two previous chapters. First, the three main questions of debate are answered. Secondly, a new theory of semantic limits is worked out, based on the concept of meaning as developed in the second chapter. The problem of the limits of the wording is analysed in Brandomian terms, most notably by means of 'deontic scorekeeping'. Semantically clear and semantically unclear cases are differentiated. This makes it possible to develop a clear concept of 'easy cases', which is useful because jurisprudence has so far mainly focused on 'hard cases'.[142] The new system of semantic limits is illustrated with examples from German jurisdiction. These results also support the thesis of the externality of language to the law. Lastly, consequences are derived for the problem of the objectivity of legal argumentation.

---

[142] For the 'lack of concern with easy cases' in jurisprudence, see W Lucy, 'Adjudication' in JL Coleman, S Shapiro and KE Himma (eds), *The Oxford Handbook of Jurisprudence and Philosophy of Law* (Oxford, 2002) 209.

Chapter 1

The Doctrine of the Limits of the Wording

A verbis legis non est recedendum.[1]

IN GERMAN LEGAL theory, three distinct positions on the limits of the wording are held: The traditional-hermeneutic (I), the analytic (II), and the critical (III). In the following text, they will be introduced in this order. The chapter concludes with an overview of the issues which, according to current academic discourse, are still in need of clarification (IV).

I. THE LIMITS OF THE WORDING IN HERMENEUTIC LEGAL THEORY

Hans-Georg Gadamer was the key influence on the current concept of hermeneutic legal theory.

A. The Reception of Ontological Hermeneutics in Legal Theory

Gadamer's hermeneutics were enthusiastically received in German legal theory, in particular by Josef Esser, Arthur Kaufmann,[2] Karl Larenz,[3]

---

[1] Latin legal provision dating back to Marcellus, see Just Dig 32, 69 pr.
[2] It is commonly accepted that Kaufmann's first publication on hermeneutics was 'Analogie und "Natur der Sache"', see M Frommel, *Die Rezeption der Hermeneutik bei Karl Larenz und Josef Esser* (Ebelsbach, 1981) 44. Busse, however, has pointed out that there is no reference to Gadamer in 'Analogie und "Natur der Sache"' and that Kaufmann's second-edition 'efforts at redefining his book as an early contribution to new hermeneutics' are incorrect. See D Busse, *Juristische Semantik. Grundfragen der juristischen Interpretationstheorie in sprachwissenschaftlicher Sicht* (Berlin, 1993) 79 fn 15.
[3] Ever since the third edition of his 'Methodenlehre der Rechtswissenschaft'. The hermeneutic influences on Larenz' legal theory have been examined by Frommel. She states that in the case of Larenz, hermeneutics meet 'a well-elaborated conception of types, resulting in an idiosyncratic combination of Hegelian and hermeneutic elements': Frommel, *Die*

34 The Doctrine of the Limits of the Wording

Joachim Hruschka,[4] and Winfried Hassemer.[5] Since Gadamer's aim was to provide a comprehensive philosophy, legal scholars cooperated in drawing up a universal legal philosophy.[6] In the following, I will single out those aspects which are interesting with regard to methodology, and examine their significance for the limits of the wording.

The key to the reception of hermeneutics can be found in the pre-Gadamer situation in legal theory.[7] Esser, in his *Grundsatz und Norm*, had criticised the idea that codified legal norms (*Rechtssätze*) were overrated. A norm, he stated, was not a constant factor because it was interacting with extra-legal reasons for decisions.[8]

The significance and effectiveness of the *canons* of traditional legal hermeneutics were also disputed.[9] It was said that they could be played off against each other and that they provided 'the judge neither with help nor control' because there was no clear rule of precedence.[10] Finally, the traditional subsumption model had also come under fire. It was objected that the role of logic in law was overrated, and that both inductive and deductive models had been found wanting.[11]

This criticism put the overall rationality of legal decision-making at risk.[12] Kriele stated with regard to constitutional law methodology that

---

Rezeption der Hermeneutik bei Karl Larenz und Josef Esser (n 2 above) 4. For criticism on the 'remoteness' of Larenz' hermeneutics from language see D Busse, *Juristische Semantik* (n 2 above) 81–8.

[4] In the same year that the second edition of *Wahrheit und Methode* was published, Hruschka published his *Die Konstitution des Rechtsfalles*. See also J Hruschka, *Das Verstehen von Rechtstexten. Zur hermeneutischen Transpositivität des positiven Rechts* (München, 1972). For a critical assessment from the standpoint of analytic legal theory see H Rottleuthner, 'Hermeneutik und Jurisprudenz' in H-J Koch (ed), *Juristische Methodenlehre und analytische Philosophie* (Kronberg/Ts., 1976) 14–18.

[5] W Hassemer, *Tatbestand und Typus. Untersuchungen zur strafrechtlichen Hermeneutik* (Köln, 1967).

[6] Most of the work on the universality of a legal hermeneutics aligned towards a philosophy of law was done by Arthur Kaufmann. See generally W Hassemer, 'Juristische Hermeneutik' (1986) 72 *Archiv für Rechts- und Sozialphilosophie* 195 at 205.

[7] See Rottleuthner, 'Hermeneutik und Jurisprudenz' (n 4 above) 11 f.

[8] J Esser, *Grundsatz und Norm in der richterlichen Fortbildung des Privatrechts* (Tübingen 1956) 20; J Esser, *Vorverständnis und Methodenwahl in der Rechtsfindung. Rationalitätsgrundlagen richterlicher Entscheidungspraxis*, 2nd edn (Frankfurt am Main, 1972) 80–83. See Frommel, *Die Rezeption der Hermeneutik bei Karl Larenz und Josef Esser* (n 2 above) 116–18.

[9] Rottleuthner, 'Hermeneutik und Jurisprudenz' (n 4 above) 11.

[10] Esser, *Vorverständnis und Methodenwahl in der Rechtsfindung* (n 8 above) 7.

[11] Rottleuthner, 'Hermeneutik und Jurisprudenz' (n 4 above) 11 f.

[12] See also R Dreier, 'Zur Problematik und Situation der Verfassungsinterpretation' in R Dreier (ed), *Recht, Moral, Ideologie. Studien zur Rechtstheorie* (Frankfurt am Main, 1981) 108 f.

the approach to creation of precedent has become so fundamentally problematic that there is hardly a single norm among the traditional tenet which remains undisputed.[13]

And, according to Larenz, it

> appears as if the doctrine of free law ... [had] privily become the creed of choice among a major part of the practitioners.[14]

The key landmarks of legal methodology had come under suspicion, and it was under the shadow of this situation that the reception of philosophical hermeneutics took place. The practitioners of legal hermeneutics focused on the issues of the relationship between rules and the facts of a case, and the openness of language. Both Gadamer's ontological hermeneutics and an increasingly common critical position with regard to the subsumption model were evident in the *three development directions* of legal hermeneutics: in Esser's teachings of *Pre-judgements* (i); in the typology formulated, in particular, by Larenz (ii); and in Arthur Kaufmann's studies on analogy (iii).

(i) The Limits of the Wording and Pre-Judgements

In his *Vorverständnis und Methodenwahl in der Rechtsfindung*, Josef Esser framed a fundamental hermeneutic criticism of traditional legal theory. Esser found the critical situation described above corroborated in his analysis of the practice of the *Bundesgerichtshof* (BGH) (German Federal Court of Justice). He detected the need of a 'theory of the practical application of law'.[15] In the spirit of ontological hermeneutics, he was not interested in creating a new legal theory, but in pinpointing the conditions for rational legal decisions. Esser examined Gadamer's philosophy with regard to the significance of those conditions for jurisprudence (a) and translates its basic principles for the reading of legal texts (b) and (c).

(a) Ontological Prerequisites for the Understanding of Normative Texts

Esser frames the expression *legal application*. Just as other interpreters, members of the judiciary are subject to a text's historical impact.[16] They operate in a legal tradition composed of laws, adjudications, and other

---

[13] M Kriele, *Theorie der Rechtsgewinnung. Entwickelt am Problem der Verfassungsinterpretation* (Berlin, 1967) 13.
[14] K Larenz, 'Entwicklungstendenzen der heutigen Zivilrechtsdogmatik' (1962) *Juristenzeitung* 105.
[15] Esser, *Vorverständnis und Methodenwahl in der Rechtsfindung* (n 8 above) 7.
[16] HG Gadamer, *Wahrheit und Methode. Grundzüge einer philosophischen Hermeneutik*, 6th edn (Tübingen, 1990) 305.

judicial paradigms, and are affected by them.[17] Within this history of events, 'judges [adapt] laws handed down to them to the requirements of the present' and connect the 'law's legal policy with the present'.[18] It is this mediating process that Esser, in reference to Gadamer, calls 'application'. Interpreting and applying laws are one and the same; they coincide.[19]

The hermeneutic circle also applies to the application of law. Any understanding of a legal text is established by the anticipating movement of the Pre-judgements with regard to the necessity of regulating the issue at hand and the regulatory objective of the rule.[20]

According to Esser, *legal pre-judgements* are the

> categorical ... apparatus ... which—itself a result of social experience—helps judges to unconsciously chose, register, and classify the obviously relevant features of a case and the 'appropriate' norms.[21]

The sources of this apparatus are

> many different learning curves, ranging from vocational training to key scientific material, ie cases of conflicts which are recognised to be particularly illustrative.[22]

It includes the interpreter's expectation of correctness, which inevitably anticipates any just result.

(b) Significance for the Application of Law in General

On the basis of the above ontological preconditions for the understanding of legal texts, Esser criticises the self-image of traditional legal theory. Applying the law cannot be limited in scope to the logical pattern of legal subsumption. Rather, he says, pre-judgements provide a pre-legal horizon. Based on this horizon, norms will be chosen and, gradually, the major premise formed, depending on the particular facts of the case.

Thus, Esser states, the key factors of legal argumentation turn out to be controlled by the legal practitioner's pre-judgements and value judgements.[23] For Esser, the logically consistent question is how one may rationally establish these extra-legal value judgements. The usefulness of any interpretation would depend 'on identifying a rational link between judicial Pre-judgements and tamper-proof posits of justice'.[24]

---

[17] Esser, *Vorverständnis und Methodenwahl in der Rechtsfindung* (n 8 above) 140.
[18] Esser, *Vorverständnis und Methodenwahl in der Rechtsfindung* (n 8 above) 136 f.
[19] Esser, *Vorverständnis und Methodenwahl in der Rechtsfindung* (n 8 above) 119, 136.
[20] Esser, *Vorverständnis und Methodenwahl in der Rechtsfindung* (n 8 above) 30, 136.
[21] Esser, *Vorverständnis und Methodenwahl in der Rechtsfindung* (n 8 above) 10.
[22] Esser, *Vorverständnis und Methodenwahl in der Rechtsfindung* (n 8 above) 10.
[23] Esser, *Vorverständnis und Methodenwahl in der Rechtsfindung* (n 8 above) 31, 53 f.
[24] Esser, *Vorverständnis und Methodenwahl in der Rechtsfindung* (n 8 above) 117.

Esser goes on to develop three of these posits: First, the compilation of relevant material would have to be absolute. Secondly, any interpretation would have to dovetail with existing dogmatic regulatory tradition.[25] Thirdly, during the verification of correctness, it would be necessary for the decision to meet widespread agreement, be plausible, and be reasonable.[26]

The verification of correctness is, according to Esser, the key element of rationalisation. He states that it means nothing less than 'suspending dogmatic authority in favour of "legal policy" arguments on justice'.[27]

(c) Significance for the Limits of the Wording

For Esser, language, too, is 'an integral part of Pre-judgements'.[28] Whenever we employ language, he says, traditional ways of usage are updated with regard to the horizon of their application. According to Gadamer, understanding only becomes possible because we have presuppositional knowledge (ie Pre-judgements) with regard to the problem in question:

> Considering a specific regulatory issue in view of the possible authority of a text is *the* pivotal act. If we forgo this step, we remain utterly unable to deduce the regulatory spirit behind the language of law.[29]

The significance of a term, Esser states, is not determined by 'given semantic properties' of any kind whatsoever, but rather by the evaluation of interests.[30] While these follow the know-how acquired through precedents and science, the actual regulatory task resulting from the case at hand remains crucial. It is this task, according to Esser, which determines the definitions we select for given legal concepts.[31] He declares:

> Accordingly, the 'semantic examination' of a concept of law is always absolute with regard to the regulatory context that is relevant to its conceptual use.[32]

> [T]he semantic performance of any concept is fully determined by its specific previous treatment and examination.[33]

As a consequence, Esser argues, legal practitioners are unable to determine the true or correct meaning of legal texts if they rely on semantics alone. Rather, they themselves established norms through the hermeneutic circle.[34] Interpreters, Esser states, base their normative definitions of concepts

---

[25] Esser, *Vorverständnis und Methodenwahl in der Rechtsfindung* (n 8 above) 19.
[26] Esser, *Vorverständnis und Methodenwahl in der Rechtsfindung* (n 8 above) 9.
[27] Esser, *Vorverständnis und Methodenwahl in der Rechtsfindung* (n 8 above) 19.
[28] Esser, *Vorverständnis und Methodenwahl in der Rechtsfindung* (n 8 above) 10.
[29] Esser, *Vorverständnis und Methodenwahl in der Rechtsfindung* (n 8 above) 138.
[30] Esser, *Vorverständnis und Methodenwahl in der Rechtsfindung* (n 8 above) 56 f.
[31] Esser, *Vorverständnis und Methodenwahl in der Rechtsfindung* (n 8 above) 58.
[32] Esser, *Vorverständnis und Methodenwahl in der Rechtsfindung* (n 8 above) 103.
[33] Esser, *Vorverständnis und Methodenwahl in der Rechtsfindung* (n 8 above) 104.
[34] Esser, *Vorverständnis und Methodenwahl in der Rechtsfindung* (n 8 above) 41 f.

38 The Doctrine of the Limits of the Wording

on value judgements. Because of these ontological preconditions, he considers making a distinction between cognitive and volitive elements of language unfeasible, similar to differentiating between descriptive and normative concepts.[35] This opinion leads him to a general relativisation of the significance of semantics for the practical application of law:

> The regulatory meaning of a law which is to be applied is, in general, not considered to be an issue of a rule's formal quality, and neither one of the linguistic expression used in a particular text to describe a rule, but rather one of the regulatory motive communicated by said expression or form ... it may even lack a norm text.[36]

For Esser, this remains true even in cases where the result is critically influenced by the semantic argument, as,

> [i]n each case, the significance of a legal concept depends on the demands made on its legal permeability or dogmatic rigidity by the will to justice.[37]

For Esser, the hermeneutic context described above leads to the following conclusion regarding the limits of the wording:

> Thus fade the ideas of the limits of positive law which had to be part and parcel of legislative ideology.[38]

In *Grundsatz und Norm*—with reference to the volitive elements of interpretation—Esser had already described any application of a rule as the creation of a new rule. He had also denied the existence of any fundamental difference between extensive interpretation and the use of analogies to close gaps.[39] The difference between interpretation and further development of the law, as Esser added in *Vorverständnis und Methodenwahl*, is not one of quality, but rather only a very slight one[40] and, all-in-all, 'indefinable'.[41]

The conclusions drawn by Esser for the limits of the wording have often been interpreted incorrectly. It has been claimed that Esser referred to the limits of the wording as 'fluid'.[42] The complete quotation, however, runs as follows:

---

[35] Esser, *Vorverständnis und Methodenwahl in der Rechtsfindung* (n 8 above) 10, 57.
[36] Esser, *Vorverständnis und Methodenwahl in der Rechtsfindung* (n 8 above) 33.
[37] Esser, *Vorverständnis und Methodenwahl in der Rechtsfindung* (n 8 above) 102.
[38] Esser, *Vorverständnis und Methodenwahl in der Rechtsfindung* (n 8 above) 177.
[39] Esser, *Grundsatz und Norm in der richterlichen Fortbildung des Privatrechts* (n 8 above) 255 f, 259.
[40] Esser, *Vorverständnis und Methodenwahl in der Rechtsfindung* (n 8 above) 178.
[41] Esser, *Vorverständnis und Methodenwahl in der Rechtsfindung* (n 8 above) 120 fn 6, referring to Larenz, Canaris, and Kriele.
[42] K Engisch and T Würtenberger, *Einführung in das juristische Denken*, 9th edn (Stuttgart, 1997) 122 fn 47; H-M Pawlowski, *Methodenlehre für Juristen. Theorie der Norm und des Gesetzes*, 3rd edn (Heidelberg, 1999) para 458, and fn 11.

The Limits of the Wording in Hermeneutic Legal Theory 39

[Thus], everything depends on understanding rules within their accepted range of interpretation and their concepts' approved dogmatic regulatory capacity. The constant changes in this interpretative and dogmatic understanding are the reasons why any legal theory which assumed a predetermined 'content of the law' would have to consider the limit between extensive interpretation and filling gaps to be 'fluid'.[43]

Esser does not share this view of a 'fluid' limit. Rather, he uses this term to describe a position which a view he *rejects* would have to take if followed through to its logical conclusion: ie, any legal theory which assumes that the content of law is predetermined. Esser's reserved position on this matter suggests that he is unwilling to share this assumption, in other words, that he completely rejects the principle of limits. Esser says so himself in a passage which has often been overlooked:

> Thus, it is not enough to describe the limit between extensive interpretation and filling gaps as 'fluid'. One has to admit that filling gaps is nothing less than 'the continuation of interpretation', albeit on 'a different level'.[44]

According to Esser, the limit to judicial activity assumed in the principle of the separation of powers which grants judges solely the right to interpret—leaving further development of the law to the legislative branch or (as in case law) to specific courts of interpretation—is mere fiction.[45] While older legal theories considered crucial the issue of the compatibility of juridical development of the law with the words of the law, Esser regards this point to be irrelevant. In his eyes, the *qualitative* control of correctness is pivotal.[46] Esser not only considers the issue of the limits of the wording to be impossible to solve; from his point of view, it remains trivial.

In the light of this position, one cannot help enquiring into just what Esser's opinion on the law's binding force on the courts is. In his remarks on language, Esser already emphasised that on no account did he assume an arbitrary 'anything goes'. Rather, he spoke of a 'binding regulatory significance' of norms—one which was beyond legal practitioners' authority.[47] If semantic observations are always final and under the formative influence of Pre-judgements, then how would this regulatory significance come about? Esser expressively dismisses the idea of fixed, objective meaning that would only have to be applied 'to the case at hand'. The binding effect, he says, is the result of working with the law while

---

[43] Esser, *Vorverständnis und Methodenwahl in der Rechtsfindung* (n 8 above) 180.
[44] Esser, *Vorverständnis und Methodenwahl in der Rechtsfindung* (n 8 above) 182, quoting C-W Canaris, *Die Feststellung von Lücken im Gesetz. Eine methodologische Studie über Voraussetzungen und Grenzen der richterlichen Rechtsfortbildung praeter legem* (Berlin, 1964).
[45] Esser, *Vorverständnis und Methodenwahl in der Rechtsfindung* (n 8 above) 178.
[46] Esser, *Vorverständnis und Methodenwahl in der Rechtsfindung* (n 8 above) 186.
[47] Esser, *Vorverständnis und Methodenwahl in der Rechtsfindung* (n 8 above) 34.

including the value judgements of casuistry.[48] Thus, the 'authority of a system of legal awareness' is to take the place of the 'rule of the legal text'.[49] Esser is of the opinion that this would not attach too little value to the text itself. In no way, he states, would it become a 'mere backdrop to decisions which are the product of irrational and emotional aspirations', since no decision is lawful unless it refers to the text.[50] Esser continues:

> [Y]et this, precisely, is the moot point: To what extent does the wording determine the outcome? We will only be able to resolve this issue if we include all hermeneutic and political pre-assessments. There is no use hoping for ... a doctrinal formulatory which would determine the binding character of the wording in terms of verbal flexibility. The verbal limit fully depends upon the limits of significance of the rule's purpose. The extent of the latter, in turn, relies on the understanding of the judge, who never acts on his own authority, but conscientiously processes the statutory motive both with regard to its dogmatic aspects and legal policy.[51]

Ultimately, the degree to which a judge is bound to the law is (only) determined by his or her sense of responsibility. Depending on hermeneutic and political pre-assessment, limits of significance will be extended or shrunk. The fact that Esser still feels entitled to call this approach 'never act[ing] on [one's] own authority' is connected with his concept of non-manipulable principles of justice, presented above.[52]

(ii) Limits of the Wording and Typology

In his essay on being bound by the law as a problem of hermeneutics, Larenz objects to the conclusions Esser had drawn from Gadamer's hermeneutics. First, he emphasises his commitment to Gadamer's 'fundamental hermeneutic insight'.[53] For Larenz, legal determination is in no way beyond rationality. Even if Pre-judgements, as an indispensable precondition of understanding, were constantly reformed and changed, our tradition of language and culture would still remain a workable foundation for inter-subjective communication and, also, for the interpretation of laws.[54] Larenz continues that hard cases should not be declared archetypal for

---

[48] Esser, *Vorverständnis und Methodenwahl in der Rechtsfindung* (n 8 above) 197.
[49] Esser, *Vorverständnis und Methodenwahl in der Rechtsfindung* (n 8 above) 190.
[50] Esser, *Vorverständnis und Methodenwahl in der Rechtsfindung* (n 8 above) 197.
[51] Esser, *Vorverständnis und Methodenwahl in der Rechtsfindung* (n 8 above) 197.
[52] *Cf* p 37 above.
[53] K Larenz, 'Die Bindung des Richters an das Gesetz als hermeneutisches Problem' in E Forsthoff, W Weber and F Wieacker (eds), *Festschrift für Ernst Rudolf Huber* (Göttingen, 1973) 292.
[54] *Ibid*, 296, 298.

The Limits of the Wording in Hermeneutic Legal Theory 41

legal determination.[55] Furthermore, the final standards were determined by the positive legal system and 'the results . . . of the judiciary'.[56] Whether Larenz is correct in his interpretation of Esser remains doubtful with regard to Esser's remarks on the issue of being bound by the law. More important are Larenz's own remarks on the limits of the wording, which are closely connected to the typology he developed.

Legal typology goes back to Georg Jellinek's political science and Max Weber's sociology of politics and government.[57] Hermeneutics compare the type with the concept. While the latter was defined in abstract terms by a limited number of characteristics, the former occupied the middle ground between the general and the specific.[58] As opposed to the concept, types were clearer and more practical; they could not be defined but only described.[59] According to Larenz, the characteristics of a type can never be completely determined; they remain variable and gradable.[60] Thus, subsumption under a type was impossible. Rather, the application of law was effected by way of assignment to an overall picture.[61]

Larenz aims to understand the limits of the wording not in conceptual terms, but typologically.[62] However, he remains silent on the details of this typological definition. Even though Larenz, with reference to Gadamer and Esser, also submits meaning to the hermeneutic circle, he wants to adhere to the limits of the wording:

> We have to make a distinction between interpretation and juridical development of the law, precisely because the latter has to be bound by specific preconditions, if the law is to keep its natural role as the prime regulation . . . There is no other limit to be found . . . than that of the semantically possible meaning.[63]

---

[55] Larenz, 'Die Bindung des Richters an das Gesetz als hermeneutisches Problem' (n 53 above) 300.
[56] Larenz, 'Die Bindung des Richters an das Gesetz als hermeneutisches Problem' (n 53 above) 307 f.
[57] G Jellinek, *Allgemeine Staatslehre*, 3rd edn (Berlin, 1921) 34 ff; M Weber, 'Die "Objektivität" sozialwissenschaftlicher und sozialpolitischer Erkenntnis' (1904) 19 *Archiv für Sozialwissenschaft und Sozialpolitik* 43. See also G Radbruch, 'Klassenbegriffe und Ordnungsbegriffe im Rechtsdenken' in G Radbruch (ed), *Rechtsphilosophie III* (Heidelberg 1990); HJ Wolff, 'Typen im Recht und in der Rechtswissenschaft' (1952) 5 *Studium Generale* 195.
[58] A Kaufmann, *Analogie und 'Natur der Sache'. Zugleich ein Beitrag zur Lehre vom Typus*, 2nd edn (Publisher, Heidelberg, 1982) 47 f.
[59] K Larenz, *Methodenlehre der Rechtswissenschaft*, 6th edn (Berlin, 1991) 218.
[60] K Engisch, *Die Idee der Konkretisierung in Recht und Rechtswissenschaft unserer Zeit*, 2nd edn, (Heidelberg, 1968) 242.
[61] Larenz, *Methodenlehre der Rechtswissenschaft* (n 59 above) 221.
[62] Larenz, *Methodenlehre der Rechtswissenschaft* (n 59 above) 322. See also G Hassold, 'Strukturen der Gesetzesauslegung' in C-W Canaris and U Diederichsen (eds), *Festschrift für Karl Larenz zum 80. Geburtstag* (München, 1983) 219.
[63] Larenz, *Methodenlehre der Rechtswissenschaft* (n 59 above) 323.

According to Larenz, drawing precise limits remains impossible, yet 'in the overwhelming majority of all cases' it can be clearly shown whether a statement lies outside the meaning of a term. Negative assertions such as these were 'self-explanatory for anyone proficient in a language'.[64] The number of marginal cases in which a clear line could not be drawn is, according to Larenz, 'minute'.[65]

(iii)   The Limits of the Wording and the Analogicity of Language

Arthur Kaufmann offers a more elaborated version of Larenz's notion of a typological determination of the limits of the wording. In his philosophy of law, Kaufmann applies the principle of 'analogicity', which he considers to be characteristic of our existence, to language.[66] Since it was based on detecting similarities between forms of usage, any use of language must proceed analogously. This, Kaufmann states, is especially relevant in legal terminology, which consists, to a large degree, of abstract terms. According to Kaufmann, analogies are not merely a part of judicial development of the law, unconnected to the general application of law. Rather, any application of law was based on analogies. There was no room for a limit to possible meaning. There was but one crucial issue, namely whether it was at all possible to draw a line *within* analogies, separating permitted and inadmissibly extensive applications of law.[67] This line, according to Kaufmann, is the *type* on which the statutory elements of an offence are based.[68]

As a consequence Kaufmann sees not semantic aspects, but primarily the nature of the matter as crucial for the application of law. Rules were related to the actual state of affairs, with the 'meaning of the law' determined by the factual structure of the actual state of affairs.[69] Types, Kaufmann continues, are at no-one's disposition, they are the fixed 'root causes and objects' of legislation.[70] Legislators' only option is to describe

---

[64]   Larenz, *Methodenlehre der Rechtswissenschaft* (n 59 above) 322 with fn 19a. See also K Larenz, 'Über das Verhältnis von Interpretation und richterlicher Rechtsfortbildung' in F Lejman (ed), *Festskrift tillägnad Professor, Juris Doktor Karl Olivecrona* (Stockholm, 1964) 385, 404.

[65]   Larenz, 'Über das Verhältnis von Interpretation und richterlicher Rechtsfortbildung' (n 64 above) 394.

[66]   *Cf* concerning this matter and with regard to the following Kaufmann, *Analogie und 'Natur der Sache'* (n 58 above) 29–32.

[67]   Kaufmann, *Analogie und 'Natur der Sache'* (n 58 above) 6.

[68]   Kaufmann, *Analogie und 'Natur der Sache'* (n 58 above) 52. However, Kaufmann admits in his afterword that this limit is ultimately set by the interpreter, and that for this reason the limits of types are of little more use than the limits of the wording, see Kaufmann, *Analogie und 'Natur der Sache'* (n 58 above) 68.

[69]   Kaufmann, *Analogie und 'Natur der Sache'* (n 58 above) 42.

[70]   Kaufmann, *Analogie und 'Natur der Sache'* (n 58 above) 48.

types. These descriptions, in turn, are what legal practitioners are bound to. They determine the limits of the admissible application of the law.

Even within typology this position is controversial. Hassemer objects that, with types themselves being the outcome of a hermeneutic process of construction, they can hardly be used to set limits on it.[71] Nevertheless, he also wants to retain the notion of a limit of the possible meaning, as it to some degree has a controlling function 'within the horizon of a typological approach to the hermeneutic process' and is an essential element of judicial argumentation.[72] Hruschka, on the other hand, objects to the limits of the wording in principle. With reference to Kaufmann and Hassemer, he declares that it is impossible to separate interpretation and analogy since any application of the law proceeded analogously.[73]

B. Hermeneutics and Legal Interpretation

Hermeneuts in the tradition of Gadamer share an emphasis on the volitive elements in any application of the law. The meaning of the wording of the law is not beyond evaluation. Therefore, the limits of the wording are not settled once and for all. According to the hermeneuts' perception, legal practitioners themselves ultimately decide on the meaning of a norm and thus on the limits of the wording. Depending on their legal-political or hermeneutic pre-assessment, they consider the wording of the law to be more or less flexible. Hassold thus describes the 'typological differentiation' between interpretation and juridical development of the law advocated by Larenz as a 'judgemental classification'.[74] For hermeneuts, the meaning of the words—conveyed through language use, doctrine, and judicial precedents—is but one aspect among others; one which has to come second to considerations of justice. It is only during the actual process of the application of the law that the up-to-date meaning of the words is constructed.[75] Needless to say that *this* meaning will never be able to limit interpretation. After all, it is an outcome of said interpretation.

With regard to the separation of powers, this result is shocking. However, hermeneuts feel not in the least troubled. Rather, they consider

---

[71] Hassemer, *Tatbestand und Typus* (n 5 above) 161. In his afterword, Kaufmann essentially agreed to this criticism, see Kaufmann, *Analogie und 'Natur der Sache'* (n 58 above) 67 f.
[72] Hassemer, *Tatbestand und Typus* (n 5 above) 164 f.
[73] Hruschka, *Das Verstehen von Rechtstexten* (n 4 above) 102.
[74] Hassold, 'Strukturen der Gesetzesauslegung' (n 62 above) 219.
[75] See also M von Hoecke, *Norm, Kontext und Entscheidung. Die Interpretationsfreiheit des Richters* (Publisher, Leuven, 1988) 227.

the vagueness of legal language to be an advantage.[76] With regard to the binding to the law, they rely on the judges' responsibility and the necessity of justification within the discourse of justice. Following Heidegger, Hassemer stipulates that one needs not to get out of the circle, but to enter it.[77] Incidences of Pre-judgements and concealed reasons for judgement have to be disclosed and examined in the discourse of interpretation.[78]

II. THE LIMITS OF THE WORDING IN ANALYTIC LEGAL THEORY

Since the beginning of the 1970s, speech analysis theories have become a part of legal theory. They prompted analytic legal philosophers to criticise legal hermeneutics. They demanded the separation of the individual problems, which had been syncretically mingled in hermeneutics, and that they should be assigned to the various specialist fields, eg semantics, legal sociology, et al.[79] With regard to the issue of the limits of the wording, the approaches of speech analysis proved to be seminal. The classification of unclear semantic terms by Koch, Rüßmann, and Herberger led to a specification of the limits of the wording (A). With his word usage rule (theory of the rule of the use of words) Robert Alexy made a significant contribution to the clarification of the role of the limits of the wording within the so-called internal justification (B).

A. The Clarification of the Limits of the Wording by Koch, Rüßmann, and Herberger

Using the methods of speech analysis, Koch and Rüßmann were able to specify the limits of the wording more precisely. Their understanding is

---

[76] A Kaufmann, *Rechtsphilosophie*, 2nd edn (München, 1997) 117; R Zippelius, *Juristische Methodenlehre. Eine Einführung*, 7th edn (München, 1999) 48. Along the same lines J Waldron, 'Vagueness in Law and Language. Some Philosophical Issues' (1994) *California Law Review* 509 at 532; T Williamson, 'Vagueness' in PV Lamarque and RE Asher (eds), *Concise Encyclopedia of Philosophy of Language* (Oxford, 1997) 204. With regard to the latter, see also B Bix, *Law, Language, and Legal Determinacy* (Oxford, 1995) 55–9. For an *economic analysis of law* with regard to the costs and advantages of semantic precision in laws see GK Hadfield, 'Weighing the Value of Vagueness. An Economic Perspective on Precision in the Law' (1994) *California Law Review* 541.

[77] Hassemer, 'Juristische Hermeneutik' (n 6 above) 211.

[78] Hassemer, 'Juristische Hermeneutik' (n 6 above) 211; Kriele, *Theorie der Rechtsgewinnung* (n 13 above) 315 f.

[79] Rottleuthner, 'Hermeneutik und Jurisprudenz' (n 4 above) 28. For reasons of clarity, this classification strictly separates hermeneutic and analytic legal theory. However, this accurate discrimination has already been quashed, in the main thanks to the integrating works of Georg Henrik von Wright. See GH von Wright, *Erklären und Verstehen*, 3rd edn (Frankfurt am Main, 1991) 38–41. On 'analytic hermeneutics' see also R Alexy, 'Juristische Interpretation' in R Alexy (ed), *Recht, Vernunft, Diskurs. Studien zur Rechtsphilosophie* (Frankfurt am Main, 1995) 75.

The Limits of the Wording in Analytic Legal Theory 45

based on the philosophy of language and the debates and basic premises it yielded for legal theory. Therefore, we will begin by discussing the concept of meaning and its implications for the application of law (i) and (ii), before we come to a discussion of the model of the limits of the wording (iii).

(i) Establishing and Assigning Meaning

According to Koch and Rüßmann, there are only two approaches to the semantic interpretation of legal expressions: Either to *establish* habitual language use empirically, or to *assign* meaning.[80] This difference is integrated into their model of the application of the law. Hence, there are two feasible ways of assigning meaning—the result of the three objectives of interpretation defined by Koch and Rüßmann: What has been said, what is desired, and what is reasonable.[81] These objectives match the three criteria: interpretation of the wording, subjective-teleological interpretation, and objective-teleological interpretation. This results in the following tiered model for the *application of the law*[82]:

1   Establishing what the legislator *said*.
2   Meaning is assigned, taking into account the legislator's subjective purposes (ie what is *intended*).
3   Assigning meaning in light of the objective purposes, ie what is *reasonable*.

As judges are bound by the law, this model has to be considered hierarchical, ie one is only allowed to progress to the lower level if decision-making was impossible on the higher one.[83] With regard to the limits of the wording, two essential questions result from this process: How can we establish what has been said? And how are we to distinguish between unambiguous and vague wording?

With regard to establishing what has been said, two conclusions can be drawn from the concept of meaning argued by Koch and Rüßmann. First, if we establish what has been said empirically, this has to mean determining linguistic conventions. Secondly, we need to make a 'detour' and

---

[80] H-J Koch and H Rüssmann, *Juristische Begründungslehre. Eine Einführung in die Grundprobleme der Rechtswissenschaft* (München, 1982) 163. See also E von Savigny, *Grundkurs im wissenschaftlichen Definieren. Übungen zum Selbststudium* (München, 1970) 22–5.
[81] Koch and Rüssmann, *Juristische Begründungslehre* (n 80 above) 7.
[82] Koch and Rüssmann, *Juristische Begründungslehre* (n 80 above) 182, 210 and 211.
[83] Koch and Rüssmann, *Juristische Begründungslehre* (n 80 above) 182. In contrast, Neuner remains very unclear about the relationship between the three objectives of interpretation. According to him, 'in the case of conflicts between what the legislature said and what he desired, unambiguous wording takes precedence if ... it implicates a reasonable settlement', see J Neuner, *Die Rechtsfindung contra legem* (München, 1992) 184.

identify extension in order to specify intention.[84] However, Koch and Rüßmann do not consider empirical research of extensions to be feasible: '[R]easons of time and money definitely' ruled out commissioning linguists to research appropriate language use.[85] Furthermore, Koch has shown in another work that from a given extension, it is not automatically possible to infer the matching intention.[86] With regard to determining meaning, Koch and Rüßmann also argue for a tiered approach: To begin with, one has to peruse legal literature for information on terminological conventions. Where this is insufficient, one may consider referring to dictionaries. *Expressively* referring to personal assumptions about common language use is only acceptable as a subordinate step.

The latter procedure, which has been discredited as the 'armchair approach', may contain some arbitrary elements. Koch and Rüßmann, however, consider this tolerable, as both judicial discourse and interventions by the legislator offered the opportunity of corrections (*correction argument*). Furthermore, the only available alternative, ie ignoring linguistic content, was absurd. Experience showed that in many cases the linguistic content of a norm was enough to achieve clarity among participants whether or not it could be applied (*argument of clear cases*). It was this experience alone that made the legislator's work meaningful. And even in unclear cases, Koch and Rüßmann add, where there is no evidence for a precise use of language or where it is beyond the competence of native speakers to provide such evidence, the meaning of a word still has a binding force. Linguistic indefiniteness was not the equivalent of triviality (*argument of controlling force in unclear cases*).[87]

Thus, the problem of establishing meaning leads to the second question mentioned above, ie how to distinguish unambiguous and vague wording (or clear and unclear instances of interpretation). We will deal with this issue in the next section.

(ii) Classification of Unclear Usage Rules

Koch and Rüßmann offer no definition of what they would consider to be non-ambiguous wording. They rely on a negative determination. The classification they present is to include every case of unclear wording. For

---

[84] Koch and Rüssmann, *Juristische Begründungslehre* (n 80 above) 189.
[85] Koch and Rüssmann, *Juristische Begründungslehre* (n 80 above) 190.
[86] H-J Koch (ed), *Die juristische Methode im Staatsrecht. Über Grenzen von Verfassungs- und Gesetzesbindung* (Frankfurt am Main, 1997).
[87] Koch and Rüssmann, *Juristische Begründungslehre* (n 80 above) 191.

the limits of the wording, this classification is highly significant, as any precise description of this theory depends upon distinguishing between the different cases of unclear meaning.[88]

Koch and Rüßmann distinguish three cases of unclear meaning: Ambiguity, inconsistency, and vagueness.[89] In these cases, usage rules and thus the meaning of a term are unclear.[90] Consequently, interpretation is impossible on semantic grounds, ie the judges establish the meaning of the law for the first time, proceeding according to the step model shown above.[91]

(a) Ambiguity

A term is ambiguous if it may take on different meanings in different contexts. In German, for instance, the expression 'Sicke' stands for, with regard to technology, a swage (a steel block with grooved sides), while in hunter's jargon, it is a female bird. In German judicial terminology, the term 'Wegnahme' (privation or seizure) is used differently in § 289 I of the Criminal Code (StGB) on the one hand and in § 17 II number 1c Act Against Unfair Practices (Gesetz gegen den unlauteren Wettbewerb (UWG)) on the other.[92]

(b) Inconsistency

A term is considered to be inconsistent if it is used within the same context by different speakers with different meanings. Within judicial terminology, we speak of inconsistency if the precise meaning of a legal term has not yet been clarified by the supreme court. Their use varies between different courts, or, in the case of *dissenting votes* of individual judges, also within

---

[88] Koch and Rüßmann, *Juristische Begründungslehre* (n 80 above) 194.
[89] Koch and Rüßmann, *Juristische Begründungslehre* (n 80 above) 191–201. Three extensions to this classification are discussed. To begin with, Koch and Rüßmann introduce a fourth class of unclear terms: Forecast terms. Their distinctive feature is that their use implies laying down a probability factor and empirically-based probability judgement. Problems of interpretation, however, do not go beyond common vagueness. Hence, with regard to the context that is relevant to this book, this is no original category. Secondly, in other publications, Koch mentions porosity as a fifth category, see H-J Koch, 'Das Postulat der Gesetzesbindung im Lichte sprachphilosophischer Überlegungen' (1975) 61 *Archiv für Rechts- und Sozialphilosophie* 37; Koch (ed), *Die juristische Methode im Staatsrecht* (n 86 above). It constitutes, however, a 'potential vagueness' and may be conceptualised with the instruments developed for vagueness. Finally, similar to Koch in earlier publications, Alexy assumes evaluative openness as an independent category. We will go into this when we get to Alexy's theory.
[90] See Koch (ed), *Die juristische Methode im Staatsrecht* (n 86 above).
[91] Koch, 'Das Postulat der Gesetzesbindung im Lichte sprachphilosophischer Überlegungen' (n 89 above) 41.
[92] Regarding § 289 I StGB see BayObLG NJW 1981, 1745 f; regarding § 17 II no1 c UWG see BayObLG NJW 1992, 1777.

courts. One example from German law would be the use of 'Bande' (gang) by the criminal divisions of the Federal Court of Justice (*Bundesgerichtshof* (*BGH*)).[93]

(c) Vagueness

Following Walter Jellinek, Koch and Rüßmann describe the term vagueness by further developing Heck's core-corona-model into a three-sphere model.[94] According to this model, there are three categories of vagueness[95]:

1. There are individuals to which the concept undoubtedly applies (so-called positive candidates).

2. There are individuals to which the concept does undoubtedly not apply (so-called negative candidates).

3. There are individuals as to which it is debateable whether the concept applies or not (so-called neutral candidates).

Using modal logic, the term 'neutral candidate' can be defined more precisely. A candidate would be called neutral if it possessed properties which, according to the concept, are sufficient conditions both to assign and not to assign the term.

(iii) The Limits of the Wording According to Koch, Rüßmann, and Herberger

Having presented Koch and Rüßmann's theory of the application of the law and their terminology, we will now move on to their concept of the limits of the wording. Following on from their differentiation between non-ambiguous and ambiguous meaning, we have to distinguish two types of limits: The limits of the wording in semantically clear cases and the

---

[93] *Cf* the order for referral of the 4th Criminal Division (Strafsenat), NJW 2001, 380–4, and the subsequent decision of the High Senate for Criminal Matters (*Großer Senat für Strafsachen*), BGHSt 46, 321.

[94] Koch and Rüssmann, *Juristische Begründungslehre* (n 80 above) 195. Jellinek, however, using different terminology, distinguished 'spheres' of positive certainty, negative certainty, and possible doubt, see W Jellinek, *Gesetz, Gesetzesanwendung und Zweckmäßigkeitserwägung* (Tübingen, 1913) 37 f. Criticism of the three-spheres model comes from U Neumann, *Rechtsontologie und juristische Argumentation. Zu den ontologischen Implikationen juristischen Argumentierens* (Heidelberg, 1979) 72–7. Neumann's overall conclusion is that the significance of semantic rules for the application of the law is overrated, Neumann, *Rechtsontologie und juristische Argumentation* at 51. The three-candidate model has also been discussed in Anglo-American legal theory, see Waldron, 'Vagueness in Law and Language. Some Philosophical Issues' (n 76 above) 520 f.

[95] Koch and Rüssmann, *Juristische Begründungslehre* (n 80 above) 195.

limits of the wording in semantically unclear cases. The latter can be further divided according to the various types of ambiguity, which have been described above.

A case is semantically clear if, according to the defined usage rules, it is clear without ambiguity whether or not a term applies to an individual. Koch and Rüßmann do not elaborate explicitly on the significance of the limits of the wording in these cases. We can, however, find it in their tiered model of the application of the law: Non-ambiguous wording serves as a barrier against the other canons of interpretation which are excluded from being considered.[96]

In unclear cases, we have to distinguish between different types of ambiguity. Strictly speaking, the limit of the wording gives *two boundaries* for the sphere of vagueness:

> Once meaning has been established, neutral candidates are the only vague terms that may be interpreted using the other judicial rules of interpretation. They may then be defined to be either positive or neutral. With regard to vague terms, 'possible meaning' as the 'boundary of interpretation' thus marks off *two boundaries of interpretation: Interpretation* may neither exclude positive candidates from a norm's area of application, nor include negative candidates in the norm's area of application.[97]

According to Herberger and Koch, the three-sphere model can also be of benefit when determining the limits of the wording for terms which are used ambiguously or inconsistently.[98] It may not, however, simply be copied because other categories of ambiguity lack one key characteristic of vague terms, ie the existence of neutral candidates. Hence, the authors modify their model by framing the concepts of the three candidates differently. With regard to ambiguity and inconsistency, the problem in the application of the law is identical. In both cases, the significant meaning or usage has to be chosen from a number of alternatives. Hence, the authors consider a positive candidate to be an individual which for any of its alternative meanings or usages could be categorised as ambiguous, while a negative candidate would be one which could never be categorised as ambiguous. Similarly, neutral candidates would be ambiguous for at least one but never for all their alternatives. Here, too, the limits of the wording have the twin effects shown above, which means that any assignment relying on other interpretative arguments may only be used for neutral candidates.[99]

---

[96] Koch and Rüssmann, *Juristische Begründungslehre* (n 80 above) 182.
[97] M Herberger and H-J Koch, 'Zur Einführung: Juristische Methodenlehre und Sprachphilosophie' (1978) *Juristische Schulung* 810 at 813.
[98] *Ibid*, 814.
[99] Herberger and Koch, 'Zur Einführung: Juristische Methodenlehre und Sprachphilosophie' (n 97 above) 814.

50 *The Doctrine of the Limits of the Wording*

Finally, it has to be mentioned that a combination of ambiguity and vagueness occurs if one or several of the alternative meanings is in itself vague, ie contains neutral candidates.[100]

B. The Role of the Limits of the Wording in Alexy's Theory of Legal Argumentation

In his theory of legal argumentation, Robert Alexy has produced a comprehensive and philosophically well-founded theory of legal methodology. It is based on his understanding of interpretation as a discourse (i) and consists of a theory of the application of the law which does not explicitly deal with the limits of the wording, yet clarifies that theory's premises (ii).

(i) The Discursive Character of Interpretation

In his study on the concept of judicial interpretation, Robert Alexy distinguishes the interpretation *sensu largissimo*, *sensu largo*, and *sensu stricto*.[101] In its widest sense, interpretation applies to the general understanding of those objects with which subjects associate meaning. Interpretation in its wide sense applies only to understanding of linguistic statements. According to Alexy, this understanding can either be direct or indirect. We talk of direct understanding if linguistic statements are understood without questions or doubts arising. Indirect understanding, on the other hand, is forced to deal with doubts or questions and has to solve these in the course of the process of understanding. The concept of wider interpretation includes both direct and indirect understanding. Finally, interpretation in its narrow sense becomes necessary if a statement is open to several readings and it remains unclear which one would be correct. Therefore, in its narrow sense interpretation refers solely to indirect understanding. It is the key issue of judicial interpretation.

According to Alexy, the interpretation of laws is discursive in character.[102] Discourse is defined by rule-governed activities. Alexy combines speech act theory with Habermas's consensus theory of truth and arrives at a universal pragmatic rationale for specific basic rules in discourse. It follows from these basic rules that every interpretation is a statement on the meaning of a concept. These statements are made with a claim to

---

[100] The authors are aware of this combination, yet do not examine it more closely, Herberger and Koch, 'Zur Einführung: Juristische Methodenlehre und Sprachphilosophie' (n 97 above) 814 fn 55.
[101] Alexy, 'Juristische Interpretation' (n 79 above) 71–3.
[102] Similar BVerfGE 82, 30 (38); R Zippelius, *Juristische Methodenlehre. Eine Einführung*, 7th edn (München, 1999) 48 f.

correctness and with reasons given.[103] In common practical discourse, these reasons are supposed to prove correctness per se. In the special case of legal discourse, it is only claimed that they show the correctness of the interpretation within the framework of the legal system in force.[104] Thus, interpretation (in its narrow sense) is the argument-based choice between different possible meanings.[105]

(ii) Main Features of the Theory of Legal Argumentation

As has been shown above, the indirect understanding of interpretation *sensu stricto* stands for a well-founded choice between various possible meanings. As to how the grounds for this choice are structured, analytic legal theory in general distinguishes between internal and external justification.[106] Internal justification consists of the logically correct inference of the judgement from the premises (a). External justification is concerned with the correctness of said premises (b).

(a) Internal Justification and the Word Usage Rule

The simplest structure for internal justification is[107]:

(1)   (x) (Tx → ORx)   [Rule R]
(2)   T*a*
(3)   OR*a*   (1), (2)

Depending on the complexity of the statutory elements of the offence T, this causal structure has to be broken into further steps. Prior to actual subsumption (shown here as the second premise), it would in many cases be necessary to elaborate on T using a catalogue of alternative or cumulative criteria. For each of these criteria, a rule could be defined as to when it would be considered to have been satisfied, etc. In this manner, a string of ever more precise rules emerges.

In the context at hand, what concerns us most are those rules within this string which are rules on the meaning of the expressions used in the

---

[103] R Alexy, *Theorie der juristischen Argumentation. Die Theorie des rationalen Diskurses als Theorie der juristischen Begründung* (Frankfurt am Main,1978) 264–72, 428 f; Alexy, 'Juristische Interpretation' (n 79 above) 77.
[104] Alexy, *Theorie der juristischen Argumentation* (n 103 above) 264.
[105] Already stated by J Kohler, 'Über die Interpretation von Gesetzen' (1886) 13 *Zeitschrift für das Privat- und Öffentliche Recht der Gegenwart* 1 at 35.
[106] Even though they agree in principle, the terminology used is different. Koch and Rüßmann use the terms Hauptschema and Nebenschema (primary and secondary structure), see Koch and Rüssmann, *Juristische Begründungslehre* (n 80 above) 48–58. MacCormick distinguishes between *first-order justification* and *second-order justification*, see N MacCormick, *Legal Reasoning and Legal Theory* (Oxford, 1978) 19, 100.
[107] For an explanation of the symbols used see Alexy, *Theorie der juristischen Argumentation* (n 103 above) 274.

preceding causal steps. In line with Alexy's reference to the linguistic philosophy of the later Wittgenstein, these rules refer to a particular use of said expressions. For this reason, Alexy has christened them *word usage rules*.[108] Using the word usage rule W, we can deduce a more precise rule R' from R[109]:

(1) (x) (Tx → ORx) [R]
(2) (x) (Mx → Tx) [W]
(3) (x) (Mx → ORx) [R'] (1), (2)

Alexy calls R' the 'interpretation of R by W (I_{RW})'. Following the principle of universalisability, he frames *three rules of formal justice* regarding the use of the word usage rules in the internal justification[110]:

1. A word usage rule has to be given whenever doubts remain as to whether an individual complies with the elements of an offence or a feature of a definition.

2. The number of unfolding steps given has to be sufficient for the statements in the last unfolding step to be no longer contentious, so that they apply to the case at hand.[111]

3. As many development steps as possible have to be given.

The word usage rule can not be deduced from the statute. Like all premises, it has to be justified externally.

(b) External Justification and Semantic Arguments

External justification is concerned with accounting for the premises used in the internal justification. Alexy distinguishes six different groups of external justification rules.[112] In the context of this book, the first group which consists of the canons of interpretation is most interesting. Its most important task is the justification of propositions I_{RW}(=R'), ie the interpretations of a legal norm using word usage rules.[113]

According to Alexy's classification, the semantic argument is the first form of argument of the six canons. One of these is at hand if R' is justified

---

[108] Alexy, *Theorie der juristischen Argumentation* (n 103 above) 278. See also H-J Koch, 'Ansätze einer juristischen Argumentationstheorie?' (1977) 36 *Archiv für Rechts- und Sozialphilosophie* 364. Against U Neumann, *Juristische Argumentationslehre* (Darmstadt, 1986) 47 f.
[109] Alexy, *Theorie der juristischen Argumentation* (n 103 above) 288.
[110] Alexy, *Theorie der juristischen Argumentation* (n 103 above) 279 f.
[111] On this objective of evidence see R Alexy, 'Die logische Analyse juristischer Entscheidungen' (1980) NF 14 *Archiv für Rechts- und Sozialphilosophie: Beiheft* 26 f; H Rüßmann, 'Sprache und Recht. Sprachtheoretische Überlegungen zum Gesetzesbindungspostulat' in J Zimmermann (ed), *Sprache und Welterfahrung* (München,1978) 221.
[112] Alexy, *Theorie der juristischen Argumentation* (n 103 above) 285.
[113] Alexy, *Theorie der juristischen Argumentation* (n 103 above) 288.

The Limits of the Wording in Analytic Legal Theory 53

or criticised with reference to linguistic meaning. Alexy, too, distinguishes between establishing and assigning meaning. The defined use of a word can be determined empirically. Once it has been established, it can be used to justify a word usage rule externally and hence, according to the structure shown above, a specific rule R'. We would only speak of a semantic argument if one comes to a conclusion on the way a term is used. On the other hand, W can not be *assigned* on the basis of semantics alone, but only with the help of the other forms of argument.

Alexy distinguishes three forms of semantic arguments[114]:

1 Due to W, R' *has* to be accepted as an interpretation of R.
2 Due to W_2, R' *can not* be accepted as an interpretation of R.
3 Both 1. and 2. are *possible* because neither W_1 nor W_2 can be determined.

The argument forms 1 and 2 are definite, ie the semantic argument already decides whether an individual falls under a rule or not. In the third case, however, a decision cannot be based on the semantic argument alone. A word usage rule has to be *assigned*, and this can only be done with the help of the other forms of argument.[115] This third case applies if no word usage rule can be established, eg because usage is inconsistent or one lacks rules for the sphere of vagueness. Furthermore, assigning meaning can be necessary for reasons of practicability, ie especially considerations of justice, if these necessitate a deviation from the established word usage rule. The latter raises the question of how the individual arguments of interpretation are ranked. On account of the binding to the law, Alexy argues a rule for *allocating the burden of argument*:

> Arguments which express a binding to the wording of the law or to the intention of the historical legislature rank higher than other arguments, unless sound reasons can be given to let other arguments take priority over them.[116]

---

[114] Alexy, *Theorie der juristischen Argumentation* (n 103 above) 289.
[115] Alexy, *Theorie der juristischen Argumentation* (n 103 above) 290 f. Waldron objects to the option of assigning meaning in the sphere of vagueness. However, he also states 'One should not exaggerate the problem. If vagueness is in general ineliminable, it does not follow that it is irreducible in a given area, or with respect to a given speech community': Waldron, 'Vagueness in Law and Language. Some Philosophical Issues' (n 76 above) 524 f.
[116] Alexy, *Theorie der juristischen Argumentation* (n 103 above) 305. Koch and Rüß-mann, on the other hand, opt for stricter seniority, see Koch and Rüssmann, *Juristische Begründungslehre* (n 80 above) 182. *Cf* p 45 above. Neumann is critical of both suggestions, see Neumann, *Juristische Argumentationslehre* (n 108 above) 89.

Whether these sound reasons exist can only be assessed in legal discourse if all argument forms are considered. Hence, we have the postulate of taking all arguments fully into account.[117]

As we have seen, the semantic argument is used for the external justification of I_{RW}. In turn, it depends on the justification of the claimed word usage rule W. Just how this may be done is a question Alexy explicitly leaves unanswered. However, he lists three possible options: The interpreter's reference to his own linguistic competence, empirical inquiries, and taking recourse to dictionaries.[118]

III. THE DECONSTRUCTIVISTIC CHALLENGE OF THE STRUCTURING LEGAL THEORY (SLT)

Structuring legal theory was founded by Friedrich Müller. In his workgroup on 'legal linguistics', linguists and jurists teamed up in interdisciplinary co-operation. Based on their observations of how language worked in the field of law, they inductively developed very independent, basic assumptions on legal theory (A).

The openness of language and the influence of the legal practitioner's Pre-judgements had already been emphasised by new hermeneutics. For Müller's school, however, this conceptualisation of the loss of certainty of language did not go far enough (B). Further, they passionately attacked analytic legal theory (C), (D). In contradistinction to all the theories presented above, SLT argued its very own concept of the limits of the wording (E).

A. Basic Premises of Structuring Legal Theory

Structuring Legal Theory considers itself to be a 'post-positivistic' idea of legal theory. Müller observes the continuing influence of legal positivism in legal theory and states that while it was no longer held expressively as a view, it was still implicitly present in many elements.[119] He considers positivism to be a persisting problem in jurisprudence, one that structuring legal theory intends to solve with a new overall concept of the theory of legal reasoning.

---

[117] Alexy, *Theorie der juristischen Argumentation* (n 103 above) 306. Here, too, Koch and Rüßmann differ. In their tiered model, they only consider subordinate arguments in case of doubt, see Koch and Rüssmann, *Juristische Begründungslehre* (n 80 above) 182, and p 45 above.

[118] Alexy, *Theorie der juristischen Argumentation* (n 103 above) 290.

[119] F Müller, *Juristische Methodik*, 7th edn (Berlin, 1997) paras 75 f.

Deconstructivistic Challenge of the Structuring Legal Theory (SLT) 55

Structuring legal theory is opposed to the assumption shared by the subjective and objective theories of interpretation, which is that rules are predefined for legal practitioners. The key thesis of SLT is the non-identity of the text of a rule and the rule itself.[120] The text is only a 'guideline', as such it has no claim to normativity. For SLT, the rule is not the beginning, but the product of the process of the application of the law. It is developed during the act of applying law. Thus, its focus is on legal practice. SLT understands its own task to be a 'deliberation on creative decision-making',[121] as a 'theory of practice'.[122] It begins by describing legal procedure, and in a second step compares this with the rule of the law, and (re)structures it according to the latter's standards.

In this process, the structure developed is one of doing 'legal work' with texts. According to SLT, it showed that the text of a rule was not synonymous with the law, but rather the linguistic date of receipt for decision-making.[123] It is the legal practitioners, SLT claims, that make rules by using interpretation to extract from the legal text of a rule its 'normative program', and using the latter to select the rule's 'normative sphere', ie those actual facts which, based on the normative program, are normatively significant. Only at this stage was the rule complete, consisting of normative program and normative sphere. The facts of the case in question could then be subsumed under it.[124]

Correspondingly, interpretation does not hold the key role it has according to other schools of theory. For structuring legal theory, concretisation takes the place of interpretation.[125] Legal practitioners put a rule in concrete terms and in this way initiate it.[126] Several elements of concretisation are part of this process, the canons being just one element group among others. After all, not only the legal text which has been analysed with the help of the canons is incorporated into legal work. Also considered are structural elements of the normative sphere related to the case, as well as other elements of concretisation, eg dogmatic aspects or those of legal policy.[127]

---

[120] *Ibid*, para 162.
[121] Müller, *Juristische Methodik* (n 119 above) para 214.
[122] Busse, *Juristische Semantik* (n 2 above) 228 f.
[123] Müller, *Juristische Methodik* (n 119 above) para 224.
[124] Müller, *Juristische Methodik* (n 119 above) paras 232 f. Rüthers criticises this model as 'a self-chosen terminological dissociation', see B Rüthers, 'Richterrecht—rechtswidrig oder notwendig?' (1988) 112 *Archiv des öffentlichen Rechts* 268 at 282.
[125] Müller, *Juristische Methodik* (n 119 above) paras 248–88.
[126] Particularly explicit F Müller, *Strukturierende Rechtslehre*, 2nd edn (Berlin, 1994) 174: 'putting a legal rule in specific terms means designing a legal rule'.
[127] Müller, *Juristische Methodik* (n 119 above) paras 248 f.

Overall, structuring legal theory aims to replace the dogma of traditional legal theory—ie the determinateness of the statutory text—with the determinability of legal rules as a normative task directed at the legal practitioner.[128] Here, Müller particularly refers to Quine and Davidson.[129]

B. Criticism of New Hermeneutics

Busse in particular has summed up the structuring legal theory's criticism of new hermeneutics. He discusses Hruschka, Larenz, Esser, and Kaufmann and arrives at a scathing conclusion. By using the concept of Prejudgements to make explicit the prejudices, which had in actual fact always been powerful, and elevating them to the lofty heights of a philosophical rationale, new hermeneutics, he claims, permitted lawyers to cling to an outdated code of practice.[130] He criticises the 'debordering of hermeneutics', which let the understanding of texts disappear in the understanding of the world, and belittled semantic interpretation through argumentative figures, eg 'the nature of things', analogies, and the hermeneutic circle.[131] Busse indeed admits that new hermeneutics aimed to get away from the isolated observation of the meaning of individual words by emphasising frames of reference.[132] Yet in terms of theory of language, he maintains, this effort actually means going to back to pre-Gadamer hermeneutics, a result of clinging to the ideal of objectivity, neglecting the understanding of text in favour of a general merging of horizons.[133]

C. Criticism of the Theory of Legal Reasoning According to Koch and Rüßmann

Structuring legal theory objects to the concepts of semantic interpretation and the limits of the wording developed by Koch and Rüßmann. Its criticism focuses in particular on the three-candidate model.[134]

Classifying subject-matter as a positive, negative, or neutral candidate is criticised as being a merely extensional determination of meaning which implies the existence of meaning in the first place. After all, it is argued, in

---

[128] Müller, *Juristische Methodik* (n 119 above) para 166.
[129] Müller, *Juristische Methodik* (n 119 above) paras 167–72.
[130] Busse, *Juristische Semantik* (n 2 above) 77, 95.
[131] Busse, *Juristische Semantik* (n 2 above) 81 fn 29, 90, 97.
[132] Busse, *Juristische Semantik* (n 2 above) 86.
[133] Busse, *Juristische Semantik* (n 2 above) 81, 87, 100.
[134] With regard to this specification, see p 48 above.

order to specify the extension, meaning has to be known already. Therefore, this theory would be unable to make any contribution to a theory of interpretation which aimed at finding out first what the meaning of a statement was.[135]

Furthermore, any assignment to the spheres of positive and negative candidates according to this model is only possible if one is absolutely certain. By definition, even the slightest doubt necessitates an assignment to the group of neutral candidates. According to Busse, this means that the concept of semantic certainty held is much too narrow, resulting in a massively inflated sphere of neutral candidates. This extension does not, he maintains, correspond to the actual semantic situation, and, furthermore, resulted in the spheres of the negative and positive candidates remaining almost bare.[136] Also, this problem could not be resolved by Koch's reference to predominant language use or relevant speaker groups:

Just what we are supposed to have in mind when we consider 'predominant language use' on the one hand and 'relevant speaker groups' on the other, Koch does not say. Would this include all members of the judiciary, all members of parliament, or even the entire population of the Federal Republic of Germany? Have we got to forsake 'certainty' if a single individual out of these 80 million has 'doubts'?[137]

Busse, in contrast, does see the potential for semantic arguments even in case of doubts.[138] After all, he argues, even vague language is rule-governed. Koch and Rüßmann, Busse says, are mistaken in their definition of the sphere of vagueness as the absence of conventions. Vagueness is the result of vague conventions, and is directed at the usage rule itself. Therefore, it cannot be defined as the lack of a usage rule.[139]

Finally, structuring legal theory also objects to the dichotomy between establishing and assigning meaning.[140] In combination with the identified extension of the neutral sphere, in which, according to Koch and Rüßmann, meaning has to be assigned, this would signify an increase of arbitrariness, which is diametrically opposed to the demand for precision.[141] Furthermore, they are accused of completely abandoning the option of establishing meaning through the empirical instruments offered by linguistics. Instead, they brought personal prejudice to bear.[142]

---

[135] Busse, *Juristische Semantik* (n 2 above) 127.
[136] Busse, *Juristische Semantik* (n 2 above) 128.
[137] Busse, *Juristische Semantik* (n 2 above).
[138] Busse, *Juristische Semantik* (n 2 above) 135.
[139] Busse, *Juristische Semantik* (n 2 above) 129.
[140] Müller, *Juristische Methodik* (n 119 above) para 184.
[141] Busse, *Juristische Semantik* (n 2 above) 130.
[142] For similar criticism see R Christensen, 'Gesetzesbindung oder Bindung an das Gesetzbuch der praktischen Vernunft. Eine skeptische Widerrede zur Vorstellung des sprechenden Textes' in R Mellinghoff and H-H Trute (eds), *Die Leistungsfähigkeit des Rechts:*

D. Criticism of Alexy's Theory of Legal Argumentation

From a language-theoretical point of view, SLT considers the theory of legal argumentation developed by Alexy to be untenable. The authors generally regret that by switching its focus from interpretation to argumentation Alexy was reforming legal theory. This resulted in severing all links between meaning and interpretation.[143] Furthermore, his theory substituted the postulate of judges being bound by the law with a philosophical theory of truth, leading to an exchange of the binding to statutory texts with a code of practical reason.[144]

In particular, objections focus on the role of the semantic argument assumed by Alexy. According to Alexy, the semantic argument is drawn upon to empirically establish meaning during the external justification of the premises used in the judicial syllogism. Busse considers it worthless, as the linguistic-empirical research effort involved made it impossible to verify.[145] Once normative power was attached to semantics, ie when it came to assigning meaning, any attempt at creating non-normative arguments by switching to a language-analytical debate would fail. The semantic discourse, which had previously been intended to be merely descriptive, would automatically turn normative. This, in turn, threatened an infinite retrogression of arguments, which was precisely the development the semantic argument had been supposed to help avoid.

According to Müller, Alexy's version of the semantic argument is based on a positivistic misconception, namely, that there is by necessity a connection between the text of a rule and its meaning.[146] Alexy's view, he claims, is limited to an external, additive combination of semantics and argument. Yet the route from the text of a rule to the legal norm was no mere application of objective semantic rules, but rather an active process of semantisation. It was only through argumentation that a text acquired meaning. As a consequence, Müller calls for replacing, as a semantic practice, the additive model of semantics plus argumentation, with an integral analysis of legal argumentation.[147]

The concept of the word usage rule has also met with criticism. Alexy defines word usage rules to be rules for the use of statements used in

---

Methodik, Gentechnologie, internationales Verwaltungsrecht (Heidelberg, 1988) 75. See also R Wank, *Die juristische Begriffsbildung* (München, 1985) 21 f.

[143] According to Busse, *Juristische Semantik* (n 2 above) 175.
[144] Christensen, 'Gesetzesbindung oder Bindung an das Gesetzbuch der praktischen Vernunft' (n 142 above) 184.
[145] Busse, *Juristische Semantik* (n 2 above) 183.
[146] Müller, *Juristische Methodik* (n 119 above) para 255.
[147] Müller, *Juristische Methodik* (n 119 above) para 256.

previous premises.[148] Busse agrees that explications of meaning in dogmatic texts, eg in annotations or legal precedents, are semantic tasks. However, these explications of meaning could not be authoritative for judges. Otherwise, the principle of being bound to the law would amount to a binding to majority opinion or prevailing doctrine.[149] Busse also claims that Alexy remained silent with regard to the issue of how word usage rules are empirically established. By only mentioning options—eg the legal practitioner's reference to his own linguistic competence, or the use of dictionaries—Alexy, similar to Koch and Rüßmann, left the key problem of legal semantics unsolved. After all, if the semantic argument as such was to be of any use, it was precisely the option of empirically establishing meaning that mattered. Since many alleged establishments were de facto assignments, Busse says, Alexy's theory would have the unbearable consequence of generally excluding semantic arguments from legal reasoning.[150]

E. Structuring Legal Theory and the Limits of the Wording

The position of SLT on the limits of the wording will be developed in four steps (i)-(iv).

(i) The Limits of the Wording as a Result of the Concretisation of Rules

In the eyes of structuring legal theory, the principle of the limits of the wording highlights the shortcomings of existing legal theory. Christensen emphasises that the relation which existed between the meaning of a legal text and the linguistic actions of the legal practitioner was not external but internal.[151] In a creative—not perceptive—act, meaning rules were drafted by the legal practitioners themselves. For SLT, meaning is not a linguistic variable which a legal practitioner comes across. Rather, he has to develop it himself:

> Not only ... in borderline cases, but by necessity and invariably the meaning of linguistic signs depends on the language's speakers, on their understanding of reality, their foreknowledge. Even more so: The signs' meaning and usefulness used are not only not discovered or modified in actual speech acts, but ... created in the first place.[152]

Since the text of a rule did not provide legal practitioners with meaning, the principle of the limits of the wording was impossible to uphold. Before

---
[148] See p 52 above.
[149] Busse, *Juristische Semantik* (n 2 above) 185.
[150] Busse, *Juristische Semantik* (n 2 above) 186 f.
[151] Christensen, 'Gesetzesbindung oder Bindung an das Gesetzbuch der praktischen Vernunft' (n 142 above) 269, 272.
[152] Müller, *Strukturierende Rechtslehre*, 2nd edn (Berlin, 1994) 377 f.

a rule was put into concrete terms, and if examined independent of context, its text was so indistinct that the limits of the wording proved to be an illusion.[153] Both meaning and the limits of the wording were only created during the act of concretisation. They were not the starting point, but the result of 'law work'.[154]

(ii) Binding Effects of Legal Culture

Legal theory does not draw the conclusion from the above structuring that the limits of the wording are useless as a border-line criterion. Müller does indeed declare that the traditional concept of the limits of the wording would have to go,[155] yet he also aims to rephrase it from a 'language-theoretical point of view'.[156] So SLT does retain the limits of the wording, but compared to the schools of theory, it has a fundamentally different understanding: The limiting effect is not an inherent quality of the legal text or its individual expressions. Language does not determine this boundary, rather, it is only erected in, and by speaking, the language.[157]

> Hence, the limits of the wording are not the limits of the language. Words as such know no bounds which would exclude particular ways of using them. Language *itself* does not determine the limits of its use. Rather, these limits are determined *in* the language by the people who are a part of a speech community.[158]

Müller makes it clear in no uncertain terms that SLT does grant the wording a limiting effect, 'not only in particular cases, but throughout'. This is precisely where Müller sees the difference between his school and the Topic, which only considered the text of a rule as the 'starting point' for problem solving.[159] Elsewhere, however, Müller——having extensive recourse to Derrida—declares the text of the rule to be a mere 'date of receipt',[160] and Busse considers the wording of the law to be a mere 'piece

---

[153] F Laudenklos, 'Rechtsarbeit ist Textarbeit. Einige Bemerkungen zur Arbeitsweise der Strukturierenden Rechtslehre' (1997) *Kritische Justiz* 142 at 151. See also Jeand'Heur, who has 'great sympathies' for the view that meaning is nothing but a 'chimera', a 'metaphysical construct', B Jeand'Heur, 'Bedeutungstheorie in Sprachwissenschaft und Rechtswissenschaft. Der Kruzifix-Beschluß aus rechtslinguistischer Sicht' in W Brugger and S Huster (eds), *Der Streit um das Kreuz in der Schule. Zur religiös-weltanschaulichen Neutralität des Staates* (Baden-Baden, 1998) 162.
[154] Müller, *Juristische Methodik* (n 119 above) para 534.
[155] Müller, *Juristische Methodik* (n 119 above) para 535. Similar Busse, *Juristische Semantik* (n 2 above) 248; Christensen, 'Gesetzesbindung oder Bindung an das Gesetzbuch der praktischen Vernunft' (n 142 above) 285.
[156] Müller, *Juristische Methodik* (n 119 above) para 328.
[157] Müller, *Juristische Methodik* (n 119 above) para 533.
[158] Christensen, 'Gesetzesbindung oder Bindung an das Gesetzbuch der praktischen Vernunft' (n 142 above) 285.
[159] Müller, *Juristische Methodik* (n 119 above) para 310.
[160] Müller, *Juristische Methodik* (n 119 above) paras 507–10.

of scenery' among others within the process of specifying a rule.[161] Finally, Müller refers to Umberto Eco when distancing himself from Richard Rorty's pragmatic theory and from deconstructivistic textual criticism, which erred in their efforts at upsetting the presence of the text as a reliable limit.[162]

In the face of these inconsistent statements, one has to ask what binding effects structuring legal theory actually does attach to the legal text and how it aims to achieve these, the language-theoretical assumption presented above notwithstanding. The answer can be found in the following remarks of Müller:

> A limit to the constitution of meaning carried out by the judge only results from the legal text, published by the legislature as a character string, and the given standards of the culture of legal reasoning, safeguarded by constitutional law.[163]
>
> The binding to the law does . . . not . . . refer to the allegedly provided content of the law, but is realised within the process of the *creation* of the legal norm . . . In the first instance, a judge is bound by the legal text as a string of characters, created by the legislator . . . He . . . has to develop the crucial *meaning* of the text for the case at hand himself. He is, however, not wholly unrestricted, but bound to the standards of a culture of legal reasoning, which in turn are sanctioned by the guidelines given by the constitution.[164]

Thus, the limiting effect does not come from the legal text alone. It is the result of the interplay between the legal text and the standards of legal reasoning, which take effect during specification and are in turn determined by constitutional guidelines. Müller's clarity in committing himself, at least in some places, to the limiting effect of the wording, should not hide the fact that compared to the majority opinion of scholars he holds a fundamentally different view. No legal text can on its own guarantee a binding effect. In principle, meaning is always open linguistically; there needs to be a 'legal culture' which narrows it down.[165] Unlike analytic legal

---

[161] Busse, *Juristische Semantik* (n 2 above) 257.
[162] Müller, *Juristische Methodik* (n 119 above) paras 341–6.
[163] Müller, *Juristische Methodik* (n 119 above) para 325.
[164] Müller, *Juristische Methodik* (n 119 above) para 346. See also Christensen, 'Gesetzesbindung oder Bindung an das Gesetzbuch der praktischen Vernunft' (n 142 above) 287: 'But that is not to say that the wording holds no discriminatory power with regard to the justifiability of interpretations. However, it only has this power in combination with methodological standards, not by itself. It is only in combination with the standards of interpretation developed through science and practical experience that the legal text may exclude particular alternative understandings as less well justified'.
[165] According to Christensen, the limits of the wording are determined by legal culture and, as a consequence, are not left to the discretion of the individual, see Christensen, 'Gesetzesbindung oder Bindung an das Gesetzbuch der praktischen Vernunft' (n 142 above) 286 f.

62 The Doctrine of the Limits of the Wording

theory, this is expressly not supposed to be habitual language use.[166] Rather, legal culture covers all activities of the judicial interpretative community in connection with reasoning. While this community may be unable to develop substantial meaning through doctrine and precedents, it would still restrict legal practitioners' freedom and arbitrariness.[167] In this respect, Busse elaborates that even though any application of a concept's usage rule could be considered a modification of the same, said modification would still be recognisable. He comments:

> Hence, maintaining the differentiation between *interpretation* and *further development* of the law is not obsolete as such. Constitutional considerations alone demand that we not be rash in jettisoning it. However, we lack a clear criterion which would define the limits from outside judicial interpretation practices ... It is only in and through our *practical experience* that the difference appears, one criterion being, as *Wittgenstein* framed for the rule, the manner in which the other participants of the game react to the application of the rule.[168]

This makes the 'explicit or tacit consensus of the interpretative community' the crucial criterion for the differentiation of interpretation and further development of the law.[169]

(iii) The Limits of the Wording as the Limits of the Normative Program

Müller elaborates on how the limits of the wording, which have to be developed in the process of legal reasoning, operate. Müller's position is consistent with traditional legal theory in that he declares the limiting effect to be negative, ie the result may not go beyond the scope offered by the wording.[170] Furthermore, Müller distinguishes between normal and special cases. For him, special cases are characterised by the fact that the limiting function is based solely on the grammatical element, as the latter

---

[166] Language usage cannot endow the legal text with limiting powers, see Müller, *Juristische Methodik* (n 119 above) para 535. In this respect, Christensen differs. He includes 'semantic fields' and 'habitual ways of use' among the limiting factors, see Christensen, 'Gesetzesbindung oder Bindung an das Gesetzbuch der praktischen Vernunft' (n 142 above) 282 f.

[167] Christensen, 'Gesetzesbindung oder Bindung an das Gesetzbuch der praktischen Vernunft' (n 142 above) 282 f; Müller, *Juristische Methodik* (n 119 above) para 526.

[168] D Busse, 'Zum Regel-Charakter von Normtextbedeutungen und Rechtsnormen' (1988) *Rechtstheorie* 318.

[169] D Busse, 'Was ist die Bedeutung eines Gesetzestextes? Sprachwissenschaftliche Argumente im Methodenstreit der juristischen Auslegungslehre—linguistisch gesehen' in F Müller (ed), *Untersuchungen zur Rechtslinguistik. Interdisziplinäre Studien zur praktischen Semantik und Strukturierender Rechtslehre in Grundfragen der juristischen Methodik* (Berlin, 1989) 147. On the stabilising influence of *habits* on the practice of interpretation according to Peirce's pragmatism, see J Lege, *Pragmatismus und Jurisprudenz. Über die Philosophie des Charles Sanders Peirce und über das Verhältnis von Logik, Wertung und Kreativität im Recht* (Tübingen, 1999) 534 f.

[170] Müller, *Juristische Methodik* (n 119 above) para 311.

prevail in the determination of the normative program over other elements of concretisation.[171] In normal cases, on the other hand, '*several* specifying elements of a primarily linguistic nature (language data) [lead] to the same conclusion'.[172] Here, he says, the limits of the wording are also the limits of the normative program. In normal cases, a decision's consistency with the wording would not only depend on the grammatical element, but could only be assessed by means of the normative program.[173] Strictly speaking, Müller also assumes for exceptions that the limits of the wording are inherent in the normative program because the issue of whether the normative program can be determined by the grammatical element alone can only be resolved once the concretisation has been completed.

(iv) The Role of the Limits of the Normative Program

Müller's definition of the role of the limits of the normative program also differs from traditional legal theory. For him, it is not a matter of establishing a boundary between interpretation and further development of the law, but of drawing a line between the admissible and the inadmissible specification of norms; between construction and using the law as a tool of power. Similar to dominant legal theory, Müller considers this interpretation of the process of delimitation to be of crucial importance for any constitutional state based on the principle of the separation of powers.

Hence, distinguishing mere interpretation and use as a tool of power carries a heavy political burden: What depends on it is nothing less than keeping the democratic promise. Therefore, any approach to distinguishing justified and unjustified governmental power has to pass this litmus test, ie being able to discriminate between the law's interpretation and its use as a tool of power.[174]

F. Structuring Legal Theory—Summary

In the view of structuring legal theory, all other schools of legal methodology are closely attached to legal positivism. By contrast, it aims to present a 'post-positivistic' theory of practical legal work, which is to bring nothing less than a 'paradigm change'.[175] Based on an all-new theory of

---

[171] Müller, *Juristische Methodik* (n 119 above) para 312.
[172] Müller, *Juristische Methodik* (n 119 above) para 312.
[173] Müller, *Juristische Methodik* (n 119 above) paras 448, 312. The normative program is the normative guiding principle of a norm. It may be established by interpreting the legal text, see p 55 above.
[174] Müller, *Juristische Methodik* (n 119 above) para 338.
[175] R Christensen, 'Der Richter als Mund des sprechenden Textes. Zur Kritik des gesetzespositivistischen Textmodells' in F Müller (ed), *Untersuchungen zur Rechtslinguistik*.

legal rules, its proponents consider not interpreting, but the putting of rules in specific terms to be the key element of methodology. SLT is opposed to the ideal of objectivity held by previous legal theory, as the latter was mistaken in its belief in the possibility of an empirically firm, precise, historically true, in sum accurate determination of literal meanings.[176] In addition to disapproving of post-Gadamer ontological hermeneutics and recent subjective interpretation theory, the main target of SLT's criticism is analytic legal theory.

The objection is raised against analytic legal theory that it relies on incorrect language-philosophical assumptions and that it leaves unanswered *the* main interpretation-theoretical question, ie how to determine an expression's meaning rule. According to SLT, specification using the three-candidate model and the model of the word usage rule fails on account of a positivistic misconception, which assumes a fixed connection between a rule and its meaning. The meaning of a rule, SLT claims, is not known prior to its legal application, but rather it is assigned by the legal practitioner. Accordingly, the limits of the wording, or the normative program, have to be constantly re-developed. In this process, however, the standards of legal reasoning—safeguarded by the constitution, as well as doctrine and precedents—assure that the legal practitioner's arbitrariness is reduced to a degree sufficient to keep him bound by the law.

IV. THE RESULTS OF THE FIRST CHAPTER

The first chapter will be concluded with an overview of the current state of research (A). Afterwards, I will critically assess both positions and arguments (B).

A. State of Research

The emergence of Gadamer's ontological hermeneutics severely shook the traditional hermeneutic position of an objective theory of interpretation. Within legal theory, its reception led to emphasis being placed on the volitive elements in the course of justice. However, this brought about an expansion of the legal practitioner's freedom, a fact criticised by analytic legal theory. The latter's advocates, Koch, Rüßmann, Herberger, and Alexy, developed the three-candidate model and the model of the word usage rule as more precise models of the application of the law.

Interdisziplinäre Studien zu praktischer Semantik und Strukturierender Rechtslehre in Grundfragen der juristischen Methodik (Berlin, 1989) 73.
[176] Cf Busse, *Juristische Semantik* (n 2 above) 225 f, 251.

The specification in analytic legal theory has been intensely criticised. Friedrich Müller's structuring legal theory has presented an original overall concept which completely breaks with previous opinions.

The three positions on the limits of the wording are summed up in their key arguments (i) to (iii). There follows an overview of all objections raised against the principle of the limits of the wording (iv).

(i) The Hermeneutic Position

(a) Pre-Judgements and Typology

In hermeneutic legal theory, there is no uniform assessment of the influence of Pre-judgements, which in particular Esser also applies to language. To some extent, a limiting effect of the wording is disputed on account of the legal practitioner's influence on the meaning of a text.[177] Some consider it possible to use typology to differentiate between interpretation and further development of the law.[178] In general, however, it is accepted that this differentiation is based on the legal practitioner's judgemental classification.[179] During the process of applying the law, legal practitioners themselves laid down the standards both for the meaning of the legal text and the limits of the wording. This result is explicitly approved, since the Pre-judgements had to be revealed in the interpretative discourse and could thus be restrained.[180] Hence, judicial authority was bound to the law.

(b) Arguments in Support of the Hermeneutic Position

Here, I will only list the arguments supporting the views of hermeneutics which retain the limits of the wording. Opposing views will be considered in Section (iv).

(1) Argument of Ontological Hermeneutics Gadamer claims the hermeneutic circle to be the ontological structural characteristic of any

---

[177] Esser, *Vorverständnis und Methodenwahl in der Rechtsfindung* (n 8 above) 178, 120 fn 6; Hruschka, *Das Verstehen von Rechtstexten* (n 4 above) 102; Kriele, *Theorie der Rechtsgewinnung* (n 13 above) 223; Pawlowski, *Methodenlehre für Juristen* (n 42 above) paras 458, 507.
[178] W Fikentscher, *Methoden des Rechts in vergleichender Darstellung. Band IV: Dogmatischer Teil. Anhang* (Tübingen, 1977) 202–10, 288–302; Hassemer, *Tatbestand und Typus* (n 5 above) 164 f; Hassold, 'Strukturen der Gesetzesauslegung' (n 62 above) 219; Kaufmann, *Analogie und 'Natur der Sache'* (n 58 above) 52; Larenz, *Methodenlehre der Rechtswissenschaft* (n 59 above) 322.
[179] See p 39 f above.
[180] Hassemer, 'Juristische Hermeneutik' (n 6 above) 211; Kriele, *Theorie der Rechtsgewinnung* (n 13 above) 315 f.

process of understanding.[181] According to this, understanding is only possible because the subjects of this process approach the text equipped with presuppositional opinions on substance and linguistics. As a consequence, the meaning of a norm may not be considered a given semantic reality. Rather, it is based on value judgements made by the interpreter.

(2) Argument of Analogicity According to Kaufmann, all use of language is by necessity analogous in nature, as it is based on detecting similarities between ways of application. Not only the judicial development of the law, but also its interpretation rests on analogies. Consequently, Kaufmann deduces, it is impossible to distinguish the two by setting a limit to possible meaning. Rather, this line was drawn within the analogy between legitimate and illegitimate application of the law. It was demarcated by the type of the statutory elements of an offence.[182]

(3) Argument of Procedural Correctness It is claimed that the hermeneutic circle and the influence of Pre-judgements do not result in arbitrariness because the legal practitioner's value classifications can be scrutinised during the interpretational discourse, thus safeguarding the procedural correctness of judicial decision-making.[183]

(4) Argument of Normative Necessity Notwithstanding the uncertainties resulting from the ontological preconditions of understanding, constitutional considerations make it imperative to retain the limits of the wording.[184]

(ii) The Analytic Position

(a) Establishing and Assigning Meaning

One has to distinguish semantically clear and unclear cases. The latter may be classified according to ambiguity, inconsistency, vagueness, and evaluative openness.[185] With regard to unclear concepts, one can distinguish positive, negative, and neutral candidates, with candidates classified according to the word usage rules. Since meaning can be established in the spheres of positive and negative candidates, the limits of the wording in the

---

[181] Gadamer, *Wahrheit und Methode* (n 16 above) 272, 299.
[182] Kaufmann, *Analogie und 'Natur der Sache'* (n 58 above) 52.
[183] J Esser, *Vorverständnis und Methodenwahl in der Rechtsfindung* (n 8 above) 197.
[184] F Bydlinski, *Juristische Methodenlehre und Rechtsbegriff* (2nd edn, Wien 1991) 468; Engisch and Würtenberger, *Einführung in das juristische Denken* (n 42 above) 100 fn 47, 121 fn 47; J Neuner, *Die Rechtsfindung contra legem* (München, 1992) 84.

[185] Only Alexy assumes a category of evaluative openness, Koch and Rüßmann, however, dismiss it. See p 47 above.

strict sense consist of two boundaries, a positive and a negative one.[186] With regard to the sphere of neutral candidates, the limits of the wording have no effect. Here, a word usage rule has to be assigned.[187]

(b) Arguments for the Analytic Viewpoint

(1) Argument of Clear Cases The argument of clear cases[188] consists of three hypotheses. One: There are clear cases which leave no doubt about the use of a concept.[189] Two: There is only a small number of *hard cases* in which doubts emerge. Three: Even in hard cases, the legal text and its meaning develop a binding force. Linguistic indefiniteness can not be equalled with triviality.[190]

(2) Argument of the Empirical Discernibility of Meaning There are three variations of this argument. We find the first at Koch and Rüßmann. Their hypothesis is that intention plays the role of assigning extension.[191] Hence, the intention of a concept determines the subject sphere of its use. Therefore, it is possible to establish the meaning of a concept by examining its subject sphere.

The second variant is argued by Robert Alexy. According to his model, word usage rules, ie linguistic conventions within the language game, can be determined empirically.[192] The process of determination has a tiered structure. First and foremost, the juridical literature's terminological conventions are authoritative. In addition, it is possible to consult dictionaries. Any expressive reference, based one's own linguistic competence, to an assumed general language use has to remain subordinate.[193] In this way, it is possible to distinguish between establishing meaning and assigning meaning.

With specific regard to normative statements, Alexy uses the argument of speech acts. According to him, meaning in the sense of the speech act

---

[186] Herberger and Koch, 'Zur Einführung: Juristische Methodenlehre und Sprachphilosophie' (n 97 above) 813, and p 49 above.
[187] Alexy, *Theorie der juristischen Argumentation* (n 103 above) 290 f. See also n 115 above.
[188] This argument is also used by several adherents to hermeneutics, see K Larenz, 'Die Bindung des Richters an das Gesetz als hermeneutisches Problem' in E Forsthoff, W Weber and F Wieacker (eds), *Festschrift für Ernst Rudolf Huber* (Göttingen, 1973) 296, 298, 300.
[189] Alexy, *Theorie der juristischen Argumentation* (n 103 above) 289; Koch and Rüssmann, *Juristische Begründungslehre* (n 80 above) 163.
[190] Here, this is called the argument of guiding force in unclear cases, see Koch and Rüssmann, *Juristische Begründungslehre* (n 80 above) 191, and p 46 above.
[191] *Cf* p 46 above.
[192] Alexy, *Theorie der juristischen Argumentation* (n 103 above) 71–5. See p 54 above.
[193] Koch and Rüssmann, *Juristische Begründungslehre* (n 80 above) 191. This opinion is shared by some within modern hermeneutic legal theory, see B Rüthers, *Rechtstheorie. Begriff, Geltung und Anwendung des Rechts* (München, 1999) 413.

theory is rule-based.[194] Hare argues that significant differences with regard to conventions of use can already be determined on a speech act's locutionary level. They also make it possible to assess normative statements according to the 'true/false' criterion.

(3) Argument of Possible Corrections The approach to the determination of meaning presented above might have been unable to eliminate completely the arbitrariness resulting from referring to one's own linguistic competence. However, it could be argued that there are options for corrections both within the legal discourse and through the legislature's intervention.[195] This argument corresponds to the argument of procedural correctness put forward by more modern hermeneutics.[196]

(iii) The Structuring Legal Theory Position

(a) Putting Rules in Specific Terms and the Limits of the Normative Program

Only the normative program, ie a rule's guiding principles established by interpretation, may exert a limiting function. This limit of the normative program is not something legal practitioners discover. Rather, they create it when putting a rule in specific terms.[197] In the process, legal practitioners' freedom and arbitrariness are checked by the standards of judicial argumentation.

(b) Arguments in Support of Structuring Legal Theory

(1) Argument of the Indefiniteness of the Legal Text Prior to specification, legal texts are too indefinite to possibly provide a limiting function.[198]

(2) Argument of Legal Culture The standards of argumentation within jurisprudence's interpretative community, reflected in the given constitutional paradigms as well as doctrine and precedents, reduce the linguistic openness of legal texts and the freedom of legal practitioners.[199]

---

[194] Alexy, *Theorie der juristischen Argumentation* (n 103 above) 85. See p 50 above.
[195] Koch and Rüssmann, *Juristische Begründungslehre* (n 80 above) 191.
[196] With regard to this argument, see p 37 f above.
[197] Müller, *Juristische Methodik* (n 119 above) paras 448, 312.
[198] R Christensen, *Was heißt Gesetzesbindung? Eine rechtslinguistische Untersuchung* (Berlin, 1989) 285; Müller, *Juristische Methodik* (n 119 above) paras 553, 507–10.
[199] Müller, *Juristische Methodik* (n 119 above) paras 325, 346. See also M Vocke, *Verfassungsinterpretation und Normbegründung. Grundlegung zu einer prozeduralen Theorie der Verfassungsgerichtsbarkeit* (Frankfurt am Main, 1995) 28 f.

(iv) Arguments Against the Limits of the Wording

Below is a compilation of the arguments given against the hermeneutic and the analytic theory of the limits of the wording.

(a) Argument of Practical Ineffectiveness

In the practical experience of legal work, the principle of the limits of the wording does not result in any restrictions.[200]

(b) Argument of Necessary Failure

It is only in clear cases that meaning is so firm as to provide a limiting function. In these cases, however, distinguishing interpretation and judicial development of the law never present a problem. In unclear cases, on the other hand, meaning is so uncertain that the limits of the wording are of little help. By necessity, the principle of the limits of the wording fails precisely where it is supposed to take effect.[201]

(c) Argument of the Lacking Normative Necessity

Claims that the limiting function of the wording is essential remain unconvincing. Arguments of legal certainty and protection of confidence are invalid, as they focus not on a rule's text, but on its content.[202] After all, what matters is not whether a decision is consistent with a potential meaning, but whether it can be reconciled with material criteria of justice.[203]

(d) Argument of Reversal

The principle of the limits of the wording reverses the relationship of interpretation and judicial development of the law. A decision which followed ancient legislative intent would possibly qualify as judicial

---

[200] O Depenheuer, *Der Wortlaut als Grenze. Thesen zu einem Topos der Verfassungsinterpretation* (Heidelberg, 1988) 41. *Cf* also Neumann's empirical research of judgements by the BGH's criminal division, U Neumann, 'Der "mögliche Wortsinn" als Auslegungsgrenze in der Rechtsprechung der Strafsenate des BGH' in Ev Savigny (ed), *Juristische Dogmatik und Wissenschaftstheorie* (München, 1976) 42.

[201] Depenheuer, *Der Wortlaut als Grenze* (n 200 above) 40; M Herbert, *Rechtstheorie als Sprachkritik. Zum Einfluß Wittgensteins auf die Rechtstheorie* (Baden-Baden, 1995) 239 f.

[202] Depenheuer, *Der Wortlaut als Grenze* (n 200 above) 42 f.

[203] Esser, *Vorverständnis und Methodenwahl in der Rechtsfindung* (n 8 above) 186; Kriele, *Theorie der Rechtsgewinnung* (n 13 above) 223, 311; Pawlowski, *Methodenlehre für Juristen* (n 42 above) paras 458, 507, with some qualifications in para 508.

70 *The Doctrine of the Limits of the Wording*

development of the law, whereas one which is inconsistent with this intent would possibly be considered an interpretation.[204]

(e) The Language Game Argument

The language game argument, following the later Wittgenstein, refers to the openness of meaning within language games. It is produced in four variants:

(1) Argument of Openness The use of language is never restricted by fixed boundaries, but is always open.[205]

(2) Argument of Innovation Members of a language game are always liable to change its rules. Hence, conventions do not lend themselves to disciplinarian instruments. Establishing a language rule is not an act of perception, but one of creation, and always results in assigning meaning.[206]

(3) Argument of Context-Dependency Embedding a word in a particular frame of reference and a particular communicative situation reduces conventionally possible, lexical meaning to topical meaning. Hence, one is mistaken in applying the principle of the limits of the wording to lexical meaning.[207]

(4) Argument of Circularity Language is tied to presuppositional knowledge. Meaning is not given but is determined by assessments of interests and application. Legal practitioners do not come across it, they assign it. Correct meaning can not be determined through semantics alone. Rather, legal practitioners lay it down as a rule in a hermeneutic circle.[208]

---

[204] This argumentum is defended *ad absurdum* by recent subjective interpretation theory, see R Hegenbarth, *Juristische Hermeneutik und linguistische Pragmatik. Dargestellt am Beispiel der Lehre vom Wortlaut als Grenze der Auslegung* (Königstein/Ts, 1982) 142–5; Herbert, *Rechtstheorie als Sprachkritik* (n 201 above) 243. See also Busse, *Juristische Semantik* (n 2 above) 271.

[205] Herbert, *Rechtstheorie als Sprachkritik* (n 201 above) 239 f.

[206] R Christensen, *Was heißt Gesetzesbindung?* (n 198 above) 198; Hegenbarth, *Juristische Hermeneutik und linguistische Pragmatik* (n 204 above) 51; Herbert, *Rechtstheorie als Sprachkritik* (n 201 above) 240 f; Müller, *Juristische Methodik* (n 119 above) para 184; P Schiffauer, *Wortbedeutung und Rechtserkenntnis. Entwickelt an Hand einer Studie zum Verhältnis von verfassungskonformer Auslegung und Analogie* (Berlin, 1979) 102–4.

[207] Hegenbarth, *Juristische Hermeneutik und linguistische Pragmatik* (n 204 above) 97–101; Herbert, *Rechtstheorie als Sprachkritik* (n 201 above) 241–50. Fuller directs the argument of context dependency against Hart's early *open texture* theory, see LL Fuller, 'Positivism and Fidelity to Law. A Reply to Professor Hart' (1958) 71 *Harvard Law Review* 630 at 662 f. For a critical view see Bix, *Law, Language, and Legal Determinacy* (n 76 above) 29–31.

[208] Busse, 'Was ist die Bedeutung eines Gesetzestextes?' (n 169 above) 100; Christensen, *Was heißt Gesetzesbindung?* (n 198 above) 75. In this respect, Busse speaks of 'arbitrariness',

(f) Argument that Meaning Remains Unclarified

The principle of the limits of the wording is dependent on a convincing language-philosophical clarification of the problem of meaning. No plausible explanation has so far been forthcoming. The following arguments are brought to bear against the dominant legal theory's language-philosophical posits:

(1) Argument of Objectivism In general, dominant legal theory is characterised by an objectivistic approach to meaning. Both objective and subjective interpretation theory assume that the meaning of a rule is definite prior to any practical application of the law. However, it is only created in the process of the application of the law.[209]

(2) Argument of Features Semantics Any isolated examination of individual words and a focus on definitions with particular characteristics will give rise to checklist semantics and traditional Platonic realism.[210]

(3) Argument of the Incorrect Reception of the Speech Act Theory It is claimed that Alexy is mistaken in concluding from the speech act theory that, similarly to descriptive statements, normative statements could be assessed using the 'true/false' criterion. Hare's principle of universalisability was flawed, and could not be drawn on to justify performative inconsistencies independent of the language game.[211]

(4) Argument of Excessive Commitment If one subscribes to the idea of the word usage rule according to Alexy, this must result in binding oneself to the explications of meaning in dogmatic texts, ie precedents and scientific works. This amounts to an excessive commitment to majority opinion.[212]

(5) Argument of the Impossibility of the Empirical Determination of Meaning Meaning cannot be determined empirically. If dominating legal theory pretends that meaning is something one comes across or can

---

see Busse, *Juristische Semantik* (n 2 above) 130 f; Esser, *Vorverständnis und Methodenwahl in der Rechtsfindung* (n 8 above) 41 f; KF Röhl, *Allgemeine Rechtslehre. Ein Lehrbuch* (Köln, 1995) 663, 657; R Zippelius, *Juristische Methodenlehre. Eine Einführung*, 7th edn (München, 1999) 47 f.

[209] D Busse, 'Was ist die Bedeutung eines Gesetzestextes?' (n 169 above) 100; Christensen, *Was heißt Gesetzesbindung?* (n 198 above) 75.

[210] Busse, *Juristische Semantik* (n 2 above) 107–11; Christensen, *Was heißt Gesetzesbindung?* (n 198 above) 198.

[211] Busse, *Juristische Semantik* (n 2 above) 178; Christensen, *Was heißt Gesetzesbindung?* (n 198 above) 198.

[212] Busse, *Juristische Semantik* (n 2 above) 185. See p 58f above.

72 The Doctrine of the Limits of the Wording

establish, the result is 'free decision-making' and arbitrariness.[213] There are two versions of this argument. The *complexity argument* is: The linguistic research effort for the determination of a rule's meaning is excessive and plagued with technical problems.[214]

The *argument of participation* emphasises that the relationship between the meaning of a legal text and the linguistic actions of legal practitioners is not external, but internal in nature.[215] From this, it would follow that only participants in the language game may hermeneutically research meaning from within. They can not determine it from outside.[216]

B. Criticism

The controversy on the limits of the wording can be summarised in opposing camps (i). This will be followed by a critical look at structuring legal theory (ii). Finally, the three key issues will be pieced together (iii).

(i) Analytic Versus Post-Positivistic Legal Theory

It has already become obvious that the arguments of ontological hermeneutics and those of the Müller school coincide in many respects. Both emphasise the influence exerted by legal practitioners, and come to the conclusion that the meaning of a rule and the limits of the wording are both determined by legal practitioners themselves.[217] Structuring legal theory repeats the arguments raised by ontological hermeneutics, but does so in language-philosophical terms and within the framework of a different overall concept.[218]

---

[213] Busse, *Juristische Semantik* (n 2 above) 130; Christensen, *Was heißt Gesetzesbindung?* (n 198 above) 180 f.

[214] R Hegenbarth, *Juristische Hermeneutik und linguistische Pragmatik. Dargestellt am Beispiel der Lehre vom Wortlaut als Grenze der Auslegung* (Königstein/Ts, 1982) 132; Koch and Rüssmann, *Juristische Begründungslehre* (n 80 above) 190. See also Christensen, *Was heißt Gesetzesbindung?* (n 198 above) 7.

[215] Christensen, *Was heißt Gesetzesbindung?* (n 198 above) 269, 272.

[216] Herbert, *Rechtstheorie als Sprachkritik* (n 201 above) 90.

[217] Even though this would not include those advocates of legal hermeneutics who rely on typology to establish the limits of the wording, fundamental objections to typology make it unnecessary to include this position in the debate, see Koch and Rüssmann, *Juristische Begründungslehre* (n 80 above) 73–7, 209 f. For further analyses see Herbert, *Rechtstheorie als Sprachkritik* (n 201 above) 253 fn 90.

[218] The argument of ontological hermeneutics (see p 65 above) matches the arguments of circularity and objectivism, both of which are raised by Structuring Legal Theory (see p 70 f above). The hermeneutic argument of procedural correctness (see p 66 above) corresponds to the argument of legal culture held by the Müller school (see p 68 above).

The current state of research can thus be boiled down to the dispute between analytic legal theory and structuring legal theory. Here one finds three instances of common ground between analytic and post-positivistic legal theory.

First, they agree with regard to the normative fundamentals. According to both schools, constitutional reasons alone make it prudent to retain the limits of the wording.[219] Secondly, Müller's concept of concretisation is redolent of Alexy's structure of internal justification. Alexy also aims at expressing rules in ever more precise terms.[220] Thirdly, in order to bind judges to the law, structuring legal theory also affirms that elements of concretisation, or arguments which are closer to the wording of the rule, respectively, take priority.[221]

However, this common ground does not extend very far. With regard to the second aspect, one has to mention that according to Alexy, a *rule* is put in specific terms. Müller, on the other hand, sees concretisation *turn* the text as such into a rule. If we look at the third aspect, we find that there is a surprising element to the position of structuring legal theory: If the legal text does not imply anything, how may arguments be closer to or further away from its wording? Structuring legal theory will have to face further, fundamental objections.

(ii) A Critical Look at Structuring Legal Theory

Structuring legal theory faces fundamental, norm-theoretical objections (a). Furthermore, two important arguments which SLT has brought forward against analytic legal theory may also be raised against SLT itself (b) and (c).

One has to grant to structuring legal theory that references to 'well-defined' limits of the wording or to 'ordinary, unprejudiced speakers' often hide the fact that judges unthinkingly take their very own language usage as a basis. However, this is by no means a fresh insight, but has been well known ever since the hermeneutic turn.

Furthermore, one cannot escape the impression that SLT, using the arguments of objectivism[222] and of features semantics,[223] accuses dominant legal theory of relying on an objective concept of meaning which the latter has not resorted to since the hermeneutic turn.[224] Even for adherents to the

---

[219] For analytic legal theory see p 45 above. For structuring legal theory see p 60 above.
[220] *Cf* p 55 above.
[221] Christensen, 'Der Richter als Mund des sprechenden Textes' (n 175 above) 90; Müller, *Juristische Methodik* (n 119 above) para 445.
[222] See p 71 above.
[223] See p 71 above.
[224] See W Gast, 'Rezension' (1991) 77 *Archiv für Rechts- und Sozialphilosophie* 556 at 557.

traditional structure of interpretation and subsumption, there can be no doubt that rules are not identical with their text and that meaning is (also) at the legal practitioner's disposal.[225] However, this descriptive perception should in no way be used as a go-ahead for the normative conclusion that interpreters, as it were, are *supposed* to assign the meaning of the norm, and thus the limits of the wording—just as the fact that all interpreters, by definition, have Pre-judgements cannot be taken as a licence to assume that they should follow said Pre-judgements when interpreting a text.[226] A similar misunderstanding of the analytic position is also evident from Busse's charge that the model of the word usage rule resulted in a commitment to majority opinion (d).

Finally, one has to take issue with the inconsistency of the methodological concepts of structuring legal theory (e). This criticism is extended in a concluding remark (f).

(a) The Basic Norm

According to structuring legal theory, rules consist of legal text, normative program, and normative sphere. Alexy offers a convincing criticism of this theory of norms.[227] In his objection, he is correct in emphasising the difference between normative and significantly normative. Not everything which is relevant for judicial decision-making would, by necessity, be part of the basic norm. For Müller, however, normative program and normative sphere are equally important with regard to a rule's composition. However, this would give the legislator's directives and the area of life they regulate 'equal methodological significance and equal legal validity, making them only relatively distinguishable'.[228] Therefore, attempts to construct the limits of the wording as the limits of the normative program are problematic, especially with regard to the theoretical basis of norms.[229]

---

[225] B Schlink, 'Juristische Methodik zwischen Verfassungstheorie und Wissenschaftstheorie' (1975) 6 *Rechtstheorie* 94 at 98.

[226] M Herbert, 'Buchbesprechung' (1993) 24 *Rechtstheorie* 533 at 546.

[227] R Alexy, *Theorie der Grundrechte*, 3rd edn (Frankfurt am Main, 1996) 67 f.

[228] B Schlink, 'Juristische Methodik zwischen Verfassungstheorie und Wissenschaftstheorie' (1975) 6 *Rechtstheorie* 94 at 97 f.

[229] There are also democratic-theoretical reasons against using a 'sociological approach to the identification of norms', see I Maus, 'Zur Problematik des Rationalitäts- und Rechtsstaatspostulats in der gegenwärtigen juristischen Methodik am Beispiel Friedrich Müllers' in D Deiseroth (ed), *Ordnungsmacht. Über das Verhältnis von Legalität, Konsens und Herrschaft* (Frankfurt am Main, 1981) 165, 171 f.

(b) Circularity

According to Müller, the legal text sets the limits of the scope of permissible concretization,[230] a role it can only play as long as the determination of its meaning remains independent of the concretisation process.[231] However, this is precisely what structuring legal theory considers to be impossible. SLT regards not the 'mere', but the 'specified' wording to be definitive. After all, it was the normative program which sets the limits. The normative program, in turn, is established by putting the legal text in specific terms. In other words: The limits of concretisation are found by putting the legal text in specific terms. All Müller's school does is to present a new description of the hermeneutic circle.[232] Simultaneously, structuring legal theory has to admit to the accusation of circularity,[233] an argument it had levelled against the hermeneutic and the analytic concepts of the limits of the wording.[234]

Christensen has put forward two arguments to counter these accusations. First, he emphasises the difference between the object level and the meta-level.[235] This is correct insofar as the body of constitutional law establishes meta-rules for the methodological approach to legal norms. However, this consideration would only refute the circularity argument if the given linguistic facts—ie that legal practitioners in all cases assign the meaning of norms—applied only to the object level and not to the meta-level. But this distinction would not only be very difficult to justify, it would also be diametrically opposed to structuring legal theory's basic language-philosophical premise.

Christensen's second argument also fails to convince. He emphasises that the starting point for the interpretation of the methodology-related rules of constitutional law was not 'a vacuum', but was based on a particular Pre-judgement.[236] This is an explicit admission of a hermeneutic circle. A lot can be said in favour of the hermeneutic portrayal of the practical

---

[230] Müller, *Juristische Methodik* (n 119 above) para 480.
[231] J Harenburg, *Die Rechtsdogmatik zwischen Wissenschaft und Praxis. Ein Beitrag zur Theorie der Rechtsdogmatik* (Stuttgart, 1986) 268; B Schlink, 'Bemerkungen zum Stand der Methodendiskussion in der Verfassungsrechtswissenschaft' (1980) 19 *Der Staat* 73 at 100.
[232] Similar findings also in J Harenburg, *Die Rechtsdogmatik zwischen Wissenschaft und Praxis. Ein Beitrag zur Theorie der Rechtsdogmatik* (Stuttgart, 1986) 267; Schlink, 'Bemerkungen zum Stand der Methodendiskussion in der Verfassungsrechtswissenschaft' (n 231 above) 96.
[233] With regard to the argument of circularity, see p 70 above.
[234] Maus also observes: 'The circular structure of the process of concretization ... undermines the democratic and constitutional intentions of Müller's overall methodology'. I Maus, 'Zur Problematik des Rationalitäts- und Rechtsstaatspostulats in der gegenwärtigen juristischen Methodik am Beispiel Friedrich Müllers' in D Deiseroth (ed), *Ordnungsmacht. Über das Verhältnis von Legalität, Konsens und Herrschaft* (Frankfurt am Main, 1981) 163.
[235] Christensen, *Was heißt Gesetzesbindung?* (n 198 above) 221 f.
[236] Christensen, *Was heißt Gesetzesbindung?* (n 198 above) 222 fn 20.

application of law as circular. However, it remains remarkable how vehemently structuring legal theory brings circularity to bear against previous legal theory. And yet it not only in principle shares this notion, but even explicitly relies on Pre-judgements.

Müller, too, indirectly admits to the circularity of his approach, but is of the opinion that

> this paradox, ie that judicial interpretatory work has to begin by establishing the limits it is bound to, and by which it has to be measured ... [is] only superficial.[237]

After all, he continues, it would only prove that the question for the limits of the wording was procedural in nature. This rationale, however, can do nothing to remove the charge of circularity. Quite to the contrary, it is a confirmation. The limits of the wording are established in a hermeneutic process. It thus has to fall short of its key role, ie to restrict the very same process. Any concept of the limits of the wording which leaves the determination of these limits to the legal practitioners is worthless with regard to the constitutional task of this undertaking. We are left with the result that structuring legal theory, based on its idiosyncratic theory of norms, only delivers a novel description of the hermeneutic circle. With regard to concretisation, it has even less potential than analytic legal theory.

(c) Normal and Exceptional Cases

Using the argument of the indefiniteness of the legal text, as well as the language game argument, structuring legal theory raises the objection to analytic legal theory that distinguishing between clear and unclear cases is impossible. Yet at the same time structuring legal theory also distinguishes between normal and exceptional cases when it comes to the limits of the wording.

In their traditional version, Müller claims, the limits of the wording emerge only in exceptional cases, ie if the grammatical element wins precedence over the other elements of concretisation. In normal cases, on the other hand, the limiting function is rooted solely in the normative program, which includes all elements of concretisation.[238] However, upon taking a closer look, one finds that structuring legal theory is unable to come up with a criterion for distinguishing normal and exceptional cases. Yet the actual role of the limits of the wording is to be that of an argument in the dispute on which element is to have priority over the others. In this

---

[237] Müller, *Juristische Methodik* (n 119 above) para 532.
[238] How structuring legal theory distinguishes normal and exceptional cases was explained on p 61 f above.

dispute, it is not feasible to rely on the *result* of the conflict between several elements of concretisation as a yardstick for whether the limits of interpretation were exceeded or not. Therefore, the objection arises that it is impossible to follow Müller's model and distinguish exceptional cases, in which the limits of the wording are based on the grammatical element alone, from normal cases, where the limits of the normative program (as the product of all elements) are crucial. Müller admits this explicitly in stating that, ultimately, a normative program which 'has shrunk to include only the grammatical element' also decided exceptional cases.[239] In other words: In exceptional cases, too, the limits of interpretation are not determined until the end of the process of concretisation. The terminology used wrongly creates the impression that, at least in exceptional cases, structuring legal theory was not at odds with dominant legal theory.

(d) Commitment to the Majority Opinion

Busse argues that Alexy's concept of the word usage rule resulted in a commitment to majority opinion.[240] This is patently untrue, if only for the fact that Alexy never regards an established word usage rule, ie the semantic argument, to be cast in stone. Rather, other forms of argument, in particular considerations of justice, may justify deviating from established word usage rules.[241] Consequently, Alexy does not argue in favour of a strong commitment principle, according to which legal practitioners may never defy an established word usage rule, but a weaker one which binds legal practitioners to consider all arguments. In this process, the rules for allocating the burden of argument demand that particular emphasis be placed on the semantic argument.

Structuring legal theory, however, also advocates a weaker principle of commitment. Its own legal culture argument assumes that with legal practitioners assigning the limits of wording, the only thing that stands in the way of arbitrariness is the stabilising role of doctrine and precedent. This stabilising role can only mean that legal practitioners have to take into account the argumentative state-of-the-art in jurisprudence. To sum up: The principle of commitment in its strong form is not argued by analytic legal theory, whereas in its weak form, it is also argued by structuring legal theory. As a result, Busse's argument against Alexy comes to nothing.

---

[239] See also Müller, *Juristische Methodik* (n 119 above) para 448. *Cf* p 61 above.
[240] See p 58 f above.
[241] See p 52 f above.

(e) Inconsistency

Structuring legal theory does not fully implement its own language-philosophical a priori statements and, consequently, arrives at an inconsistent position.

On the one hand, Müller declares with reference to deconstructivist positions and arguments that with judges incapable of *recognising* solutions to a case, they have to make decisions 'without the option of justifying their actions by resorting to an objective fact in either text or language'.[242] On the other hand, according to the legal culture argument,[243] the objectivity of decisions and the judges' commitment are safeguarded by the standards of the culture of legal reasoning and by holding proceedings in accordance with the rule of law. This was feasible since said standards were not at the disposition of legal practitioners, but remained the exclusive domain of the legislator.[244] To sum up: In the view of structuring legal theory, language is incapable of guaranteeing reliability in the application of the law. Instead, this is to be provided by method- and proceedings-based standards of constitutional law.

This position is not only similar to the argument of procedural correctness—which has been advanced by ontological hermeneutics and is vehemently derided by structuring legal theory[245]—but it is inconsistent to boot, as the reliability aspired to by structuring legal theory is only conceivable if it can be based on linguistic certainties. The culture of legal reasoning and standards in the practical application of the law have to be governed by norms in order to be capable of safeguarding a reliability independent of the disposition of individual legal practitioners. However, said norms have no controlling force if their linguistic scope is assigned by the legal practitioner.

Hence, structuring legal theory, having for language-philosophical reasons made meaning something to be assigned by the legal practitioner, has to resort to the culture of legal reasoning to conjure a restriction which is not only ill-founded,[246] but which also seems to be hardly reasonable with regard to the language-game argument and to the theory of the non-identity of the legal text and of the rule. How might the norms set by constitutional law be beyond the reach of the legal practitioner if standard

---

[242] Müller, *Juristische Methodik* (n 119 above) para 181. References to the deconstructivists Derrida and Lyotard can be found in paras 507–21. See also Christensen, 'Der Richter als Mund des sprechenden Textes' (n 175 above) 49 fn 7.
[243] With regard to this argument, see p 68 above.
[244] Christensen, *Was heißt Gesetzesbindung?* (n 198 above) 287.
[245] See p 58 f above.
[246] This argumentative deficit only applies to structuring legal theory as such. In this context, one has to refer to the extensive grounds for rules of argumentation given by Alexy in his theory of argumentation.

practice demands that he constitute the meaning of any rule? The norms of constitutional law, which in turn are the subject of concretisation and of the interpretation controversy, become in the hands of structuring legal theory a deus ex machina, used to safeguard the binding to the law as if they had a fixed meaning. Based on SLT's own language-philosophical assumptions, this position is untenable.[247]

Christensen states:

> Constitutional law has a constitutive effect on the substance and the reach of any legal culture. Not only the practical application of law is bound to it.[248]

How can this binding effect be safeguarded if the meaning of constitutional norms is also only established during the process of concretisation? If structuring legal theory was to remain consistent, it would have to arrive at the direct opposite of the result stated by Christensen: It is not constitutional law that is constitutive for practice, but practice is constitutive for the substance of constitutional law.

Christensen's statement that the legal culture of reasoning came equipped with 'pragmatic values', as well as with 'results of linguistic action consolidated by tradition and institutional practice'[249] is, in the face of the fierce and fundamental criticism SLT metes out to dominant legal theory,[250] a surprising return to the safe shores of majority opinion. We may only speculate as to the reasons for this homecoming. More significant is the conclusion that structuring legal theory is unable to produce a consistent theory of the limits of wording fully based on its own language-theoretical assumptions.

(f) Concluding Remarks

Finally, one has to consider the consequences arising from structuring legal theory. Müller's opinion leads to banishing the semantic argument from juridical interpretation. If the meaning of a rule is only established as the result of juridical interpretation, it follows that it may not be used as an argument during that interpretation. Should this view of structuring legal theory be correct, it would follow that there could be no 'grammatical interpretation', as proposed by hermeneutic legal theory, nor, in the terms

---

[247] Consequently, Müller describes the effect of the limits of the wording as 'orders to stop the discourse of reasoning, administered with reference to a yardstick of closeness to the legal text' and as 'violence entering the world of letters', which resulted in a 'violent arrest of the discursively unstoppable discourse', see Müller, *Juristische Methodik* (n 119 above) paras 517 f. H. Albert would call this the 'breakdown of proceedings'.
[248] Christensen, *Was heißt Gesetzesbindung?* (n 198 above) 287.
[249] Christensen, *Was heißt Gesetzesbindung?* (n 198 above) 216, 282 f.
[250] See, eg, Christensen's charge that the theory of the application of law resulted in 'autonomous positing of legal texts' and in 'free decision-making', Christensen, *Was heißt Gesetzesbindung?* (n 198 above) 180 f.

of analytic legal theory, a 'semantic argument'[251]. This corresponds to Busse's downgrading the legal text to the status of a 'piece of scenery'.[252] Ultimately, this concept of structuring legal theory almost literally leads to an inversion of binding to the law: If interpreters create the rules in the first place, they bind the laws to themselves.[253]

Structuring legal theory is not unaware of this circularity. Christensen puts the question thus: 'How may judges be subject to the law once they have been granted the authority to create legal rules?'[254] However, structuring legal theory fails to find a satisfactory solution to this issue. The school's view that 'the methodological standards set by constitutional law' were to safeguard judges' binding to the law[255] is too much of a generality to let it off the hook.[256] The German Basic Law (Grundgesetz) only states *that* binding to the law is to prevail, but not how this is to be achieved. According to Müller, the limits of the wording are exceeded if it is no longer possible to attribute the ruling to the legal text.[257] But how is this attribution to proceed, and which criteria are supposed to ensure the binding to the law? Structuring legal theory is unable to find a satisfactory answer to this important question. A blanket reference to the methodological standards set by constitutional law and the standards of the culture of legal reasoning fall short. There is no demonstration of how these norms and standards would effect their limiting function. Yet this precisely is the issue that needs to be clarified: Are the limits of the wording a valid argument in the debate on *whether* a decision can still be attributed to a legal text? The answer given by structuring legal theory is: Whether it is attributable or not depends on whether it is attributable or not. This reply is not in the least enlightening.

---

[251] By embracing the traditional canons, however, Müller also includes grammatical interpretation among the elements of concretisation, see Müller, *Juristische Methodik* (n 119 above) paras 351–9. The fact that he does so may be explained with the inconsistency of structuring legal theory described above.

[252] Busse, *Juristische Semantik* (n 2 above) 257.

[253] In this regard, the description of structuring legal theory offered by Laudenklos is telling indeed: 'The text as such has no authority over the decision. Rather, *the legal practitioner is in control of the text* and, within the process of ruling, bends it to his will' (emphasis added): Laudenklos, 'Rechtsarbeit ist Textarbeit' (n 153 above) 157.

[254] Christensen, *Was heißt Gesetzesbindung?* (n 198 above) 183.

[255] Christensen, *Was heißt Gesetzesbindung?* (n 198 above) 220.

[256] Schlink even considers the emphasis on methodology-related standards in constitutional law to be 'not only questionable, but downright unnecessary. As regards the commitment to clarity, certainty, and rationality in juridical statements, Müller is erroneous in asserting the need for methodology to rely on constitutional theory and the latter, in turn, on the constitutional state. All insights are based on clarity, certainty, and rationality, and juridical insight, too, may only be had at the price of conforming to these conditions': Schlink, 'Bemerkungen zum Stand der Methodendiskussion in der Verfassungsrechtswissenschaft' (n 231 above) 97.

[257] Müller, *Juristische Methodik* (n 119 above) para 311.

One only has to agree with the criticism voiced by structuring legal theory insofar as it states that the principle of the wording would have to be discarded if it were found to be untenable in terms of language philosophy.[258] However, a radical turn of this kind in fundamental methodological and constitutional doctrine would not be justified unless it had been proven that the concept of the limits of the wording was impossible. This is something that structuring legal theory has failed to accomplish.

As a result, it has to be emphasised that the hypothesis advanced by structuring legal theory is inconsistent and, with regard to the theory of norms, questionable. SLT never fully implements its own language-philosophical assumptions, and hovers between deconstructivist and traditional positions. In doing so, it has to accept being countered by a substantial number of the arguments it has raised against the hermeneutic and analytic concepts of the limits of the wording.

In consequence, structuring legal theory is unable to provide a solution to the issue of the limits of the wording. Nevertheless, it does raise some important questions vis-à-vis previous legal theory. Its objections can not be dismissed easily; they have to be examined closely. In conclusion, the crucial issues will be summed up.

(iii) Controversial Issues

It is from the arguments offered in support and against the various positions that the contentious issues stem, reflecting the state-of-the-art in current legal theory, which are to be settled within the scope of this book.[259] These arguments may be classified according to type into empirical, normative, and analytic arguments.

Depenheuer, Kriele, Esser, and Pawlowski rely on a normative argument which claims that it is impossible to give a convincing normative explanation for the limits of the wording.[260] This argument can be countered with reference to the constitutional basis of the limits of wording, which was presented in the introduction.[261] Therefore, concurring with the overwhelming majority in legal theory, one may support the argument of normative necessity. There can be no doubt that the principle of the limits

---

[258] This follows from the fact that something can only be necessary if it is possible, ie the so-called 'ought implies can' formula: $Op \rightarrow Mp$ The contraposition the text to this footnote based upon is: $\neg Mp \rightarrow \neg Op$ Cf Kant, I Kant, *Kritik der praktischen Vernunft*, 10th edn (Hamburg, 1990) 54, 171, 283.

[259] Cf the overview of arguments pp 64 ff above.

[260] Esser, *Vorverständnis und Methodenwahl in der Rechtsfindung* (n 8 above) 178, 186; Kriele, *Theorie der Rechtsgewinnung* (n 13 above) 311; Pawlowski, *Methodenlehre für Juristen* (n 42 above) paras 458. 507. Depenheuer, *Der Wortlaut als Grenze* (n 200 above) 42 f, 45.

[261] See p 18 above.

of the wording is of fundamental importance in normative terms. The only point in dispute is whether there are language-philosophical arguments in its support, and whether it is empirically enforceable. Rather than engaging in a normative discussion, we need one focusing on analytic and empirical issues.

The argument of the limits of the wording's practical ineffectiveness is empirical in nature.[262] It claims that the principle of the limits of the wording does not result in limitations being placed on the practical application of the law. This argument is refuted by a claim that is likewise empirical, ie the argument of legal culture, which declares that there is a factual binding potential effected by doctrine and precedent.[263] If we assume the diagnosis of practical ineffectiveness to be correct, we may continue by enquiring as to the cause underlying this ineffectiveness.[264] This issue can be researched using the instruments offered by legal sociology.

Empirical arguments can be powerful indicators of a theory's weaknesses. On the one hand, the point of legal theory is to provide guidelines for legal practitioners which make allowances for the practical conditions of legal rulings. Yet, on the other hand, the guidelines aim at changing these conditions and making them conform with constitutional requirements. It is essential here that one construct a consistent concept of the limits of the wording. The first hurdle on the way to successful practical application is that legal theory should actually present a workable concept. This, precisely, remains a matter of some debate. Consequently, we will focus first and foremost on solving this issue of theory, and in the scope of this book ignore the controversy surrounding the empirical effectiveness of the principle of the limits of the wording.

What remains are the analytical arguments. According to current research, the fundamental discussion on the principle of the limits of the wording is language-philosophical in nature. Therefore, the preconditions of the limits of the wording will be clarified in the second chapter, based on the latest developments in the philosophy of language. The most important controversial issues can be identified from the arguments compiled above:

---

[262] Depenheuer, *Der Wortlaut als Grenze* (n 200 above) 41; Neumann, 'Der "mögliche Wortsinn" als Auslegungsgrenze in der Rechtsprechung der Strafsenate des BGH' (n 200 above) 42.

[263] Müller, *Juristische Methodik* (n 119 above) paras 325, 246. Along the same lines also Vocke, *Verfassungsinterpretation und Normbegründung* (n 199 above) 28 f. With regard to this argument, see p 68 above. The argument of legal culture is not solely empirical in nature; rather, it is also analytical. It does, however, include an empirical part.

[264] Neumann, in particular, discusses possible causes based on an analysis of court decisions, see Neumann, 'Der "mögliche Wortsinn" als Auslegungsgrenze in der Rechtsprechung der Strafsenate des BGH' (n 200 above) 50–52.

1   Can we distinguish clear and unclear cases of semantic interpretation? This is where the argument of clear cases and the argument of necessary failure clash.
2   Can the meaning of rules be determined empirically? The argument that it is empirically possible to establish meaning makes this claim, whilst the language-game argument and the argument that meaning remains unclarified negate it.
3   Can the meaning of rules be objectified within the juridical interpreters' language game? The language-game argument is at odds with the arguments of possible corrections, legal culture, and procedural correctness.

In view of these controversial issues, we have to clarify whether, as critics have claimed, the limits of the wording have completely outlived their usefulness. Objections along these lines can be refuted using the argument of clear cases and the argument of legal culture: Quite often, there is intersubjective consensus on the possible uses of a word within the juridical community of interpretation.[265] Language in general may be open, but any interpretation of laws always takes place within a particular legal system, within a specific 'language game', and thus the openness of terms is reduced. Wittgenstein himself emphasised that in normal cases, rules worked and facilitated understanding, even without having to take recourse to Platonism.[266] Any normative conclusion which abandons the limits of wording, therefore, ignores the stabilising role of a doctrine which systematically analyses the ways in which words are used. It would be wrongly based on Wittgenstein.[267]

This rationale, however, is challenged by the argument of necessary failure, which claims that conventions of language use, even within a single branch of science, would only in normal cases be sufficiently stable to be able to explicitly exclude particular ways of using a word as wrong.[268] The fact that they are sufficiently stable in normal cases is evident if we consider that all acts of communication are doomed to failure unless there is agreement on the use of words. But in clear cases, the argument goes,

---

[265] D Busse, 'Zum Regel-Charakter von Normtextbedeutungen und Rechtsnormen' (n 168 above) 318; W Heun, 'Original intent und Wille des historischen Verfassungsgebers. Zur Problematik einer Maxime im amerikanischen und deutschen Verfassungsrecht' (1991) 116 *Archiv des öffentlichen Rechts* 185 at 203.

[266] This follows from §§ 198–242 of the *Philosophical Investigations*. Here, Wittgenstein elaborates on the characteristics of rule-following, see in particular §§ 208, 215. With regard to the overall issue, see Herbert, *Rechtstheorie als Sprachkritik* (n 201 above) 86–91.

[267] See Ibid 262; B Schünemann, 'Die Gesetzesinterpretation im Schnittfeld von Sprachphilosophie, Staatsverfassung und juristischer Methodenlehre' in G Kohlmann (ed), *Festschrift für Ulrich Klug. Band 1* (Köln, 1983) 179. This argument of doctrine is also put forward by structuring legal theory, see Laudenklos, 'Rechtsarbeit ist Textarbeit' (n 153 above) 156.

[268] Herbert, *Rechtstheorie als Sprachkritik* (n 201 above) 239.

there is no necessity to draw on the limits of the wording as a delimitation factor. The issue of the limits of wording only becomes relevant the moment doubts emerge as to the use of a term. In these cases, there was no linguistic convention to refer to within the legal language game. It would follow from this that the concept of the limits of the wording was incapable of providing the delimitation of interpretation and further development of the law in intrinsically difficult cases.

Against this view it must be postulated that, to begin with, the concepts of clear cases and consensus have to be more subtly differentiated. The latter can either refer to the wording or to the fact that justice demands a particular result, whether it is consistent with the wording or not.[269] We have to differentiate between consensus on the wording and consensus with regard to justice. Along the same lines, normal cases with regard to wording and justice have to be distinguished. Therefore, we may only speak of clear cases, ie cases in which there is no need to use the limits of the wording, if there is consensus on a decision's compatibility with both the wording and with the idea of justice. A case would have to be called unclear not only if its compatibility with the wording was in dispute, but also if clarity existed with regard to the wording, yet extra-linguistic reasons cast doubts on the solution which the consensus on the wording would suggest. In the latter case, too, the limits of the wording matter. Hence, the assumption that the issue of the limits of the wording would only become relevant if there were doubts as to the use of a concept is based on too narrow a view. There can thus be no question of the concept of the limits of the wording being unworkable in intrinsically problematic cases.

What remains to be clarified is the first group of unclear cases. If, due to the lack of the limits of the wording, there are doubts as to the proper use of a term, the concept of the limits of the wording seems to be invalidated. After all, it is based on a use-theory of meaning. Given *this* group of unclear cases, one understands the hypothesis that in many instances the limits of the wording cannot be used as a criterion for distinguishing interpretation and further development of the law.[270]

Having said that, the size of this group of unclear cases is uncertain. Among other things, this issue sums up the controversy between structuring legal theory and traditional legal theory. While traditional legal theory

---

[269] Schauer introduced a similar discrimination into the debate, see F Schauer, *Playing by the Rules. A Philosophical Examination of Rule-Based Decision-Making in Law and in Life* (Oxford, 1991) 209–11. See M Stone, 'Focusing the Law: What Legal Interpretation Is Not' in A Marmor (ed), *Law and Interpretation. Essays in Legal Philosophy* (Oxford, 1995) 67.
[270] Herbert, *Rechtstheorie als Sprachkritik* (n 201 above) 250.

assumes that it was possible to determine most legal cases by establishing word usage rules, structuring legal theory claims that hardly a single meaning is open to determination.

Concerning this question, one may draw the following dividing line based on the argument of legal culture and the argument of procedural correctness: The extent to which the limits of the wording may be used as an effective differentiator depends on the existing opportunities for the determination of word usage rules, ie the scope and quality of the interpretative community's linguistic consensus. The limits of the wording divide interpretation and further development of the law wherever, but only wherever, there is a stable interpretative code of practice.

However, it remains to be seen whether structuring legal theory would concur with this dividing line. In the controversy on assessing the capability of the juridical interpretative community's linguistic consensus, SLT argues that this assessment amounts to 'a rather subjective feeling concerned with acts of understanding meaning which move dynamically on a linear scale'.[271] Whether this was called interpretation or further development of the law was nothing but 'a part of the game for legitimacy'[272] and persuasiveness within the juridical discourse.[273]

This position is unsatisfactory. It falls far short of the constitutional requirements for juridical discourse. With the dividing line summarised above—according to which the scope of the limits of the wording is restricted to the consensus of the interpretative community—structuring legal theory concurs with the hermeneutic positions and its argument of procedural correctness. It is questionable whether this constitutes a workable criterion for the distinction between interpretation and further development of the law. Legal practitioners are unable to wait and see if a change they suggest to the usage rule of a concept will win wide recognition. The given criterion, ie the other participants' (in the juridical practice) response to a juridical ruling,[274] only results in a vague ex-post assessment which is too uncertain with regard to the judges' binding to the law.

The rationale of structuring legal theory and hermeneutic legal theory stands here in the tradition of Quine. Pursuant to this holistic way of thinking, there is no analyticity, no meaning, no a priori established

---

[271] Busse, 'Was ist die Bedeutung eines Gesetzestextes?' (n 169 above) 146.
[272] Busse, 'Was ist die Bedeutung eines Gesetzestextes?' (n 169 above) 130.
[273] Heun, 'Original intent und Wille des historischen Verfassungsgebers' (n 265 above) 204; Müller, *Juristische Methodik* (n 119 above) para 526.
[274] See D Busse, 'Zum Regel-Charakter von Normtextbedeutungen und Rechtsnormen' (n 168 above) 313: 'Only practical application will show if our action is covered by the rule. We have to observe the reactions of others and see whether they consider our actions to be in accordance with the practice in question'. See also Herbert, *Rechtstheorie als Sprachkritik* (n 201 above) 207.

content; there are only seamless transitions. This is explicitly expressed in Busse's formula of dynamic movement on a linear scale, quoted above. In this case, one may refer to analytic legal theory and put categorical thinking to this brand of holistic thinking. The argument of procedural correctness can be accepted insofar as any juridical decision may possibly be the subject of an argumentative discourse on whether the limits of interpretation were observed or exceeded. However, we have to distinguish two types of discourse. A discourse may either pertain to establishing meaning, or concern the question of whether one should comply with a particular, established meaning. Structuring legal theory is wrong in claiming that it is impossible to distinguish these two types of discourse.

These reflections complete the identification of the limits of the wording as a core problem of both legal theory and the philosophy of language. It concerns the question of the structure and the ways in which we may perceive meaning. Is the meaning of a rule fixed, at least within the confines of a particular language game? Is there a bridge between a text and its meaning, between the wording of a rule and its content? These very fundamental questions make it clear that in using the principle of the limits of the wording one also examines how objective and how absolutely or relatively correct juridical rulings may be. The key arguments against the principle of the limits of the wording are rooted in the philosophy of language. They may only be refuted by language-philosophical reflections.

Chapter 2

Normativity and Objectivity of Linguistic Meaning

Logic is the organ of semantic self-consciousness.[1]

I. INTRODUCTION

BELOW, I WILL state more precisely the reasons for the second chapter's language-philosophical focus (A). This will be followed by an analysis of the most crucial individual issues of the overall 'meaning' complex (B). Subsequently, I will give an outline of theories of meaning, their significance for the limits of the wording, and their problems (C). Finally, I will present this chapter's main thesis, and I will survey the second chapter's main points (D).

A. Meaning Scepticism and the Indeterminacy Thesis

The key objections raised against the posit of the limits of the wording are language-philosophical in nature: They claim that there are no semantically clear cases; that the meaning of norms is always open, cannot be empirically determined, and is not objectifiable. Structuring legal theory refers to Quine's meaning scepticism, and to deconstructive authors, such as Derrida or Foucault.[2] In Anglo-American legal theory, semantic indeterminacy theses are *the* crucial arguments in support of the positions of

---

[1] RB Brandom, *Making It Explicit. Reasoning, Representing, and Discursive Commitment* (Cambridge MA, 1994) XIX.
[2] R Christensen, 'Der Richter als Mund des sprechenden Textes. Zur Kritik des gesetzespositivistischen Textmodells' in F Müller (ed), *Untersuchungen zur Rechtslinguistik. Interdisziplinäre Studien zu praktischer Semantik und Strukturierender Rechtslehre in Grundfragen der juristischen Methodik* (Berlin, 1989) 49; F Müller, *Juristische Methodik*, 7th edn (Berlin, 1997) paras 166 f, 507–18.

Legal Realism and *Critical Legal Studies*.³ From Quine's *Two Dogmas of Empiricism*, via Kripke's *sceptical paradox*, and culminating in Wright's repudiation of any attempt to constitute meaning as *investigation-independent*, meaning scepticism has long been framing serious objections to efforts at awarding meaning with normativity and objectivity.⁴

Meaning scepticism's deconstructive challenge upsets the posit of the limits of the wording. If meaning is not objective, and there is no difference between correct and incorrect use of a concept, a theory of indeterminism results. A premise that linguistic meaning does not determine the use of a concept (ie, in a legal context, subsumption) may be used in four variations, according to scope:

1. Linguistic meaning may never determine use.
2. Linguistic meaning may determine every use.
3. Linguistic meaning may never determine a single use.
4. Linguistic meaning may not determine a single use only in hard cases.

Predominantly, legal theory accepts indeterminacy of the first kind, as semantic arguments are always subject to the proviso that teleological considerations require a different result.⁵ Indeterminacy of the first kind would only be a problem for strict subjectivists who assume an exact ranking of canones. Thus, indeterminacy of the first kind holds no interest.

The result of indeterminacy of the third kind is that, for semantic reasons alone, it will never be possible to identify one use as the only feasible one, ie there is always semantic leeway. This denies the possibility of semantically easy cases, in which the semantic argument alone offers sufficient grounds for decision-making. Indeterminacy of the fourth kind confines that of the third kind to hard cases. This position is held by Hart and by analytic legal theory. Both assume that in hard cases, meaning is by necessity determined by extra-semantic arguments. Müller's school, on the other hand, negates the difference between easy and hard cases by referring

---

³ See DO Brink, 'Legal Interpretation, Objectivity and Morality' in B Leiter (ed), *Objectivity in Law and Morals* (Cambridge, 1997) 14 f, 17; JL Coleman and B Leiter, 'Determinacy, Objectivity, and Authority' in A Marmor (ed), *Law and Interpretation. Essays in Legal Philosophy* (Oxford, 1995) 203–5.

⁴ P Carruthers, 'Baker and Hacker's Wittgenstein' (1984) 58 *Synthese* 451 at 467 f; SA Kripke, *Wittgenstein on Rules and Private Language. An Elementary Exposition* (Oxford, 1982) 7–11; WVO Quine, 'Two Dogmas of Empiricism' in WVO Quine (ed), *From a Logical Point of View. Nine Logico-Philosophical Essays* (Cambridge MA, 1999) 36 f; C Wright, 'Rule-following, Objectivity and the Theory of Meaning' in SH Holtzman and CM Leich (eds), *Wittgenstein: To follow a Rule* (London, 1981) 100; C Wright, 'Rule-following, Meaning and Constructivism' in C Travis (ed), *Meaning and Interpretation* (Oxford, 1986) 290–92.

⁵ See Alexy's rule on the burden of proof in argumentation, R Alexy, *A Theory of Legal Argumentation. The Theory of Rational Discourse as Theory of Legal Justification* (Oxford, 1989) 305.

to use-theory, according to which every speech act constitutes its own meaning. Müller's school thus approximates to the indeterminacy thesis of the second kind.

With regard to the issue of the limits of the wording, the consequences of variants two to four vary. The second thesis argues the most far-reaching indeterminacy, disposing of the semantic-limiting function. The third thesis means that there is leeway in all cases, but that there is a limit to said leeway. Thesis four assumes that in easy cases, one single use is correct, while hard cases leave some leeway. According to the fourth thesis, there is only room for the limits of the wording in hard cases.

Meaning scepticism can be based on ontological or epistemological reasons.[6] Therefore, we have to distinguish constitutive meaning scepticism and epistemological scepticism. The variants of the indeterminacy thesis can all be understood either ontologically or epistemologically. The theory of the limits of the wording will already be unsettled should epistemological scepticism be correct. In other words: the theory of the limits of the wording depends on the constitutive *and* epistemological objectivity of both meaning and linguistic judgements. The legal theory of the limits of the wording presupposes that meaning cannot only be explained, but is also intersubjectively accessible and communicable.

B. Meaning as a Problem of the Philosophy of Language

Linguistic meaning is a highly complex issue and of great relevance to a large number of philosophical questions.[7] Philosophy of language, action theory, and the philosophy of mind are very closely connected. However, it still crucial to distinguish the individual issues analytically. Here, on a very general level, the most obvious option would be to use the language-philosophical triangle which links the key points of 'language', 'mind', and 'world'.[8] The link between 'mind' and 'world' touches upon issues such as perception, behaviour, the structure of mind, representation, and intentionality. The philosophy of mind and the philosophy of consciousness both

---

[6] See PA Boghossian, 'The Rule-Following Considerations' (1989) 98 *Mind* 507 at 515; K Glüer, *Sprache und Regeln. Zur Normativität von Bedeutung* (Berlin, 1999) 33; BC Smith, 'Meaning and Rule-Following' in E Craig (ed), *Routledge Encyclopedia of Philosophy*, vol 6 (London, 1998) 214.

[7] Dummett has called the development of a satisfactory theory of meaning 'the most pressing task of contemporary analytical philosophy', see M Dummett, 'Introduction' in M Dummett (ed), *The Logical Basis of Metaphysics* (London, 1991) 18.

[8] M Crimmins, 'Language, Philosophy of' in Craig (ed), *Routledge Encyclopedia of Philosophy*, vol 5 (n 6 above) 409. The language-philosophical triangle with the corners 'symbol', 'thought/reference', and 'referent' is known in linguistics as the semiotic triangle.

deal with these questions.[9] In the present book, they will at best be touched upon indirectly, as will the influence of language on consciousness, ie the question of the extent to which language mediates and empowers the mind to hold thoughts.[10]

The present work focuses on the relation between the world and language, and the influence of consciousness on language. Using and understanding a language is a mental task. Hence, many language philosophers have made the influence of consciousness on language the focus of their deliberations by considering the understanding of language as their core issue. Independent of the question of how a concept of understanding may look in detail, it is met with a fundamental criticism. Wittgenstein's private language argument and Quine's indeterminacy thesis both deny the ability of consciousness to constitute or define linguistic meaning.

The second major issue of theories of meaning concerns the relation between the world and language. With language, which is the vehicle of describing and explaining reality, language philosophy concentrates on whether and by what means language may give a correct, true, or adequate description of the world. Linguistic meaning is accordingly closely connected to the nature of truth and reality. With regard to these problems, the present work will leave many questions unresolved. Nevertheless, individual aspects of reference, truth, and the debate between realism and anti-realism will play an important role. The quarrel between realism and anti-realism, in particular, remains too abstract and sweeping to warrant a more extensive treatment on these pages.

In addition to the crucial lines of problems identified in the language-philosophical triangle, I will go into questions of analyticity, the possibility of *substantial disagreement*, the relations between meaning and logic, and the relations between propositional and subsentential meaning.

C. Language-Philosophical Theories of Meaning

Many sciences carry out research into linguistic meaning: Linguistics, philosophy, logic, psychology, etc. Within the context of this work, aspects of linguistic meaning take centre-stage which are not genuinely a part of

---

[9] D Braddon-Mitchell and F Jackson, *The Philosophy of Mind and Cognition* (Oxford, 1996); J Locke, *Essay Concerning Human Understanding* (1690) (London, 1997); C MacDonald and G MacDonald, *Philosophy of Psychology* (Oxford, 1995); C McGinn, *The Problem of Consciousness* (Oxford, 1991); G Ryle, *The Concept of Mind* (London, 2000).

[10] This issue is the object of the discussion of the Sapir-Whorf hypothesis, see JJ Gumperz and SC Levinson, *Rethinking Linguistic Relativity* (Cambridge, 1996); JA Lucy, *Language Diversity and Thought. A Reformulation of the Linguistic Relativity Hypothesis* (Cambridge, 1992).

linguistics,[11] but rather of philosophy. Thus, the approach I have selected—differing from the method chosen by Friedrich Müller's workgroup on legal linguistics—is based on non-linguistic, philosophical semantics.[12]

(i) Classification in Categories

Language-philosophical theories of meaning can be classified according to various criteria.[13] Possible options are: a tripartite classification using referent, idea, and behaviour (a)[14]; according to the dichotomy of realism and antirealism (b)[15]; and according to the functions of language (c).[16]

(a) Referent, Idea, and Behaviour

Reference theories identify the meaning of a term with its referent, ie with the relation of words to the world.[17] This relation may, first, consist between singular expressions such as names, or definite descriptions and individual objects. This reference is singular because it refers to one particular object, eg the name 'Aristotle'. Secondly, reference may exist between general terms, eg 'table' or 'proton', and a class of objects or their common properties.

We can distinguish four variants of reference theories. The theory of names holds that the meaning of a name or subject term is its referent. This view was held by the early Wittgenstein and Russell.[18]

---

[11] On the concept and history of linguistic semantics see J Lyons, 'Bedeutungstheorien' in AV Stechow and D Wunderlich (eds), *Semantik. Ein internationales Handbuch der zeitgenössischen Forschung* (Berlin, 1991) 17.
[12] On the concept of non-linguistic semantics see *ibid*, 4.
[13] The categories presented below facilitate terminological classification and specify the remit for this chapter's deliberations. Nevertheless, one has to point out the problems brought by schematical assignments, namely, not counting overlaps as regards content, that the categories are unable to account for every theory. A classification according to referent, idea, and behaviour, for instance, is unable to account for either pragmatic approaches or a theory of truth conditions.
[14] WP Alston, 'Meaning' in P Edwards (ed), *The Encyclopedia of Philosophy* (New York, 1967) 233; Lyons, 'Bedeutungstheorien' (n 11 above) 8.
[15] G Meggle and G Siegwart, 'Der Streit um die Bedeutungstheorien' in M Dascal, D Gerhardus, K Lorenz and G Meggle (eds), *Sprachphilosophie. 2. Halbband* (Berlin, 1995) 965.
[16] Williams relies on this criterion, SG Williams, 'Meaning and Truth' in Craig (ed), *Routledge Encyclopedia of Philosophy, vol 6* (n 6 above) 220.
[17] For an overview of reference theories see K Sterelny, 'Reference. Philosophical Issues ' in PV Lamarque and RE Asher (eds), *Concise Encyclopedia of Philosophy of Language* (Oxford, 1997).
[18] L Wittgenstein, *Tractatus logico-philosophicus. Werkausgabe Band 1* (Frankfurt am Main, 1997) 3.203: 'A name means an object. The object is its meaning'. *Cf* B Russell, 'The Philosophy of Logical Atomism ' in B Russell (ed), *Logic and Knowledge. Essays 1901–1950* (London, 1956) 244: 'A name is a simple symbol ... used to designate a certain particular or by extension an object'.

Verification theory, which has its seeds in the Vienna circle's logical positivism, primarily assigns meaning not to words, but to propositions. Language is reduced to that of scientific observation. A proposition is only meaningful if it can be verified—with its meaning determined by the method it is empirically verified.[19] In Dummett's modern (anti-realistic) version, the meaning of a proposition is determined by the conditions under which a speaker has sufficient reasons for his assertion (*assertability conditions*).[20]

Causal theories of reference see a causal connection between the use of a term and its referent. According to the view held by Kripke and Putnam, especially names and *natural kind terms* are introduced by ostensive definitions. Ostensive definitions refer to all objects having the same internal structure as the object ostensively 'dubbed' during the 'initial baptism'.[21]

Naturalism, finally, assumes that meaning can be completely reduced to empirically accessible data. Forming part of this category of reference theories are psychological theories that equate meaning with the intentions and opinions of speakers.[22]

While reference theories view meaning to be the relation between language and the world, *idea theories* focus on ideas or concepts which are connected to a linguistic expression.[23] *Behaviourist theories* cannot be assigned to the language-philosophical triangle. They explain meaning using a behaviourist stimulus-response model.[24]

---

[19] AJ Ayer, Language, Truth and Logic (London 1936); R Carnap, *Der logische Aufbau der Welt* (Hamburg, 1998) para 161, 179; Wittgenstein, *Tractatus logico-philosophicus* (n 18 above) 4.022, 4.024, 4.061, 4.2.

[20] M Dummett (ed), *Truth and Other Enigmas* (Cambridge, MA 1978).

[21] SA Kripke, *Naming and Necessity* (Oxford, 1980); H Putnam (ed), *Mind, Language and Reality. Philosophical Papers, vol 2* (Cambridge, 1975).

[22] P Grice, 'Meaning' (1957) 66 *The Philosophical Review* 377; D Lewis, *Convention. A Philosophical Study* (Cambridge MA, 1969). See the connection to Papineau's or Millikan's evolution-theoretical assumptions: RG Millikan, *Language, Thought, and Other Biological Categories. New Foundations for Realism* (Cambridge MA, 1984); D Papineau, *Philosophical Naturalism* (Oxford, 1993).

[23] J Locke, *Essay Concerning Human Understanding* (1690) (London, 1997) II 2 1 f 'The use then of words, is to be sensible Marks of Ideas; and the Ideas they stand for, are their proper and immediate Signification ... Words in their primary or immediate Signification stand for nothing, but the Ideas in the Mind of him that uses them'. See also G Frege, 'Über Sinn und Bedeutung' in G Frege (ed), *Funktion, Begriff, Bedeutung. Fünf logische Studien* (Göttingen, 1994) 40–65.

[24] CK Ogden and IA Richards, *The Meaning of Meaning. A Study of the Influence of Language upon Thought and of the Science of Symbolism*, 5th edn (London 1938); BF Skinner, *Verbal behavior* (London 1957).

(b) Realism and Anti-Realism

Any separation of meaning theories according to their position with regard to the realism problem has to be rooted in a clear concept of 'realism'. Three fundamental meanings can be distinguished. First, in the problem of universals, realism—as opposed to nominalism—stands for the conviction that universals (eg a property or relation), abstract objects (eg numbers, propositions), or collective particulars (sets, types) exist as irreducible components of reality.[25] Secondly, realism—as opposed to idealism—is used to label the view that reality is independent of subjective, mental performances such as thinking, cognition, or language.[26] Thirdly, realism—as opposed to anti-realism—is, according to Dummett, the theory that the truth of a statement (identical with its meaning) is independent of the possibility of its verification or justification.[27] This latter, modern meaning considers the realism problem not to be concerned with the existence of entities, but with the character of the truth that is attributed or awarded to a particular class of sentences. Dummett considers the previous two concepts of realism to be based on this semantic perspective.[28]

Realist and anti-realist positions can be global or limited to specific spheres, eg the debates concerning scientific realism or moral realism. Dummett, on the other hand, considers realism to be by necessity a global problem affecting all spheres of thought, since it applies to linguistic meaning.

Language-philosophical realism will take centre-stage in the present work. All reference theories can be attributed to realism. According to the respective concepts of realism, they are based either on the irreducible or mind-independent existence of referents, or on treating truth as an independent property of sentences.[29] Idea theories can be understood to be realist or anti-realist, depending on whether or not one awards ideas or their truth-values an independent existence. Behaviourist theories are anti-realist, in a similar way to pragmatic theories.

---

[25] On the problem of universals see DM Armstrong, *Universals and Scientific Realism* (Cambridge, 1978); W Künne, *Abstrakte Gegenstände. Semantik und Ontologie* (Frankfurt am Main, 1983); WVO Quine, 'On What There Is' in Quine (ed), *From a Logical Point of View* (n 4 above), WVO Quine, 'Logic and the Reification of Universals' in Quine (ed), *From a Logical Point of View* (n 4 above).

[26] H Putnam and J Conant, *Realism with a Human Face* (Cambridge MA, 1990).

[27] M Dummett, 'Realism' in Dummett (ed), *Truth and Other Enigmas* (n 20 above) 146. On Dummett's language philosophy see D Gunson, *Michael Dummett and the Theory of Meaning* (Aldershot, 1998). On Dummett's overall antirealism see A Matar, *From Dummett's Philosophical Perspective* (Berlin, 1997).

[28] Dummett's reconstruction is controversial, see B Hale, 'Realism and its Oppositions' in B Hale and C Wright (eds), *A Companion to the Philosophy of Language* (Oxford, 1997) 283–8.

[29] Meggle/Siegwart, however, place verification theory in the realist school, see Meggle and Siegwart, 'Der Streit um die Bedeutungstheorien' (n 15 above) 964.

(c) Functions of Language

Meaning theories can also be classified according to which functions of language they consider fundamental. Three important, overlapping functions of language can be distinguished: the function of language in communication, in thinking, and in making assertions. Hence, meaning may first be equated with the communicative intentions of speakers, following the analysis propagated by speech act theory.[30] Secondly, the psychological-functionalistic relations between mind states can be considered to constitute concepts and meanings. The assertive function of language, on the other hand, is central to the theory of truth conditions.

(ii) Significance for the Limits of the Wording

It is evident that a limiting function can be designed according to each of the above meaning theories. For reference theories, the semantic limit is set by the nature of the world, which by referring to the methods of science simultaneously also clarifies the issue of epistemic access. Both realist and anti-realist idea theories can also refer to the limits of ideas or concepts, but run into difficulties when having to explain how this limit may be recognised. For Davidsonian theories, the limits of the wording are situated between truth conditions and non-truth conditions, while pragmatic theories simply refer to a language community's use practices, which may be determined using socio-linguistic tools.

This result might suggest the conclusion that it made little difference to which theory of meaning one had subscribed, as long as one was able to refute meaning-sceptic arguments. However, this would be a premature conclusion, as legal theory depends not only on the existence of the limits of the wording, but also on epistemic access to these limits. A judge has to be aware of how he or she may determine the limits of the wording. Hence, it is not sufficient to merely refute sceptical arguments. Moreover, one has to decide on an authoritative theory of meaning in order to use its epistemic assumptions to ascertain the position of the limits of the wording.

D. An Integrative Theory of Meaning

Each of the meaning theories presented above has its own problems to overcome. Reference theories can be accused of leaving the relation between word and the world unexplained, and of simply taking it for

---

[30] HP Grice, *Studies in the Way of Words* (Cambridge, MA 1989); JR Searle, *Speech Acts. An Essay in the Philosophy of Language* (Cambridge, 1969).

granted. The only account possible would be some sort of physical reductionism. However, this option meets with grave objections. Intentionalism is unable to break the semantic circle; it merely shifts the meaning problem to the level of the mind. Intentionalism presupposes on the level of mind what has to be explained on the level of language. The theory of truth conditions is unable to clarify why the truth conditions of synonyms should vary even if their meanings are identical. Another accusation levelled at this theory is that specifying truth conditions will only help those who already comprehend the expression. A simple use theory remains unable to explain the normativity of meaning.

These are the problems we face when trying to define the requirements that a theory of meaning for natural languages would have to meet. It has already been stressed that not only constitutive, but also epistemic questions will have to be clarified. Furthermore, we have to emphasise that linguistic meaning has many aspects. One fails to see why each meaning theory would have to consider these aspects in isolation, and, as it were, pit them against each other in the language-philosophical arena. These controversies do not do justice to the complex phenomenon that is language. Sophisticated meaning theories, by contrast, would allow for both conventional and intentional elements, grasping both the world-relatedness of language and its rule-governedness.[31] An *integrative theory of meaning* has to be developed, one which combines both approaches, even if at first glance—and in traditional language-philosophical classification—they appear to be antithetic.[32]

The integrative theory described in this work combines several deliberations on the topic of normativity and the objectivity of linguistic meaning, focussing on Robert Brandom's theory, presented in his 1994 volume *Making It Explicit*, and on theories developed by Wittgenstein, Davidson, Dummett, Putnam, and Habermas. Brandom's theory is also integrative in nature. Another focal point of the second chapter is the repudiation of meaning-sceptical arguments, which have most notably been put forward by Quine and Kripke.

This integrative theory of meaning will be developed in three stages, mirrored in the three-tiered structure of this chapter. Its first part will be devoted to an examination of normativity (II); the second will focus on the objectivity of linguistic meaning (III). Introducing these two principal parts will be surveys on the concept of normativity and objectivity, respectively,

---

[31] With regard to a sophisticated theory of meaning see C Demmerling, 'Bedeutung' in HJ Sandkühler (ed), *Enzyklopädie Philosophie. Band 1* (Hamburg, 1999) 113; B Loewer, 'A Guide to Naturalizing Semantics' in Hale and Wright (eds), *A Companion to the Philosophy of Language* (n 28 above) 110.
[32] Lyons also discusses a possible complementarity, see Lyons, 'Bedeutungstheorien' (n 11 above) 23.

followed by a closer look at the relations each aspect has with linguistic meaning. Finally, the most important objections will be discussed. In the third part, I will summarise the results of the two principal parts (IV).

II. THE NORMATIVITY OF LINGUISTIC MEANING

Whether and how linguistic meaning is normative remains unclear and has been a matter of some debate. As yet, there is no generally acknowledged explanation of the concept.[33] In one way or another, all theories on normativity follow Wittgenstein's middle or late phase. Here, too, in addition to other important elements, his use-theory of meaning with its deliberations on rule-following will provide the basis for an integrative theory of normativity (A). Building on that, I will focus on Robert Brandom's large-scale defence of the normativity postulate (B). In conclusion, the three key objections to the normativity postulate will be discussed (C).

A. The Concept of Semantic Normativity

The concept of semantic normativity is elucidated in four stages. Based on broad previous considerations, a general normativity thesis—shared by all normativity theories—is formulated (i). The conditions that any theory of normativity would have to meet will be set down subsequently (ii). On that basis, four strategies for the argumentation of semantic normativity can be distinguished (iii), which finally, using a connection thesis, are combined to form an integrative theory of normativity (iv).

(i) The General Thesis of Normativity

The concept of normativity describes the evaluative or prescriptive property of judgements.[34] Normative judgements differ from empirical judgements, which may be 'true' or 'false' depending on the degree to which they are consistent with the facts of a case.

---

[33] In 1957, Cavell complained that 'The way philosophers have practised with the word 'normative' in recent years seems to me lamentable'. S Cavell, 'Must We Mean What We Say?' in S Cavell (ed), *Must We Mean What We Say? A Book of Essays* (Cambridge, 1976) 21 f.
[34] RM Hare, *The Language of Morals* (Oxford, 1972) 1–3; W Vossenkuhl, 'Artikel "normativ/deskriptiv"' in J Ritter, G Bien and R Eisler (eds), *Historisches Wörterbuch der Philosophie, Band 6* (1984) 931.

Even in the most recent language-philosophical works, the question of the normativity of semantic meaning remains a hotly contested subject.[35] The concept of normativity as such is already unclear.[36] What remains fundamental for all theories, however, is the thought that it is impossible to express meaningful content unless is it possible to use words incorrectly. Thus, there is consensus with regard to a very broad concept of normativity. The *general normativity thesis* based on this is[37]: 'There is an intersubjectively valid way of distinguishing correct and incorrect uses of concepts and propositions'. According to this thesis, any actual or potential use of a concept can either be awarded the property 'correct' or the property 'incorrect'.[38] Blackburn declares that

> [i]t is not seriously open to a philosopher to deny that, in this minimal sense, there is such a thing as correctness and incorrectness. The entire question is the conception we have.[39]

This minimum consensus has two fundamental qualities. One: The relation between the meaning of a proposition and its use is specified to be normative.[40] Two: The thesis that there are correctness conditions is not exactly far-reaching. These conditions might vary widely, making it necessary to distinguish between a great number of normativity theses. Before we begin discussing individual specifications for correctness conditions, three conditions for normativity theories have to be laid down.

---

[35] Critical with regard to the thesis of the normativity of linguistic meaning are: A Bilgrami, 'Norms and Meaning' in R Stoecker (ed), *Reflecting Davidson. Donald Davidson Responding to an International Forum of Philosophers* (Berlin, 1993) 144; P Coates, 'Kripke's Sceptical Paradox: Normativeness and Meaning ' (1986) 95 *Mind* 77 at 78; K Glüer, *Sprache und Regeln* (n 6 above) 234 f; K Glüer and P Pagin, 'Rules of Meaning and Practical Reasoning' (1999) 118 *Synthese* 207 at 224 f; P Horwich, 'Meaning, Use and Truth' (1995) 104 *Mind* 355 at 357; AM Wikforss, 'Semantic Normativity' (2001) 102 *Philosophical Studies* 203 at 220. For normativity: S Blackburn, 'The Individual Strikes Back' (1984) 58 *Synthese* 281 at 291; Boghossian, 'The Rule-Following Considerations' (n 6 above) 532; Brandom, *Making It Explicit* (n 1 above) 29; EH Gampel, 'The Normativity of Meaning' (1997) 86 *Philosophical Studies* 221; MN Lance and J Hawthorne, *The Grammar of Meaning. Normativy and Semantic Discourse* (Cambridge, 1997) 13; J McDowell, 'Wittgenstein on Following a Rule' (1984) 58 *Synthese* 325 at 329; C Wright, 'Kripke's Account of the Argument Against Private Language' (1984) 81 *Journal of Philosophy* 759 at 771 f.
[36] See GH von Wright, *Norm and Action. A Logical Enquiry* (New York, 1963) 1.
[37] Boghossian, 'The Rule-Following Considerations' (n 6 above) 513; J McDowell, 'Wittgenstein on Following a Rule' (n 35 above) 358 fn 3. See also K Glüer, 'Sense and Prescriptivity' (1999) 14 *Acta Analytica* 111 at 121; Glüer, *Sprache und Regeln* (n 6 above) 38.
[38] C McGinn, *Mental Content* (Oxford, 1989) 160.
[39] Blackburn, 'The Individual Strikes Back' (n 35 above) 281 f.
[40] See Glüer, *Sprache und Regeln* (n 6 above) 159.

(ii) The Three Conditions for Normativity Theories

Ironically, the credit for having put the normativity of meaning at the focus of the language-philosophical discourse goes to one of its severest critics: Saul Kripke. Kripke considers the normativity of linguistic meaning not as an integral part of a theory of meaning, but as a meta-level, pre-theoretical condition for the tenability of any sort of theory of meaning.[41] In his eyes, any theory not meeting the normativity condition is invalid. The sceptical conclusion that Kripke draws from the normativity condition will have to be discussed in detail later. Here, it suffices to point out that the approach used in this work differs from Kripke's. The emphasis is not on checking whether a theory meets a requirement, but on the question preceding this requirement, namely, whether and how meaning may be normative. This depends on the conditions a normativity thesis would have to meet. We have to distinguish three of these conditions (a)-(c).

(a) The Condition of Anti-Reductionist Supervenience

The condition of anti-reductionism implies that correctness conditions cannot be determined by empirical means alone.[42] Any effort at a naturalist reduction must lead to identifying what is correct with empirical facts. The distinguishing feature of normativity, ie the anti-reductionist supervenience,[43] is lost.[44] Normativity reduced to naturalist facts does not constitute normativity in the sense of the general thesis of normativity.[45] The possibility and the power of this position will be discussed in detail

---

[41] See K Puhl, 'Introduction' in K Puhl (ed), *Meaning Scepticism* (Berlin, 1991) 4; Wikforss, 'Semantic Normativity' (n 35 above) 203.

[42] With regard to this question see Boghossian, 'The Rule-Following Considerations' (n 6 above) 537; Glüer, *Sprache und Regeln* (n 6 above) 166. It follows that the concept of normativity held by McGinn has to be rejected. According to McGinn, Kripkean normativity consists in a speaker maintaining steady the meaning of his concepts over a period of time. This view, however, does not meet the normativity condition. See C McGinn, *Wittgenstein on Meaning* (Oxford, 1984) 174. Critical, Boghossian, 'The Rule-Following Considerations' (n 6 above) 512 f.

[43] With regard to the concept of antireductionist supervenience see SL Hurley, *Natural Reasons. Personality and Polity* (New York, 1989) 299 f. The key advantage of an antireductionist supervenience—which will be claimed below for normativity—lies in its making possible, in the words of Blackburn, 'a path between full-scale reduction of upper-level and lower-level properties, and an uncomfortable dualism'. S Blackburn, 'Supervenience' in Craig (ed), *Routledge Encyclopedia of Philosophy, vol 9* (n 6 above) 237. On the concept of supervenience in general, see Hare, *The Language of Morals* (n 34 above) 80 f; J Kim, 'Concepts of Supervenience' (1984) 45 *Philosophy and Phenomenological Research* 153. Compare TR Grimes, 'The Myth of Supervenience' (1988) 69 *Pacific Philosophical Quarterly* 152.

[44] See G Rosen, 'Who Makes the Rules Around Here?' (1997) 57 *Philosophy and Phenomenological Research* 163.

[45] See Gampel, 'The Normativity of Meaning' (n 35 above) 237.

later. For the moment, it is enough to note that the correct conditions necessary to ensure normativity must be non-empirical in nature.[46]

(b) The Condition of Internality

There are various ways of justifying normative requirements on the use of language. Theories of normativity are thus open to a categorical mistake.[47] We have to distinguish explanations for normativity that are internal to semantics and those which are external. Among the latter are, eg, general rationality postulates, but also moral or legal demands on the use of linguistic expressions. However, explanations that are semantic-external such as these cannot be used to justify the thesis of the normativity of linguistic meaning. The intrinsic normativity of linguistic meaning can only be grounded in semantic-internal arguments.[48]

Gibbard and Horwich, for instance, commit category mistakes in the form shown above. Both hold a notion of linguistic normativity based on semantic-external arguments. Gibbard looks at linguistic meaning from a meta-ethical perspective. In case of disagreement, he claims, meta-languages are used to assess the meaning of a proposition, with meaning used normatively within said meta-language.[49] Gibbard ignores the fact that this thesis is defeated by his very separation of primary and secondary language. If we distinguish two levels, normativity on the secondary level would not necessarily also exist on the primary level. The general normativity thesis, however, is concerned with normativity in *primary* language. With regard to normativity in secondary language, we have to note that, on the meta-level, discourse could also be conducted in purely empirical terms. This would necessitate further premises beyond the discrimination of levels, but Gibbard does not go into this.

---

[46] In this context, Coleman and Leiter discuss the problem of rational disagreement. Theories which focus purely on conventions have to assume that any dissent removes the rule adhered to by the community's majority, and are thus unable to explain how rational dissent may be at all possible. Coleman and Leiter, 'Determinacy, Objectivity, and Authority' (n 3 above) 262 f.

[47] See Glüer, 'Sense and Prescriptivity' (n 37 above) 124 f; Glüer, *Sprache und Regeln* (n 6 above) 110.

[48] Dummett puts the requirement of internality thus: 'The paradoxical character of language lies in the fact that while its practice must be subject to standards of correctness, there is no ultimate authority to impose those standards from without'. M Dummett, 'Meaning, Knowledge, and Understanding' in M Dummett (ed), *The Logical Basis of Metaphysics* (London, 1991) 85.

[49] A Gibbard, 'Meaning and Normativity' (1994) 5 *Philosophical Issues* 95 at 104.

Horwich bases his notion of normativity on the premises, among others, that one has to endorse the truth.[50] This rationality postulate, however, is also an argument which is semantic-external, and hence inadequate to justify normativity.[51]

(c) The Condition of Possible Semantic Mistakes

If a speaker, S, asserts earnestly that a red ball is, in fact, a 'green cone', there are two possible causes for his mistake. S may actually think that the red ball is a green cone, and hence call it a 'green cone'. On the other hand, he may equally assume that the meaning of the term 'green cone' is red ball. Both assumptions are wrong, but they belong to different categories. In the first case of the speech act, S commits an *empirical* mistake, and in the second a *semantic* mistake.

Normativity in terms of non-empirical correctness conditions is based on the premise that it is possible to use a linguistic term that is empirically wrong and, simultaneously, semantically correct, or that is empirically correct and, simultaneously, semantically wrong.[52] A normativity theory would have to allow for a discrete category of semantic mistakes, independent of that of empirical mistakes.[53]

(iii) Four Strategies of Arguing Semantic Normativity

In order to describe normativity, Kripke uses the concepts of justification, linguistic correctness, obligation, enforcement, and correctness.[54] A general normativity thesis may thus refer to three different dichotomies, depending one's respective choice of correctness conditions.[55] One may distinguish between 'true' and 'false', between 'semantically correct' and 'semantically incorrect', and between 'necessary' and 'actual performance'. In a similar vein, Boghossian lists, as sub-types of correctness conditions, truth conditions, and justification conditions.[56]

Within the context of these varied types of correctness conditions, four strategies of justifying linguistic normativity can be distinguished. The first strategy attempts to ground a connection between empirical truth and normativity (a). Two further strategies refer to specific explanations of

---

[50] P Horwich, 'Wittgenstein and Kripke on the Nature of Meaning' (1990) 5 *Mind and Language* 105 at 113.
[51] According to Glüer, Horwich has already admitted as much at a convention, see Glüer, 'Sense and Prescriptivity' (n 37 above) 125 fn 13.
[52] Glüer, 'Sense and Prescriptivity' (n 37 above) 122.
[53] Boghossian, 'The Rule-Following Considerations' (n 6 above) 519; Glüer, *Sprache und Regeln* (n 6 above) 37 f.
[54] See Glüer, *Sprache und Regeln* (n 6 above) 109.
[55] See Glüer, *Sprache und Regeln* (n 6 above) 110.
[56] Boghossian, 'The Rule-Following Considerations' (n 6 above) 517 fn 18.

intentionality, ie actions based on reasons. One takes up Wittgenstein's remarks on the internal relations between intentions and resulting actions (b); the other focuses on the link between rationality and intentionality (c). Underlying all three strategies, and thus uniting them, is a specific understanding of rules. This fundamental strategy—the fourth argumentative approach—takes up Wittgenstein's considerations on rule-following and will conclude this section (d).

(a) Normativity and Truth

A philosophy of language predominantly concerned with reference relies on object properties to arrive at specific correctness conditions. Hence, it is close to a theory of truth. Boghossian has characterised this approach as follows:

> Suppose the expression 'green' means green. It follows immediately that the expression 'green' applies *correctly* only to *these* things (the green ones) and not to *those* (the non-greens). The fact that the expression means something implies, that is, a whole set of *normative truths* about my behaviour with that expression: namely, that my use of it is correct in application to certain objects and not in application to others.[57] (emphasis added)

In Boghossian's view, the use of an expression is *semantically incorrect* if it refers to an object to which it truthfully does not apply. Relying on this strategy to argue normativity means equating semantic and empirical mistakes, as one is unable to distinguish these two categories.[58] As we have seen above, however, being able to do so is one of the prerequisites to be met by any theory which aims to explain *normativity*. In order to escape the naturalistic fallacy, the connection between empirical truth and normativity may not be a direct one. We need an *additional* rule, one which determines that linguistic terms are only to be used in their empirically true meaning. Boghossian implies this rule when writing that

> [t]o be told that 'horse' means horse implies that the speaker ought to be motivated to apply the expression only to horses.[59]

In the context of rational discourse we have good reason to assume the existence of this rule.[60] However, it does remain difficult to determine to what extent this obligation to be truthful is a semantic-internal or semantic-external rule. The condition of internality—a prerequisite for any theory of normativity—would be met only in the former case. Hence, the

---

[57] Boghossian, 'The Rule-Following Considerations' (n 6 above) 514.
[58] Glüer, 'Sense and Prescriptivity' (n 37 above) 122.
[59] Boghossian, 'The Rule-Following Considerations' (n 6 above) 533. See also P Horwich, 'What It Is Like to Be a Deflationary Theory of Meaning?' (1994) 5 *Philosophical Issues* 149.
[60] Alexy, *A Theory of Legal Argumentation* (n 5 above) 188 f.

problem can be put thus: Is the truth of statement p a semantic-internal, normative correctness condition of p?

This question can be answered in the affirmative, based on the fact that linguistic practice is essentially based on assertional speech acts. By necessity, every practitioner makes a claim to the truth when uttering a proposition.[61] Hence, our assertional practice is governed by rules which create the necessary connection between the use of language and truth. Examples of these rules are Searle's preparatory rule ('Do not agree to p until you have good reasons for p'), his sincerity rule ('Only agree to p if you believe in p'), and Alexy's partly similar basic rules of practical discourse.[62]

There are two main arguments against this position. The first counter-argument claims that there is a rigid separation of pragmatics and semantics. The assertion rules presented above, it is said, were mere co-operation principles and hence a part of pragmatics and of no concern for semantics. Anyone who infers the normativity of meaning from the existence of these rules, Wikforss states, walks right into the trap of Searle's *assertion fallacy*, ie confusing the conditions for the utterance of assertional speech acts with the analysis of meaning.[63]

This counter-argument is unconvincing. It assumes that semantics and pragmatics can be separated at a very basic level, a possibility inconsistent with Wittgensteinian convention theory and with Robert Brandom's analysis of assertional practice. In the context of methodological pragmatism, particular linguistic phenomena can no longer be reliably distinguished as pragmatic or semantic.[64] We have to assume that there is an intrinsic link between semantics and pragmatics.[65]

---

[61] Alexy, *A Theory of Legal Argumentation* (n 5 above) 127. Rorty asks for the abolition of this claim to the truth, See W Welsch, 'Richard Rorty: Philosophie jenseits von Argumentation und Wahrheit?' in M Sandbothe (ed), *Die Renaissance des Pragmatismus. Aktuelle Verflechtungen zwischen analytischer und kontinentaler Philosophie* (Weilerswist, 2000) 188 f.

[62] Alexy, *A Theory of Legal Argumentation* (n 5 above) 188; Searle, *Speech Acts. An Essay in the Philosophy of Language* (n 30 above) 62–4.

[63] Wikforss, 'Semantic Normativity' (n 35 above) 206. The term 'cooperation principle' is Grice's, see Grice, *Studies in the Way of Words* (n 30 above) 26. Searle's assertion fallacy can be found in Searle, *Speech Acts. An Essay in the Philosophy of Language* (n 30 above) 141.

[64] See Brandom, *Making It Explicit* (n 1 above) 592.

[65] Similar A Bilgrami, 'Meaning, Holism and Use' in E LePore (ed), *Truth and Interpretation. Perspectives on the Philosophy of Donald Davidson* (Oxford, 1986) 119 f; M Dummett, 'What Does the Appeal to Use Do for the Theory of Meaning?' and 'What Is a Theory of Meaning? (II)' in M Dummett (ed), *The Seas of Language* (Oxford, 1993) 108, and 36 at 51.

The second counter-argument refers to assertion rules being able to forge only a very weak link between meaning and truth.[66] There can be no doubt that it is feasible to follow Searle's preparatory rule, and yet utter a wrong assertion, just as it is possible to make a true utterance and still breach the preparatory rule. However, we would only be correct in inferring from this fact the utter impossibility of a link between truth and meaning if this link really consisted of a mere identification of truth and meaning. But the assertion rules never make this claim. On the contrary, they show that the link is indirect, and yet the rules are intrinsic to any assertional practice. They refer to empirical truth and make it a part of the correct conditions for assertions, but they amount to more than just empirical truth. Hence, the interaction of pragmatically necessary assertional rules and empirical truth as their object results in the truth of a statement p being a semantic-*internal* normative correctness condition of p.[67]

This settles the problem outlined above. The claim for truth inherent in every assertion creates a necessary connection between truth and the normatively interpreted linguistic meaning. The empirical properties of the objects that assertions refer to are not only relevant to the statements' truthfulness, but also to their semantic correctness. The object-relatedness of linguistic meaning can be used to define the boundary of linguistic meaning. Here, this object-related normativity will be considered the objectivity of linguistic meaning.

(b) Normativity and Internal Relation

In his middle period, Wittgenstein defined the relation between an intention and its implementation to be 'internal', distancing himself from Russell, whose theory of intentional states he calls 'external'.[68] His view is best illustrated by Kripke's addition example: Whether an individual's intention of adding two numbers is realized amounts to more than the merely empirical issue of which behaviour would be in accordance with that intention. Rather, it is normatively compulsory that the indivicual *has*

---

[66] Wikforss, 'Semantic Normativity' (n 35 above) 206 f. The third counter-argument described by Wikforss is of no interest here. In the present book, normativity is to be developed within the framework of a concrete theory of meaning, and is not understood to be a Kripkean pre-theoretical requirement.

[67] This internality is also supported by Ebbs and Millikan, see G Ebbs, Rule-Following and Realism (Cambridge MA, 1997) 18; RG Millikan, 'Truth Rules, Hoverflies, and the Kripke-Wittgenstein Paradox' (1990) 99 *Philosophical Review* 323 at 350 f. Criticism comes from P Horwich, 'What It Is Like to Be a Deflationary Theory of Meaning?' (1994) 5 *Philosophical Issues* 133 at 149; Wikforss, 'Semantic Normativity' (n 35 above) 205 f.

[68] L Wittgenstein, *Philosophical Remarks* (Oxford, 1975) para 21. See also L Wittgenstein, *Philosophical Investigations*, 2nd edn (Oxford, 1963) paras 420, 440 f.

104 Normativity and Objectivity of Linguistic Meaning

to act in accordance with his oder her intentions. From this internal relation, it is concluded that linguistic meaning is normative.[69]

Baker and Hacker show that there are internal relations between the concepts of a language. These relations, called 'grammatical sentences', determined which connections between words would be considered meaningful, and which inferences may be drawn from propositions.[70]

> What philosophers have called 'necessary truths' are, in Wittgenstein's view, typically rules of grammar, norms of representation, ie they fix concepts. They are expressions of internal relations between concepts which are themselves used in stating truths about the world.[71]

Basing normativity on internal relations provides important support, especially to Brandom's inferential semantics.

The key objection to this account of normativity is that internal relations only gave a *constitutive*, not a *prescriptive* connection.[72] The fact that the relation between the intention of adding numbers and the correct answer is internal was merely a description of what it means to add numbers. On no account, however, was there any sort of prescription. The correct answer was not prescribed in a normative sense.

This criticism is based on a specific definition of normativity. It assumes that any normativity thesis would have to give proof of *prescriptivity*. This assumption is in need of substantiation. The concept of prescriptivity and the justification of a rule model based on it refer to the debate on Wittgenstein's thoughts on rule-following, which will be discussed as the fourth justification strategy (d). The strategy of justifying normativity using internal relations depends upon the strategy of justification via rule-following. Hence, I will analyse these objections later.

(c) Normativity and Rationality

The notion that normativity is anchored in general rationality is based on the explanation of intentionality and *mental content* by Davidson and his successors. McDowell writes that

---

[69] Kripke, *Wittgenstein on Rules and Private Language* (n 4 above) 37; J McDowell, 'Intentionality and Interiority in Wittgenstein' in Puhl (ed), *Meaning Scepticism* (n 41 above) 152; Wright, 'Kripke's Account of the Argument Against Private Language' (n 35 above).

[70] An extensive account of Wittgenstein's internal relations and their interpretation by Baker and Hacker can be found in Glüer, *Sprache und Regeln* (n 6 above) 124–37.

[71] GP Baker and PMS Hacker, *Wittgenstein: Rules, Grammar and Necessity. An Analytical Commentary on the Philosophical Investigations*, vol 2 (Oxford, 1985) 269.

[72] Glüer, *Sprache und Regeln* (n 6 above) 136; Wikforss, 'Semantic Normativity' (n 35 above) 231 f.

our dealings with content must be understood in terms of the idea that mental activity is undertaken under the aspect of allegiance to norms.[73]

According to this view, meaning rules serve as fundamental standards of rationality. Semantic rules define what it means to act intentionally, ie based on reasons.[74]

Joseph Raz also emphasised the close relation between normativity and rationality. He defined rationality as the capability to recognise the normative significance of facts in the world, and to respond to it.[75] The normative significance of facts, he states, consists in their constituting reasons; the capability of responding appropriately consists in deciding what the reasons are and what behaviour they entail.[76] Even Glüer emphasises how closely connected the concepts of semantic normativity and general rationality are: If sceptical arguments lead to the rejection of one of the two, this would also apply to the other.[77]

There are two counter-arguments to grounding semantic normativity in rationality: First, rationality scepticism questions the very concepts of reasons, rational argumentation, and reasonable discourse.[78] Joseph Raz has countered these attacks impressively. He demonstrates that while radical rational scepticism may be a conscious and deliberate decision, it still remains impossible to justify this position using rational arguments:

> Rational thought did not stop, was not abandoned, in spite of the awareness that, for all one knew, there were contradictions at its foundations. I do not know of any serious, let alone successful, argument that that was irrational, that it was irrational of people to carry on using reason, although they were aware of unresolved paradoxes concerning its basic features ... People can take action deliberately in order to be rational no more, but they cannot get there simply by reasoning their way into scepticism about reason.[79]

Secondly, critics emphasise that rationality requirements were limited to demonstrating a constitutive connection between meaning and rationality,

---

[73] J McDowell, *Mind and World* (Cambridge MA, 1994) 11.
[74] See Glüer, 'Sense and Prescriptivity' (n 37 above) 114.
[75] J Raz, 'Explaining Normativity. On Rationality and the Justification of Reason' in J Raz (ed), *Engaging Reason. On the Theory of Value and Action* (Oxford, 1999) 68.
[76] *Ibid*, 70.
[77] Glüer, 'Sense and Prescriptivity' (n 37 above) 117. See also V Mayer, 'Regeln, Normen, Gebräuche. Reflexionen über Ludwig Wittgensteins "Über Gewißheit"' (2000) *Deutsche Zeitschrift für Philosophie* 409 at 411.
[78] Arguments against the language dependency of rational performances come, eg, from AC MacIntyre, *Dependent Rational Animals. Why Human Beings Need the Virtues* (London, 1999) 54.
[79] Raz, 'Explaining Normativity. On Rationality and the Justification of Reason' (n 75 above) 80. Another convincing argumentation against rational scepticism can be found in R Dworkin, 'Objectivity and Truth: You'd Better Believe It' (1996) 25 *Philosophy & Public Affairs* 87 at 128.

whereas the assumption of semantic normativity made prescriptivity necessary.[80] With this, the issue of the significance and role of semantic rules returns to our agenda. The dividing line runs between a constitutive and a prescriptive rule model. We will take a closer look at this below. At the same time, the fourth basic strategy of arguing semantic normativity will be addressed.

(d) Normativity and Regularity

Searle states that

> speaking a language is engaging in a rule-guided form of behaviour. To put it more briskly, talking is performing acts according to rules.[81]

This significant argument for a linguistic normativity grounded in regularity (1) has met with two important objections (2) and (3).

(1) Semantic Normativity According to the Rule Model Using a rule model to define linguistic normativity continues Wittgenstein's late philosophy. In his *Philosophical Investigations* and in the *Remarks on the Foundations of Mathematics*, Wittgenstein shows that the meaning of a sign lies in its use in language. This use is governed by rules which determine the meaning of terms. Being a competent speaker means being able to act in accordance with these meaning rules. The rules show how a term has to be used in order to have a specific meaning.[82] They are the standards according to which the correctness of speech acts is assessed.

The mere rule-governedness of language use within a language community would be insufficient in order to constitute normativity in this way. According to the conditions of anti-reductionist supervenience, one has to show that the rules do not simply *describe* use, but *prescribe* a particular use.[83] This requirement is reflected in Wittgenstein's terminology, where he distinguishes between a mere convergence of opinion, and a shared form of life:

> 'So you are saying that human agreement decides what is true and what is false?'—It is what human beings *say* that is true and false; and they agree in the *language* they use. That is not agreement in opinions but in form of life.[84]

---

[80] Wikforss, 'Semantic Normativity' (n 35 above) 215.
[81] Searle, *Speech Acts. An Essay in the Philosophy of Language* (n 30 above) 22.
[82] See Glüer, 'Sense and Prescriptivity' (n 37 above) 113.
[83] See BC Smith, 'Meaning and Rule-Following' (n 6 above) 214.
[84] Wittgenstein, *Philosophical Investigations* (n 68 above) para 241. See Davidson's criticism: 'What is conventional about language, if anything is, is that people tend to speak much as their neighbours do. But in indicating this element of the conventional, or of the conditioning process that makes speakers rough linguistic facsimiles of their friends and parents, we explain no more than the convergence; we throw no light on the essential nature

Mere similarity or overlapping of idiolects can be explained by empirical science. Normativity, however, can only be constituted if rules can be considered 'supra-individual use-governing authorities'.[85] If we can interpret any imaginable use as conforming to rules, the result, according to Wittgenstein, is that

> whatever is going to seem right to me is right. And that only means that here we can't talk about 'right'.[86]

Normativity of linguistic meaning requires that the difference between what 'seems right to me' and what *is* right can be justified. It remains controversial whether this can be achieved through a normative understanding of meaning rules. The objections of the analytic priority of individualism (2) and incoherence (3) have been raised.

(2) Objection of the Analytic Priority of Individualism Lewis's statement that the conventionality of language is 'a platitude—something only a philosopher would dream of denying'[87] has never stopped philosophers from doing precisely that. The rule model of normativity has been rejected based on the argument that linguistic meaning was by no means determined by a community's shared use of language. Rather, the individual language use of each speaker was fundamental and sufficient.

One has to agree insofar as the term 'use' in Wittgenstein's famous remark leaves open, in his wording, whether he refers to individual or common practice.[88] The form taken by a use-theory of meaning may vary widely, depending on the design of the relation between term and use and the language community called upon.[89] Here, the relevance of the debate on whether conventionalism or individualism takes explanatory precedence is not due to the fact that a normativity theory of meaning was compatible with only one of these positions. Rather, we need to distinguish

---

of the skills that are thus made to converge': D Davidson, 'Communication and Convention' in D Davidson (ed), *Inquiries into Truth and Interpretation* (Oxford, 1984) 265 at 278.

[85] As Glüer succinctly put it, Glüer, *Sprache und Regeln* (n 6 above) 12.

[86] Wittgenstein, *Philosophical Investigations* (n 68 above) para 258.

[87] D Lewis, 'Languages and Language' in K Gunderson (ed), *Language, Mind, and Knowledge* (Minneapolis, 1975) 37.

[88] Wittgenstein, *Philosophical Investigations* (n 68 above) para 43. The meaning had already been determined by the use of the term in Wittgenstein's Tractatus, see Wittgenstein, *Tractatus logico-philosophicus* (n 18 above) 3.326, 3.328. This 'use theory' of meaning has achieved great popularity in legal theory, often degenerating to a mere buzzword. Neuner is of the opinion that this 'trend towards absoluteness' has to be checked and refers to Wittgenstein's own restriction of his use theory ('For a large class of cases—though not for all'), J Neuner, *Die Rechtsfindung contra legem* (München, 1992) 97 fn 57. Herbert, by contrast, is correct in emphasising that this restriction is of no concern within the context of language-philosophical theories of meaning, see M Herbert, *Rechtstheorie als Sprachkritik. Zum Einfluß Wittgensteins auf die Rechtstheorie* (Baden-Baden, 1995) 55.

[89] Glüer, *Sprache und Regeln* (n 6 above) 10.

systematically between the question of conventionality and that of normativity.[90] Here, I will argue a theory of normativity based on rules of convention. Hence, attacks against the fundamental conventionality of language would also apply to the concept of normativity developed on these pages.

Davidson has two basic arguments for the meaning-theoretical priority of the idiolect. First, he rejects the assumption of a prescriptive attitude implicit in the rule model, as it was possible to explain a speaker's intention to speak like others without recourse to normative responsibility.[91] Secondly, and foremost, it was not necessary to have a shared meaning convention in order to communicate successfully. Two speakers, Davidson claims, in no way needed to associate the same meaning with the same speech act. It was enough to know which meaning one meant, and which was intended by the other speaker. Also, this knowledge did not need to extend into the future use of rules. It was enough to rely on methodical principles to acquire knowledge of meaning in a presuppositionless *radical interpretation*.[92]

I will differ from Davidson in maintaining the explanatory precedence of the shared language. The fact that speakers have prescriptive attitudes cannot be denied.[93] A speaker using a term while not fully familiar with its meaning

> holds himself responsible to the established use and would withdraw what he had said if it could be shown to be wrong by the standard of that use.[94]

Dummett concludes that

> [t]here is no describing any individual's employment of his words without account being taken of his willingness to subordinate his use to that generally agreed as correct. That is, one cannot so much as explain what an idiolect is without invoking the notion of language as a social phenomenon.[95]

---

[90] Glüer, *Sprache und Regeln* (n 6 above) 41.
[91] 'What magic ingredient does holding oneself responsible to the usual way of speaking add to the usual way of speaking? ... It is absurd to be obligated to a language'. D Davidson, 'The Social Aspect of Language' in B McGuiness and G Olivieri (eds), *The Philosophy of Michael Dummett* (Dordrecht, 1994) 8 f.
[92] D Davidson, 'Communication and Convention' in Davidson (ed), *Inquiries into Truth and Interpretation* (n 84 above) 277.
[93] Brandom, *Making It Explicit* (n 1 above) 30–32. See p 119 below. M Dummett, 'Reply to Davidson' in McGuiness and Olivieri (eds), *The Philosophy of Michael Dummett* (n 91 above) 265.
[94] Dummett, 'Meaning, Knowledge, and Understanding' (n 48 above) 84.
[95] M Dummett, 'The Social Character of Meaning' in Dummett (ed), *Truth and Other Enigmas* (n 20 above) 425.

Davidson's theory is phenomenologically inappropriate, also with regard to the attribution of a paradigmatic role to the exceptional condition of *radical interpretation*.[96]

Furthermore, it is only within a language community which provides standards independent of the individual opinion of speakers that the objective of successful communication can be attained.[97] Countering Davidson's rejection of the speakers' 'responsibility', one has to agree with Alexy's statement that

> the requirements ... placed on speech acts do not depend on the speakers' wishes, but on the rules which form the basis of speech acts.[98]

The practice of asserting and reasoning, which is fundamental to linguistic meaning, would not be conceivable without the backdrop of linguistic rule-following.[99] While one has to concur with Rawls that rule-following can only be explained against the backdrop of a particular stage-setting of the practice in question,[100] the universality of the 'game of giving and taking reasons' is so absolute that this aspect does not limit the model of rule-following in any way.

(3) Objection of the Incoherence of Prescriptivity and Constitutivity
Present-day critics of normativity have raised the objection of incoherence in a stronger and a weaker form. For a better understanding, I will make a few remarks on the concept of rules in advance. With regard to norms of conduct, we will follow a widely accepted classification and distinguish particularly between prescriptive and constitutive rules.[101] Prescriptions stipulate, in the sense of the three deontic operators, particular conduct as permitted, forbidden, or obligatory.[102] Constitutive rules, on the other hand, 'neither describe nor prescribe, but *determine* something'.[103] They define what it means to put a particular activity into practice. Thus, both rule types differ fundamentally in the way they understand the relation

---

[96] M Dummett, 'A nice derangement of epitaphs. Some comments on Davidson and Hacking' in LePore (ed), *Truth and Interpretation. Perspectives on the Philosophy of Donald Davidson* (n 65 above) 464.

[97] Dummett, 'Meaning, Knowledge, and Understanding' (n 48 above) 85; H-J Glock, 'Wittgenstein vs Quine on Logical Necessity' in S Teghrarian (ed), *Wittgenstein and Contemporary Philosophy* (Bristol, 1994) 94 ff.

[98] Alexy, *A Theory of Legal Argumentation* (n 5 above) 127.

[99] Alexy, *A Theory of Legal Argumentation* (n 5 above) 129 f; Brandom, *Making It Explicit* (n 1 above) 30.

[100] J Rawls, 'Two Concepts of Rules' (1955) 64 *The Philosophical Review* 3 at 27.

[101] For a detailed description of the various forms of object norms and norms of conduct, and their role in a theory of linguistic meaning see Glüer, *Sprache und Regeln* (n 6 above) 160–205. On the concept of rules in general See P Pagin, 'Rules' in Lamarque and Asher (eds), *Concise Encyclopedia of Philosophy of Language* (n 17 above) 170 f.

[102] von Wright, *Norm and Action. A Logical Enquiry* (n 36 above) 7.

[103] von Wright, *Norm and Action. A Logical Enquiry* (n 36 above) 6.

between norm and activity. Searle, who calls prescriptive rules *regulative rules*, summarises said difference as follows:

> Regulative rules regulate a pre-existing activity whose existence is logically independent of the rules. Constitutive rules constitute ... an activity the existence of which is logically dependent on the rules.[104]

Theories which base the normativity of linguistic meaning on its regularity see language first and foremost as determined by *constitutive* rules:

> Using language and playing a game are not like doing one's hair and taking a bath. One may do either of the last two things as one likes and still be doing it. But if the game ceases to have rules, it ceases to be a game, and, if there cease to be right and wrong uses of a word, the word loses its meaning.[105]

> It is grammatical rules that determine meaning (constitute it) and so they themselves are not answerable to any meaning and to that extent are arbitrary ... For without these rules the word has as yet no meaning; and if we change the rules, it now has another meaning (or none), and in that case we may as well change the word too.[106]

The objection of the incoherence of constitutivity and prescriptivity opposes basing normativity on constitutive rules. In its stronger form, this objection has been mentioned several times below. It is fundamental to the criticism of the strategies of grounding normativity on the connections of language practice on the one hand, and truth or rationality on the other.[107] This criticism consists of two theses. One: Semantic normativity stipulates prescriptivity. Two: Linguistic rules are constitutive, not prescriptive.[108]

In its weaker form, this objection does not go so far as to assume a necessary connection between normativity and prescriptivity and, hence, rejects the stronger form's first thesis. Neither does it support the second thesis. Rather, this form argues a non-combinability of both rule types, using also two theses. One: Semantic normativity stipulates *both* prescriptivity *and* constitutivity of rules. Two: Linguistic rules can be *either* prescriptive *or* constitutive, but cannot be both simultaneously.[109]

---

[104] Searle, *Speech Acts. An Essay in the Philosophy of Language* (n 30 above) 34.
[105] Dummett, 'Meaning, Knowledge, and Understanding' (n 48 above) 85.
[106] L Wittgenstein, *Philosophical Grammar* (Oxford, 1974) 184 f. See also L Wittgenstein, *On Certainty* (Oxford, 1974) paras 61–5.
[107] See p 103 f above.
[108] Glüer, 'Sense and Prescriptivity' (n 37 above) 127; Wikforss, 'Semantic Normativity' (n 35 above) 203 f.
[109] Glüer and Pagin, 'Rules of Meaning and Practical Reasoning' (n 35 above) 207. It is of interest that Glüer argues both the stronger and the weaker forms of the incoherence objection. It remains doubtful whether a theory might actually assume both forms simultaneously without becoming incoherent itself.

The reasoning of the incoherence objection in either form focuses on the second thesis, ie concerning the character of rules as either constitutive or prescriptive. Constitutive rules have the general form

(CR$_a$) In context C, speech act x has the meaning p.[110]

An example for a meaning-constitutive Rule would be

(CR$_1$) The speech act 'Red ball' has the meaning of the term red ball.

Rules of this kind *constitute* meaning. There is, however, the objection that they completely lack motivational power.[111] They neither request nor prescribe. The speech act 'Red Ball' could not be considered adherence to the rule CR$_1$ because the rule CR$_1$ did not *prescribe* said speech act. The motivational power to utter 'Red Ball' was solely the result of a further attitude on the part of the speaker, which took the form

(SA$_a$) I would like to say that p.

It was only this additional rule which gave the whole picture of a practical conclusion:

(SA$_a$) I would like to say that p.
(CR$_a$) In context C, speech act x has meaning p.

Hence, I would like to perform speech act x.

This full picture revealed that the constitutive rule CR$_a$ played no motivational role, but rather remained limited to a doxastic role,[112] making it possible to make the transition from a general, performance-related speech attitude to a specific attitude. Prescriptivity was hence the result of the general speech attitude, and not that of the constitutive meaning rule.

In its stronger form, the objection leaves it at that. Identifying normativity with prescriptivity, it considers the argument that normative rules cannot be prescriptive to constitute sufficient proof against the assumption of linguistic normativity. The weaker objection, however, still needs the reversed form of the argument to support its thesis of the non-combinability of both rule types. In addition, it has to show that constitutive rules could never be prescriptive. This is achieved as follows: The key factor in giving rules a prescriptive aspect was that they played the role of reasons for speech acts, ie had motivational power over speakers. This,

---

[110] See Searle, *Speech Acts. An Essay in the Philosophy of Language* (n 30 above) 35.
[111] Glüer and Pagin, 'Rules of Meaning and Practical Reasoning' (n 35 above) 217 f.
[112] This corresponds to Raz's analysis, who in his terminology distinguishes between auxiliary reasons and operative reasons, see J Raz, *Practical Reason and Norms* (Oxford, 1999) 33–5.

however, assumed that meaning had already been established independently of these rules. Hence, prescriptive rules were unable to determine meaning themselves, and thus could not be meaning-constitutive.[113]

The objection of incoherence remains unconvincing. Without clearly stating it, it is based on two premises. One: Semantics and pragmatics can be clearly distinguished. Two: Prescriptivity and constitutivity can be clearly distinguished. Both premises are wrong.

Arguments against the separation of semantics and pragmatics can be found above.[114] Furthermore, the key insight gained by Wittgensteinian use theory is that the meaning of any linguistic performance is constituted through practice.[115] Hence, rule CR_a is only conceivable within a linguistic practice. This stipulation renders void the argument that a constitutive rule could not be broken as it only played a doxastic role. In practice, constitutive rules are invariably connected to prescriptive rules. Thus, we may expressively acknowledge the first thesis of the objection's weak form, according to which semantic normativity presupposes both prescriptivity and constitutivity. In contrast, the second thesis—which says that rules cannot be constitutive and prescriptive simultaneously—has to be rejected. The *prescriptive* rule: 'If S wants to express meaning p, S has to utter speech act x' is expressly violated by the fact that the *constitutive* rule which connects p and x is not observed in the context of the speaker's motivational attitude SA_a. *Because* rules are constitutive for meaning, S *has to* observe these rules if he wants to express a specific meaning p. In this sense, prescriptivity depends on constitutivity. This close interconnection of the two rule types *in practice* is rendered void if one claims a strict dichotomy of semantics and pragmatics on the one hand, and prescriptivity and constitutivity on the other.

I want to reject this annulment by putting forward a *connection thesis*. The claim that prescriptivity and constitutivity are connected in linguistic practice can be based on von Wright's classification of norms. Von Wright considers the main categories to be in no way clearly partitioned from each other. Rather, he mentions sub-categories which combine the characteristics of several main categories, for instance in the case of *customs*, which define how one should dress or greet one another, but also traditions of marriage.[116] These social conventions can, on the hand, be specified in purely descriptive terms, but on the other hand can also be violated, resulting in sanctions by the community. The normative pressure exerted

---

[113] Glüer and Pagin, 'Rules of Meaning and Practical Reasoning' (n 35 above) 207.
[114] See p 102 f above.
[115] See also Glock, who considers the traditional semiotic differentiation between syntactics, semantics, and pragmatics as 'incompatible with a meaning-theoretical position'. H-J Glock, 'Wie kam die Bedeutung zur Regel?' (2000) *Deutsche Zeitschrift für Philosophie* 429 at 441.
[116] von Wright, *Norm and Action. A Logical Enquiry* (n 36 above) 8 f.

The Normativity of Linguistic Meaning 113

by the threat of sanctions makes them prescriptive, *and* they are constitutive by virtue of their constituting the institutional facts. Searle, too, awards rules a dual role: 'Constitutive rules *constitute (and also regulate) an activity*'.[117] (emphasis added)

There are many indicators that semantic rules, too, are a hybrid of this type and have a dual function in linguistic practice.[118]

This backdrop makes 'playing off' prescriptivity and constitutivity—the agenda of Glüer's and Wikforss' criticism of normativity[119]—a bad choice. It may be analytically possible to look at each aspect in isolation, yet this approach does not do justice to the practice of language use. In the language game, both rule types are closely intertwined. Prescriptive and constitutive rules complement one another in the way described above. The claim that use-theory and normativity thesis were incompatible if only for the fact that as meaning only emerged through use, it was unable to regulate the latter[120] overlooks this interaction. The paradox of the practice of use creating the standards it is subject to[121] is no counter-argument, but rather the key characteristic of a semantic normativity grounded in pragmatics.

The error of the incoherence objection lies in its fixation on prescriptivity. This is particularly apparent in the first thesis of its strong form. Here, normativity is simply considered identical to prescriptivity. This done, it is a trifle to refer to the constitutivity of linguistic rules and to reject normativity—viz the second thesis of the strong form. However, a theory of normativity's *proper* burden of argument lies in demonstrating the *constitutive* connection between rules and meaning. This is expressly admitted by Glüer.[122] For a normative theory of linguistic meaning it would fully suffice to show that a standard exists which is used to assess speech acts as either correct or incorrect. It is not necessary for normative theory of meaning to consider the further-reaching thesis that it is imperative for speakers to perform correct speech acts.[123] As Glock aptly

---

[117] Searle, *Speech Acts. An Essay in the Philosophy of Language* (n 30 above) 34.
[118] Even Glüer speculates that a regulative-prescriptive ambivalence exists. In her eyes, this is a 'typically perfect, reconstructed' and 'interesting' thesis of normativity. See Glüer, *Sprache und Regeln* (n 6 above) 165. By contrast, the incompatibility objection raised by Glüer on p 166 is grounded solely in the criticised fixing of the normativity thesis on prescriptivity as a key driving force. See immediately below.
[119] Thus expressively Glüer, *Sprache und Regeln* (n 6 above) 166 f.
[120] See Glüer, *Sprache und Regeln* (n 6 above) 11, 26. In the controversy on the limits of the wording, this has become a key argument of Müller's school, see p 68 above.
[121] See Dummett: 'The paradoxical character of language lies in the fact that while its practice must be subject to standards of correctness, there is no ultimate authority to impose those standards from without'. M Dummett, 'Meaning, Knowledge, and Understanding' (n 48 above) 85.
[122] Glüer, *Sprache und Regeln* (n 6 above).
[123] A point overlooked by Glüer, see *Sprache und Regeln* (n 6 above) 166 f.

states, constitutive rules are normative in the very simple sense that they *standardise* what the speech act 'Red Ball', 'Art Gallery', or a question mean.[124]

Within a language game, prescriptivity emerges automatically. It is the simple result of a speaker trying to express a specific meaning. This is a Wittgensteinian internal relation. We can demonstrate an *essentially semantic* motivation to use the constitutively *correct* meaning and thus fulfil the condition of internality. Correct use is the use of a term with a particular meaning which results from the constitutive rule. Overly focusing on the element of prescriptivity means assuming that theories of normativity by necessity stipulate specific ways of using terms, and prohibit others. This assumption is a priori beside the point.[125]

This means that the concept of linguistic mistakes can actually play the role of a *limiting value*. Based on this concept, speech acts can be classified as to whether they use a term x to express meaning p or not. This is absolutely sufficient for a regulatively grounded theory of normativity. The condition of the possibility of a linguistic mistake is also maintained.

(iv) Normativity and Connection Thesis

Explaining semantic normativity by recourse to rules which have both constitutive and prescriptive effects within conventional language practice has been met with objections, all of which have been found to be groundless.[126] Within the language game, one is able to perceive from the reaction of the other practitioners which meaning is accepted in which context, and which is not. Language is a system of constitutive rules, with the validity of these rules secured by their conventional realisation within a community. In terms of Searle, meaning is an *institutional fact*.[127]

Furthermore, the refusal to simply consider semantic normativity identical to prescriptivity also puts paid to the criticism raised against basing internal relations and rationality on normativity.[128]

We have shown that all four strategies can be used to explain semantic normativity. In this work, I will argue a *connection thesis* against the isolated discussion of the diverse normativity concepts. The normativity of linguistic meaning is thus equally based on the essential conventionality of language and the connection of meaning and truth, just as it is on

---

[124] Glock, 'Wie kam die Bedeutung zur Regel?' (n 115 above) 445.
[125] Glüer expressly alludes to this assumption, see Glüer, *Sprache und Regeln* (n 6 above) 167–9. See also Glüer and Pagin, 'Rules of Meaning and Practical Reasoning' (n 35 above) 224. 'It is only the meaning determining function, not the guiding function, that is relevant'.
[126] Similar Glock, 'Wie kam die Bedeutung zur Regel?' (n 115 above) 445.
[127] Searle, *Speech Acts. An Essay in the Philosophy of Language* (n 30 above) 51.
[128] See pp 103, 106 above.

regularity—in the sense of constitutive, internal relations which are able to guide the speakers' behaviour in linguistic practice, ie which have a prescriptive effect.

Based on these preliminary remarks on the concept of normativity, we will now be able to tackle Robert Brandom's sweeping defence of the normativity theory. Brandom shows how the emergence and functionality of constitutive and prescriptive rules in linguistic practice can be explained. He shows how it is precisely the paradox of a normative use theory which is essential for the possibility of meaning. And he explains how a category of linguistic mistakes would have to be designed.

B. Brandom's Linguistic Normativity

In 1994, Robert Brandom published *Making It Explicit*,[129] a landmark work which

> develops the most elaborate and systematically comprehensive philosophy of language, the world, and mind which has so far been produced by analytical philosophy.[130]

Brandom himself aims 'to present a unified vision of language and mind'.[131] Within his unified, systematic approach, Brandom discusses a multitude of key problems not limited to language philosophy and philosophy of mind, but also concerning metaphysics, logic, and anthropology. From this doctrinal wealth the present book will focus on Brandom's elucidations on linguistic meaning and normativity.

The central theme of the book is in its title. For Brandom, the task of his philosophy is to express, and thus make explicit, what already implicitly

---

[129] Brandom, *Making It Explicit* (n 1 above). A comprehensive summary of Brandom's key fundamental ideas can be found in a book based on Brandom's lectures, RB Brandom, *Articulating Reasons. An Introduction to Inferentialism* (Cambridge MA, 2000). Furthermore, there is an illuminating interview by Susanna Schellenberg with the author, RB Brandom, 'Von der Begriffsanalyse zu einer systematischen Metaphysik. Interview von Susanna Schellenberg' (1999) 6 *Deutsche Zeitschrift für Philosophie* 1005.

[130] W Kersting, 'Baseball ist unser Leben' *Frankfurter Allgemeine Zeitung* (7 August 2000) 49 See also Habermas, who considers *Making It Explicit* a landmark comparable to John Rawl's *A Theory of Justice*, J Habermas, 'Von Kant zu Hegel. Zu R. Brandoms Sprachpragmatik' in J Habermas (ed), *Wahrheit und Rechtfertigung. Philosophische Aufsätze* (Frankfurt am Main, 1999) 138.

[131] Brandom, *Making It Explicit* (n 1 above) XXIII.

exists in our practices. The methodological starting point of this explicit-making of the implicit is a phenomenological description of the manifestations of our social interactions.[132] Brandom's key statement is: Our discursive practice has an implicit, normative structure. Its key feature is the possibility to judge the speech acts occurring within a language game as correct or wrong, appropriate or inappropriate:

> The practices that confer propositional and other sorts of conceptual content implicitly contain norms concerning how it is *correct* to use expression, under what circumstances it is *appropriate* to perform various speech acts, and what the *appropriate* consequences of such performances are.[133]

> [T]o talk of practices is to talk of *proprieties* of performance, rather than of regularities; it is to prescribe, rather than describe.[134]

His research focuses on the question of how mental states, as well as linguistic and non-linguistic acts, are awarded conceptual content in social practice. By elaborating on the connection between an action's content and the practical context of its reference, Brandom develops a markedly well-crafted version of Wittgenstein's use theory of meaning, which has so often been reduced to a mere buzzword.[135]

Brandom develops his theory of linguistic normativity in two stages[136]: In a pragmatic examination of the use of concepts, he clarifies what actions agents have to take for their practices to be considered specifically linguistic. Brandom shows how linguistic norms are instituted by social-practical activity, and makes explicit the normative vocabulary used to express them. Following this normative pragmatics, he develops an inferential semantics. This describes how normative practices create conceptual content, and addresses the structure of specifically *discursive* practices, which have the distinction of using propositional contents as premises and conclusions, ie as reasons and reasoning.

Initially, Brandom discusses pragmatics and semantics separately (i) and (ii). Both levels, however, are interleaved by the guiding concept of 'making explicit' (iii).[137] Here, pragmatics is the more basic element with regard to two aspects: One, the semantic vocabulary is developed in relation to the pragmatic. Two, the conceptual content of any action is explained with regard to its practical embedding.

---

[132] With regard to the question of the extent to which *Making It Explicit* could be considered a work of pure phenomenology, or a critical project, see Brandom, 'Von der Begriffsanalyse zu einer systematischen Metaphysik. Interview von Susanna Schellenberg' (n 129 above) 1007 f.
[133] Brandom, *Making It Explicit* (n 1 above) XIII.
[134] Brandom, *Making It Explicit* (n 1 above) 159.
[135] Brandom, *Making It Explicit* (n 1 above) XII f.
[136] See Brandom, *Making It Explicit* (n 1 above) XIII f.
[137] Brandom, *Making It Explicit* (n 1 above) XVIII.

The relation between semantics and pragmatics—of what is implicit in actions and what is explicit in statements—is also discussed on two levels[138]: On the first level, the ability to use concepts and to know *that* something is the case is traced to the ability to share in a practice, ie to the knowledge of *how* to do something. Here, the guiding concept of explicit-making implies making explicit the implicit structure of linguistic practices. On the second level, Brandom elaborates on the propositional content of mental states and (speech) acts by referring to logical vocabulary. He considers the latter fundamental for the possibility of conceptual content:

> Logical vocabulary endows practitioners with the expressive power to make explicit as the contents of claims just those implicit features of linguistic practice that confer semantic contents of their utterances in the first place. Logic is the organ of semantic self-consciousness.[139]

Logical vocabulary plays a particularly expressive role. It allows for making implicit inferences explicit in the shape of statements.

In addition to the meaning-theoretical foundations that Brandom develops in the first three chapters of *Making It Explicit*, his elaborations on the meaning of subsentential expressions (iv) are of interest for the present analysis.

(i) Normative Pragmatics

In his normative pragmatics, Brandom describes how norms are constituted in social practice.

(a) Anthropologic Basis and Implicit Normativity

The starting point is an anthropological action-theoretical understanding of Man in the tradition of Kant, ie as a being defined by his ability to judge and act. Man not only responds to stimuli in his environment, but frames perception judgements; he not only reacts, but acts. Human judgement and agency are always concerned with reasons, and they are specifically conceptual actions.[140]

> The judgements that are our perceptual responses to what is going on around us differ from responses that are not propositionally contentful (and so are not in that sense intelligible) in that they can serve as reasons, as premises from which further conclusions can be drawn.

---

[138] Brandom, *Making It Explicit* (n 1 above) XVIII f.
[139] Brandom, *Making It Explicit* (n 1 above) XIX.
[140] Critical of the connection of rationality and language is most notably MacIntyre, who provocatively argues Man's 'animality'. See AC MacIntyre, *Dependent Rational Animals. Why Human Beings Need the Virtues* (London, 1999) 5–8.

> Intelligibility in the sense of propositional contentfulness ... is a matter of conceptual articulation—in the case of perception and action, that the reliably elicited response and reliably eliciting stimulus, respectively, essentially involve the use of concepts.[141]

Conceptually structured agency is distinguished by its normative character. Brandom introduces the concept of normative status for this phenomenon.[142] Intentional states and acts are essentially liable to evaluations of the 'force of the better reason'.[143] For Brandom, the relevance of reasons to the attributing and undertaking of intentional states and acts is prima facie reason to employ a normative meta-language in analysing such activity. Hence, he acts on the fundamental insight that

> the sort of intentionality characteristic of us, exhibited on the theoretical side in judgement and on the practical side in action, has an essential *normative* dimension.[144]

The concept of normativity refers to the concept of rules. Brandom observes:

> What is distinctive about judgings and doings—acts that have contents that one can take or make true and for which demand for reasons is in order—is the way they are governed by rules.[145]

Brandom, however, differs from Kant in that he assumes an *implicit* normativity. He distances himself from a regularistic stance according to which assessments on correctness or non-correctness may only be based on explicit norms.[146] Wittgenstein has rebutted *regularism* using the argument of rules regress[147]: Since rules can only be interpreted using other rules, a rule may only be supposed to offer a criterion for the correct use of a word, or more general an act, if the meaning rule was applied correctly. But, yet another interpretation rule can be specified for the latter, resulting in infinite regress. No sequence of interpretations may abolish the necessity to specify new measures of correctness for each 'final' rule. This regress may only be suspended by using a pragmatic conception to supplement explicit norms:

---

[141] Brandom, *Making It Explicit* (n 1 above) 8.
[142] Brandom, *Making It Explicit* (n 1 above) 16–18.
[143] See Brandom, *Making It Explicit* (n 1 above) 17.
[144] Brandom, *Making It Explicit* (n 1 above) 30.
[145] Brandom, *Making It Explicit* (n 1 above) 8.
[146] Critical of the concept and the epistemological status of the implicit S Schellenberg, 'Buchbesprechung "Brandom, Making It Explicit"' (1999) *Philosophischer Literaturanzeiger* 187 at 195.
[147] See Wittgenstein, *Philosophical Investigations* (n 68 above) paras 201 f.

The conclusion of the regress argument is that there is a need for a *pragmatic* conception of norms—a notion of primitive correctnesses of performance *implicit* in *practice* that precede and are presupposed by their *explicit* formulation in *rules* and *principles*.[148]

Brandom joins Sellars in refuting *regularism*. By identifying the distinction correct/incorrect with the distinction regular/irregular, the normative is traced back to the non-normative.[149] This would reduce a norm implicit in practice to a mere pattern of behaviour. This assumption remains unable to explain which possible behavioural pattern among several is to be relevant in a given case. Furthermore, this would nullify the difference between descriptive and prescriptive, eliminating *the* feature of the normative.[150]

In practice, the constitution of implicit norms has to become explicit to a degree which avoids the pitfalls of regularism and regulism.

(b) Normative Attitudes and Sanctions

This explicit-making becomes possible once we focus, following Pufendorf and Kant, on the normative assessment stance of the participants in the practice.[151] Kant shows that as rational beings, we not merely act according to rules, but significantly according to our *conception* of rules. Norms governing actions do not, unlike laws of nature, immediately force us to comply. It is not the norm as such that governs our actions, but the fact that we *acknowledge* it. To be a subject of normative attitudes, therefore, means to be capable of acknowledging proprieties and improprieties of conduct.[152]

Normative attitudes sanction performances as correct or incorrect. The normative significance of the physical world is a result of these attitudes, manifest in treating-as. Moral entities, norms governing actions, are not an intrinsic part of things. Rather, they are

> products of our practical normative attitudes, as expressed in our activity of imposing those significances and acknowledging them in assessments.[153]

These attitudes, in turn, could be understood to be explicit propositional beliefs by *asserting* an action to be correct. However, the ramification

---

[148] Brandom, *Making It Explicit* (n 1 above) 21.
[149] Brandom, *Making It Explicit* (n 1 above) 26–30.
[150] See the condition of anti-reductionistic supervenience, see p 98 above.
[151] I Kant, *Kritik der praktischen Vernunft*, 10th edn (Publisher, Hamburg, 1990) para 7; S Pufendorf, *De jure naturae et gentium (Liber primus—Liber quartus)* (Publisher, Berlin, 1998) 13–15 (ch 1 §§ 2–5).
[152] Brandom, *Making It Explicit* (n 1 above) 30–32.
[153] Brandom, *Making It Explicit* (n 1 above) 49. However, the normative statuses thus established are not simply identified in a reductionist sense with natural features; rather, they remain independent performances of our practice, open to description in non-normative terms.

would be, yet again, the regress of regulism. Brandom, in contrast, considers it to be possible for the attitudes to be implicitly understood, and thus not to be subject to the regression objection. This implicit understanding is facilitated by interpreting the attitudes pragmatically. Brandom asks the question:

> What must one be able to *do* in order to count as *taking* or *treating* a performance as correct or incorrect? What is it of such a normative attitude—attributing a normative significance or status to a performance—to be implicit in practice?[154]

The act of assessing thus becomes the key to understanding normative attitudes.

According to Brandom, the act of assessing actions essentially consists of *sanctions*.[155] An action is assessed as correct or appropriate by rewarding it, and as incorrect or inappropriate by punishing it. Practical norms are understood in terms of social configurations of dispositions having a conformist structure. This would make it possible to fully attribute any sanction, and thus also normative disposition, to pure actual occurrences. Normative attitudes would then be a psycho-social product of positive and negative behaviour reinforcement. They would be established as a result of the purely functional, descriptive effect sanctions have on the dispositions or normative attitudes of the person whose action they reinforce, ie assess.

However, this kind of reductionist understanding would yet again result in the disappearance of the normative's key element, namely, the difference between 'following a rule' and '*believing* that one is following a rule'. Thus, two crucial distinctions are removed: On the one hand, the distinction between a performance and its normative status—that is, between what is done and what ought to be done—and on the other hand, the difference between a performance's normative status and the normative attitude toward that status—ie what is correct, and what is taken to be correct.[156] Sanctioning cannot be defined as genuinely factual reactions,

---

[154] Brandom, *Making It Explicit* (n 1 above) 32.
[155] Critical with regard to the coherence of the internal sanctioning mechanism is S Knell, 'Die normativistische Wende der analytischen Philosophie. Zu Robert Brandoms Theorie begrifflichen Gehalts und diskursiver Praxis' (2000) *Allgemeine Zeitschrift für Philosophie* 225 at 240. Brandom seems to assume a common interest in discursive authority. Criticised by Habermas, 'Von Kant zu Hegel. Zu R. Brandoms Sprachpragmatik' (n 130 above) 176 f. Habermas interprets the practice of claims by relying on an internal communication orientation. This option is disputed by Brandom, see RB Brandom, 'Facts, Norms, and Normative Facts. A Reply to Habermas' (2000) 8 *European Journal of Philosophy* 356 at 363.
[156] Brandom, *Making It Explicit* (n 1 above) 41.

because sanctioning itself is something that can be done correctly or incorrectly.[157] The attitude may be incorrect in that it incorrectly assesses a performance's status.

Thus, attitudes have to be attributed to sanctions in such a way that they cannot be understood to be naturalistic. Brandom elucidates this problem by considering an archaic community. In this community, a practical norm is in force according to which one may only enter a specific hut if one displays a leaf from a certain sort of tree. Anyone violating the norm is beaten with sticks. In this case, the assessing response is fully describable in non-normative terms, ie unless the leaf is displayed, admission to the hut is refused and beatings are administered with a stick. However, punishment might also consist of making other actions inappropriate, eg, by refusing permission to attend the weekly village festival if the norm for entering the hut has been violated. Brandom remarks:

> In such a case, the normative significance of transgression is itself specified in normative terms (of what is *appropriate*, of [what] the transgressor is *entitled* to do). The punishment for violating one norm is an alternation in other normative statuses. Acting incorrectly alters what other performances are correct and incorrect.[158]

This example shows that attitudes and sanctions can be described in non-normative terms, and that this description is contingent, and, in any case, unable to explain all norms. Even if someone who is not entitled to attempt were to try to participate in the tribal festival, and hence receive a beating, only the norm regarding entitlement to attend the festival would be non-normatively intelligible. The norm concerning entitlement to enter the hut, however, is intelligible in terms of attitudes expressed as sanctions that are fully specifiable in normative terms, ie in entitlement to participate in the festival.

> In this way one norm can depend on another, as the sanctions expressing assessments of the normative significance of performances according to the first norm consist in alterations of normative status with respect to the second norm.[159]

Hence, Brandom distinguishes between external and internal sanctions.[160] A sanction is considered internal if it is only intelligible in normative terms, ie in terms of the normative statuses of other performances according to

---

[157] Brandom, *Making It Explicit* (n 1 above) 36.
[158] Brandom, *Making It Explicit* (n 1 above) 43.
[159] Brandom, *Making It Explicit* (n 1 above) 44.
[160] This is an improvement over Eike von Savigny's theory of sanctions, mentioned in the first chapter, which was accepted by Koch and Rüßmann. For both authors, conventionality is based on terms of application which have been accepted as correct. What is accepted as correct depends, among other things, on the sanctions imposed by other members of the language community.

other norms of the system of norms. An external sanction, on the other hand, can be specified without reference to a specific normative status, that is in wholly descriptive terms of what the group's members do or are disposed to do. In this terminology, the sanction of beatings with a stick is an external; the sanction of non-entitlement to participate in the festival, an internal. This *interdependency of norms* can be extended and ramified, creating a complex web of interdependent normative statuses, which has holistic characteristics.[161]

(c) Result: Principle of Instituting Norms through Social Practice

According to Brandom, norms are constituted implicitly in social practice. This theory can be called the principle of instituting norms through social practice.[162] Essential for the institution are the normative attitudes of all participants, which consist of assumptions on performance norms and lead to the use of sanctions to assess performances, or to analogous assessment dispositions. These assessing attitudes have a social structure, so that the practices in which norms are implicit ought to be understood as essentially social practices. Any description of these norms, therefore, assumes regularities of conduct and dispositions because the existence of regularities is not a part of the claims made by these norms.[163] Regularities are necessary, yet not sufficient conditions for a normative vocabulary. Mere conformance does not constitute correctness.

(ii) Inferential Semantics

Following his pragmatics, Brandom turns to the question of how intentional states, attitudes, and performances receive semantic content through the outlined normative practices. Here, Brandom assumes propositional content to take analytical precedence over subsentential content (a). An analysis of the practice of using statements as sentences leads Brandom to the concept of material inference, a crucial concept for his philosophy of meaning (b).

(a) The Pragmatic Priority of Propositional Meaning

Brandom considers propositional content to be the starting point of any semantics. He distances himself from pre-Kantian theory, which construes

---

[161] Brandom, *Making It Explicit* (n 1 above) 45.
[162] See Knell, 'Die normativistische Wende der analytischen Philosophie' (n 155 above) 235 f. Criticism of Brandom's explanation of the genesis of the normative is to be found in G Rosen, 'Who Makes the Rules Around Here?' (1997) 57 *Philosophy and Phenomenological Research* 163 at 170.
[163] Brandom, *Making It Explicit* (n 1 above) 46.

meaning based on concepts whose content can be grasped without resort to statements. In reply to this view, Kant had already stated that the smallest primary semantic category was the judgement. His argument was a pragmatic concept of understanding, of the 'faculty of judging'[164]: 'The only use which the understanding can make of concepts is to form judgements by them'.[165]

This idea was taken up by Frege.[166] For Wittgenstein, too, judgement is primary, as sentences are the only expressions whose utterance makes a move in a language game. Semantic content, therefore, is primarily assigned to propositions, and it is only from these that the meaning of individual terms may be inferred.[167]

(b) Meaning and Material Inference

Brandom accepts one of Sellar's language-philosophical leading ideas, holding an inferential concept of semantic content.[168] According to Sellar, the basis of linguistic meaning is formed by the proposition's inferential relations to other statements. This view is based on the idea that any conceptual practice consists essentially of giving and asking for reasons which justify a belief or assertion. Accordingly, a statement has been understood if its inferential role within a web of statements—each giving definitions and reasons—has been grasped. A statement's semantic content, understood in terms of inference, is by necessity holistic.[169]

It is highly important to note that Brandom does not consider inferences to be formal logical relations whose correctness is only determined by their logical validity. Rather, he takes up a basic idea gleaned both from Frege's[170] and Sellars's[171] early work, according to which linguistic correctness consists of *material* inferences. Material inferences are inferences

---

[164] On the concept of understanding see I Kant, *Kritik der reinen Vernunft*, 3rd edn (Hamburg, 1990) B94 (A69).
[165] *Ibid*, B93 (A68).
[166] 'I start out from judgements and their contents, and not from concepts . . . [I]nstead of putting a judgement together out of an individual as subject and an already previously formed concept as predicate, we do the opposite and arrive at a concept by splitting up the content of a possible judgement'. G Frege, 'Booles rechnende Logik und die Begriffsschrift' in G Frege (ed), *Nachgelassene Schriften* (Hamburg, 1969) 16–17. See also G Frege, *Die Grundlagen der Arithmetik. Eine logisch mathematische Untersuchung über den Begriff der Zahl* (Stuttgart, 1987) paras 60, 62.
[167] Here, the principle of the pragmatic priority of the propositional suffices to describe inferential semantics. Brandom goes beyond this by presenting an extensive, elaborate theory on the meaning of subsentential expressions which will be discussed in Section (iv), see p 134 below.
[168] Brandom, *Making It Explicit* (n 1 above) 89.
[169] Brandom, *Making It Explicit* (n 1 above) 89–91.
[170] See G Frege, *Begriffsschrift und andere Aufsätze. Nachdruck Halle 1879*, 3rd edn (Darmstadt, 1977) para 3.
[171] See W Sellars, 'Inference and Meaning' (1953) 62 *Mind* 313 at 317.

whose correctness essentially involves the non-logical conceptual content of premises and conclusions.[172] For instance, concluding 'Munich is to the south of Hamburg' from 'Hamburg is to the north of Munich' is correct based on the meaning of the concepts 'to the south of' and 'to the north of'. According to Brandom's pragmatic approach, the correctness of inferences is in practice by no means assessed based on logical validity. Rather, distinguishing good and bad inferences was primarily connected to content. The formalistic view, opposed by Brandom, focuses only on the conclusion's logical validity, dismissing the idea of 'material conclusions'. Brandom considers this to fall short of fully grasping the rationality of a language-practical, implicit acknowledgement of inferences.[173]

This view reverses the explanatory precedence of logical vocabulary argued by the formalist school. The material inferences implicitly contained in the practice are primary. Logical concepts have the function of making explicit the conceptual contents that are implicitly contained in the practical proprieties of inference.[174] Modal logic statements taking the shape of '$\Box(A \to B)$' are authorisations to infer. They express the correctness of inferential transfers as the content of an assertion. Their function is

> [to make] explicit, in the form of assertible rules, commitments that had hitherto remained implicit in inferential practices.[175]

This thesis regarding the expressive function of logic is part of an ambitious agenda: Developing logic from pragmatics. Referring to Frege's *Begriffsschrift*, the conditional is considered a paradigm.[176] With the conditional, one is able to make explicit material inferential relations between an antecedent and a consequent.[177] Inferential commitments are thus made explicit as the content of judgements. The crucial advantage of these explications and, thus, the point and payoff of introducing a logical vocabulary is that the conditional makes it possible to assess inferences as

---

[172] On the concept of material inference see Brandom, *Making It Explicit* (n 1 above) 97, 102.

[173] Sellar's reasoning, which will not be retraced in detail here, is based on the inferences of subjunctive conditionals, which are not logically valid, yet their material relations can still be expressed using logical vocabulary, see Brandom, *Making It Explicit* (n 1 above) 103 f.

[174] Brandom, *Making It Explicit* (n 1 above) 102.

[175] Brandom, *Making It Explicit* (n 1 above) 106.

[176] Frege emphatically distances himself from Boole's symbolic logic. He wants to express the material part of the language, not just the 'formal cement that can bind these stones [prefixes, suffixes, etc. M.K.] together', see Frege, 'Booles rechnende Logik und die Begriffsschrift' (n 166 above) 14.

[177] Brandom, *Making It Explicit* (n 1 above) 108. Brandom considers the two-valued conditional a paradigm. However, he assumes that this semantic approach can be extended to the standard logical vocabulary and traditional semantic vocabulary, such as 'true', 'refers', and the 'of' of intentional aboutness, see Brandom, *Making It Explicit* (n 1 above) 114, 116. This extension is argued in ch 5 of *Making It Explicit*, and will not be reviewed in detail here.

material content. It is only by specifying the inferential role of concepts that an evaluation of the correctness of concepts becomes possible:

> The fundamental characteristic role of logical vocabulary is to make it possible to talk and think *explicitly* about the inferentially articulated semantic contents *implicitly* conferred on expressions ... by their role in rational practice ... By its means the material inferential practices, which govern and make possible the game of giving and asking for reasons, are brought into that game (and so into consciousness) as explicit topics of discussion and justification.[178]

In order to put the inferential structure of speech acts into specific terms, Brandom resorts to a model[179] proposed by Dummett.[180] The use of any linguistic expression has two aspects: the circumstances under which it is correctly applied, and the appropriate consequences of its use. The semantic content to which a speaker is committed by using the expression is represented by the material inference he implicitly endorses by such use: the inference from circumstances of appropriate employment to the appropriate consequences of such employment.[181]

(c) Result: The Principle of the Normative Significance of Conceptual Systems

In his inferential semantics, Brandom develops two views: an expressive one on logic and an inferentialist one on propositional meaning.[182] Logical vocabulary is assigned the role of making explicit those inferences whose correctness is implicit in the meaning of non-logical concepts.[183] This meaning is considered identical with the inferential role of the proposition.

The meaning of a proposition consists thus in the proposition's material inferential role, which can be described by way of the relation between the circumstances of the appropriate use and the appropriate result.[184] According to this *Principle of the Normative Significance of Conceptual Systems*,[185] every conceptually contentful speech act is intrinsically normatively situated in two ways, which may be called conditional and

---

[178] Brandom, *Making It Explicit* (n 1 above) 117.
[179] Brandom, *Making It Explicit* (n 1 above) 116.
[180] M Dummett, *Frege. Philosophy of Language* (London, 1973) 453.
[181] Brandom, *Making It Explicit* (n 1 above) 117.
[182] See Brandom, *Making It Explicit* (n 1 above) 109.
[183] Critical on the possibility of explicit-making with regard to the possibility of assessing whether the conceptual content remains the same, Schellenberg, 'Buchbesprechung "Brandom, Making It Explicit"' (n 146 above) 195.
[184] On the normative significance of the inferential in general, see J Raz, 'Explaining Normativity. On Rationality and the Justification of Reason' (n 75 above) 60, 73 f.
[185] A term coined by Knell, 'Die normativistische Wende der analytischen Philosophie' (n 155 above) 227.

consequential normative significance. Linguistic content thus settles when it is *correct* to apply a concept, and what *correctly* follows from such an application.[186]

There are two ways in which inference can be considered significant for linguistic meaning. The weak thesis is that inferential articulation of propositions is necessary for their meaning. According to the strong thesis, this is a sufficient condition: There is nothing more to propositional content than its inferential articulation. Brandom advocates the strong inferential thesis. However, he argues the broad conception, which includes the possibility of non-inferential circumstances and consequences of application.[187]

(iii) Interlocking Normative Pragmatics and Inferential Semantics in a Discursive Practice Model

In his third chapter, Brandom interlocks pragmatics and semantics. He describes precisely how conferring propositional content can be considered an example of the principle of constituting the normative through social practice. Brandom assumes that the inferentialist strategy for the explanation of linguistic meaning has to be grounded in pragmatics with a view to the norms implicitly contained in the practice of using concepts.[188] This is so because inferential semantics refer to a concept of *materially correct* inferences. Which inferences are materially correct—ie not just logically valid, but also appropriate with regard to content—is governed by the norms used implicitly, which are explained by normative pragmatics.[189] The concept of semantic meaning has thus to be situated in a wider pragmatic framework. Content is understood in terms of proprieties of inference, and those are understood in terms of the norm-instituting attitudes of taking or treating inferential practices as appropriate or inappropriate. Brandom explains this interlocking model as follows:

> A theoretical route is accordingly made available from what people *do* to what they *mean*, from their *practice* to the *contents* of their states and expressions. In this way, a suitable pragmatic theory can ground an inferentialist semantic theory; its explanations of what it is in practice to treat inferences as correct are what ultimately license appeal to material proprieties of inference, which can then function as semantic primitives.[190]

Based on the fundamental idea of interlocking normative pragmatics and inferential semantics, we now have to make explicit, in a model of

---

[186] Brandom, *Making It Explicit* (n 1 above) 18.
[187] Brandom, *Making It Explicit* (n 1 above) 130–32.
[188] Brandom, *Making It Explicit* (n 1 above) 132.
[189] Brandom, *Making It Explicit* (n 1 above) 91.
[190] Brandom, *Making It Explicit* (n 1 above) 134.

discursive practice, how the use of implicit norms is connected to the constitution and conferral of linguistic content by practice.[191] A theory of meaning developed in this way has at its heart the thesis that propositional contentfulness can be understood in terms of the practices of giving and asking for *reasons*. The fundamental sort of move in the game of giving and asking for reasons is making a claim.[192] Brandom analyses the discursive practice of assigning the significance of claims to particular speech acts and arrives at the two deontic statuses (a).[193] They make a more sophisticated description of inferential relations possible (b). On the basis of this analysis, Brandom describes attributing and acknowledging of each other's claims in linguistic social practice in terms of deontic score-keeping (c). Propositional meaning is thus embedded in discursive practice (d).

(a) Commitment and Entitlement as Deontic Statuses

Brandom considers the game of giving and asking for reasons to be at the core of discursive practice.[194] The key elements of the game are speech acts of assertion.[195] According to Brandom, making an assertion means acknowledging inferential commitments, which he calls *doxastic commitments*. They are a sub-class of discursive commitments. From this, it follows that propositional content is picked out by the pragmatic property of being *assertable*. The starting point for Brandom's analysis of the function of assertional speech acts is the insight that assertions are, in essence, actions for which, on the one hand, reasons may be demanded, and which, on the other hand, may be used as reasons for further speech acts or extra-linguistic actions: in the context of entitlement, assertions have two roles. By defining their function thus, Brandom links to his normative pragmatics, according to which discursive practice is essentially about assessing the correctness or incorrectness of speech acts. Instituting these proprieties by practical assessments on the part of the practitioners in the linguistic practice is the source of the significance of assertions.

In order to explain this crucial thesis, Brandom develops the general notion of proprieties, which refers to implicit norms, to a finer concept. He further refines the pragmatics suggested by Dummett, which specified the

---

[191] Brandom, *Making It Explicit* (n 1 above) 133.
[192] Brandom, *Making It Explicit* (n 1 above) 141.
[193] For Brandom, the concept of claiming is essentially related to believing, thus developing an explanation for intentionality, see Brandom, *Making It Explicit* (n 1 above) 148–57.
[194] Brandom, *Making It Explicit* (n 1 above) 159.
[195] Postema offers an impressive overview of those various spheres of discursive practice in which assertions have an essential role: 'Food, hobbies, love, humour, sports, perception, medicine, science, measurement—we make assertions and express our views in lots of different contexts and others of us accept or reject or qualify them'. GJ Postema, 'Objectivity Fit for Law' in B Leiter (ed), *Objectivity in Law and Morals* (Cambridge, 1997) 99.

significance of linguistic expressions in terms of circumstances of appropriate application and appropriate consequences, in order to distinguish several different sorts of proprieties.[196] *Commitment* and *entitlement* are the two fundamental normative concepts used in this discrimination. Brandom considers being committed, eg to an assertable content, and being entitled to be *deontic statuses*. Deontic statuses are normative in character. They are instituted by the practices of the members of a language community, which, based on specific speech acts, take and treat individual speakers *as* committed or entitled.[197] Doxastic commitments and entitlements are considered reasons for further actions (*consequential normative significance*) and they distinguished in that one can ask for *their* entitlement (*conditional normative significance*).[198] Commitment and entitlement mirror the double function of speech acts of assertion on both levels of the principle of the two-fold normative significance of the conceptual. Thus, the Dummettian bipartite circumstance-consequence model is expanded to four dimensions. Both with regard to the circumstances of appropriate application, and to the appropriate consequences of application, we may now ask to what a particular speech act commits one and to what it entitles one, or under which circumstances it commits or entitles.[199]

Normative statuses are socially instituted. They are the result of the practical attitudes of the members of a language community, who award or attribute these statuses to each other, recognise or acknowledge them.[200] Doxastic commitments and entitlements are inferentially articulated; they are consequentially related. By virtue of their articulation, they deserve to be called propositionally contentful.[201] In order to illustrate this inferential articulation in terms of an internal interconnectedness, Brandom uses the example of promising, which he considers to have the same commitment-entitlement structure as assertions.[202] Promising is a way of committing oneself in a certain way. The object of this commitment has to be assertable, eg a linguistic characterisation of the performance that would count as fulfilling the promise. By committing himself, the promiser takes on a responsibility, which entitles the promisee to demand fulfilment of the

---

[196] Brandom, *Making It Explicit* (n 1 above) 159.
[197] Brandom, *Making It Explicit* (n 1 above) 142.
[198] This two-fold normative significance, including the aspect of inheritance, was already described at least in general terms by Cavell in 1957: '[S]omething does follow from the fact that a term is used in its usual way; it entitles you (or, using the term, you entitle others) to make certain inferences, draw certain conclusions'. (emphasis added) S Cavell, 'Must We Mean What We Say?' in S Cavell (ed), *Must We Mean What We Say? A Book of Essays* (Cambridge, 1976) 11.
[199] Brandom, *Making It Explicit* (n 1 above) 159.
[200] Brandom, *Making It Explicit* (n 1 above) 161, 166.
[201] Brandom, *Making It Explicit* (n 1 above) 142.
[202] Brandom, *Making It Explicit* (n 1 above) 163–5.

promise.203 Making a promise means both committing oneself to a particular responsibility, and acknowledging a particular entitlement of the opposite side. Contrariwise, the promisee considers the promiser to be committed, and derives a particular entitlement for himself. The deontic commitments of attributing and acknowledging commitment and entitlement are internally connected aspects of a single social practice.

This internal connectedness is especially evident in the promisee's disposition to sanction non-performance of the promise. Such a sanction may be exclusively externally intelligible. This would be the case if the sanction referred only to the actual results, eg by not inviting the promiser to the next outing with friends because he did not fulfil his promise of lending a hand when someone moved flat. However, it is also possible to internally sanction failure to perform as promised by withholding recognition of the individual's entitlement to undertake such (promise-related) commitments. The cost of not fulfilling a previous commitment is that the promisees will not (or will be less disposed to) recognise future promises of the failed commitment undertaker as normatively significant, ie as committing and making entitled. Such a sanction is defined as internal to the practice considered, since apart from the practice of promising, one cannot specify what the sanction is.[204] *Normatively internal sanctions*, which react to changes in deontic status (non-fulfilment of a commitment) in terms of further changes of deontic statuses (withholding the entitlement to undertake commitments), link various statuses and attitudes into systems of interdefined practices.[205] In complex interactions, mutual commitments and entitlements to other performances or attitudes are reciprocally attributed and acknowledged.

(b) Three Types and Three Dimensions of Inferential Structure

Based on the fundamental terms of commitment and entitlement, Brandom gives a more nuanced description of the inferential articulation of assertional speech acts. He develops the abstract concept of inferential role into a more full-blooded notion of propositional content.[206] Conceptual content is defined by the normative statuses of commitment and entitlement. These, in turn, are elements of complex normative structures, insofar as they share various consequential and exclusive relations. Brandom distinguishes three types of inferential relations.[207] If, in the case of two assertions p and q, commitment p has the consequence of commitment q, q

---

[203] See Brandom, *Making It Explicit* (n 1 above) 164.
[204] Brandom, *Making It Explicit* (n 1 above) 165.
[205] Brandom, *Making It Explicit* (n 1 above) 163.
[206] See Brandom, *Making It Explicit* (n 1 above) 138.
[207] Brandom, *Making It Explicit* (n 1 above) 168 f.

is deemed to inherit this commitment (*committive*, or *commitment-preserving relation*). In the case of entitlement p having the consequence of entitlement q, this relation is *permissive*, or *entitlement-preserving*. There is also the relation of *incompatibility*, if the commitment to p precludes commitment to q.[208]

These three types of inferential relations are also characteristic of the *first dimension* of the structure of discursive interaction.[209] In this dimension, propositional content is explained in terms of the interaction of the two deontic statuses 'commitment' and 'entitlement', and the three types of their inferential relations described above. The *second dimension* turns on the distinction between the concomitant and the communicative inheritance of deontic statuses. Assertions have intrapersonal and interpersonal consequences. In the first case, undertaking a commitment or acquiring an entitlement has consequences for the person whose statuses those are. One commitment carries with it other concomitant commitments, a consequence of the commitment-preserving relations. Entitlement to commitments can legitimate the entitlement to further commitments, and, finally, undertaking a commitment can also lead to the loss of entitlement to incompatible commitments. In each of these cases, changes to the deontic status are exclusively intrapersonal. Communicative inheritance of deontic statuses, on the other hand, results in social changes of the significance of assertional performances, as one commitment entitles others to attribute this commitment, and to deduce entitlement to other assertions.

The *third dimension* of the inferential articulation of assertional practice concerns the link between discursive *authority* and corresponding *responsibility*. In asserting a claim, one authorises further claims (and non-linguistic performances) by having a concomitant and communicative entitlement-preserving effect. Simultaneously, however, the person uttering the assertion commits himself to the responsibility to vindicate the original claim by showing that he is entitled to make it.[210] Authority is directly dependent on responsibility. Entitlement to asserting can only be inherited if the person making the assertion is in possession of it.

The interplay of authority and responsibility can be used to explain semantic content. The commitment expressed in the assertional speech act—that the authority claimed and the responsibility assumed have the content p, and not q—consists precisely in the inferential articulation. Linguistic meaning thus consists of the further commitments to which an assertion entitles the asserter and his audience, what might be considered its vindication, etc. With the third dimension of the inferential structure of

---

[208] Brandom argues a material concept of incompatibility, analogous to his concept of material inference, see *Making It Explicit* (n 1 above) 160.
[209] On the three dimensions see Brandom, *Making It Explicit* (n 1 above) 168–70.
[210] Brandom, *Making It Explicit* (n 1 above) 171.

linguistic practice, Brandom specifies the slogan of use theory of meaning and determines the specific pragmatic significance of asserting, which lies in the interconnection (when socially articulated) of authority and responsibility, mirroring the dual function of speech acts in the game of giving and asking for reasons.[211]

Brandom describes the aspect of responsibility carried by the third dimension by distinguishing two ways of demonstrating one's entitlement to a claim.[212] The first option is justifying by giving reasons. These are more claims, which serve as premises from which the original claim follows as a conclusion. The second option is to appeal to the authority of another asserter.

Based on three dimensions of inferential structure, we can explain the pragmatic significance of the distinction between warranted and unwarranted assertional commitment, ie what it means if one makes an assertion to which one is not entitled.[213] An assertion's inferential authority to license further commitments only exists if the performer was entitled to make it. The deontic attitudes of the participants in the language practice determine the entitlement. They express entitlement to specific claims, ie they accept some claims as satisfactorily justified, while rejecting others. If the asserter fails to shoulder the justificatory responsibility successfully, he is internally sanctioned within the linguistic practice. The claim's authority as an inferential warrant for further commitments is rendered void. Furthermore, differing from the case of the non-fulfilment of a promise, the internal sanction will also cover the original claim. It will not only be treated as non-warranting, but also as not warranted.

(c) The Deontic Score-keeping Model

In order to explain the particular way in which the pragmatic significance of speech acts and deontic statuses is related to their semantic contents, Brandom refers to a version of deontic score-keeping developed by David Lewis, in his paper 'Scorekeeping in a Language Game'.[214] The basic idea behind this model is that all participants in a language game, as it were, keep score of attitudes, commitments, and entitlements. In this way, a picture results of what the community considers to be correct and incorrect

---

[211] Brandom, *Making It Explicit* (n 1 above) 173.
[212] Brandom, *Making It Explicit* (n 1 above) 174 f. Brandom also mentions a third way of demonstrating entitlement; however, as this is only relevant in the context of non-inferential conditions, it will not be discussed here.
[213] Brandom, *Making It Explicit* (n 1 above) 179.
[214] D Lewis, 'Scorekeeping in a Language Game' in D Lewis (ed), *Philosophical Papers. vol I* (Oxford, 1983) 238 f.

speech acts. In the form of a score function, implicit norms can be made explicit, making it possible to consider linguistic practice in terms of deontic score-keeping.[215]

The normative significance of speech acts and actors' deontic statuses is established by social practice. The participants in the language game adopt deontic attitudes of acknowledging and attributing with a view to these statuses. In doing so, actors keep score, both for themselves and for each other, by changing their practical deontic attitudes of attributing and undertaking assertional commitments. The normative significance of a performance thus consists in the difference it makes for the deontic score,[216] which measures configurations of deontic statuses of various participants in a language game. The appropriateness of any speech act (what one is permitted to do) depends on the score.[217]

The changes which an assertion effects on the scores depend substantially on the semantic content of the assertional commitment[218] which results from the inferential articulation. We can thus use the three different sorts of inferential structure (commitment-preserving and entitlement-preserving inference, as well as incompatibility) to describe alterations in deontic scores.[219]

This connection can be explained using the following example.[220] Scorekeeper A maps changes resulting from the assertion 'p' by B, an asserter. To begin with, A must add p to the commitments attributed to B. Furthermore, A has to add any claims 'q' that are committive-inferential consequences of p. Hence, A will need the further premises consisting of the commitments already attributed to B. Next, using an incompatibility test, A checks which of the commitments on the account maintained for B are precluded by the newly attributed commitment p, and thus have to be struck from his account because B's entitlement to these incompatible commitments can no longer be acknowledged. Furthermore, A can attribute to B entitlements to any claims that are committive-inferential consequences of commitments to which B is already entitled according to his score.

A can only make these changes to B's score if he assesses B's entitlement to the claim of p. This assessment consists of looking at good inferences having p as a conclusion and at premises to which B is entitled and committed.[221] If the assessment shows that B is entitled to the assertion, A may not only change B's score in the way described above. Besides these

---

[215] Brandom, *Making It Explicit* (n 1 above) 181.
[216] Brandom, *Making It Explicit* (n 1 above) 166.
[217] Brandom, *Making It Explicit* (n 1 above) 183.
[218] Brandom, *Making It Explicit* (n 1 above) 186.
[219] Brandom, *Making It Explicit* (n 1 above) 188.
[220] Brandom, *Making It Explicit* (n 1 above) 190 f.
[221] Brandom, *Making It Explicit* (n 1 above) 191.

intercontent, intrapersonal score-keeping consequences of B's speech act, the assertion may also have intracontent interpersonal consequences regarding A's attitudes. The entitlement to the claim p may also be communicatively inherited by other persons, including A.[222]

We also have to note that the changes effected by a speech act in the deontic attitudes by means of which the score-keepers keep score on the deontic statuses of various interlocutors depend both on the antecedent score and on the semantic content of the speech act.[223]

The propositional content of assertions takes centre-stage in a linguistic practice analysed using the score-keeping model. Assertions are enriched by four auxiliary sorts of speech act, which play an important role in score-keeping. These are the speech acts of deferrals, disavowals, queries, and challenges.[224] As a result of these *auxiliary speech acts*, no new sorts of content need be considered. Rather, they are associated with the semantic content of the assertion. It is the significance of the auxiliary speech acts for score-keeping that is different.

Deferrals to other entitlements have already been mentioned. They can be used by the asserter to defer his responsibility to vindicate his assertion to a third party. A deferral's success depends on whether the claim made by the third party is justified, and whether the requirements for the communicative inheritance of authority have been met. The latter would not be the case, if eg C defers to A's entitlement his claim p, yet differs from A in that he is committed to some claim incompatible with p, and thus does not meet one of the conditions for inheriting A's authority.

Disavowals repudiate or disclaim a commitment one has previously acknowledged. A disavowal of p can only be successful if not just p but any entitlement-preserving, inferentially attributed claims q, r, s are also disavowed. Thus, if one disavows p, but persists in asserting r, it is impossible to use the disavowal to attain other entitlements which were withheld only because of p.

Queries can be used by score-keepers to elicit the avowal or disavowal of a particular claim. Challenges might consist of making an incompatible assertion or explicitly questioning the attribution of an entitlement.

(d) *Propositional Meaning in Discursive Practice*

Brandom firmly roots propositional meaning in discursive practice by intertwining inferential semantics and normative pragmatics. In this practice, assertions have a dual function: On the one hand, they are the objects

---

[222] Brandom, *Making It Explicit* (n 1 above) 186.
[223] Brandom, *Making It Explicit* (n 1 above) 186.
[224] Brandom, *Making It Explicit* (n 1 above) 191–3.

134 Normativity and Objectivity of Linguistic Meaning

of justification. On the other hand, they are available as reasons for other speech acts. As a part of inferences, they can take on the role of premises or conclusions.

For speech acts to take on the latter function the assertional commitment to something must entitle the speaker to other commitments. Their heritability is the basis of inferential articulation, by virtue of which they count as semantically contentful.[225] The deontic statuses of commitment and entitlement, instituted by the practical attitudes of the practitioners, are basic semantic concepts. They make it possible to authorise discursively and take on responsibility discursively. In this way, propositional meaning results from a dual embedding into the contexts of intrapersonal, intercontent justification and of interpersonal, intracontent deferral.[226]

In the deontic score-keeping model, complex dynamic configurations of the deontic statuses and corresponding normative attitudes can be analysed down to sub-structures.[227] The participants in a language game use the practice of score-keeping to confer propositional content to specific statements. Thus, Brandom's model of discursive practice makes it possible to analyse propositional meaning solely in terms of normative concepts.

(iv) Theory of the Meaning of Subsentential Expressions

In chapters 6 and 7 of *Making It Explicit*, Brandom discusses the meaning of subsentential expressions.[228] According to the principle of the explanatory precedence of the propositional, subsentential expressions only receive semantic content indirectly.[229] In general, one can say that the meaning of individual expressions can be derived from the meaning of the sentence in which they appear, and not vice versa. This ranking has considerable consequences. It is a reversal of the explanation sequence often used during semantic arguments. The principle of the explanatory precedence of

---

[225] Brandom, *Making It Explicit* (n 1 above) 168.
[226] See Knell, 'Die normativistische Wende der analytischen Philosophie' (n 155 above) 237.
[227] Brandom, *Making It Explicit* (n 1 above) 175.
[228] Here, expressions are called subsentential if they are at a sub-sentence level. Their meaning is important for the cognitive interest of the present work, given that, in the interpretation of the law, the meaning of individual concepts is often paramount. With regard to the concept of the subsentential term and its function within language, see Brandom, *Making It Explicit* (n 1 above) 375–84, 400–404. Critical on Brandom's theory of subsentential expressions see PJ Graham, 'Brandom on Singular Terms' (1999) 93 *Philosophical Studies* 247.
[229] This kind of derivation is familiar to legal theory: The semantic-systematic interpretation includes the context of a sentence when determining the meaning of individual expressions. Nevertheless, there are important differences between Brandom's analysis and the majority approach in legal theory, which concern analytic precedence between propositional and subsentential expressions.

propositional meaning has been discussed previously.[230] Based on this, we will now describe how the derivation of subsentential meaning from propositional meaning can be understood.

Brandom relies on Frege's substitution method to show how the semantic, ie inferential, content of sentences can be expanded to include the expressions found in it (a). Afterwards, he introduces another structural level, the anaphora, in order to include contents which are expressed token-reflexively or indexical (b). In conclusion, the theory of subsentential expressions will be summarised (c).

(a) Substitution

Brandom elaborates on the concept of inferential articulation by supplementing it with an apparatus of substitutional mechanisms. Subsentential expressions, like singular terms and predicates, cannot be used in inferences as premises or conclusions. They can, however, appear in sentences having this function. Hence, they have a derivative, indirect meaning:

> [T]he utterance of an essentially subsentential expression, such a singular term ... does not by itself make a move in the language game, does not alter the score of commitments and attitudes that it is appropriate for an audience to attribute to the speaker. Accordingly, such expressions cannot have semantic contents in the same sense in which sentences can. They can be taken to be semantically contentful only in a derivative sense, insofar as their occurrence as components in sentences contributes to the contents ... of those sentences.[231]

Following Frege,[232] Brandom uses the notion of substitution to analyse this indirect meaning, which Dummett called a 'contribution' to the propositional content of sentences in which these expressions appear.[233] As a method, substitution can be used on two levels. On the one hand, premises and conclusions in claim inferences can be substituted for others. Here, the object of substitution is one sentence. On the other hand, subsentential expressions in a sentence can be substituted for others. Here, the object of substitution is formed by subsentential expressions.[234] Summarising both levels, one arrives at the following *guiding principle*:

---

[230] See p 122 above.
[231] Brandom, *Making It Explicit* (n 1 above)364.
[232] See Frege, *Die Grundlagen der Arithmetik* (n 166 above) 97 f, 136 f. Frege refers to Leibniz, who wrote in the fragment Non inelegans: 'Eadem sunt quorum unum potest substitui alteri salva veritate. ('Those things are identical of which one can be substituted for the other without loss of truth [of the statement in which the substitution is effected]'). GW Leibniz, 'Non inelegans specimen demonstrandi in abstractis' in GW Leibniz (ed), *Opera Philosophica Omnia* (Aalen, 1959) 94.
[233] See M Dummett, 'What Do I Know When I Know a Language?' in Dummett (ed), *The Seas of Language* (n 65 above) 100.
[234] Brandom makes an intermediate step between the examination of propositional content and that of the content of expressions such as singular terms and predicates. He

136 Normativity and Objectivity of Linguistic Meaning

> The meaning of any subsentential expression is determined by the number of words it can be substituted by, whilst the content of the sentences in which it appears remains unchanged.

This guiding principle can be explained as follows: If the only difference between two sentences p and q is that the subsentential expression a in sentence p is replaced by a subsentential expression in sentence q, then a and b have the same meaning if p and q have the same meaning. p and q have the same meaning if substituting one for the other never changes the pragmatic significance of inferences in which p or q appear, ie if substituting a for b never turns a good inference into a bad one.[235] This interconnectedness between the two levels justifies speaking of an indirect inferential significance of subsentential expressions.

Subsentential sets of expressions can play three roles in this substitution-theoretical structure[236]: An expression can be *substituted for* another; it can *substitute* another with regard to the latter's function as a compound expression; and finally, it can act as a sentence frame, *into* which other expressions may be *substituted*.[237] These varying substitution-structural roles can be used to distinguish different subsentential expressions. Frege was the first to describe how predicates are substitutional sentence frames formed when singular terms are substituted for in sentences.[238]

The notion of substitution can, in turn, be considered an inference, as the following example shows:

(1) Benjamin Franklin invented bifocals.
(2) Benjamin Franklin was the first postmaster general of the United States.
(3) The first Postmaster General of the United States invented bifocals. (1), (2)

Here, the substitution is *into* the sentence frame of the premised sentence (1) 'invented bifocals', with 'Benjamin Franklin' *substituted for* the singular term. Inferences such as this, which relate substitutionally variant substituted-in sentences as premise (1) and conclusion (3), are called *substitution inferences* by Brandom.[239] As these inferences can be used to substitute both singular terms and sentence frames, we have to distinguish two variants of substitution inferences. The example above substitutes a

---

begins by looking at other, complete sentences which are constituent parts of composite sentences. See Brandom, *Making It Explicit* (n 1 above) 338–54.

[235] Brandom, *Making It Explicit* (n 1 above) 354.
[236] See Brandom, *Making It Explicit* (n 1 above) 368.
[237] See Brandom, *Making It Explicit* (n 1 above). However, Brandom defines the three roles somewhat differently.
[238] See Brandom, *Making It Explicit* (n 1 above) 369.
[239] Brandom, *Making It Explicit* (n 1 above) 370.

singular term. The inference from 'Benjamin Franklin went for a walk' to 'Benjamin Franklin moved' creates a *frame-variant* of the premise by substitution of the predicate.

It is extremely important to note that the two variants of substitution inference differ in their formal structure.[240] A substitution inference which substitutes a singular term is reversible, ie it is good in both directions. If the inference from 'Benjamin Franklin went for a walk' to 'The first Postmaster General of the United States went for walk' is a good one, then so is the reversed inference. Substitution inferences which substitute singular expressions can accordingly be called symmetrical. This is not necessarily the case with inferences substituting predicates. If the inference from 'Benjamin Franklin went for a walk' to 'Benjamin Franklin moved' is a good one, it does not follow that the inference from 'Benjamin Franklin moved' to 'Benjamin Franklin went for a walk' has to be a good one, too. Replacement of predicates need not yield reversible inferences. If they are not reversible, substitution inferences can be called asymmetrical.

Singular terms are grouped into equivalence classes by the good substitution inferences in sentences in which the terms are substituted for each other (intersubstitution), while predicates are grouped into asymmetrical families.[241] According to the guiding principle given above, an equivalence class consists of a set of singular terms that share the same meaning. Their interchangeability can be mapped by good substitution inferences, ie by the fact that the significance of the inferences in which the sentences containing them appear remains unchanged. Brandom states that

> the route from pragmatics to semantics is that of assimilating expressions according to invariance (of pragmatic significance of some sort) under substitution. This same substitutional path that leads from inference to sentential conceptual content leads as well from the possession of freestanding inferential content by compound sentences to the possession of component-inferential content by embedded ingredient sentences and … from sentential content to the content of subsentential expressions such as singular terms and predicates.[242]

> Assimilating sentences accordingly as their intersubstitution in inferences preserves the material goodness of inferences yields freestanding content equivalence classes, and assimilating them accordingly as their intersubstitution in sentential compounds preserves freestanding content, yields component or ingredient content-equivalence classes.[243]

Relations within an equivalence class can be called *substitution-inferential commitments*. If these commitments are made explicit by claims, they take

---

[240] Brandom, *Making It Explicit* (n 1 above) 371; Brandom, *Articulating Reasons. An Introduction to Inferentialism* (n 129 above) 150 f.
[241] Brandom, *Making It Explicit* (n 1 above) 372.
[242] Brandom, *Making It Explicit* (n 1 above) 354.
[243] Brandom, *Making It Explicit* (n 1 above) 348.

the shape of identity claims, eg 'Benjamin Franklin is the first Postmaster General of the United States' or 'a = b'. We can consider these identity claims to be licences for intersubstitution. Weaker inferences, on the other hand, which state the asymmetric substitution of predicates can be made assertionally explicit using the conditional: 'Everything that takes a walk, moves' or (x) (Px → Qx).

Brandom has termed these commitments 'simple material substitution-inferential commitments' (SMSICs).[244] Commitments such as 'Benjamin Franklin is the first Postmaster General of the United States' are material in that their correctness is externally justified, and thus depends on the goodness of this justification.[245] This goodness, in turn, is a matter of normative force, of deontic status, and so of the normative attitudes existing in social practice. Ultimately, the goodness of substitution inference is a matter of pragmatics.[246] Hence, Brandom is able to make explicit the connection of normative pragmatics and inferential semantics also on the subsentential level.

SMSICs express the relations between subsentential expressions, and thus determine the correctness of substitution inferences.[247] An SMSIC may, for instance, determine that the relation between the singular terms a and b is a relation to the effect that for any sentence frame F, the inference from Fa to Fb is good. With regard to the predicates F and G, however, the SMSIC may determine that for any term a, the inference from Fa to Ga is good. The guiding principle[248] for the meaning of subsentential expressions may thus be phrased more precisely:

> The content of each subsentential expression is represented by the set of SMSICs that relate it to other expressions. The correctness of the substitution inferences in which a sentence occurs as a premise or conclusion is thus determined by the collaboration between all of the SMSICs corresponding to subsentential expressions having occurrence in the sentence.[249]

---

[244] Brandom, *Making It Explicit* (n 1 above) 373.

[245] While designating substitution-inferential commitments, 'material' is self-explanatory, whilst the designation 'simple' is anything but. Robert Brandom was so kind as to elucidate on his terminology when asked by the author. On 4 July 2001, he wrote in an email that the designation 'simple' for MSICs served to distinguish them from complex or compound MSICs. This complementary term was not used in *Making It Explicit*, which makes it difficult to understand the designation 'simple'. According to Brandom's explanations, complex MSICs differ in that they concern predicates, not singular terms. Commitments concerning predicates are made explicit by complex conditionals, which, among other things, set explicit restrictions for the contexts of substitution inferences. With regard to this complementary term, MSICs concerning singular terms may be called 'simple' as they are both 'not complex' and also 'basic' in the sense that they are fundamental to the understanding of subsentential expressions. I am grateful to R Brandom for this explanation.

[246] Brandom, *Making It Explicit* (n 1 above) 354.

[247] Brandom, *Making It Explicit* (n 1 above) 374.

[248] See above, p 74.

[249] Brandom, *Making It Explicit* (n 1 above) 374.

(b) Anaphora

In order to be an object of substitution, an expression tokening has to be repeatable, ie able to occur in various contexts, such as 'Benjamin Franklin' or 'the inventor of the bifocals'. This token recurrence is an implicit presupposition for the reidentifiability of singular terms.[250] This substitution can only be called a general theory of the meaning of subsentential expressions if it also applies to unrepeatable tokenings, such as 'the man' or 'it'. We now have to explain how such unrepeatables are grouped together into term repeatables. That claims are articulated according to substitution inferences presupposes a further level of structure responsible for this task.[251] As this complementary level, Brandom introduces the *anaphor*.[252]

Tokenings of subsentential expressions can be linked to form anaphoric chains,[253] as the following example shows[254]:

> A man in a brown suit approached me on the street yesterday and offered to buy my briefcase. When I declined to sell it, the man doubled his offer. Since he wanted the case so badly, I sold it to him.

Two anaphoric chains are intertwined here, one corresponding to the buyer, and one to the briefcase:

> A man in a brown suit ... the man ... he ... him and my briefcase ... it ... the case ... it.

In such anaphoric chains, not all singular terms have reference independently. Rather, some of the chain's links are related to their referents only in a derivate manner, in virtue of their anaphoric links to other expressions. Only the terms which initiate the chain ('a man', and 'my briefcase') have reference immediately. The deictic tokenings 'the man', 'it', etc, on the other hand, are anaphoric dependents. Singular term tokens can play eight different roles in anaphoric chains.[255] Here, however, it will suffice to record a key characteristic of anaphoric reference which is crucial to the inferential integration of unrepeatables, and hence to their semantic content:

> Just as it is their potential for inferential involvements that makes sentence repeatables bearers of contents, so it is the potential for anaphoric involvements

---

[250] Brandom, *Making It Explicit* (n 1 above) 451.
[251] Brandom, *Making It Explicit* (n 1 above) 449.
[252] Brandom, *Making It Explicit* (n 1 above) 450.
[253] On the concept of anaphoric chains see C Chastain, 'Reference and Context ' in K Gunderson (ed), *Language, Mind, and Knowledge* (Minneapolis, 1975) 204–9, 214–19.
[254] Brandom, *Making It Explicit* (n 1 above) 307.
[255] With regard to the various roles see Brandom, *Making It Explicit* (n 1 above) 309 f.

that makes unrepeatable tokenings bearers of contents ... Unrepeatable tokenings, paradigmatically demonstrative, can now be seen to be *conceptually* articulated, for they can stand in *anaphoric* relations to other tokenings, and the chains thus formed can be involved in substitutional, and hence inferential, commitments.[256]

For one term to be anaphorically dependent on another is for it to inherit from that antecedent the substitution-inferential commitments (SMSICs).[257] The use of an anaphoric successor is assessed in terms of its antecedent's commitments.[258] Deictic expressions, ie unrepeatables, can become chains of tokenings through anaphora. These chains of unrepeatables are themselves repeatables and thus able to enter substitution inferences.[259] Using anaphora, an expression may inherit the substitution-inferential potential of an unrepeatable tokening. Thus, unrepeatable tokenings may serve as premises or conclusions. This explains how subsentential expressions may be semantically contentful even if unrepeatable.

(c) Results of the Theory of the Meaning of Subsentential Expressions

Brandom adds two further levels to his theory of linguistic meaning, which focuses on the concept of material inference: substitution and anaphora. Using substitution, the concept of conceptual content is spread to include subsentential expressions such as singular terms and predicates. While the latter may not appear as premises and conclusions, substitution gives them an indirect inferential role. Anaphora make it possible to consider links between tokenings of subsentential expressions which make unrepeatables repeatable, and explain the inheritance of substitution-inferential commitments. The result is an analysis of the practice of discursive commitment which uses three key concepts—inference, substitution, and anaphora—to differentiate linguistic meaning. Therefore, Brandom has termed his own model the 'ISA approach to semantics'.[260]

The theory of linguistic meaning accordingly has three layers.[261] At the top are sentences, which are propositionally contentful in virtue of their use in expressing claims. Here, the key concept at this level is *inference*, for the meaning of sentences results from their role in giving and asking for reasons. Inferential connections among assertional sentences can be understood pragmatically, by means of keeping score on commitments and entitlements.

[256] Brandom, *Making It Explicit* (n 1 above) 466.
[257] Brandom, *Making It Explicit* (n 1 above) 455.
[258] Brandom, *Making It Explicit* (n 1 above) 432.
[259] Brandom, *Making It Explicit* (n 1 above) 621.
[260] Brandom, *Making It Explicit* (n 1 above) 632. See also *Making It Explicit*, 198, 432.
[261] Brandom, *Making It Explicit* (n 1 above) 472 f.

The second level transfers semantic content to subsentential expressions, by virtue of the systematic contribution they make to the correctness of those inferences which serve as premises and conclusions to the sentences they occur in. The goodness of these inferences depends on the invariance in substituting subsentential expressions. Thus, *substitution* is the key concept at this level.

The third level considers unrepeatable tokenings to be grouped into repeatable recurrence chains that are involved in substitution inferences, and so are indirectly inferentially contentful. Here, a key characteristic is the inheritance of substitutional commitments in anaphoric chains, which makes *anaphora* the key concept at this level.

C. Objections against the Theory of Normativity

Any theory accepting the normativity of linguistic meaning must, in one way or another, presuppose that meaning has a determining effect. The determinacy thesis indicates that the meaning of a term determines which of its possible uses is correct, independently of the respective speaker.

WVO Quine and Saul Kripke, in particular, have argued against the adoption of normativity and determinacy. Quine's indeterminacy thesis is directed at the distinctions between synthetic and analytic sentences, and between knowledge of facts and knowledge of meaning. With a radically sceptical reading of Wittgenstein's thoughts on rule-following, Kripke supports the indeterminacy thesis.[262]

Combined, Quine and Kripke offer the three central objections of meaning scepticism.[263] Below, I will discuss Kripke's theory of rule-following (i), Quine's objections of semantic holism (ii), and of the impossibility of analyticity (iii).

All three objections are the subject of a vast body of literature, which in never-ending debates fathoms the strengths and weaknesses of each argument down to the last minute detail. Quine's and Kripke's objections have all the crucial and still-valid considerations; they deserve to receive special attention.[264] The examination of meaning-sceptical objections allows for a fine-tuning or more precise localisation of the position acceptable for a Brandomian theory of normativity.

---

[262] See Coleman and Leiter, 'Determinacy, Objectivity, and Authority' (n 3 above) 219–23.

[263] Other individual details of Brandom's theory have also been the object of criticism, which will not be examined in detail here. See Habermas, 'Von Kant zu Hegel. Zu R. Brandoms Sprachpragmatik' (n 130 above) 161–85; Knell, 'Die normativistische Wende der analytischen Philosophie' (n 155 above) 240; Schellenberg, 'Buchbesprechung Brandom, "Making It Explicit"' (n 146 above) 190.

[264] This is apparent e.g. in the fact that Glüer's modern criticism of normativity is still predominantly rooted in Quine's work, see Glüer, *Sprache und Regeln* (n 6 above) 234 f.

(i) Kripke's Theory of Rule-Following

In *Wittgenstein on Rules and Private Language*, Kripke interprets key passages of the *Philosophical Investigations* (§§ 184–202) to the effect that they develop a 'sceptical paradox' of meaning. For him, Wittgenstein's theory of meaning forces us to abandon the belief that an individual's use of a concept can be judged as right or wrong. There is general consent that Kripke's reading of Wittgenstein is exegetically indefensible.[265] However, Kripke's meaning-sceptical arguments are still of systematic interest. Kripke differs from other objecters to the theory of normativity in that he does not doubt its existence. Rather, he takes it as a basis for his deliberations.[266] Kripke interprets normativity in such a way as constitutive for meaning that its theoretical non-obtainability entails radical meaning-scepticism.[267] This effect makes Kripke's deliberation on rule-following a key challenge to any theory which assumes that it is possible to explicate the normativity of linguistic meaning.

Kripke's argument has two stages. First, he develops a paradox (a), which is then resolved in a sceptical approach (b). Kripke's theory of rule-following, however, is to be criticised in a way that renders his meaning-sceptical argument superfluous (c).

(a) Kripke's Sceptical Paradox

Kripke bases his *sceptical paradox* on a single example,[268] which, so as to emphasise the infinite character of rules, is taken from mathematics. The expression of a mathematical series creates an infinite sequence of clear cases in which the expression may be used correctly. In order to illustrate rules of this kind, Kripke chooses addition, symbolised by the expressions 'plus' or '+'. In Kripke's model, a speaker claims that his past usage of '+' was used to denote addition, and that he had thus followed this mathematical rule. Now, a radical sceptic confronts him with an addition problem he has never had to solve before. This is possible, as the speaker could only have solved a finite number of problems, yet computation allows for an infinite number of applications. Kripke gives as the problem

---

[265] B Bix, *Law, Language, and Legal Determinacy* (Oxford, 1995) 37 fn 4; Blackburn, 'The Individual Strikes Back' (n 35 above) 281; Glock, 'Wie kam die Bedeutung zur Regel?' (n 115 above) 431 f; W Goldfarb, 'Kripke on Wittgenstein on Rules' (1985) 82 *Journal of Philosophy* 471 at 471 f; McDowell, 'Wittgenstein on Following a Rule' (n 35 above) 330 f. Boghossian considers Wittgenstein's deliberations on rule-following uninterpretable in toto, see Boghossian, 'The Rule-Following Considerations' (n 6 above) 507 fn 3.

[266] However, the concept of normativity remains unclear in Kripke, see Glüer, *Sprache und Regeln* (n 6 above) 109–12.

[267] See Glüer, *Sprache und Regeln* (n 6 above) 85.

[268] Kripke, *Wittgenstein on Rules and Private Language* (n 4 above) 7–11.

'68 + 57 = ?'. If the speaker has understood the mathematical operation of addition correctly, his answer will of course be '125'.

The sceptic, however, considers this answer to be wrong. He claims that now and in the past, the speaker had not been following the rule of addition, but of quussing, which Kripke denotes as the symbol '⊕'. It is defined by:

$$x \oplus y = x + y, \text{ if } x, y < 57$$
$$x \oplus y = 5, \text{ if } x, y \geq 57$$

Any normativity theory claiming that there is a correct solution to this problem, and that this solution is '125', has to refute the sceptic's hypothesis, ie that the speaker followed the rule of quussing. According to the sceptic, a rebuttal would only be possible if the speaker were able to mention a fact from which the meaning of 'plus' can be explicitly concluded. This meaning fact has to satisfy specific conditions.[269] First, it has to clearly define the fact which characterises the answer as correct. Secondly, this characterisation has to be normative because '[t]he relation of meaning and intention to future action is *normative*, not *descriptive*'.[270] Furthermore, Kripke considers the missing meaning fact to be that which, in terms of an imperative, determines the speaker's actions. Hence, he thirdly demands this fact to be directly, epistemically accessible from the first person's perspective.

The sceptic game played between speaker and sceptic now consists of examining possibly relevant facts according to these conditions. Kripke proceeds according to the conclusion principle. Every possible fact is now contemplated and rejected. Kripke then arrives at his sceptical conclusion that

> there is no fact about me that distinguishes between my meaning a definite function by 'plus' ... and my meaning nothing at all.[271]

The facts examined can be divided into two classes.[272] Hence, they all fail to clear two key hurdles. All signs or representations have to be justified in their use, resulting in an infinite regress of justification. Naturalist reductions, on the other hand, miss the normative character of the distinction between correct and incorrect.

---

[269] On these conditions see Boghossian, 'The Rule-Following Considerations' (n 6 above) 533 f; Glüer, *Sprache und Regeln* (n 6 above) 91 f. Kripke considers the second condition crucial for his reasoning, see Kripke, *Wittgenstein on Rules and Private Language* (n 4 above) 40.
[270] Kripke, *Wittgenstein on Rules and Private Language* (n 4 above) 37.
[271] Kripke, *Wittgenstein on Rules and Private Language* (n 4 above) 21.
[272] See Glüer, *Sprache und Regeln* (n 6 above) 94.

144 *Normativity and Objectivity of Linguistic Meaning*

The regress argument[273] defeats both platonic copy theories of meaning and those theories which call on the speakers' inner states as meaning facts. A reduction of meaning to probable behaviour argued by disposition theory, on the other hand, gives a merely descriptive account of the relation between meaning and use, and thus falls short of the second condition.[274] Normativity assumes that the rule can be violated, that there is a difference between what is done and what ought to be done. For Brandom, too, this is the crucial defect of the disposition theories:

> No one ever acts incorrectly in the sense of violating his or her own dispositions. Indeed, to talk of 'violating' dispositions is illicitly to import normative vocabulary into a purely descriptive context.[275]

Because the speaker is unable to advance any argument which would support the meaning of 'plus', the result of the sceptical discussion is: There are facts which determine the meaning of a term, and hence there are no facts which would determine the correct use of a term.[276] Kripke writes:

> The sceptical argument, then, remains unanswered. There can be no such thing as meaning anything by any word. Each new application we make is a leap in the dark; any present intention could be interpreted so as to accord with anything we may choose to do. So there can be neither accord, nor conflict.[277]

Thus, no sign has a meaning; no use may be accounted for as normatively correct. This sceptical result is paradox and seems to defeat itself[278] because the claim that no one may express meaning using language also applies to the sceptic.[279] Hence, the question is how language may be possible after all.[280] The answer, Kripke says, lies in a 'sceptical solution'.

---

[273] On the argument of infinite regress see Kant, *Kritik der praktischen Vernunft* (n 151 above) A 132/B171; Wittgenstein, *Philosophical Investigations* (n 68 above) para 210. The regress argument is decisive because the actual use of a sign can always be subsumed under a great number of rules, see Brandom, *Making It Explicit* (n 1 above) 28.

[274] See Boghossian, 'The Rule-Following Considerations' (n 6 above) 509.

[275] Brandom, *Making It Explicit* (n 1 above) 29.

[276] Kripke, *Wittgenstein on Rules and Private Language* (n 4 above) 21. One has to note that Kripke argues a constitutive, not an epistemological scepticism, see B Hale, 'Rule-Following, Objectivity and Meaning' in Hale and Wright (eds), *A Companion to the Philosophy of Language* (n 28 above) 371; Wright, 'Rule-following, Objectivity and the Theory of Meaning' (n 4 above) 515.

[277] Kripke, *Wittgenstein on Rules and Private Language* (n 4 above) 55.

[278] Kripke, *Wittgenstein on Rules and Private Language* (n 4 above) 71.

[279] See K Puhl, 'Introduction' in Puhl (ed), *Meaning Scepticism* (n 41 above) 4.

[280] Kripke, *Wittgenstein on Rules and Private Language* (n 4 above) 62. Kripke's scepticism is not only directed against the possibility of meaning, but also against the possibility of a content of consciousness, see Boghossian, 'The Rule-Following Considerations' (n 6 above) 509 f; K Puhl, 'Introduction' in Puhl (ed), *Meaning Scepticism* (n 41 above) 3. Against McGinn, *Wittgenstein on Meaning* (n 42 above) 144–6.

(b) Kripke's Sceptical Solution

The *sceptical solution* advanced by Kripke in view of the paradox consists of two parts. To begin with, one simply has to accept the sceptical solution: There can be no meaning facts. In the subsequent part, Kripke wants to demonstrate how the concept of meaning may be redeemed without presupposing semantic facts.[281] This second parts consist of a sceptical replacement for the truth-conditional model of meaning. Explaining meaning through philosophical analysis is impossible. Kripke substitutes it with the mere description of the conditions under which claims—ie also assertions on the meaning of propositions and signs—may be considered justified. This avoids the sceptical conclusion:

> All that is needed to legitimize assertions that someone means something is for there to be roughly specifiable circumstances under which they are legitimately assertable, and that the game of asserting them under such conditions has a role in our lives. No supposition that 'facts correspond' to those assertions is needed.[282]

This sceptical solution consists of abandoning any attempt towards a constitutive theory of meaning due to its susceptibility to scepticism, and to replace it with a description of the use practice of meaning attributions.[283] This, however, may only serve as a substitute for the dichotomies of true and false, justified and unjustified, if it provides a standard which may be used to distinguish actual and normatively correct use of language. As all facts regarding the individual's behaviour and consciousness invoke the sceptical conclusion, an isolated observation of a single speaker could never provide this standard.[284] The sceptical solution will only allow for normativity if interactions in language communities are observed.[285] Agreement or divergence between the answers given by individual speakers makes it possible to assess an utterance as justified or unjustified. An explanation of meaning is not achieved; this remains impossible. But it has been shown how language is possible.

(c) Criticism

At first glace it seems as if Kripke's *sceptical solution* did not stray too far from Brandom's normative pragmatics. Kripke, too, presupposes the

---

[281] See Boghossian, 'The Rule-Following Considerations' (n 6 above) 518.
[282] Kripke, *Wittgenstein on Rules and Private Language* (n 4 above) 77 f.
[283] See Boghossian, 'The Rule-Following Considerations' (n 6 above) 520.
[284] This is Kripke's famous thesis that Wittgenstein's deliberations on rule-following had already demonstrated the impossibility of solitary and private languages. Kripke, *Wittgenstein on Rules and Private Language* (n 4 above) 68 f.
[285] See A McKinlay, 'Agreement and Normativity' in Puhl (ed), *Meaning Scepticism* (n 41 above) 191. Hale, 'Rule-Following, Objectivity and Meaning' (n 276 above) 373.

normativity of meaning. Kripke's and Brandom's theories have much in common, especially with regard to their description of social interaction serving as a standard for the dichotomy of correct and incorrect. Kripke describes how individuals are punished when deviating from the standards of their language community.[286] This aspect is also central to Brandom's concept of normativity.

Nevertheless, there are three fundamental differences which these shared features cannot hide. First, Kripke's position is far more sceptical than Brandom's. In Kripke's view, normativity is inaccessible to philosophical analysis. It is a *black box*, something that can be recognised, but not explained. Brandom's concept of normativity is considerably more elaborate. More important, secondly, is that in Brandom's work normativity is a genuine property of linguistic meaning, whereas Kripke's factual scepticism means he sees it as nothing but a substitute. Thirdly, there remains a substantial difference with regard to ontological theses. In Kripke's eyes, *semantic facts* do not exist, while according to Brandom, meanings are instituted in the framework of normative facts.

In view of these fundamental contradictions, Kripke's scepticism is a key challenge to a theory of normativity inspired by Brandom. Should Kripke's assumptions apply, an analysis of normative statuses and their inferential relations would be impossible, as would be a detailed examination of deontic score-keeping, all the more so since the sceptical solution offered by Kripke is untenable (1). Therefore, the paradox continues to veto explanations of linguistic normativity (2).

(1) Normativity and Agreement The sceptical solution has come under attack mostly by those who assume that Wittgenstein intended not to accept, but to suspend the sceptical paradox. The paradox was based on a faulty understanding of what is necessary for competent rule-following.[287] Independent of any interpretational issues, Kripke's sceptical solution is intrinsically indefensible. Goldfarb has shown how Kripke's solution, contrary to his claim, is neither communitarian nor sceptical, and that it does not do justice to the normativity of meaning.

Kripke states explicitly that the *sceptical solution* can only ascribe meaning using purely descriptive, sufficient conditions. As a result, there is uncertainty as to its modal power for the thesis that solitary languages are

---

[286] See Glüer, *Sprache und Regeln* (n 6 above) 106.
[287] Goldfarb, 'Kripke on Wittgenstein on Rules' (n 265 above) 486; BC Smith, 'Meaning and Rule-Following' (n 6 above) 218; Wright, 'Kripke's Account of the Argument Against Private Language' (n 35 above) 777 f.

impossible.[288] Furthermore, the attribution conditions anchored by Kripke in society are based on individualistic conditions, effectively collapsing Kripke's communitarism.[289]

Even more crucial is the thought that in the community's practice, it would only be possible to determine agreement if a speaker's utterance could be subsumed under one particular among many potential rules. Alas, following the sceptical solution, this is precisely what remains impossible. Therefore, Kripke presupposes a fundamental part of a *non*-sceptical solution.[290]

All criticism of Kripke's sceptical solution has at its core the fact that mere agreement in use—descriptively understood by Kripke—is unable to provide normativity.[291] As such, de facto conformity remains a contingent condition, and cannot constitute an ought.[292] Hence, the sceptic argument can be simply repeated on the level of the community.[293] Kripke may have passionately and commendably put normativity of linguistic meaning under the focus of language-philosophical debate, but he sacrifices the normative of normativity. In view of these weaknesses, his sceptical solution has to be rejected.

(2) Naturalism, Reductionism, and Regress If the sceptical solution is unavailable, the objection of the sceptical paradox will resurface. We still have to deal with the question of whether a non-reductive theory of meaning and a normative analysis of meaning are possible, notwithstanding the fact that the sceptical paradox has grave flaws.[294]

There are three approaches open to the critics of Kripke's line of argument.[295] First, they can try to defend the meaning facts tested by Kripke against the sceptical argument. Secondly, there is the option of

---

[288] Boghossian, 'The Rule-Following Considerations' (n 6 above) 519 f; Glüer, *Sprache und Regeln* (n 6 above) 107.

[289] Boghossian, 'The Rule-Following Considerations' (n 6 above) 521 f; Goldfarb, 'Kripke on Wittgenstein on Rules' (n 265 above) 482 f; McGinn, *Wittgenstein on Meaning* (n 42 above) 185–7.

[290] See Glüer, *Sprache und Regeln* (n 6 above) 109.

[291] A McKinlay, 'Agreement and Normativity' (n 285 above) 193 f.

[292] On the difference between agreement in the sense of mere regulism and normativity, see p 118 above.

[293] Hale, 'Rule-Following, Objectivity and Meaning' (n 276 above) 374.

[294] Blackburn has shown that the sceptical paradox cannot be phrased in the first person, see S Blackburn, 'Theory, Observation and Drama' (1992) 7 *Mind and Language* 187 at 199. Wright and Boghossian have proven in detail the incoherence of Kripke's position of semantic irrealism, Boghossian, 'The Rule-Following Considerations' (n 6 above) 522; Wright, 'Kripke's Account of the Argument Against Private Language' (n 35 above) 796 f. See also Hale, 'Rule-Following, Objectivity and Meaning' (n 276 above) 374–9.

[295] See Boghossian, 'The Rule-Following Considerations' (n 6 above) 527; B Hale, 'Rule-Following, Objectivity and Meaning' (n 276 above) 374.

proving that Kripke fails to cover all existing facts in his discussion.[296] These two approaches follow a naturalist strategy. They accept Kripke's assumption that linguistic meaning is constituted by determinable facts that can be described by non-meaning-specific concepts. The naturalist strategy amounts to taking a disposition theory of meaning, or a causal reference theory, or something along those lines. All naturalist efforts at tracing back the normativity of meaning to facts fail because they remain unable to incorporate the difference between correct and incorrect usage.[297] They do not fulfil the condition of anti-reductionist supervenience.[298] The possibility of incorrect use is factored out *ex definitio*. Hence, the naturalist strategy is by necessity a non-normative strategy, a fact overlooked by Kripke.

It is only the third potential approach—characteristic of the anti-naturalist strategy chosen here—which takes up the normativity of meaning. In view of Kripke's futile search for meaning facts, the conclusion that there was no way of explaining normativity is in no way compulsory. Rather, it stands to reason that the premise may be at fault. It is based on a reductionist model. Normativity, however, cannot be fully dissolved into facticity. Seen from this perspective, the only thing Kripke does show is that meaning cannot be reduced to naturalistic facts. A *sceptical* conclusion would only be sufficiently justified if one demonstrated in addition that it was solely naturalistic facts which might be held to be existent. Kripke does not come forward with proof to this effect.[299]

The critics' third approach may fall back on two ideas that differ in range. On the one hand, one may limit oneself to the irreducibility thesis and consider any further analysis of rule-following to be impossible. This is the approach chosen by McDowell's *quietism*, based on Wittgenstein's bedrock argument.[300] By contrast, a much higher explanatory value is offered by theories which, being based on anti-reductionism, aim for a more precise explanation of linguistic normativity. Among these is also numbered Brandom's theory.

Defending Brandom against Kripke's objection of the sceptical paradox means demonstrating how it may be possible to normatively distinguish the meanings of the sign '+', ie 'plus' or 'quus'. The key lies in connecting normative pragmatics and inferential semantics. The normative attitudes of the members of a language community assign correct conditions of use and

---

[296] This is the approach chosen by McGinn and Goldfarb, see Goldfarb, 'Kripke on Wittgenstein on Rules' (n 265 above) 478 and fn 13; McGinn, *Wittgenstein on Meaning* (n 42 above) 168–74. Critical, Boghossian, 'The Rule-Following Considerations' (n 6 above) 538.
[297] Boghossian, 'The Rule-Following Considerations' (n 6 above) 538; BC Smith, 'Meaning and Rule-Following' (n 6 above) 217.
[298] See p 98 above.
[299] Boghossian, 'The Rule-Following Considerations' (n 6 above) 540 f.
[300] McDowell, 'Wittgenstein on Following a Rule' (n 35 above) 341.

The Normativity of Linguistic Meaning   149

correct consequences to specific speech acts. Whether or not speakers are entitled to state '57 + 68 = 5' is proved in discursive practice. Whether speakers attribute an adding or quussing meaning to the sign '+' can be perceived in the fact which other statements containing the sign '+' are accepted. The inferential relations between these statements, especially the relation of incompatibility, make explicit whether entitlement to an adding statement in the number domain R_1 (x, y < 57) is inherited or not by a statement in the number domain R_2 (x, y ≥57). In this way, the full meaning of the rule is deduced, making it possible to distinguish adding and quussing-meanings. The speakers' normative attitudes are made explicit by their actions of assessment in linguistic practice, a factor completely ignored by Kripke who in particular neglects to contemplate them the missing meaning facts.[301] Mutual score-keeping of the normative statuses of +-speech acts makes it possible to assess these as right or wrong.

At first glance, Brandom's analysis seems to be frustrated by Kripke's regress argument.[302] According to Brandom, an essential role of the propositions' normative statuses lies precisely in inheriting entitlements to other propositions. Brandom's key justification strategy—whereby a speaker adduces premises of different content as reasons for a claim—may trigger a regression of assertional contents.

It certainly is a prerequisite for any theory of normativity that the process of explanation is brought to a standstill at a certain point for certain propositions.[303] However, it is not necessary for this standstill to be irreversible. It suffices if one is able to distinguish in this way old and new explanations, ie to determine a *change* in meaning.

This is precisely what Brandom does with his so-called *default-and-challenge structure of entitlement*, which he explicitly refers to in countering the regress argument. It is based on the pragmatic attitude that the normative status of entitlement is an implicit element of the social practices of giving and taking reasons. Hence, specific propositions are considered to be those to which speakers are entitled prima facie. The prima facie status is neither permanent nor unshakeable; it can be challenged by doubts. However, these doubts have to be reasoned. In deontic score-keeping, a claim's inferential and communicative authority is annulled only if the doubts submitted are legitimate. The claim then loses the ability to inherit entitlements. This default-and-challenge structure of entitlement makes Brandom's theory immune to Kripke's regress argument:

> Claims such as 'there have been black dogs' and 'I have ten fingers' are ones to which interlocutors are treated as *prima facie* entitled. They are not immune to

---

[301] See Glüer, *Sprache und Regeln* (n 6 above) 96.
[302] A charge levelled by Schellenberg, 'Buchbesprechung "Brandom, Making It Explicit"' (n 146 above) 190.
[303] See McKinlay, 'Agreement and Normativity' (n 285 above) 197.

doubt in the form of questions about entitlement, but such questions themselves stand in need of some sort of warrant or justification.

If many claims are treated as innocent until proven guilty—taken to be entitled commitments until and unless someone is in a position to raise a legitimate question about them—the global threat of regress dissolves.[304]

Furthermore, Brandom is right in emphasising that any preliminary end to the spiral of justification, which Kripke considered impossible, is nothing less than a prerequisite for rational discourse:

> Practices in which that status is attributed only upon actual vindication by appeal to inheritance from other commitments are simply unworkable; nothing recognizable as a game of giving and asking for reasons results if justifications are not permitted to come to an end.[305]

This is where Brandom presents the two decisive pieces of theory which Kripke had been looking for. Within the language game, regress is not infinite. Other speakers award the entitlement to make specific +-statements as a prima facie status, with no further justification necessary. It is thus that the meaning of '+' emerges. By means of the deontic score-keeping used in a specific language community, we are able to refute the sceptic's hypothesis, ie that the speaker had acted according to the rules of quussing. Deontic score-keeping provides precisely that meaning fact that Kripke had been looking for. It makes clear distinctions possible, based on its providing evidence of subtly differentiated inferential relations, and its listing of both interpersonal and intrapersonal conditions and consequences. Deontic score-keeping is normative and epistemologically open to the first person. Thus the three conditions put forward by Kripke are met.

There is, however, the prerequisite that Brandom's theory may not fall victim to Kripke's criticism of reference to a language community. It is obvious that merely coincidental, regular use within the community is out of the question as a standard for normative correctness because 'the community itself does not go right or wrong, it simply goes'.[306] However, this kind of regularity theory is in no way the sum total of Brandom's theory.[307] Rather, Brandom is able to show how a *normative* use of language emerges within a language community. It may remain contingent whether the '+'-sign is attributed the meaning of adding, or quussing, or even guussing. Yet from the fact that the entitlement attributions chosen *in*

---

[304] Brandom, *Making It Explicit* (n 1 above) 177.
[305] Brandom, *Making It Explicit* (n 1 above) 177.
[306] BC Smith, 'Meaning and Rule-Following' (n 6 above) 217. This important aspect is overlooked by Coleman and Leiter, 'Determinacy, Objectivity, and Authority' (n 3 above) 222.
[307] See pp 119 f above.

concreto are contingent it does not necessarily follow that it is contingent that the attributions are chosen *at all*.[308] Linguistic meaning substantially consists in these attributions, which create inferential relations between propositions. From the language game's perspective, meaning is normative.

Kripke states as the measure of every theory of meaning that it has to do justice to the normativity of linguistic meaning, and argues by elimination.[309] We have shown that Brandom's theory is an alternative which has not been taken into account by Kripke. Hence, Kripke's sceptical conclusion is unfounded.

(ii) The Objection of Semantic Holism

The doctrine of semantic holism (a) has characteristics in common with Brandomian inferentialism. Hence, one might suspect at first glance that Quine's deconstruction of linguistic meaning would disprove Brandom's theory (b). However, we can show that Brandom only advances a moderate holism which is not affected by Quine's meaning-sceptical arguments (c).

(a) The Doctrine of Semantic Holism

It is hard to classify a theory which has been attributed to such a diverse group of philosophers, including Quine, Putnam, Davidson, Gadamer, and Heidegger. In general, holism is defined as

> the philosophical tendency to consider something as a whole which is not composed of parts which may exist independently of the complete entity.[310]

Holist positions are advanced in many fields of philosophy. While ontological holism[311] looks at the world as a whole, justification holism[312] considers as a whole a theory which is justified by internal coherence. At this point, epistemological and semantic holism are most important. Epistemological holism is traced back to Duhem.[313] It says that a single

---

[308] 'So it is a contingent matter that we apply the expression in the way that we do. It is, therefore, a contingent matter that we follow the rules that we do. But this does not imply that, following the rule that we do, whether we apply the expression in such and such a way is a contingent matter. For, given our own agreement in judgement, to follow a certain rule just is to apply the relevant expression in such and such a way'. McKinlay, 'Agreement and Normativity' (n 285 above) 196.
[309] See K Puhl, 'Introduction' in Puhl (ed), *Meaning Scepticism* (n 41 above) 4.
[310] M Esfeld, 'Semantischer Holismus' in GW Bertram and J Liptow (eds), *Holismus in der Philosophie. Ein zentrales Motiv der Gegenwartsphilosophie* (Weilerswist, 2002) 238.
[311] Examples of ontological holism are the cosmological period of Greek philosophy (Parmenides, Heraclites), and Spinoza's substance monism.
[312] A coherence theory of knowledge is advanced by Neurath and Bonjour, see L BonJour, *The Structure of Empirical Knowledge* (Cambridge MA, 1985); O Neurath, 'Soziologie im Physikalismus' (1931) 2 *Erkenntnis* 393.
[313] P Duhem, *Ziel und Struktur der physikalischen Theorien (1908)* (Hamburg, 1978).

sentence of a theory cannot be refuted or confirmed in isolation, a test of one sentence always applies to the theory as a whole. Quine applied this thesis to human knowledge as a whole, and drew conclusions for the knowledge of language. This gave rise to semantic holism, which in its most general form was defined by Peacocke as *global holism*:

> The meaning of an expression depends constitutively on its relations to all other expressions in the language, where these relations may need to take account of such facts about the use of these other expressions as their relations to the non-linguistic world, to action and to perception.[314]

The meaning and propositional content of a concept or statement are thus never conceived in isolation, but only in the context of a whole cluster of other statements. Depending on whether the meaning of a sentence is considered to be contingent on the meaning of all other elements of a language, or only a more or less sizeable part of it, we may frame holism theses of varying strength.

One has to note that the global holism thesis is a *constitutive* thesis on what it means that a term has a specific meaning. It is epistemologically open, admitting both sceptical and optimistic assessments with regard to the perceptibility of each individual meaning. An optimistic holist position is advanced, for example, by Davidson.[315] The actual challenge of semantic holism for the position on normativity held in this work lies in the meaning-sceptical conclusions drawn, in particular, by Quine.

(b) WVO Quine's Two Dogmas of Empiricism

Starting with his *Two Dogmas of Empiricism*, Quine developed a new holistic empiricism with which to criticise the concepts of meaning, synonymity, and analyticity. In *Word and Object*, he developed the thesis of translational indeterminacy as a further criticism of these concepts. The arguments Quine directed against the supposition of analyticity in *Word and Object* will be subject of Section III. Here, the focus will be on the

---

[314] C Peacocke, 'Holism' in Hale and Wright (eds), *A Companion to the Philosophy of Language* (n 28 above) 227. See also R Weir, 'Holism' in Lamarque and Asher (eds), *Concise Encyclopedia of Philosophy of Language* (n 17 above) 117.
[315] D Davidson, 'Mental Events' in D Davidson (ed), *Essays on Actions and Events* (Oxford, 2001) 225. D Davidson, 'The Method of Truth in Metaphysics' in Davidson (ed), *Inquiries into Truth and Interpretation* (n 84 above) 200, 205, 214. Davidson's proximity to Quine is particularly obvious in D Davidson, 'The Inscrutability of Reference' in Davidson (ed), *Inquiries into Truth and Interpretation* (n 84 above) 227. Important criticism comes from J Fodor and E LePore, *Holism. A Shopper's Guide* (Oxford, 1993). Fodor and Lapore turn especially against combining semantic holism with confirmation holism. The criticism is rejected in favour of Quine by Okasha, see S Okasha, 'Holism About Meaning and About Evidence. In Defence of W.V. Quine' (2000) 52 *Erkenntnis* 39 at 58.

holistic empiricism advanced in *Two Dogmas*, as its meaning-sceptical argumentation could be directed against Brandom's inferentialism.

Quine considers the relations between theory and practice, as well as those between language and the world, to be holistic. A language's empirical content consists in the web of relations between all its statements. No single sentence, but only the language as a whole may be considered meaningful.

> [I]n taking the statement as a unit we have drawn our grid too finely. The unit of empirical significance is the whole of science.[316]

> The dogma of reductionism survives in the supposition that each statement, taken in isolation from its fellows, can admit of confirmation or information at all. My counter-suggestion ... is that our statements about the external world face the tribunal of sense experience not individually but only as a corporate body.[317]

According to Michael Dummett's analysis, Quine advances two theses in justification of his holism in *Two Dogmas*.[318] The first thesis is: Experience and statement are never sufficiently closely connected for any experience to be able to imperatively determine the ascription of a truth-value to a sentence. Here, this thesis will be called the *indeterminacy thesis*. The second thesis is: Every sentence of a language is reversible. This may be called the *reversibility thesis*.

According to Shieh and Dummett, there are two ways of interpreting Quine's holism based on these theories.[319] Using the first thesis, one may advance a *moderate Quinean holism*. From his indeterminacy thesis, Quine infers that the sentence cannot be the primary linguistic unit, but only a theory as a whole—ie the totality of all truth-value attributions to all sentences of a language—since according to the indeterminacy thesis, experience may only verify a theory as a whole. Quine reasons that no individual concepts or sentences, but only the totality of all sentences is fundamental. This conclusion already puts him at a far greater distance to atomistic concepts than Brandom, who considers sentences to be primary.[320]

Except for this difference, moderate Quinean holism is actually rather close to Brandom's meaning concept. Quine's indeterminacy thesis can be interpreted along the lines of Frege's explanation of the reference of

---

[316] Quine, 'Two Dogmas of Empiricism' (n 4 above) 42.
[317] Quine, 'Two Dogmas of Empiricism' (n 4 above) 41.
[318] See Dummett, *Frege. Philosophy of Language* (n 180 above) 597.
[319] Dummett, *Frege. Philosophy of Language* (n 180 above) 595 f; S Shieh, 'Some Senses of Holism. An Anti-Realist's Guide to Quine' in R Heck (ed), *Language, Thought and Logic. Essays in Honour of Michael Dummett* (Oxford, 1997) 83, 85.
[320] See p 122 above.

sentences.[321] Modelled on this, we can attribute a meaning to individual sentences which consists of the sentences' contribution to the overall theory. Furthermore, direct relations between a sentence and an experience, as well as relations between a language's individual sentences, can also be specified. According to this moderate holism, it is possible to assess whether a sentence meaning matches an experience or not, and how it may have to be modified to adapt it to the newly-made experience.

The moderate holism is very reminiscent of Brandom's inferentialism, if we disregard the fundamental difference between a pragmatic and an empirical understanding of language. Both positions have in common that they consider it possible to understand the inferential relations between the sentences of language, and hence attribute meaning to individual sentences that consist of their contribution to the totality of the language. Brandom has noted himself that

> inferentialist semantics is resolutely *holist*. On an inferentialist account of conceptual content, one cannot have *any* concepts unless one has *many* concepts. For the content of each concept is articulated by its inferential links to *other* concepts.[322]

We can call Brandom's inferentialism moderately holist. This shared ground is the reason why Quine's indeterminacy thesis cannot be considered a crucial challenge to Brandom's theory.

The situation is totally different with regard to the reversibility thesis, which forms the foundation of a second interpretation of Quine which can be called *radical Quinean holism*. According to Dummett, Quine's thesis that any sentence whatsoever in a language, including the sentences of logic, may be reversed based on experience, has the consequence that the model of inferential relations between sentences becomes untenable. This puts a key part of Brandom's theory under criticism. His inferential semantics are based to a large part on the thesis that it is possible to understand inferential relations. According to Brandom's strong inferential thesis, propositional content does not extend beyond the inferential structure that can be made explicit using logical vocabulary.[323] Similarly, subsentential content is also accessible through inferences, using simple material substitution-inferential commitments (SMSICs).[324] Using Quine's reversibility thesis, we have identified radical semantic holism's central objection to Brandom's inferentialism. We will take a closer look at it below.

---

[321] See Dummett, *Frege. Philosophy of Language* (n 180 above) 595 f.
[322] Brandom, *Articulating Reasons. An Introduction to Inferentialism* (n 129 above) 15 f.
[323] See p 123 above.
[324] See p 138 above.

The Normativity of Linguistic Meaning   155

According to Dummett's analysis, Quine argues as follows against the supposition of inferential relations, based on his reversibility thesis:

> The principles governing deductive connections themselves form part of the total theory, which, as a whole, confronts experience ... But, in that case, there is nothing for the inferential links between the sentences to consist in. They cannot be replaced by superinferential links, compelling us, if we accept certain logical principles, to accept the consequences under those principles of other sentences we accept: for any such superlogical laws could in turn be formulated and considered as sentences no more immune to revision than any other.[325]

This is a surprising line of argument. If we assume the thesis—that the laws of logic are subject to revision—to be correct, any revision would only result in a new group of inferential relations. The most far-reaching consequence possibly drawn from the reversibility thesis seems to be that inferential relations are modifiable—but not that these relations do not exist. The reversibility thesis cannot implicitly be sufficient reason for a thesis of non-existence.[326]

Shieh has provided an examination which makes it possible to understand Dummett's above-cited description of Quine's argumentation, and shows the last reason of its meaning-sceptical bottom line.[327] According to Shieh, Quine's argumentation is based on four premises:

1   An inferential relation within a language is a boundary for the correct attribution of truth-values to that language's sentences.
2   Every inferential relation assumed by a speaker results from supposition of the laws of logic.
3   Supposing a logical law means ascribing the value true ($\top$) to the sentence expressing that law. Conversely, the revision of such a law means ascribing the value false ($\bot$) to the sentence expressing the law.
4   If a speaker revises a logical law, the boundaries for the correct attribution of truth-values to sentences, ie the inferential relations, also change.

Using these premises, which also seem to form the basis of Brandom's theory, the reversibility thesis line of argument runs as follows: A speaker S considers that in his language, there is an inferential relation between the statements p and q such that it is impossible for both statements to be false. Following the second premise, this boundary to the attribution of truth-values to p and q is the result of supposing a logical law. According

---

[325] Quine, 'Two Dogmas of Empiricism' (n 4 above) 41.
[326] Fricker goes so far as to put the significance of a revision of a proposition's meaning on a level with the significance of a change in spelling, see E Fricker, 'Analyticity, Linguistic Practice and Philosophical Method' in Puhl (ed), *Meaning Scepticism* (n 41 above) 225.
[327] Shieh, 'Some Senses of Holism. An Anti-Realist's Guide to Quine' (n 319 above) 88–91.

to the third premise, S attributes the value ⊤ to the sentence L expressing this logical law. However, following the reversibility thesis, L is subject to the possibility of change. It is possible that S no longer attributes ⊤, but rather ⊥ to sentence L. According to the fourth premise, S would then no longer be bound to the original relation and would thus be able to make the attribution (p = ⊥; q = ⊥). The inferential relation is hence not between p and q, because both sentences may receive widely varying attributions of truth-values if attribution to L is changed accordingly. Rather, an inferential relation exists between p, q, *and* L which precludes the attribution (L = ⊤; p = ⊥; q = ⊥).

However, this conclusion can be repeated for the inferential relation between L, p, and q which would then be the result of supposing a sentence L', called a *superlogical law* by Dummett, which would in turn be possibly subject to change. Hence, the inferential relation exists not between the sentences (L, p, q), but between (L', L, p, q). Shieh summarises the key thought of the Quinean reversibility thesis as follows:

> Generalizing from this, it follows that, given *any* set of sentences in S's language, the claim that there exist inferential links among these sentences can be shown to be false ... a speaker cannot state all the principles underlying her inferential dispositions ... *no speaker of a language can make fully explicit* the principles underlying her linguistic practice.[328] (emphasis added)

For Dummett, this deficiency in explicit-making, diametrically opposed as it is to Brandom's theory, is the last reason for Quine's holist meaning scepticism:

> Meaning thus becomes for Quine something essentially ineffable. We cannot say what meaning our language has.[329]

> [Holism is the view that] the smallest unit which can be taken as saying something is the totality of sentences [...] and of what this complex totality says no representation is possible – we are part of the mechanism, and cannot view it from outside.[330]

(c) Criticism

Quinean holism has been subject to varying criticism, both in its moderate and, even more so, in its radical form. Hence, it is evident that two of Quine's basic principles can be considered problematic. On the one hand, his meaning holism is the result of connecting an epistemological thesis, the Quine-Duhem thesis, with the verification theory of meaning. The latter

---

[328] Shieh, 'Some Senses of Holism. An Anti-Realist's Guide to Quine' (n 319 above) 89 f.
[329] Dummett, *Frege. Philosophy of Language* (n 180 above) 596.
[330] M Dummett, 'The Justification of Deduction' in Dummett (ed), *Truth and Other Enigmas* (n 20 above) 309.

has been subjected to copious objections.[331] On the other hand, a rejection of Quine's naturalism is self-evident from the position of Brandom and discursive theory, just as from that of Davidson's meaning-optimistic holism. It is especially in their rationality that humans differ from stars or nuclear particles, a fact to which naturalist theories of language cannot do sufficient justice. Finally, there is a certain nonchalance to denying point-blank that (radical) holism has the quality necessary for a theory of meaning,[332] or to classify the thesis of meaning scepticism as a self-refuting *reduction ad absurdum*.[333]

None of these deliberations will be centre-stage here. Rather, we will begin by juxtaposing the two chains of argument in order to reveal the actual issue of the controversy (1) which will then be discussed (2) to (4).

(1) The Central Chains of Argument Quinean meaning scepticism argues as follows[334]:

(1) Some of an expression's inferential relations are relevant to fixing its meaning.
(2) There is no principled distinction between those inferential relations that are constitutive and those that are not.
(3) Therefore, all of an expression's inferential relations are relevant to fixing its meaning. (moderate semantic holism)
(4) We cannot know all of an expression's inferential relations.
(5) Therefore, we cannot know an expression's meaning. (radical semantic holism)

The view argued in this book, however, arrives at a meaning-optimistic conclusion:

---

[331] Boghossian uses this approach to argue against meaning holism, see PA Boghossian, 'Analyticity' in Hale and Wright (eds), *A Companion to the Philosophy of Language* (n 28 above) 345.
[332] Something done by, eg, Dummett: 'The theory of meaning ... attempts to explain the way in which we contrive to represent reality by means of language. It does so by giving a model for the content of a sentence ... Holism is not, in this sense, a theory of meaning: it is the denial that a theory of meaning is possible'. M Dummett, 'The Justification of Deduction' in Dummett (ed), *Truth and Other Enigmas* (n 20 above) 309. Against Shieh, 'Some Senses of Holism. An Anti-Realist's Guide to Quine' (n 319 above) 97.
[333] This is the line of argument followed by Boghossian, 'Analyticity' (n 331 above) 345; L BonJour, *In Defense of Pure Reason. A Rationalist Account of A Priori Justification* (Publisher, Cambridge, 1998) 79. Convincing reasons against the sceptical consequences of this type of argument come from J Raz, 'Explaining Normativity. On Rationality and the Justification of Reason' (n 75 above) 78–80.
[334] The first three premises correspond with Fodor and Lepore's reconstruction of the traditional argument of semantic holism. Here, they are supplemented by the pursuant premise (4), leading to the meaning-sceptical conclusion (5). With regard to the first three premises, see Fodor and LePore, *Holism. A Shopper's Guide* (n 315 above) 23–5.

(a) All its inferential relations to other expressions of a given language fix the meaning of an expression. (Brandom's principle of the normative significance of the conceptual)
(b) We can know the inferences by making them explicit.
(c) Therefore, we can know the meaning of a sentence.

Some remarks have to be made with regard to these conclusions. First: In the wording chosen here, the conclusions refer to the possibility of knowing linguistic meaning. However, they can also be worded more strongly, and used to deny or support the existence of linguistic meaning. Here, this difference shall be disregarded. Secondly: Quine's starting premise (1) is rejected by Brandom. In his view, all inferences of a claim are a priori meaning-constitutive, and not just a few. Quine's first intermediate conclusion (3), however, matches Brandom's starting premise (a), so in this respect, there is agreement.[335] Thirdly: Boghossian is correct in criticising that the argumentation of meaning-scepticism is not stringent.[336] The intermediate conclusion (3) that all of an expression's inferential relations are constitutive for its meaning cannot be deduced from premise (2) that there is no way of identifying constitutive inferential relations. If it remains unclear which inferences are constitutive, the claim that all inferences are constitutive is inconsistent. Fourthly: It is evident from the above comparison of the two arguments as to which the crucial step within the conclusions is, and hence which is the most important difference between Quine's and Brandom's position: It is between premises (4) and (b). The crucial point of contention is thus the question whether and how a claim's inferential relations may be made explicit. Quine's key argument for his premise (4), and hence for his meaning scepticism, is the reversibility thesis. This will have to be discussed in more detail.

(2) Reversibility and the Status of Logical Laws The key aspect of Quine's reversibility thesis lies in the supposition that *all* sentences of a language are subject to the possibility of revision. According to Quine, we do not have the option of referring to putatively fixed sentences, eg those of logic, in order to use them as meta-rules for inferential relations. He argues that even logical sentences in the form listed above, ie $L, L', L''-L^n$, are reversible. Ultimately, the attribution of truth-values to assertions was controlled by the totality of all inferences of a language. This totality, however, could not be accessed: 'No speaker of a language can make fully explicit the principles underlying her linguistic practice'.[337]

---

[335] For this reason, Brandom's theory has been described as 'moderate holism', see p 154 above.
[336] See Boghossian, 'Analyticity' (n 331 above) 355.
[337] See Shieh, 'Some Senses of Holism. An Anti-Realist's Guide to Quine' (n 319 above) 90.

There are only two conditions under which one may avoid drawing the meaning-sceptical conclusion from the reversibility thesis. Either one is able to show that the purported reversibility does not exist, or that speakers do have the ability to access the totality of all inferences. Our strategy will combine both options of refuting meaning-scepticism.

With regard to Quine's assertion that every sentence is reversible, one can object that this thesis was never conclusively justified. In *Two Dogmas of Empiricism*, Quine writes that

> [e]ven a statement very close to the periphery can be held true in the face of recalcitrant experience ... Conversely, by the same token, no statement is immune to revision.[338]

Fricker has rightly pointed out that this is a fallacy.[339] If we have the premise—based on holism—that in the face of experience to the contrary, every sentence can be saved by giving up other sentences, it by no means follows that no sentence is immune to revision. This is a point we will have to revisit later.

Apart from that, there is naturally no denying that *many* attributions of truth-values to the sentences of a language are changed in the light of new experience. However, in order for Quine's line of argument to remain valid it is imperative that these changes apply in principle to *all* sentences.[340] This necessary criterion would not be met if a particular set of sentences in a language was found to be immune to changes. Once some sentences in a language are beyond reversibility, then the spiral of reference to an ever longer list of *superlogical laws* L, L', L'', L''', etc is broken. In other words: If reversibility cannot be denied for all sentences of a language, it has to be limited. This would satisfy the first condition of the strategy for the rejection of meaning-scepticism presented above.

We are now confronted with the *problem of the possibility of limiting reversibility*. The first question has to be what it actually means if a sentence is immune to revision. Following Brandom, the answer is: Sentences are immune if the language community treats them as such. Speakers have discursive attitudes regarding the reversibility of truth-value attributions, which—according to the principle of instituting the normative through social practice—assign immunity to revision to a specific set of sentences. Similar to other, non-immune attributions, these attributions are evident in mutual deontic score-keeping. They are hence both interpersonally and intrapersonally binding. In this respect, discursive authority is implicitly acknowledged, ie speakers of the same language and within the

---

[338] Quine, 'Two Dogmas of Empiricism' (n 4 above) 43.
[339] Fricker, 'Analyticity, Linguistic Practice and Philosophical Method' (n 326 above) 225.
[340] See Peacocke, 'Holism' (n 314 above) 233.

same language community are considered to be and treated as prima facie entitled to use the 'immune' sentences.

We have thus made clear what it means if individual sentences are immune to revision. The next step is to find out whether there are, or can be, sentences with this immunity in a language. Here, we distinguish between primary (immune to revision) and non-primary sentences in a language. Brandom's phenomenological analysis of language has demonstrated the special role of the sentences of logic. They are primary not only in the sense of being the instrument of explication by means of which propositional content in the semantic sense is developed. The thesis advanced here is that logic sentences are precisely that set of sentences immune to revision which robs meaning-scepticism of its crucial basis. Brandom's theory does not depend on the unchangeability of the speakers' normative attitudes. Quite to the contrary, his analysis of deontic scorekeeping shows that entitlement attributions are subject to constant change. Brandom expressly excludes logic from this process.[341]

By contrast, Quine does not distinguish between a language's primary and peripheral sentences. In his view, all assertions which could possibly be made in a language are *equally* uncertain. They are *to the same degree* subject to the possibility of revision. This undifferentiated view does not do justice to reality or to fundamental characteristics of linguistic discourse. Brandom's analysis has shown that the explicative apparatus which emerges by necessity through the use of language makes a *normative* assessment of the validity of specific inferences possible. Quine ignores the fact that speakers make a distinction in their normative attitudes between primary and peripheral propositions. This makes the Quinean line of argument amenable only to a playful discussion of remote possibilities, but for the analysis of linguistic practice. It lacks the prerequisite measure of pragmatic foundation which any post-Wittgensteinian theory of language must have.

And this is not all. One would only be correct in concluding from the fact of the possibility of a change to the primary sentences of our language that *all* meanings of our language are indeterminate, if such change actually did and could happen at any time and repeatedly. In view of the stability of the meaning of primary sentences, however, this remains very implausible. Linguistic meaning is limited in two ways, but with regard to its primary sentences, it remains robust and stable in both the social and

---

[341] Shapiro also argues against Resnik and Wright in favour of the objectivity of logical sentences, see S Shapiro, 'The Status of Logic' in PA Boghossian and C Peacocke (eds), *New Essays on the A Priori* (Oxford, 2000) 335. By contrast, Horwich's efforts at saving apriority simply by limiting Quine's reversibility argument to the field of science are not convincing, see P Horwich, 'Stipulation, Meaning, and Apriority' in Boghossian and Peacocke (eds), *New Essays on the A priori* at 166 f.

the temporal dimensions to such a degree that it would be unjustified to infer the non-existence of inferential relations from reversibility.

The criticism levelled at Quine can be expanded considerably. Dummett offers reasons why logical laws have the special role within a language that Brandom assumed them to have. Dummett's reasons come as an answer to Putnam, who had claimed that the empirical verification of quantum mechanics, combined with the fact that quantum mechanics has consequences which disagree with the distributive law of classical logic, were sufficient grounds to scrap this law. Dummett writes that

> anyone will be quite right to resist the suggestion that we simply drop the distributive law, or any other previously recognised logical principle, without further explanation. He has, after all, learned to use deductive arguments as part of the procedure for testing any empirical hypothesis ... If, when this procedure leads a given theory to apparent antinomies, this is suddenly taken, not as a ground for revising the theory, but for adjusting the rules for deriving consequences, it is not merely a natural, but a justifiable reaction to feel that we no longer know what is the content of calling a theory correct or incorrect.[342]

Dummett begins by describing a specific method used to test every empirical hypothesis, namely the use of deductions. Using logical laws, consequences are derived from a hypothesis which is to be tested. The truth of these consequences is then empirically verified. If the consequences can be successfully confirmed, the hypothesis becomes proven knowledge. If, on the other hand, the consequences cannot be confirmed empirically, the hypothesis is considered to be disproved. The crucial point in this approach is that we have to presuppose the validity of the logical laws used in the process of deduction. Otherwise, the empirical result could not be used in any way to revise the theory. Hence, it is impossible to understand how someone might consider the empirical refutation of a theory to be a reason for the revision of the logical laws. After all, this revision would mean that the logical law is to be considered valid no longer, resulting in a *petitio principii*: The reason for the revision presupposes its opposite.

Therefore, Dummett writes that once logic is revised based on empirical grounds, 'we no longer know what is the content of calling a theory correct or incorrect'.[343] Logic has to be presupposed as *the* instrument, as *the*

---

[342] M Dummett, 'Is Logic Empirical?' in Dummett (ed), *Truth and Other Enigmas* (n 20 above) 281.
[343] M Dummett, 'Is Logic Empirical?' in Dummett (ed), *Truth and Other Enigmas* (n 20 above). See also Kripke's unpublished objection, which he raised according to Putnam: 'Why should we accept the view that quantum mechanics requires us to change logic? If nothing is a priori, why do we not instead conclude that we should revise the statement that quantum mechanics requires us to change our logic?', H Putnam, 'Analyticity and Apriority. Beyond Wittgenstein and Quine' in PK Moser (ed), *A Priori Knowledge* (Oxford, 1987) 109.

162 *Normativity and Objectivity of Linguistic Meaning*

measure for the truth of a theory, if it is not to lose precisely this role as a standard. This is the argument against following Quine in subjecting logic to revision.

The only approach left to Quine in countering this argument would lie in claiming that the underlying theory of science does not apply. The reversibility thesis, Quine might argue, implicated a concept of verifying and refuting theories that did not presuppose a part of a theory to be true before applying the concept of empirical proof to them. It is, however, absolutely unclear what such a theory might look like.

I will call the possibility of changing meaning through revision the *thesis of the dual limitation of semantics*. Linguistic meaning has a temporal and a social dimension, and is thus limited in two ways. It is valid within a specific language community[344] and for a particular time span. The third premise which was attributed to Quine[345] can be readily acknowledged: Logical sentences are drafted in our language, they are part of our language, and as such they are also subject to revision. In this regard there is no difference between a language's primary and peripheral sentences. However, a change made to the primary sentences of our language, ie to logic, would be—and this is where the key difference between the primary and peripheral sentences of a language comes in—an extremely essential change, and hence recognisable and describable.[346] A new language would emerge, with a different concept of propositional meaning. This is the primary reasoning of all critics of Quine, on which Dummett comments as follows:

---

[344] Brandom's following remark on the singular term can be used to explain the range of the limitation of the social dimension of semantics. He refers to Quine's claim that what followed from the gavagai-example was that 'the very notion of term ... is ... provincial to our culture', WVO Quine, *Word and Object* (Cambridge MA, 1960) 53. The key characteristic of the concept of the singular term is that it refers to a concrete, individual object. Quine argues that the reference of gavagai could, depending on the subtlety of the system of concepts, not only be 'rabbit', but also 'undetached rabbit-part'. The sentence 'Lo, a rabbit' could also be translated as 'Lo, an undetached rabbit-part of a large contiguous collection of such parts!'. Brandom counters this argument by demonstrating that Quine uses a concept of the singular term which cannot play the role of a sortal. In the gavagai example, the identity commitment is only made via the fact that parts belong to a whole. Substituting one term for another, however, is only possible if the commitments used are based on a finer discrimination than of their belonging to the same contiguous whole. If 'gavagai' is to be able to sort objects as a singular term, it must have some individuative strategy which makes sure that parts can be distinguished. Yet should Quine's argumentation not relate to a singular term, his consequence of the cultural relativity of the singular term would be invalid. See Brandom, *Making It Explicit* (n 1 above) 409–12.

[345] See p 157 above.

[346] Critical with regard to embarking on a strategy of language game or convention arguments to save the revision immunity of language is Putnam, 'Analyticity and Apriority. Beyond Wittgenstein and Quine' (n 343 above) 110.

> No one has ever supposed that there are any sentences which ... are intrinsically assailable: the most that has ever been claimed is that there are sentences which cannot be rejected without a change of meaning.[347]

Here, Dummett describes precisely the change of meaning mentioned above, ie the change of the concept of meaning. It is in the asymmetry of the types of reasons given for the revision of sentences. By today's standards, we have such a change of meaning if there is no empirical objection which it would make sense to give as a reason. If, on the other hand, the revision can be based on an empirical objection without this resulting in the circular reasoning described above, no change of meaning has occurred. This is the decisive point ignored by Quine's meaning-sceptical argumentation, which considers all sentence revisions to be equal, even if some revisions presuppose other sentences to remain stable.[348]

According to the view argued here, which follows Brandom and Dummett, the logical laws are sentences which make explicit the standard for the normative assessment of propositions. It must be said against Quine's meaning scepticism that he errs in his assessment of the status of the relation between these sentences and the speakers. This relation has been called 'acknowledgment'.[349] Dummett shows that this acknowledgment cannot be subject to an assessment along the same standards that makes these sentences explicit. Rather, acknowledging the standards presupposes acknowledgment of the sentences that make them explicit.

Naturally it is possible to reject the standards themselves, ie the logical laws. This rejection would be evident in the fact that the explicit-making sentences would no longer be acknowledged. The core of the rebuttal of Quine is that this rejection cannot be *justified* by assessing the speech act of acknowledgment to be false. With reference to Carnap's distinction between external questions which concern the rules of a language theory, and internal questions which are asked under reference to these rules,[350] Shieh summarises this aspect as follows:

> So the acknowledgment of the laws of logic must be a different linguistic action ... from those actions governed by rules expressed by the laws.[351]

Contrary to Quine's claims, sentences which express the logical laws as standards for the assessment of propositions are unable to be assessed

---

[347] Dummett, *Frege. Philosophy of Language* (n 180 above) 603.
[348] See Shieh, 'Some Senses of Holism. An Anti-Realist's Guide to Quine' (n 319 above) 99.
[349] See Brandom, *Making It Explicit* (n 1 above) 31 f. An identical designation is chosen, without reference to Brandom, by Shieh, 'Some Senses of Holism. An Anti-Realist's Guide to Quine' (n 319 above) 101.
[350] With regard to Carnap's distinction see TG Ricketts, 'Rationality, Translation, and Epistemology Naturalized' (1982) 79 *Journal of Philosophy* 117 at 119.
[351] Shieh, 'Some Senses of Holism. An Anti-Realist's Guide to Quine' (n 319 above) 101.

according to the same standards as other sentences. This distinction resurrects the differences which Quine had levelled. We are able to distinguish between a revision of logic and the revision of a theory.

We now have to explain why these reflections could be a reason for assuming that the circle of *superlogical laws* could be broken. The key argument against the Quinean circle is this: It does not matter *which* sentences speakers of a language consider primary (in the sense of being immune to revision). The only requisite is that such a set of sentences *exists* in every language. That this would also be possible from a holistic worldview is evident from Fricker's thought mentioned earlier: Quine himself demonstrated that primary sentences can be maintained even in the face of disproving experience.[352]

It goes without saying that it is conceivable that even a language community such as ours might one day change its attitudes in a way that would revise logic and gave rise to a wholly new set of primary sentences. With regard to explicative power, this new set might be superior or inferior to today's logic, either increasing or decreasing the variety of our language. However, it is unconceivable that this kind of change would do completely without such a set of primary sentences. It might be possible for our language's fundamental sentences to be changed so radically that new ways of expression are chosen. But if this new language is to contain something akin to linguistic meaning, it will have to contain a set of immune sentences. In order that there are a language and a possibility of communication and meaning, some sentences have to make up the foundation, and be immune. A language is only imaginable if it contains immune sentences. We will call this the *thesis of the inevitable incorporation of immune sentences*.[353]

With this intermediate conclusion we have completed the first stage of the strategy for the rebuttal of holist meaning scepticism. We have shown that not all of a language's sentences are reversible. Simultaneously, this means that *there are* inferential relations between a language's propositions. Still, language would be all ignorant babble, and in discourse speakers would be doomed to be talking at cross purposes, unless they had

---

[352] See nn 326, 339 above.

[353] In recent epistemology we can find an argument mirroring this thesis. Bonjour discusses that every empirically rooted item of knowledge of necessity contains an aprioric component, see BonJour, *In Defense of Pure Reason* (n 333 above) 3. See also Railton, who argues as follows for 'The need for the a priori': '[W]e need to be able to regulate our practices by normae that fit various purposes and can be used as standards for our often actual imperfect performance, that do not simply bend to fit that performance a posteriori, as empirical generalizations must if they are to be correct'. P Railton, 'A Priori Rules. Wittgenstein on the Normativity of Logic' in Boghossian and Peacocke (eds), *New Essays on the A priori* (n 341 above) 194.

knowledge of these inferences.[354] This problem concerns the key issue between premises (4) and (b) brought up above. The answer to the second part of this strategy comes from what has already been mentioned. Brandom has shown that using logical vocabulary, it is possible to make explicit the implicit inferential relations existing between assertions. That this does not happen in everyday speech is no counter-argument. One only had to show that it was possible in principle.

(3) Dummett's Argument of the Possibility of Communication   In order to illustrate the reflections on the reversibility thesis and the role of primary sentences we will discuss one of Dummett's arguments. He raised this point against Quine's radical holism, but it could just as well be directed against Brandom's moderate holism. Dummett considers it a challenge for any holist position to explain the possibility of communication, because

> while it is only the total theory which has empirical significance, all that we know of another's total theory is some fairly small finite subset of the sentences he considers true.[355]

The fact that speakers know little about one another's theories, ie about the meanings which they assign to propositions, makes it difficult to classify divergence between speakers correctly. Dummett distinguishes two types of divergences. The first is based upon choosing different words while maintaining the same background theory on meanings (so-called 'real divergence'). The second divergence, on the other hand, concerns the background theory itself (so-called 'false divergence'). A divergence between two speakers A and B is real if they, first, utter two speech acts p_a and q_b which are obviously contrary; secondly, they share the same background theory on the standards of assessing a speech act as true or false; and thirdly, according to this theory, both speech acts cannot be true. It would be false divergence if the second or third condition were missing. Dummett's argument against holism is that communication can only be successful if the speakers are able to decide which type of divergence occurs. This, however, is impossible because of the little knowledge they have of the theories of their communication partner.

Based on his theory of *radical interpretation*, Davidson was able to show that this line of argument is not convincing, if only because communication in no way requires the speakers to have full knowledge about their

---

[354] On this problem see Shieh, 'Some Senses of Holism. An Anti-Realist's Guide to Quine' (n 319 above) 102.
[355] Dummett, *Frege. Philosophy of Language* (n 180 above) 598.

opposite number's background assumptions. According to Davidson's *principle of charity*, it is enough for them to assume a sufficient agreement.[356]

Apart from this, we can establish that Dummett's line of argument is unable to affect Brandomian theories of normativity, since the speakers have every opportunity to validate their assumptions on the relation of mutual background theories. Using the two auxiliary speech acts[357] of queries and challenges, they may request a speaker to make explicit the key background theories supporting his assertion. The inferences which then come to light can be controlled for entitlement based on the three structural types of inferential articulation,[358] ie inheritance of commitment, inheritance of entitlement, and incompatibility, and in this way the speech act's conditional significance as positive or negative can be assessed. Within the framework of this discourse it becomes manifest which background assumptions are mutual, and which are not, thus enabling the speakers to decide whether real or false divergence has occurred. With regard to moderate holism, Dummett's argument of the inability of holism to explain the possibility of communication is moot.

(4) Canonical Standards in Moderate Holism Our strategy against meaning-scepticism has proved to be a success. Distinguishing between a language's primary and non-primary sentences made it possible to rebut Quine's argument that inferential relation between the propositions of a language either does not exist or cannot be made explicit by the speakers. Primary sentences, eg the logical laws, have the role of making explicit propositional meaning within a language. According to the *thesis of the inevitable incorporation of immune sentences*, every language of necessity contains such primary sentences. Even though primary sentences are also subject to revision, as the *thesis of the dual limitation of semantics* has it, yet this revision can be distinguished from the revision of sentences of theory. Dummett has shown that it leads to a new concept of meaning. The decision in favour of this radical holism can only be made; it cannot be reasoned. In this respect, reversibility is limited. Quine's thesis of reversibility is hence unable to buttress his premise that the inferential relations of a proposition cannot be made explicit. This completes the rebuttal of radical Quinean holism.

Brandom may argue some sort of semantic holism, but in a weak form, which has been called *moderate holism*. Compared to radical holism,

---

[356] D Davidson, 'Radical Interpretation ' in Davidson (ed), *Inquiries into Truth and Interpretation* (n 84 above) 127 f, 136 f.
[357] On the auxiliary speech acts see Brandom, *Making It Explicit* (n 1 above) 191–3, and p 133 above.
[358] On the three types of inferential structure see Brandom, *Making It Explicit* (n 1 above) 168 f, and p 129 above.

moderate holism only advances a limited reversibility thesis.[359] This limitation excludes primary sentences from reversibility. Following Peacocke, the latter can be referred to as *canonical methods*,[360] or canonical standards. Brandom has defined these standards as the normative statuses of commitment and entitlement, created by the normative attitudes of the participants in a language game. They are connected by inferential relations and can be made explicit by means of logic. They make it possible to assess speech acts as true or false, but cannot be assessed themselves. Hence, Brandom's theory could be categorised as a form of *global holism*, which Peacocke characterised as follows:

> One kind is that variety which recognizes certain methods of establishing sentences containing a given expression, or certain methods of deriving consequences from them, as canonical. It writes these methods into the relevant understanding-conditions.[361]

According to Brandom, inferential relations open propositional meaning to a logical-analytical apparatus. For this reason, moderate holism does not have the far-reaching meaning-sceptical consequences which can be drawn from radical Quinean holism. The objection of semantic holism cannot invalidate Brandomian linguistic normativity.

(iii) The Objection of the Impossibility of Analyticity

Wedded to the objection of semantic holism is the objection of a lack of analyticity. Quine's holistic arguments are coupled to his criticism of analyticity. In its most general from, the objection of a lack of analyticity runs as follows: Any position supporting the existence of some form of linguistic normativity has, of necessity, to presuppose an analyticity which it is impossible to justify. Hence, the assumption of linguistic normativity cannot be upheld.[362]

Linguistic theories of normativity, on the other hand, often rely on analytic truths in addition to logics as a measure of linguistic correctness.[363] This makes it possible to have mistakes which are purely semantic. If a speaker should, for example, deny the fact that a bachelor is an unmarried man, he has not only chosen a different definition for this term, but he has also failed to understand the concept. According to the theories of normativity, he has committed a semantic mistake.

---

[359] See Peacocke, 'Holism' (n 314 above) 233.
[360] See Peacocke, 'Holism' (n 314 above) 233.
[361] Peacocke, 'Holism' (n 314 above) 228.
[362] One example of this line of argument is Glüer, *Sprache und Regeln* (n 6 above) 234 f.
[363] See Shieh, 'Some Senses of Holism. An Anti-Realist's Guide to Quine' (n 319 above) 101; A Millar, 'Analyticity' in Lamarque and Asher (eds), *Concise Encyclopedia of Philosophy of Language* (n 17 above) 94.

Following some remarks on the set of problems concerning analyticity (a), we will present Quine's counter-arguments (b) and analyse them.

(a) Analyticity, Aprioricity, Modality

Ever since Kripke published *Naming and Necessity*, it has become obvious that *the* problem of analyticity does not exist, but that there is, rather, a complex, intertwined web of ontological, epistemological, and semantic questions.[364] These can be classified according to three distinctions: analytic/synthetic, *a priori/a posteriori*, and necessary/contingent. The precise relation[365] of these conceptual pairs is no less contentious than the issue of how well they might be distinguished.[366] I will endorse a clear terminology,[367] according to which an analytic proposition is true by reason of its linguistic meaning alone, while the truth of a synthetic sentence with a given meaning depends on the world.[368] The conceptual pair analytic/synthetic hence pertains to a semantic question.

From this, we have to distinguish the epistemological question of the dependency of knowledge on experience. A sentence is true a priori if its truth does not depend on experience.[369] A proposition, on the other hand, can only be found to be true or false by experience. We can distinguish a weak and a strong apriority thesis.[370] The weak thesis is limited to claiming that a sentence p is true independent of experience. The strong thesis goes beyond this in claiming that even future empirical experience will not be able to change the attribution of truth to p.

The literature discusses three types of a priori knowledge: logical sentences, eg the sentence 'p v ¬ p', mathematical sentences, eg '8 + 3 = 11', and conceptual truths, eg 'All bachelors are unmarried'.[371] The third

---

[364] Bealer lists no less than eleven different meanings of the concept of analyticity, and his inventory is far from complete. See G Bealer, 'Analyticity' in Craig (ed), *Routledge encyclopedia of philosophy, vol 1* (n 6 above) 234.

[365] Discussions focus, eg, on whether all necessary truths are analytic truths (the so-called coincidence thesis), and whether it is only possible to know analytic truths a priori. See BonJour, *In Defense of Pure Reason* (n 333 above) 12 f.

[366] The arguments against separableness are relatively unconvincing as found in G Harman, 'Quine on Meaning and Existence I' (1968) 21 *Review of Metaphysics* 124 at 131 f. Similar to the line of argument in this book BonJour, *In Defense of Pure Reason* (n 333 above) 6; SA Kripke, 'A Priori Knowledge, Necessity, and Contingency' in PK Moser (ed), *A priori Knowledge* (Oxford, 1987) 145, 148 f; EJ Lowe, 'A Priori' in Lamarque and Asher (eds), *Concise Encyclopedia of Philosophy of Language* (n 17 above) 12; PK Moser, 'A Priori' in Craig (ed), *Routledge Encyclopedia of Philosophy, vol 1* (n 6 above) 4.

[367] Blurred, by contrast, is Boghossian's. He distinguishes metaphysical and epistemological concepts of analyticity, Boghossian, 'Analyticity' (n 331 above) 332, 334.

[368] Fricker, 'Analyticity, Linguistic Practice and Philosophical Method' (n 326 above) 218.

[369] EJ Lowe, 'A Priori' in Lamarque and Asher (eds), *Concise Encyclopedia of Philosophy of Language* (n 17 above) 11.

[370] Boghossian, 'Analyticity' (n 331 above) 333.

[371] See Boghossian, 'Analyticity' (n 331 above) 334.

category shows that semantic knowledge can be made part of the realm of knowledge, and that this creates an overlapping of semantically defined analyticity and apriority.

Finally, sentences can be categorised as necessary or possible according to alethic modality. Necessity is defined as 'true in all possible worlds', while possibility sees the truth of a statement depending on the state of the world. The view held by the coincidence thesis[372] that all analytic statements are necessary has been countered by Kripke.[373]

In the context of the debate on the normativity of linguistic meaning, and the objection of a lack of analyticity targeted against it, semantics take centre-stage. Hence, we will use the narrow, purely semantic concept of analyticity described above. The issues of apriority and modality will only be touched on in passing. The main point to be clarified is whether a proposition can be true solely as a result of its meaning.

(b) WVO Quine's *Word and Object*

Quine's crucial arguments against analyticity are to be found in *Two Dogmas of Empiricism* and in the second chapter of *Word and Object*. Quine's main thesis is: It is never possible to identify an analytically true sentence in a natural language. Quine writes that

> [a] boundary between analytic and synthetic statements simply has not been drawn. That there is such a distinction to be drawn at all is an unempirical dogma of empiricists, a metaphysical article of faith.[374]

In *Two Dogmas*, Quine presents a two-tiered argument, which is developed in §§ 1–4 and §§ 5–6. Quine's holism, the meaning-consequences of which have already been rebutted,[375] is developed in the second part.

In the first part, Quine begins by rejecting as unsatisfactory various efforts at founding analyticity. None of these efforts, he claims, is able to

---

[372] A Millar, 'Analyticity' in Lamarque and Asher (eds), *Concise Encyclopedia of Philosophy of Language* (n 17 above) 93.

[373] Kripke, *Naming and Necessity* (n 21 above) 260–75. Critical, BonJour, *In Defense of Pure Reason* (n 333 above) 11–15.

[374] Quine, 'Two Dogmas of Empiricism' (n 4 above) 37. Quine, on the other hand, assumes that the concept of logical truth in his line of argument is unproblematic. However, as Strawson's example 'No unilluminated book is illuminated' has shown, the concept of synonymity is also indispensable on the level of logical truths. PF Strawson, 'Propositions, Concepts and Logical Truths' in PF Strawson (ed), *Logico-Linguistic Papers* (London, 1971) 117. Different opinion in WVO Quine, 'Truth by Convention' in WVO Quine (ed), *The Ways of Paradox and Other Essays* (Cambridge MA, 1976). and WVO Quine, 'Carnap and Logical Truth' in WVO Quine (ed), *The Ways of Paradox and Other Essays* (Cambridge MA, 1976). In both papers, Quine argues that there is no non-trivial sense in which logic could be analytic.

[375] See pp 156 ff above.

break the circle of closely interconnected, presupposed concepts (analyticity, synonymy, necessity, and rule). Grice and Strawson have shown that Quine's argumentation in the first part of *Two Dogmas* suffers from several weaknesses. For one thing, his implicit measure for the appropriateness of a foundation of analyticity is indefensible, since he, on the one hand, demands that there should be a definition in the sense of necessary and sufficient conditions, and on the other hand, rejects a close interconnection of the concepts.[376] For another thing, a form of synonymy can be sufficiently reasoned against Quine, even if no specific meaning is presupposed.[377] And finally, Quine's last argumentative step towards a radical meaning scepticism remains puzzling. Quine writes:

> For the theory of meaning a conspicuous question is the nature of its objects: what sort of things are meanings? A felt need for meant entities may derive from an earlier failure to appreciate that meaning and reference are distinct. Once the theory of meaning is sharply separated from the theory of reference, it is a short step to recognizing as the primary business of the theory of meaning simply the synonymy of linguistic forms and the analyticity of statements; meanings themselves, as obscure intermediary entities, may well be abandoned.[378]

Quine refuses to endow meaning with the quality of an entity without giving a particularly strong reason. It is more important to note that he immediately draws on this rejection to discredit, without this step being anywhere near comprehensible, the position that there was such a thing as meaning.[379]

In view of these weaknesses, recent literature is to a large extent united with regard to the unconvincing nature of the first part of the *Two Dogmas* and its rejection of analyticity.[380] In *Word and Object*, however, Quine presented a far more elaborate version of his arguments.

The starting point of Quine's deliberations in *Word and Object* is taken from Carnap. He takes the case of a linguist who sets out to test purported translation empirically and in this way aims to discover meanings in a different language. Both Carnap and Quine see a native speaker's reactive answers to specific stimuli as the relevant empirical data. Quine defines the *stimulus meaning* of a sentence for a person to be the class of all the stimulations that would prompt his assent to the sentence.[381] Quine differs from Carnap by examining the meaning of whole sentences, not of individual terms. Quine's linguist arrives at his hypotheses by equating a

---

[376] HP Grice and PF Strawson, 'In Defense of a Dogma' (1956) 65 *The Philosophical Review* 141 at 148.
[377] *Ibid*, 153.
[378] Quine, 'Two Dogmas of Empiricism' (n 4 above) 22.
[379] See BonJour, *In Defense of Pure Reason* (n 333 above) 71.
[380] See BonJour, *In Defense of Pure Reason* (n 333 above) 72 f; Fricker, 'Analyticity, Linguistic Practice and Philosophical Method' (n 326 above) 225.
[381] Quine, *Word and Object* (n 344 above) 32–6.

sentence in his own language with one of the foreign language and observing the native's assent or dissent in the face of non-verbal stimuli. Whereas Carnap chose kindred languages such as English or German for his research, Quine opted for the *radical translation* between unrelated languages that have little or nothing in common.

In *Word and Object*, Quine assumes a behaviourist explanation of reality. Since the only objective reality available to the linguist is formed by reactions, Quine considers semantic concepts to be credible insofar as they are created from this material. According to Quine, this is not the case for analyticity.

In the example presented by Quine[382] the linguist observes a native speaker of a radically foreign tribe. The native utters the one-word-sentence 'gavagai' whenever rabbits scurry by. From this observation, the linguist forms a tentative translation which equates 'gavagai' with 'rabbit' and takes both expressions as a short form of 'Lo, a rabbit'. The linguist is able to test his hypothesis—presupposing that he has learned to recognise the native's assent and dissent as such—by asking, in the presence of rabbits, 'gavagai?' and then comparing the native's reaction with the assent expected. If empirical observations then corroborate his hypothesis, it seems to be the case that the meaning of 'gavagai' corresponds to that of 'rabbit'.

Quine, however, does show that this conclusion is deceptive. The only behaviouristic data available are the native's exclamation and the stimulation, ie the presence of the rabbit. These data, Quine argues, could also be interpreted in such a way that 'gavagai' would be translated as 'rabbit part', 'temporal rabbit stage', 'contiguous collection of rabbit parts', 'rabbithood', or similar. In order to make decisions about the different possible translations, the linguist has to rely on auxiliary means. He has to be able to ask complex questions, eg 'Is this the same gavagai as that?', in order to gradually eliminate various translations as false. To do the latter, he has to rely on a wide range of background assumptions, for instance with regard to the role and translation of articles, pronouns, etc.

This is the decisive step in Quine's line of argument: These background assumptions go far beyond anything that could be accounted for by stimulus data. Depending on the background assumptions chosen by the linguist, several translations could be labelled as correct. The complex question quoted above can be translated, based on background assumptions bg_1–bg_5, as 'Is this the same rabbit as that?' or, based on assumptions bg_6–bg_9, as 'Is this a rabbit stage from the same series as that?'. In relation to their respective assumptions, both translations are equally valid, but remain incompatible with each other. The gavagai stimulation provides

---

[382] Quine, *Word and Object* (n 344 above) 28–30.

insufficient grounds for making the decision between assumptions, and hence between translations. Quine considers this situation of *radical translation* to be proof of his thesis of indeterminacy of translation.[383]

He has shown that agreement between the native speaker and the linguist with regard to stimulus meanings is not sufficient to assume that two sentences S_n and S_l are synonymous. Indeterminacy of translation, however, works both ways: S_n and S_l could be synonymous, even if stimulus meanings are not. The agreement of the latter is neither sufficient nor necessary. The background assumptions alone are crucial.

Originally, Quine develops the thesis of indeterminacy of translation for two—even radically different—languages. However, it can also be applied to two sentences S_1 and S_2 in the *same* language if stimulus meanings for two different speakers of this language are observed.[384] Only the disposition of the *individual* speaker to treat S_1 and S_2 as synonymous seems to be exempt from differences in background assumptions—an individual speaker has only a single set of background assumptions. Hence, the concept of intra-subjective stimulus synonymy might make a behaviourist construction of the synonymy of two sentences possible. Quine, however, shows in another example that this thought is also untenable.[385] The dependency on background assumptions, he reasons, is maintained—they are not by necessity analytic. This was even the case if the assumptions were shared by the whole language community and considered to be virtually constant.[386]

Quine draws the conclusion that synthetic and analytic sentences cannot be clearly separated.[387] Rather, we see the world as a continuum in which opinions are more or less deeply rooted, and we more or less flinch from abandoning them. Even if the project of *radical translation* is epistemological in nature, the consequences drawn by Quine are ontological.[388]

It is very significant that Quine does not stop here. He does not restrict the thesis of the indeterminacy of translation to deny the assumption of analyticity.[389] Rather, he is opposed to the assumption of mental objects as

---

[383] Quine, *Word and Object* (n 344 above) 71–9.
[384] Fricker, 'Analyticity, Linguistic Practice and Philosophical Method' (n 326 above) 227.
[385] Quine, *Word and Object* (n 344 above) 50 f.
[386] Quine later agreed in principle that the distinction analytic/synthetic can be used within a language, see WVO Quine, 'Use and Its Place in Meaning' in WVO Quine (ed), *Theories and Things* (Cambridge MA, 1981) 45, 54.
[387] Quine, *Word and Object* (n 344 above) 66.
[388] See Fricker, 'Analyticity, Linguistic Practice and Philosophical Method' (n 326 above) 222. The ontological indeterminacy thesis is particularly pronounced in WVO Quine, 'Ontological Relativity' (1968) 65 *The Journal of Philosophy* 185.
[389] He is joined in this by, among others, Peacocke, 'Holism' (n 314 above) 235, and N Stavropoulos, *Objectivity in Law* (Oxford, 1996) 40 fn 59.

such, and completely dismisses the existence of linguistic meaning.[390] For Quine, there is no correct answer to the question of what 'gavagai' really means to the native speaker. Following Harman, Bonjour describes this radical sceptical conclusion as follows:

> [For Quine,] psychological attitudes like belief turn out to be attitudes only to sentences, not to determinate propositions or meanings.[391]

(c) Criticism

If Quine's claim that there are no propositions, only sentences, is correctly characterised as radical scepticism,[392] initial objections are obvious. By denying propositions, we deny the possibility of defining human communication as rational discourse. This position is—especially in the light of the crucial role propositional speech acts have according to Brandom's analysis—counter-productive to a high degree. It seems reasonable to consider this a *reduction ad absurdum*, even in the face of Quine's expressed conviction to the contrary.[393]

Even if one disregards this radical scepticism, Quine's criticism of the concept of analyticity remains extremely far-reaching. Fricker has pointed to the consequences of removing apriority and analyticity from the armoury of thought.[394] Crucial philosophical questions can no longer be answered. It is therefore small wonder that Quine's thesis—that there was no way, not even in some cases, of making a determined distinction between analytic and synthetic—has been called 'absurd'.[395] Both the semantics of common sense and large areas of philosophical thought share the intuition of there being analyticity. An appeal to intuition is no strong argument. But neither is as weak as has often been claimed. One should be able to expect that, in particular, theories of meaning be intuitively plausible. Hence, the fact that intuitions of this distinction are shared by the vast majority of a language community should by all means be used as a prima facie argument for the existence of this distinction.[396]

---

[390] See BonJour, *In Defense of Pure Reason* (n 333 above) 78 f; A Orenstein, 'Quine, Willard Van Orman' in Craig (ed), *Routledge Encyclopedia of Philosophy, vol 8* (n 6 above) 12.

[391] BonJour, *In Defense of Pure Reason* (n 333 above) 79.

[392] The question of whether, according to Quine's theory, there is any way to avoid radical scepticism, is answered in the negative, BonJour, *In Defense of Pure Reason* (n 333 above) 89–97.

[393] BonJour, *In Defense of Pure Reason* (n 333 above) 79.

[394] Fricker, 'Analyticity, Linguistic Practice and Philosophical Method' (n 326 above) 237.

[395] Grice and Strawson, 'In Defense of a Dogma' (n 376 above) 143. See also H Putnam, 'The Analytic and the Synthetic (1962)' in Putnam (ed), *Mind, Language, and Reality. Philosophical Papers. vol 2* (n 21 above) 42, 69.

[396] Fricker, 'Analyticity, Linguistic Practice and Philosophical Method' (n 326 above) 219. See also W Kersting, 'Baseball ist unser Leben' Frankfurter Allgemeine Zeitung (7 August 2000) 49. A transcendental argument for the rational intuition of aprioric knowledge is

174 *Normativity and Objectivity of Linguistic Meaning*

Not only the consequences, but also the foundations of Quinean meaning scepticism seem problematical. First of all, one may challenge Quine's behaviourist basis. In a general remark on Quine's philosophy, Gibson notes that Quine's behaviourism contains significant preliminary decisions:

> Quine's behaviourism prescribes the content of almost all of his more important doctrines and theses by restricting, ahead of time, what are to count as acceptable answers to a multitude of philosophical questions.[397]

In *Word and Object*, Quine's line of argument depends significantly on behaviourist elements, as eg stimulus meaning. Once behaviourism is rejected, Quine's argumentation is robbed of its basis.[398]

Another important limitation is the result of Quine not claiming an intrinsic inconsistency of the concept of analyticity, but rather being opposed to its application to natural languages.[399] Furthermore, Quine is convinced of the relevance of the heavily idealised and conspicuously unrealistic situation of *radical translation*, even though the issue at hand is expressly the use of analyticity in natural languages.[400] The choice of *radical translation*, of all things, for an examination of meaning in natural languages may be possible to explain in view of Quine's fixation on Carnap, but it would be hard to justify.

Notwithstanding these manifold issues with Quine's argumentation, we will take a closer look at his thesis of the indeterminacy of translation. It key argumentative step lies in the claim that any translation manual is relative. We will confront this claim with the normativity thesis advanced in this book (1) and subsequently reduce the range of the former (2). Based on these considerations it will be possible to establish analyticity in a form sufficient to support the normativity thesis (3).

(1) Relativity and Normativity In his 'gavagai' example, Quine shows that it does not make sense to speak of language-independent meanings. Rather, translations from one language to another—and hence meaning as such—were always relative to a set of analytic hypotheses.[401] This point will not be denied by a thesis of the normativity of meaning.

---

discussed by Q Cassam, 'Rationalism, Empiricism, and the A Priori' in Boghossian and Peacocke (eds), *New Essays on the A priori* (n 341 above) 47.

[397] RF Gibson, *The Philosophy of WV Quine* (Gainesville FL, 1982) XX.

[398] BonJour, *In Defense of Pure Reason* (n 333 above) 81; K Puhl, 'Introduction' in Puhl (ed), *Meaning Scepticism* (n 41 above) 11.

[399] See Fricker, 'Analyticity, Linguistic Practice and Philosophical Method' (n 326 above) 218 fn 1.

[400] See Fricker, 'Analyticity, Linguistic Practice and Philosophical Method' (n 326 above) 222.

[401] See A Orenstein, 'Quine, Willard Van Orman' in Craig (ed), *Routledge Encyclopedia of Philosophy*, vol 8 (n 6 above) 12.

On the other hand, one may wonder whether Quine's relativity thesis has to result in a radical meaning scepticism which is used to attack the thesis of normativity. The translation project is not a mere description of some regularity, but rather a quest for a rule which makes communication across cultures possible. Hence, Quine's project already contains the idea of normativity.[402] With his theory of analyticity postulates, Carnap tried to establish an analyticity which was language-relative.[403] According to his theory, relations between meanings, eg the incompatibility of the predicates 'bachelor' and 'married', are determined in a set of postulates. Based on these postulates, one may make the following definition: Sentences are considered to be analytical if they are the result of the totality of meaning postulates. Thus, analyticity would refer to linguistic rules which have been made explicitly.

Carnap, however, used the analyticity postulates to set up an empirical artificial language L_E. It goes without saying that, as a rule, such precise word-use agreements are not entered into within natural languages.[404] A theory of the normativity of meaning would suggest that translation schemes, acknowledged by the participants as mandatory, have been adopted for the languages of our culture group. However, Quine vehemently opposes precisely this way of 'saving' analyticity by linguistic conventions.[405]

The central issue between Quine and the normativity theories of analyticity is exactly the question of whether analyticity can be based on linguistic norms within a language community. The key to this is how the relativity of background assumptions, and the indeterminism of linguistic meaning derived from it, are assessed. It would only be justified to arrive at a radical meaning scepticism if one had to assume a very high degree of relativity.

(2) Analyticity's Triadic Relativity In order to assess the range of Quine's relativity thesis, we will distinguish *three dimensions of the relativity of analyticity*. All three dimensions go back to the dependency of analyticity on background assumptions demonstrated by Quine.

---

[402] See Lance and Hawthorne, *The Grammar of Meaning. Normativy and Semantic Discourse* (n 35 above) 12.

[403] R Carnap, 'Meaning Postulates' in R Carnap (ed), *Meaning and Necessity. A Study in Semantics and Modal Logic* (Chicago IL, 1956) 222. See also TMV Janssen, 'Meaning Postulate' in Lamarque and Asher (eds), *Concise Encyclopedia of Philosophy of Language* (n 17 above) 2410 f; G Wolters, 'Analytizitätspostulat' in J Mittelstraß (ed), *Enzyklopädie Philosophie und Wissenschaftstheorie. Band 1* (Stuttgart, 1995) 106.

[404] F Kambartel, 'Analytisch' in J Mittelstraß (ed), *Enzyklopädie Philosophie und Wissenschaftstheorie. Band 1* (Stuttgart, 1995) 106. Compare A Orenstein, 'Quine, Willard Van Orman' in Craig (ed), *Routledge Encyclopedia of Philosophy, vol 8* (n 6 above) 11.

[405] See BonJour, *In Defense of Pure Reason* (n 333 above) 51–8.

The first dimension of relativity is the relative social validity within a specific language community. According to the reversibility thesis,[406] however, analyticity is—this is the second dimension—also only valid for a limited period of time (temporally relative), even within a language community. Finally, all or just some of a language's propositions can be marked as analytic, which gives analyticity a third dimension of relativity with regard to distribution.

Based on these three dimensions, the normativity theory of meaning is able to defend a weakened, language-relative analyticity.[407] Hence, crucial points of Quine's criticism are defused immediately. According to the first relation, one can draw conclusions from the difficulties Quine demonstrated in the case of analyticity across languages and limit analyticity to a single language community. Relying on the second dimension, Quine's reversibility thesis can be accepted. Yet simultaneously, we can claim that analyticity remains stable over limited periods of time. In the third dimension, Quine's rejection of analyticity for many, even for most of a language's sentences can be accepted.[408] A theory of normativity does not have to mark an overwhelming, or even just a larger part of language's propositions as analytical. Quine's line of reasoning relies on *not a single sentence* being analytical, especially with regard to the meaning-sceptical consequences. Quine is rebutted the moment we can show that there is so much as a single analytical sentence.

In defence of Quine it would be possible to contend that a thesis of analyticity modified to this degree will not be strong enough to support a theory of the normativity of linguistic meaning.[409] The validity of this objection depends on how much the analyticity thesis is weakened by the acceptance of the triadic relativity. This, in turn, will be crucially influenced by the constancy of analyticity within the three dimensions, which can be imagined as a value scale. It is difficult to determine the level of constancy we would need before we can speak of a normativity of linguistic meaning. There is, however, much more clarity as regards the extreme end-points of the scales, which can be elucidated using two languages, L_1 and L_2.

In L_1, the analyticity of propositions changes hourly. Furthermore, the make-up of the L_1 language community is subject to considerable change on a day-to-day basis. As a result, 80 per cent of its members are unable to

---

[406] See pp 158 ff above.

[407] On relative analyticity see Kambartel, 'Analytisch' (n 404 above) 106. Fricker distinguishes two dimensions of relative analyticity, Fricker, 'Analyticity, Linguistic Practice and Philosophical Method' (n 326 above) 243.

[408] See Fricker, 'Analyticity, Linguistic Practice and Philosophical Method' (n 326 above) 230, 233.

[409] See A Orenstein, 'Quine, Willard Van Orman' in Craig (ed), *Routledge Encyclopedia of Philosophy, vol 8* (n 6 above) 12.

The Normativity of Linguistic Meaning   177

agree to 90 per cent of the analyticity meanings they shared previously. Finally, only eight per cent of the propositions of this language can be labelled as analytic. In L_2, on the other hand, the analytic meaning of all propositions has remained constant for centuries, and the make-up of the language community also stays the same. Whilst Quine's conclusion may be justified for L_1, for L_2, it is in fact patently absurd.

Whether the normativity thesis of meaning can be maintained for a language L_x depends on the degree of constancy that analyticity has over the three dimensions. We can describe this degree of constancy as a similarity of L_x to L_1 or L_2. If a normativity thesis of meaning is to be upheld for the highly developed languages of Europe, they have to be shown to be closer to L_2 than to L_1.

The key idea of the thesis of triadic relative analyticity developed on these pages is that Brandom's theory can be used to provide this proof of similarity. Using Brandomian theory of normativity, Carnap's idea of language-relative analyticity can be transferred to natural languages, making it possible to prove that there is a sufficient degree of constancy. The most important role is played by the simple material substitution-inferential commitments (SMSICs). The meaning of propositions consists in SMSICs, and they determine whether a proposition is analytic or not. As a result of these inferential relations, every speech act is normatively situated in two ways: On the one hand, by showing the correct conditions, and on the other hand, by showing the correct consequences. The same holds true for analytic propositions. An analytic proposition's distinctive feature is the fact that the correct condition of use consists solely in its meaning, while the correct consequence consists solely in the proposition's being true without further conditions. Synthetic sentences, on the other hand, have as correct conditions of use at least one empirical factual claim.

Since the conditions and the consequences can be made explicit in inferences, a proposition's quality can also be made explicit as analytic. The inferences' correctness is assessed based on the norms created in the language community by the participants' normative attitudes. With regard to the propositions' truth, the speakers are also treated as entitled or committed. A judgement is analytic if the meaning of the proposition alone is sufficient for the speaker to be acknowledged as being entitled to make the proposition in the language game. Conversely, the commitment to a proposition's truth by meaning includes the commitment that the proposition is analytic. Hence, discursive authority and discursive taking on of responsibility refer, on the one hand, to the meaning, and on the other hand, to the analytic or synthetic quality of a proposition.

The key aspect of this analysis is that it neither assumes meanings to be static entities, nor does it suppose that analyticity is constructed independently of the attitudes taken by a language community's speakers. In parts, Quine's 'gavagai' example reads like Brandomian theory. Brandom also does not understand analyticity to be abstract or subject to change, but rather as the result of the speakers' attitudes. A sentence is analytic if the speakers treat it as one. Quine is mistaken if he bases a continuum of sentences on *this* fact. This conclusion would only be justified if the speakers' attitudes demonstrated extreme relativity of analyticity, ie if the speakers themselves made no difference. However, it is evident from the practice of deontic score-keeping that the distinction between analytic and synthetic sentences plays an important role. With regard to the theory of analyticity, this means that distinctions can be made because they are made by the language community. The most important point of Quine's criticism has no substance: The fact that the question of analyticity depends on the speakers' attitudes and background assumptions is not a challenge, but rather forms an integral part of a normativity theory of meaning that is founded in pragmatics.

The thesis of the indeterminacy of translation is unable to support Quine's far-reaching conclusions. The premise that a translation is relative to a set of analytic hypotheses may be the case. But it does not follow that rational discourse on linguistic meaning is impossible. Hypotheses can be made explicit and discussed. In this way, the quality of a conclusion can be assessed. Brandom provides the terminological system necessary for this kind of language-analytical discourse. Hence, Quine's relativity theory is not disquieting. Dependency on background assumptions not only does not unsettle normative meaning. On the contrary, it only shows how language communities create the latter. Against this background, Quinean relativity thesis can be read as a downright affirmation of Brandom's theory. There can be no question of a degree of relativity which would justify scepticism. From the perspective of Brandom's normativity thesis, Quine's example proves the exact opposite of his theses—that linguistic meaning and analyticity exist, based on implicit background assumptions within a language community.

Against this backdrop, Quine's all-or-nothing argumentation—which either constructs analyticity in terms of eternal, immutable truths, or rejects it outright as mere pretence—becomes implausible. Simultaneously, we can reject the categorical distinction between natural and artificial languages and opt to soften it. While one has to agree with Kambartel's assertion that in natural languages, definitions do not have the same precision as in artificial languages,[410] this does not mean that natural languages could or would have to do without analyticity. In this sense, Brandom's theory covers the middle ground between Carnap's analyticity postulates and Quine's radical scepticism. Our languages are halfway

---

[410] See Kambartel, 'Analytisch' (n 404 above) 105 f.

between the uncertain language L_1 and the static language L_2. The triadic relativity of analyticity is strong enough to support the normativity of linguistic meaning.

(3) OLOL Analyticity Acknowledging triadic relativity addresses some of the main points of Quine's criticism. Based on Brandom, however, we can demonstrate that we are entitled to draw the sceptical conclusion. It is important to distinguish analytic and synthetic judgements in linguistic practice. In the language game, the participants attribute truth-values to propositions through deontic score-keeping, a process that may also be based on analyticity. Following Fricker,[411] this relative, weaker analyticity may be called OLOL analyticity: The principle of 'our language is our language' emphasises the pragmatic foundation of linguistic meaning. Thus we take leave of a point of view which considered only eternal truths to be a sufficient basis for analyticity. Simultaneously, we have proved that in the language game, there is constancy and safety enough to reject Quinean relativity and indeterminism theses.[412] Quine is right in rejecting reference to mere intuition. *Semantic facts* are not just true. We need something that supervenes meaning, an external standard with a regulative potential. Quine sees this standard in behaviourism. The position argued here finds it in the implicit norms of linguistic practice.

If we take the latter understanding as a basis, the fact that the analyticity of propositions is changeable does not mean that it does not exist.[413] Davidson puts it as follows: 'Our concepts are ours, but that doesn't mean they don't truly, as well as usefully, describe an objective reality'.[414]

Relativity of background assumptions is a precondition, not a threat to a normative theory of linguistic meaning. OLOL analyticity explains, in the first place, how philosophical problems, including scepticism, arise.[415] It is a prerequisite for the possibility of rationality. In this sense, what Bonjour stated for the related problem of apriority is also true for analyticity:

---

[411] See Fricker, 'Analyticity, Linguistic Practice and Philosophical Method' (n 326 above) 231.
[412] A fact overlooked by Matthias Kaufmann, who with reference to Quine's Two Dogmas assumes 'that there is no hiatus between analytic and empirical judgement, but rather a gradual transfer'. M Kaufmann, *Rechtsphilosophie* (Freiburg, 1996) 21, 102.
[413] See Fricker, 'Analyticity, Linguistic Practice and Philosophical Method' (n 326 above) 243.
[414] D Davidson, 'Is Truth a Goal of Inquiry? Discussion with Rorty' in UM Zeglen (ed), *Donald Davidson: Truth, Meaning and Knowledge* (London, 1999) 19.
[415] BonJour, *In Defense of Pure Reason* (n 333 above) xi. Fricker, 'Analyticity, Linguistic Practice and Philosophical Method' (n 326 above) 246. K Puhl, 'Introduction' in Puhl (ed), *Meaning Scepticism* (n 41 above) 11.

Thus we see that the repudiation of all *a priori* justification is apparently tantamount to the repudiation of argument or reasoning generally, thus amounting in effect to intellectual suicide.[416]

Based on triadic relative OLOL analyticity, we are able to reject Quine's elimination argument from the first part of *Two Dogmas*. Quine never discussed this variation, which invalidates his argument. The norms of discursive practice, following Brandom, constitute substantial truth based in pragmatics, and provide the foundation for analyticity.[417]

D. Result for the Normativity of Linguistic Meaning

Sceptical objections to the theory of semantic normativity have been shown to be unsustainable. Based on the default-and-challenge structure of entitlement, a non-regressive anti-reductionist normativity can be defended against Kripke's *sceptical paradox*. The claim of universal reversibility resulting from Quine's semantic holism was countered with the thesis of the necessary incorporation of immune sentences, ie a moderate holism which assumes limited reversibility, and considers holistic structures to be accessible, as it is possible to analyse them using expressive vocabulary. Finally, we defended against the objection of non-existing analyticity a triadic relativist OLOL analyticity, which relies on the relativity of background assumptions to explain analytic meaning, and hence avoids sceptical conclusions.

The four strategies—truth, internal relations, rationality, and regularity—*collectively* support the theory of semantic normativity. In his theory, Brandom has elaborated on these reasons and their interconnections. In developing a connection between inferential semantics and normative pragmatics in discursive practice, he came across the three essential conditions for a concept of normativity.[418] First, through the principle of instituting norms through social practice, this connection assumes an anti-reductionist supervenience of semantic norms. Secondly, the principle of the normative significance of concepts satisfies the condition of internality by showing genuinely *semantic* normativity. The assertional practice of giving and asking for reasons is not a requirement external to semantics, but rather the intrinsic property of every meaningful use of language. Whenever we speak, we invariably assume that this game and its rules exist. Thirdly, in the model of deontic score-keeping, the complex configurations of inferential relations and normative statuses and

---

[416] BonJour, *In Defense of Pure Reason* (n 333 above) 5.
[417] Quine later supported the application of the concept of analyticity within a single language. See Quine, 'Use and Its Place in Meaning' (n 386 above) 43–54.
[418] On the three conditions, see pp 98 ff above.

corresponding normative attitudes create the possibility of semantic mistakes. Whenever a score-keeper errs in his classification of inferential relations, or wrongly attributes claims or entitlements—ie is at fault about deontic statuses—he makes a mistake about meaning.

The combination of all four strategies provides us with a justification to speak strongly about semantic normativity.

III. THE OBJECTIVITY OF LINGUISTIC MEANING

If we consider linguistic meaning to be irreducible, we have to enquire into the relation of the normative and the non-normative. Based on the concept of objectivity (A), we find two basic approaches (B) and (C) to discussing this relation. The connection between normative pragmatics, inferential semantics, and socially structured objectivity established on these pages will have to be defended against its critics (D) and, finally, has to be summarised in a single comprehensive thesis (E).

A. The Concept of Objectivity

The concept of objectivity is complex and diverse.[419] It is employed in a large number of philosophical disciplines, among them epistemology, semantics, and metaphysics. In current epistemological and ontological thinking, the concept of objectivity is essentially considered to be imparted through language.[420] We can elucidate on this using the positions of Davidson, Putnam, and Dummett. Davidson considers the concepts of truth and objectivity to be congruent:

> To have the concept of truth is to have the concept of objectivity, the notion of a proposition being true or false independent of one's beliefs or interests.[421]

Putnam's internal realism, however, will only admit this identity in ideal epistemological conditions. He claims that outside of these, there can be no immediate access to a reality as such. Rather, one chooses one of several competing theoretical descriptions of reality based on epistemic values—eg coherence or rational acceptability. These values

---

[419] See Coleman and Leiter, 'Determinacy, Objectivity, and Authority' (n 3 above) 242.
[420] See D Davidson, 'The Problem of Objectivity' (1995) *Tijdschrift voor filosofie* 203 at 220. On the conceptual history see S Heßbrüggen-Walter, 'Objektivität' in HJ Sandkühler (ed), *Enzyklopädie Philosophie. Band 2* (Hamburg, 1999) 975 f.
[421] Davidson, 'The Problem of Objectivity' (n 420 above) 211.

define a kind of objectivity, *objectivity for us*, even if it is not the metaphysical objectivity of the God's Eye view. Objectivity and rationality humanly speaking are what we have; they are better than nothing.[422]

Dummett, finally, emphasises the fact that objectivity is an essential condition for the possibility of communication within a language community:

> Experience can be characterized only as the experience of a common world inhabited by others as well as me; it is intrinsic to our grasp of our language that we take testimony as contributing to our stock of information.[423]

These deliberations have addressed the two central meanings of the concept of objectivity. First, objectivity—in the sense of *concreteness*—means referring to the object of perception, thinking, and language.[424] Objectivity in the sense of object-relatedness implies that objects remain independent of the performance of cognition, ie so-called *investigation independence* or *mind independence*.[425] In its second meaning, objectivity stands for matter-of-factness, impartiality, necessary general validity,[426] implying *intersubjective validity and invariability* of a statement.[427]

With reference to these two notional lines, there are two possible approaches to discussing the objectivity of linguistic meaning. The first focuses on the relation of semantics and objectivity in terms of reference (B); the second on the relation of semantics and objectivity in terms of intersubjectivity (C).

---

[422] H Putnam, *Reason, Truth and History* (Cambridge, 1981) 55.

[423] M Dummett, 'Realism and Anti-Realism' in Dummett (ed), *The Seas of Language* (n 65 above) 471.

[424] This understanding of objectivity predominated in the German-speaking world until the 19th century, see J Grimm and W Grimm, *Deutsches Wörterbuch. Band 7* (Leipzig, 1889) column 1109.

[425] Postema, 'Objectivity Fit for Law' (n 195 above) 105 f; J Raz, 'Notes on value and objectivity' in J Raz (ed), *Engaging Reason. On the Theory of Value and Action* (Oxford, 1999) 125; Wright, 'Rule-following, Objectivity and the Theory of Meaning' (n 4 above) 99.

[426] See Heßbrüggen-Walter, 'Objektivität' (n 420 above) 975; Raz, 'Notes on value and objectivity' (n 425 above) 119; C Thiel, 'Objektiv/Objektivität' in J Mittelstraß (ed), *Enzyklopädie Philosophie und Wissenschaftstheorie. Band 2* (Mannheim, 1984) 1053.

[427] Postema, 'Objectivity Fit for Law' (n 195 above) 108 f. Kant combines both readings of the concept. In his Prolegomena, he distinguishes between objective judgements of experience and subjective judgements of perception. Judgements of experience refer to an object and, due to their referring to an object, we mean them to have necessary general validity. See I Kant, *Prolegomena zu einer jeden künftigen Metaphysik, die als Wissenschaft wird auftreten können*, 6th edn (Hamburg, 1976) para 18. and P Rohs, 'Die transzendentale Deduktion als Lösung von Invarianzproblemen' in Ff Philosophie (ed), *Kants transzendentale Deduktion und die Möglichkeit von Transzendentalphilosophie* (Frankfurt am Main, 1988) 137 f.

B. Objectivity as Reference

The problem of the object-relatedness of intentionality and language concerns the question of how thought and speech are able to refer to objects and states of affairs that are not themselves in the same sense referring to anything else.[428] It concerns an explanation of the relation of language to things outside of language.

In the spectrum of theories, the extreme systematic ends are, on the one hand, a radical theory of reference, and on the other, a theory of complete independence. The radical theory of reference identifies semantic meaning with the representational dimension. Propositional content and object-relatedness are simply equated. Accordingly, representation is both a necessary and a sufficient condition for the explanation of semantic content. The opposing position considers language to be fully without reference. Words are, in Adorno's visualisation,[429] 'mere tokens' in the language game. According to this school of thought, representation is neither sufficient nor necessary to explain linguistic meaning.[430]

The position advocated on these pages rejects both extremes and suggests striking a balance, following Brandom. We have to dismiss as too one-sided the opinion of the theories of reference, ie that linguistic meaning consists solely or primarily in the representation of facts.[431] Nevertheless, the reference of a statement is one correctness condition among others, be it only on account of the connection[432] of truth and the normativity of linguistic meaning assumed in this work. Explaining how objects are picked out, and how the relation language has to the world works, ie explaining the problem of reference, is essential for a theory of linguistic meaning. According to the integrative approach advocated above,[433] object-relatedness may not be a sufficient element of an adequate theory of meaning, but it is nonetheless an essential one.[434]

This implies explaining reference in terms of inference (i). Subsequently, we will examine the principal expressive means which make possible the explicit-making of the representational dimension of meaning. The expressive vocabulary has three dimensions. It includes the relation to individual

---

[428] See Brandom, *Making It Explicit* (n 1 above) 548.
[429] TW Adorno, 'Taubstummenanstalt' in TW Adorno (ed), *Minima moralia. Reflexionen aus dem beschädigten Leben* (Frankfurt am Main, 1969) 179.
[430] See, however, Davidson: 'It is good to be rid of representations, and with them the correspondence theory of truth, for it is thinking there are representations that engenders thoughts of relativism'. D Davidson, 'The Myth of the Subjective' in M Krausz (ed), *Relativism. Interpretation and Confrontation* (Notre Dame IN, 1989) 165 f.
[431] Brandom, *Making It Explicit* (n 1 above) 121.
[432] See p 101 above.
[433] See p 114 above.
[434] The object-relatedness of language also plays an important role in legal interpretation, see DO Brink, 'Legal Interpretation, Objectivity and Morality' (n 3 above) 25.

objects using *singular termini* (ii) and the latter's integration in *de dicto* and *de re* ascriptions (iii). Due to the relativity—as regards social practice—of the object-relatedness of language (iv), the propagation of representational content is carried out in *anaphoric* chains (v).

(i) Reference and Inference

Ever since Frege, *inference* has been analysed in terms of *reference*. Brandom turns this explanatory sequence on its head and shows how reference can be explained in terms of inference.[435] According to Dummett's model mentioned above, inferences from the appropriate circumstances of a linguistic utterance to its appropriate consequences (among others) are essential to propositional and conceptual content.[436] The circumstances of using a concept do not themselves have to be linguistic in nature; according to this model, the use of *any* term will contain inferential commitments. This is especially true for empirical concepts, which are used to express perceptions and protocols of observation. Using the concept 'red ball' includes, as a non-linguistic precondition, the empirical existence of a red ball. Simultaneously, it contains the inferential commitment that inferential consequences of 'red ball', eg 'coloured ball', apply to anything that 'red ball' is properly applied to.

In this way, the representational dimension of language can be integrated into the inferentialist concept of linguistic meaning using *non-inferential, non-linguistic* empirical preconditions.[437] Using this relation of inference and reference, we can explain key aspects of Putnam's well-known twin earth thought experiment.[438] On twin earth there is a liquid called 'twater' which has properties identical to those of our substance H_2O, but is chemically different, having the molecular structure 'XYZ'. Based on this objective difference, the terms 'water' and 'twater' have *different* circumstances of correct usage and hence different *inferential* contents. So even though terms acquire meaning through their users' practices, as long as earthlings and twearthlings lack the empirical knowledge necessary to distinguish H_2O and XYZ, they remain unable to state that their concepts differ. Speakers are not omniscient about the inferential commitments implicit in their own concepts. An interpreter who is able to distinguish

---

[435] See Brandom, *Making It Explicit* (n 1 above) 136.
[436] See p 127 above.
[437] Brandom distinguishes two types of non-inferential circumstances and consequences of use: The specifically empirical conceptual content that concepts exhibit by virtue of their connection to language entries in perception and the specifically practical conceptual content that concepts exhibit in virtue of their connection to language exits in action. See Brandom, *Making It Explicit* (n 1 above) 131. It is solely the empirical content which plays a role with regard to the problem of reference.
[438] Brandom, *Making It Explicit* (n 1 above) 119 f.

H₂O and XYZ, can, however, understand earthlings transported to twearth who, confronted with XYZ, use the term 'water': He understands them as *mistaking* the XYZ they look at for H₂O and therefore, as *inappropriately* applying the concept they express with their word 'water' to that unearthly stuff.

The essential connection between inference and reference is: As *language entry moves* which have empirical content, judgements of perception are part of inferential semantics.[439] Inferential semantics are able to integrate conceptual circumstances and consequences, even where they elude inferential terms. Since deontic score-keepers differ in their ability to classify empirical circumstances correctly, understanding—as an affair which is not solely linguistic in nature—is graded according to perceptive abilities and expert knowledge. Brandom concludes:

> [T]hinking [and speaking, MK] clearly is a matter of knowing what one is committing oneself to by a certain claim, and what would entitle one to that commitment.[440]

(ii) Frege's Analysis of Picking Out Objects

Even if Frege does not do sufficient justice to the social dimension of linguistic meaning, his analysis (in *Grundlagen der Arithmetik*) of picking out objects still offers valuable insights into the problem of reference. The grammatical category of expressions which are used to refer to objects when thinking or speaking is called *Eigenname* (proper name) by Frege.[441] Proper names can be used as simple singular termini, eg 'Bach', or as definite descriptions of sortals and predicates, such as 'the composer of the Matthäus-Passion'. Frege focuses on the later, because he considers the definite article as fundamental to any explicit-making of a singular referential purport.[442]

Frege asks the question of how linguistic expressions may be used in order to be *successful* in referring to specific objects. According to Frege, the correctness of using the definite article depends on the two requirements of existence and individuation:

> If, however, we wished to use [a] concept for defining an object falling under it, it would, of course, be necessary first to show two distinct things: 1. that some object falls under this concept; 2. that only one object falls under it.[443]

---

[439] Brandom, *Making It Explicit* (n 1 above) 235. See also Brandom, *Articulating Reasons. An Introduction to Inferentialism* (n 129 above) 28 f.
[440] Dummett, 'Realism and Anti-Realism' (n 423 above) 471.
[441] Frege, *Die Grundlagen der Arithmetik* (n 166 above) para 51.
[442] Frege, *Die Grundlagen der Arithmetik* (n 166 above) para 56 and annotation to para 74.
[443] Frege, *Die Grundlagen der Arithmetik* (n 166 above) annotation to para 74.

Brandom has shown that both requirements can be understood in deontic score-keeping terms.[444] Both requirements state what sort of *commitment* is expressed by the speaker's use of the definite article, and what is required for *entitlement* to that commitment. For a full practical understanding of propositions it is essential that not only the first, but also the second commitment be included. Otherwise, it may be possible to grasp the use of whole sentences in the sense of what it is to take them to be true, yet only in connection with the condition of individuation can it be explained what it is to apply a sentence *to* something or take it to be true *of* something.

To begin with, we have to explain the individuation requirement. It declares that any judgement directed toward *what* a proposition refers to can be intelligible only in the context of practices identifying objects as the same again, and individuating them as distinct. This means that the use of expressions as singular terms essentially involves not only norms that specify criteria of *application*, but also those that specify norms of *identity*.[445] Independent of possible epistemological errors in recognition-judgements,[446] there has to be a notion of *correctness* of identifications and discriminations. This correctness can be determined using the normative practices of deontic score-keeping, which record specific types of claims and entitlement and thus determine the meaning of identity claims. Every recognition judgement can be understood as the use of identity criteria: It contains a claim of identity.

Following Frege and Brandom, identity claims can be understood as making explicit substitution licenses. Their discursive result is the undertaking of a simple material substitution-inferential commitment (SMSIC).[447] This is the explanation of reference based on inference sought for: The reference to objects intended consists in the use of substitutional commitments which combine varying terms.

For a speaker to be *entitled* to an identity claim in the shape of a recognition-judgement, at least one non-trivial recognition claim has to be *true*, ie the set of substitutional commitments associated with each term has to be non-empty. It is only in this case that referential *purport* is crowned with referential *success*.[448] The entitlement to substitution-inferential commitments depend on the appropriate circumstances of the use of singular terms. One of these circumstances is the existence of the

---

[444] Brandom, *Making It Explicit* (n 1 above) 415 f.
[445] Frege writes: 'If we are to use the symbol a to signify an object, we must have a criterion for deciding in all cases whether b is the same as a, even if it is not always in our power to apply this criterion'. Frege, *Die Grundlagen der Arithmetik* (n 166 above) para 62. See Brandom, *Making It Explicit* (n 1 above) 416.
[446] On recognition judgements as a sentence category see Frege, *Die Grundlagen der Arithmetik* (n 166 above) paras 62, 106.
[447] With regard to these commitments see p 138 below.
[448] Brandom, *Making It Explicit* (n 1 above) 425 f, 433.

object the speaker intends to refer to. We have thus reached the first of Frege's requirements: the existence requirement.

The existence requirement states that a singular term may only be successful in referring to an object if it can be shown that there exists at least one object falling under the concept.[449] Asserting an existence claim means undertaking an *existential commitment*, a species of substitutional commitments. Brandom distinguishes three sorts of existential commitment: numerical, physical, and fictional. What these commitments share is the way in which their pragmatic significance is determined by a set of expressions playing the role of canonical designators.[450] Essentially, this consists of systematically stating addresses for all existing objects belonging to the type in question, eg, in the case of a physical commitment, giving specific spatiotemporal co-ordinates.

There is no need to go into the details of this analysis. What remains important is that the role of both of Frege's requirements can be analysed in deontic score-keeping terms. The cognitive and conceptual access to individual objects can be explained in terms of the deontic score-keeper's ability to treat sentences containing singular terms in such a way that they express identity claims and existence commitments. Singular terms have been shown to be necessary for explaining the possibility of individuals. They bridge the gap between 'saying something' and 'talking *about* something'. Simultaneously, the minimal requirement of at least one true non-trivial substitutional commitment reconfirms the necessary link between normativity and truth.[451] Of necessity, the object-relatedness of language in normative practice results in the integration of truth claims into the concept of meaning.

(iii) Reference and de re Ascriptions

De re ascriptions are the essential expressive vocabulary used to make explicit the representational dimension of propositional content.[452] Ever since scholasticism, the conceptual pair *de dicto* and *de re* has been used to analyse two types of ascribing propositional attitudes.[453] The statement 'a believes *that* b has the property P' is interpreted as *de dicto* if what a

---

[449] Frege, *Die Grundlagen der Arithmetik* (n 166 above) para 95.
[450] Brandom, *Making It Explicit* (n 1 above) 440–49.
[451] See pp 101 above.
[452] Brandom, *Making It Explicit* (n 1 above) 508. Strictly speaking, Brandom distinguishes two types of expressive representational vocabulary. Next to de re ascriptions, these are expressions such as 'true' and 'refers to'. Brandom discusses these anaphoric operators in ch 5 of *Making It Explicit*. See Brandom, *Making It Explicit* (n 1 above) 138, 499. Finally, it is worth mentioning that Brandom achieves a highly interesting analysis of intentional states and actions by distinguishing de re and de dicto ascriptions. See Brandom, *Making It Explicit* (n 1 above) 520–29.
[453] See Quine, *Quantifiers*. Critical Kneale, *Modality*, 626, 632.

believes is specified by the whole part of the sentence following the belief operator, ie 'b has the property P'. *De re*, however, the statement says that a believes *of* the object b that it has the property P.

In linguistic practice, *de re* and *de dicto* ascriptions are often jumbled, with the representational dimension often only implicitly existing. The sentence

> S claims that the red ball is in the fireside room.

for example, gives no indication as to whether it is supposed to be interpreted as *de dicto* or *de re*. This ambiguity is resolved by making explicit the *de re* ascription:

> S claims of the red ball that it is in the fireside room.

Ascriptions of propositional attitudes have three parts[454]: one specifying the individual which is the target of the ascription ('S'); one specifying the what sort of performance is being ascribed ('claims that'); and finally, one specifying the propositional content. The expressions specifying content, ie the third part of the ascription, are able to play their role *de dicto* or *de re*.

If we give a deontic score-keeping account of *de re* ascription, we arrive at the following picture.[455] Every *de re* ascription contains a commitment which is *attributed* to someone else, as well as another one which is *undertaken* by the ascriber. Hence, the deontic score is influenced in two ways. That there is an object in the fireside room is part of the commitment attributed to S. That this object is a red ball is a commitment undertaken by the ascriber himself. The expressive function of *de re* ascriptions thus consists in making explicit which parts of the propositional content are expressing *attributed* substitutional commitments, and which parts are expressing *undertaken* substitutional commitments. The part of the content specification that appears within the *de dicto* that-clause describes what—according to the ascriber—the one to whom the commitment is ascribed is committed to. The part of the content specification that appears within the scope of the *de re* 'of' describes the commitment undertaken by the ascriber.

Two important insights can be gained from this dual score-keeping significance. First, using the *de re* ascriptions' expressive vocabulary, it is possible to make explicit the distribution of the *discursive responsibility* contained in the ascription. Secondly, the connection between propositional content and truth becomes obvious once more. *De re* content specifications not only indicate what a claim represents, they are also the form in which the *truth conditions* of claims are expressed. They refer to the object—from the point of view of the score-keeper attributing the

---

[454] See Brandom, *Making It Explicit* (n 1 above) 504, 534.
[455] See Brandom, *Making It Explicit* (n 1 above) 504–508.

commitment—which the claim represents. In this way, they express which properties one would need to call on to assess the claim's truth.[456]

(iv) Doxastic Gap and Objectivity

Since the use of singular terms is subject to substitution-inferential commitments, there are very different ways of determining the propositional content of *de re* ascriptions, depending on which auxiliary commitments are called upon for further inferential specification. The significance of making a claim or acquiring a commitment whose content could be expressed in a particular sentence, and the significance of when it would be appropriate to do so, and what the appropriate consequences of doing so would be, depend on what other commitments are available as further premises is assessing grounds and consequences.[457]

The distinction between *de dicto* and *de re* ascriptions makes it clear that we have to consider in particular the collateral commitments of the ascriber and of the person to which a propositional attitude is attributed. There are smaller or bigger social differences between the concomitant commitments of various speakers. What is (based on one particular set of background assumptions) considered an appropriate ground or consequence might not be so from the perspective of a different set. Brandom puts this key aspect as follows:

> Even where people share a language (and so their concepts), which is the standard case of communication, there will still be some disagreements, some differences in the commitments that people have undertaken. We each embody different perceptual and practical perspectives and so will never have exactly the same doxastic and practical commitments.[458]

We may hence speak of a *doxastic gap* between the commitments acknowledged by different participants of a discursive community, raising the issue of this gap's effect on the thesis that linguistic meaning is objective. Following Brandom, we may answer that this gap between the commitments of different score-keepers not only does not conflict with the object-relatedness of linguistic meaning, but rather makes it possible to begin with. *De re* ascriptions make explicit the social differences in the doxastic perspective of various speakers. As a form of Wittgensteinian implicit interpretation, the score-keeping practice—in which speakers keep

---

[456] Brandom, *Making It Explicit* (n 1 above) 514–17. De re ascriptions also play other important roles in communication, see *Making It Explicit*, 510–13.
[457] See Brandom, *Making It Explicit* (n 1 above) 139.
[458] Brandom, *Making It Explicit* (n 1 above) 509 f.

score of the differences in their discursive repertoires—makes communication possible in the first place.[459] Understanding propositional content can be explained by the score-keepers' ability to navigate between their own doxastic perspective and those of other speakers in precisely the way made possible by *de re* ascriptions. A claim's representational content is understood by specifying its *de re* content, which in turn permits substitutional interpretation.

Speakers are thus able to say explicitly *what* a claim would be true of if it were true, and grasp its representational content. Identifying what is being talked *about* permits speakers to extract information across a doxastic gap.[460] This bridging of the doxastic gap in social practice clearly shows the connection between inference and reference. The result of Brandom's analysis of *de re* ascriptions in deontic score-keeping terms is that representational content, too, depends on mastering the social dimension of the inferential articulation of any given conceptual content. This concerns the familiar manner in which commitments are undertaken against a background of further collateral commitments, and serve as premises for further commitments.[461]

> The context with which concern with what is thought and talked *about* arises is the assessment of how the judgements of one individual can serve as reasons for another. The thesis is that the *representational* dimension of propositional content is conferred on thought and talk by the *social* dimension of the practice of giving and asking for reasons ... [T]he representational aspect of the propositional contents that play the inferential roles of premise and conclusion is to be understood in terms of the social dimension of communicating reasons and assessing the significance of reasons offered by others.[462]

The conclusion is that the objective representational dimension of propositional content depends on the social organisation of the inferential practice of giving and asking for reasons. Only the distinction of social practice between *acknowledging* a commitment oneself and *attributing* a commitment to another makes it possible to achieve object-relatedness.[463] In this way, the concept of empirical information and the representational dimension, ie the reference part of linguistic meaning, are rooted in interpersonal discourse.[464]

---

[459] Brandom, *Making It Explicit* (n 1 above) 508–13. Critical A Gibbard, 'Thought, Norms, and Discursive Practice. Commentary on Robert Brandom, Making It Explicit' (1996) 56 *Philosophy and Phenomenological Research* 703.
[460] Brandom, *Making It Explicit* (n 1 above) 514.
[461] Brandom, *Making It Explicit* (n 1 above) 510, 517.
[462] Brandom, *Making It Explicit* (n 1 above) 496 f.
[463] Brandom, *Making It Explicit* (n 1 above) 54 f. See also Brandom's considerations on 'the relativity of extensions to various elements of context', Brandom, *Making It Explicit* (n 1 above) 482.
[464] See Brandom, *Making It Explicit* (n 1 above) 139.

(v) Reference and Interpersonal Anaphora

In linguistics, there is the distinction between intrasentential anaphors and anaphors in discourse,[465] with the latter appearing in two sub-types—intersentential and interpersonal anaphora—which leaves us with three different types. The first two have already been discussed in connection with the issue of the repeatability of unrepeatable deictic tokens.[466]

Here, our focus is on interpersonal anaphors. It plays a key role in securing the possibility of communication *about* objects across the doxastic gap.[467] Those in the audience are capable of picking up a speaker's tokening anaphorically, and so connect it to their own substitution-inferential commitments. Brandom writes:

> Anaphoric connections among tokenings that are utterances by different interlocutors provide a way of mapping their different repertoires of substitutional commitments onto one another—a structure scorekeepers can use to keep track of how each set of concomitant commitments relates to the others.[468]

Interpersonal anaphors tie different perspectives together.[469] They permit the passing on of a singular reference across different sets of background assumptions. Anaphoric chains convey *de re* ascriptions.[470] For clarification, we will look at the following sentence of a speaker S[471]:

S: 'The seventh god has risen'.

A second speaker, T, who has heard this statement, can pick up the expression anaphorically by saying:

T: 'S claims that the seventh god has risen'.

If, according to the background assumptions acknowledged by T, the sentence of S should be incomprehensible—because T's commitments neither include the existence of a god nor the option of connecting the term 'god' sensibly with the verb 'rise'—T is able to make this clear by using quotation marks to explicitly attribute to S the responsibility for the definite description of the subject:

T: 'S claims that "the seventh god" has risen'.

Or, even more explicit:

---

[465] See J Aoun, *A Grammar of Anaphora* (Cambridge MA, 1985) 1–5; J Hintikka and J Kulas (eds), *Anaphora and Definite Descriptions. Two Applications of Game-Theoretical Semantics* (Dordrecht, 1985).
[466] See p 139 above.
[467] Brandom, *Making It Explicit* (n 1 above) 474.
[468] Brandom, *Making It Explicit* (n 1 above) 474 f.
[469] Brandom, *Making It Explicit* (n 1 above) 592.
[470] Brandom, *Making It Explicit* (n 1 above) 572.
[471] An example used by Brandom, *Making It Explicit* (n 1 above) 588 f.

T: 'S claims that the one S refers to as "the seventh god" has risen'.

Using the same anaphorical capacity, a third speaker U may make an identity statement based on *his* background assumptions:

U: 'It, the one S refers to as "the seventh god", is the sun'.

This identity statement would make it possible for T and U to specify the content of the original sentence *de re*:

T, U: 'S claims of the sun ("the seventh god", the one S refers to as "the seventh god") that it has risen'.

This example explains the role of interpersonal anaphors in the communication *about* objects. The different content specifications take account of the difference in discursive perspectives between the ascribers T and U and the target person S. Communication depends on interlocutors being able to keep two sets of account books.[472] They are thus able to move back and forth between the points of view of different speakers. During their discourse, they maintain an overview of which doxastic, inferential, and substantial commitments are undertaken and attributed by the various parties. The expressive resource for connecting the perspectives of S, T, and U is the interpersonal anaphora.

C. Objectivity as Intersubjectivity

The term objectivity is understood to mean intersubjectivity where it refers to a necessary shared validity. By contrast to strict Protagorian subjectivism, which makes an individual man or woman the measure of all things,[473] the intersubjectivity thesis distinguishes between *being* correct and subjectively *appearing* to be correct. On these pages, the focus of the objectivity thesis is on semantic norms. Hence, we have to discuss whether and how semantic norms have intersubjective validity.[474] Highly significant for these questions is the range of the doxastic gap (i). This leads to the paradox of relative objectivity (ii).

---

[472] Brandom, *Making It Explicit* (n 1 above) 590.
[473] See Platon, *Theätet*, 6th edn (Hamburg, 1955) paras 152a, 166a-b
[474] In analytic philosophy of science, the concept of intersubjectivity is defined as the possibility that several individuals use the expressions of a language in the same way because they follow intersubjectively acknowledged rules. See O Schwemmer, 'Intersubjektivität' in J Mittelstraß (ed), *Enzyklopädie Philosophie und Wissenschaftstheorie. Band 2* (Mannheim, 1984) 282.

(i) The Social Perspectival Character of Conceptual Content

We have already pointed out the social differences in inferential and substitutional accompanying commitments. A doxastic gap, however, exists for all types of semantic norms, not only for existential and identificatory object-related commitments. The collaboration of normative attitudes adopted from two socially distinct perspectives is essential to establishing discursive commitments.[475] Brandom writes:

> The social distinction between the fundamental deontic attitudes of undertaking and attributing is essential to the institution of deontic statuses and the conferral of propositional contents.[476]

Hence, we can generally speak of the *social perspectival character of conceptual content*.[477] Conceptual norms are not objective in the sense of their being eternally valid, strictly immovable truths. Rather, since they are embedded in a discursive context, they are a priori relative to social perspective.[478] The objectivity of semantic norms would thus have to be constructed as *relative objectivity*, which, following Marmor, could also be termed *discursive objectivity*.[479] It is within social practice that the decision is made as to which content is to be correctly attributed to which claim. No criterion outside discursive practice is consulted in this decision.

(ii) The Paradox of Relative Objectivity

At first glance, the perspectival relativity of semantic content seems to amount to a *refutation* of the thesis that linguistic meaning is objective—in the sense of being intersubjectively valid, and having the necessary general validity. In some respects, the necessity of collaborating background-relative inferences reads like a description of Quine's sceptical holism.[480] From the fact that any reference to reality is tied to the language game,

---

[475] Brandom, *Making It Explicit* (n 1 above) 197.
[476] Brandom, *Making It Explicit* (n 1 above) 508.
[477] See Brandom, *Making It Explicit* (n 1 above) 140; A Wellmer, 'Der Streit um die Wahrheit. Pragmatismus ohne regulative Ideen' in M Sandbothe (ed), *Die Renaissance des Pragmatismus. Aktuelle Verflechtungen zwischen analytischer und kontinentaler Philosophie* (Weilerswist, 2000) 264.
[478] Brandom, *Making It Explicit* (n 1 above) 139. See J McDowell, 'Brandom on Representation and Inference' (1997) 57 *Philosophy and Phenomenological Research* 157 at 160. See also Schellenberg, 'Buchbesprechung "Brandom, Making It Explicit"' (n 146 above) 194 f. This perspective is similar to Wittgenstein's relativity of grammatical rules, See Glüer, *Sprache und Regeln* (n 6 above) (Berlin, 1999) 175.
[479] See A Marmor, 'Four Questions About the Objectivity of Law' in A Marmor (ed), *Positive Law and Objective Values* (Oxford, 2001) 131–3.
[480] See Brandom, *Making It Explicit* (n 1 above) 587.

Rorty concludes that claims to truth have to be abandoned, and that inter-conceptual argumentation is impossible.[481]

In view of semantic content's universal dependency on socially differing background assumptions and, hence, of the ubiquitous range of the doxastic gap, we have to ask how semantic content may at all be intersubjective. If its objectivity cannot be independent of social and linguistic nature, what remains of the thesis of semantic objectivity?

One solution to this paradox might lie in referring to the stability of shared background assumptions in a language community. This effort, however, would fail if it were understood to be a consensus-oriented 'counting' of meanings. Reference to a *communal understanding* consensus reduces meaning to de facto conformity, and this in turn renders absurd the thesis of the normativity and the objectivity of meaning.[482] Objectivity in the sense of intersubjective correctness cannot be equated with what is sanctioned from the majority's ostensibly privileged perspective.[483] This position is unable to account for the possibility of said majority erring. Thus collapses the concept of a *minimal objectivity*, which wholly focuses on a language community's majority.[484]

On the other hand, the background assumptions of a language community by all means provide for a stability which would support the assumption of the intersubjectivity of semantic norms. In his late work *On Certainty*, Wittgenstein developed a concept of trivial sentences. They are the basic assumptions of our view of the world and express shared beliefs. Among them are sentences like 'I have a body', 'I have never been to the moon', and 'The Earth has existed for more than a century'. This class of sentences can only be defined vaguely, and contains sentences with varying degrees of triviality; their degree of justification differs, and they are always reversible.[485] Wittgenstein hence called them the 'mythology' of our language use.[486] Their key point is that they are tacitly implied during (speech) acts. Assertional practice and the giving of and asking for reasons are only feasible against the backdrop of these trivial sentences, which can

---

[481] See Welsch, 'Richard Rorty: Philosophie jenseits von Argumentation und Wahrheit?' (n 61 above) 172, 188.

[482] Stavropoulos, *Objectivity in Law* (n 389 above) 123 f; Wright, 'Rule-following, Objectivity and the Theory of Meaning' (n 4 above) 99. See also Raz, 'Notes on value and objectivity' (n 425 above) 415 f.

[483] Brandom argues against globally privileging an I-we intersubjectivity, Brandom, *Making It Explicit* (n 1 above) 599 f.

[484] Coleman and Leiter, 'Determinacy, Objectivity, and Authority' (n 3 above) 252 f, 260–63.

[485] See V Mayer, 'Regeln, Normen, Gebräuche. Reflexionen über Ludwig Wittgensteins "Über Gewißheit"' (2000) *Deutsche Zeitschrift für Philosophie* 421 f.

[486] Wittgenstein, *On Certainty* (n 106 above) paras 93–97.

be assumed to be unquestionable. Wittgenstein writes that '[t]he reasonable man *does not* have certain doubts'.[487]

There are two other important aspects which justify the intersubjectivity of linguistic meaning. To begin with, one has to recall the object-relatedness of conceptual content. It is in no way qualified by the doxastic gap. The correctness of claims and the application of concepts depend on what is *true of* what they in fact represent or are about, rather than on what anyone or everyone *takes* to be true of whatever they take them to represent.[488]

The correct inferential role is determined not by *arbitrary* collateral claims, but only by those which are *true*.[489] It should not be inferred from the fact that background assumptions are relative that the objects to which these assumptions refer are also relative.[490] Brandom puts it thus:

> Though thoroughly social and linguistic, these representational contents are not merely *linguistic* ... The process by which commitments and concepts develop in a community over time through this sort of collaboration of the practical and empirical aspects of discursive practice is the expressing (in an inferentially articulated and hence conceptually explicit form) of the concrete constraints supplied by the fact that we think and act in an objective world.[491]

Assumptions depend for their truth on the facts about the objects they represent.[492] Concepts are perspectival, but they refer to a non-perspectival, objective world.

The second reason why the relativity of objectivity does not justify intersubjectivity scepticism emerges when we look at the subject of intersubjective validity. This subject is *not* propositional content, since the latter varies socially, due to its inferential dependency on background assumptions. The members of a discursive community do not share individual commitments by *necessity*, but merely *contingently*. *Common practice* is however of necessity intersubjective. For all score-keepers, discursive practice consists in undertaking and attributing commitments, and keeping accounts on normative statuses. It is not the content of conceptual norms that is intersubjective but their form and structure. In a Kantian argument, Brandom asserts that objectivity should be reconstructed

---

[487] Wittgenstein, *On Certainty* (n 106 above) para 220. See also 'At the foundation of well-founded belief lies belief that is not founded', *On Certainty* at para 253.
[488] Brandom, *Making It Explicit* (n 1 above) 530.
[489] Brandom, *Making It Explicit* (n 1 above) 519, 528 f.
[490] The crucial argument that conventional practice may refer to non-conventional objects is also used by Coleman and Leiter to defend their concept of 'modest objectivity', see Coleman and Leiter, 'Determinacy, Objectivity, and Authority' (n 3 above) 270.
[491] Brandom, *Making It Explicit* (n 1 above) 528 f. See also *Making It Explicit*, 594.
[492] Brandom, *Making It Explicit* (n 1 above) 517.

as consisting in a kind of perspectival *form*, rather than in a nonperspectival or cross-perspectival *content*. What is shared by all discursive perspectives is *that* there is a difference between what is objectively correct in the way of concept application and what is merely taken to be so, not *what* it is—the structure, not the content.[493]

This view corresponds to that of the later Wittgenstein, namely, that intersubjectivity is a requirement for the possibility of successful communication not in that it *suppresses* subjectivity, but—quite the contrary—that it *recognises* other subjectivities in different ways of life.[494]

D. Objections to the Objectivity Theory

Five objections will have to be examined. This will provide more precise answers to key questions—how object-relatedness and intersubjectivity are to be understood, and how correctness and consensus are correlated.

Quine has voiced criticism with regard to the deterministic force of object-relatedness (i). Furthermore, the universality of the objectivity thesis has been contested, and arguments put forward for limiting it to simple terms (ii). Two interrelated objections deny that a conventionally based theory of meaning is able to claim the objectivity of semantic norms. Wright argues that a conventional objectivity theory is impossible (iii). The objection of incompatibility opposes the *combination* of the object-relatedness of language—based on the idea of an objective, *investigation-independent* world—with a theory based on semantic norms (iv).[495] Finally, the object-relatedness of linguistic meaning is refuted on the grounds that there is no objective world available as a point of reference (v).

---

[493] Brandom, *Making It Explicit* (n 1 above) 600. On the connection between semantic perspectivism and the objective content of concepts see Brandom, 'Von der Begriffsanalyse zu einer systematischen Metaphysik. Interview von Susanna Schellenberg' (n 129 above) 1015 f.

[494] See O Schwemmer, 'Intersubjektivität' in J Mittelstraß (ed), *Enzyklopädie Philosophie und Wissenschaftstheorie. Band 2* (Mannheim, 1984) 283.

[495] Brandom declares that '[t]his issue of objectivity is perhaps the most serious conceptual challenge facing any attempt to ground the proprieties governing concept use in social practice': Brandom, *Making It Explicit* (n 1 above) 137. See also the discussion between Habermas and Brandom, Brandom, 'Facts, Norms, and Normative Facts. A Reply to Habermas' (n 155 above); Habermas, 'Von Kant zu Hegel. Zu R. Brandoms Sprachpragmatik' (n 130 above).

(i) Quine's Objection of the Indeterminism of Reference

From his holist position, Quine also draws indeterminist conclusions for reference.[496] The constraints of the outside world, via empirical observation sentences, affect language. Observation sentences, however, can only be understood holistically. The constraints could thus be kept by widely varying, yet equally plausible interpretations, which refer to different ontologies. The expression 'gavagai' could refer to rabbit, rabbit part, rabbit stage etc.[497] Two sentences' stimulus-synonymity is unable to guarantee the identity of their semantic components' reference.[498]

Quine's holistic argumentation has been refuted above.[499] His thesis of the indeterminism of reference corresponds to the social-perspectival relativity of referential reference argued on these pages, in that there is no irreversible universal reference of linguistic terms. This indeterminism, however, is—according to the moderate holism[500] advanced in this book—no obstacle to the semantic objectivity thesis. Score-keepers are able to keep track of the varying practitioners' individual referential perspectives. Using interpersonal anaphors and *de re* ascriptions, they rely on the relations between undertaken and attributed commitments to bridge the doxastic gap between the different ontologies. This capacity enables them to ensure that they talk about the same thing.[501] The moderate indeterminism of reference does not constitute a refutation of the assumption of an intersubjectively valid and object-related semantic objectivity.

(ii) The Objection of the Special Role Played by Theoretical Terms

Carnap had already stated that theoretical terms are only meaningful within the context of a theory.[502] This corresponds to the social-perspectival character of any conceptual content advanced in this book. The objection of the special role played by theoretical terms goes beyond this. It claims that the objectivity theory developed here only works for the meaning of simple concepts, eg names or *natural kind terms*, but not for so-called *semantic deep concepts* or *thick concepts*. What is questioned is not the possibility of an objectivity theory as such, but rather its range.

---

[496] See A Orenstein, 'Quine, Willard Van Orman' in Craig (ed), *Routledge Encyclopedia of Philosophy, vol 8* (n 6 above) 9.
[497] This argument was refuted by Evans, see G Evans, 'Identity and Predication' (1975) 72 *Journal of Philosophy* 343 at 363.
[498] See Fricker, 'Analyticity, Linguistic Practice and Philosophical Method' (n 326 above) 227.
[499] See pp 156 ff above.
[500] See p 166 above.
[501] Brandom, *Making It Explicit* (n 1 above) 478 f.
[502] See W Stegmüller, 'Rudolf Carnap: Induktive Wahrscheinlichkeit' in J Speck (ed), *Grundprobleme der großen Philosophen. Philosophie der Gegenwart I* (Göttingen, 1985) 54.

This objection argues that compared to names and *natural kind terms*, the reference of theoretical terms worked the other way round. With the former, object properties determined meaning, whereas in theoretical terms reference proceeded from normatively controlled content to matching object.[503] Hence, the meaning of theoretical terms was not object-depended.

One example quoted in this context is Kripke's *phlogiston* illustration. In order to explain specific chemical processes, scientists assumed that there was an element called *phlogiston*. In this case, an object-related theory of reference would have to presume that the scientists'—erroneous—assumption referred to oxygen, as this was the only probable element which actually existed. It would only be possible to avoid this absurdity if the object-relatedness of the term *phlogiston* was abandoned.

This line of argument ignores the fact that the objects to which the *phlogiston* assumption refers are, plain and simply, chemical processes.[504] It is in this regard that the scientists are mistaken, and they are the ones responsible for the object-relatedness of the term *phlogiston*. This example shows that when it comes to object-relatedness, there is no difference between theoretical terms and names or *natural kind terms*. One only has to note that they depend to a greater degree on theoretical background assumptions than on simple empirical terms. The reflections accompanying their application are more complex. Incidentally, reference using *de re* ascriptions and interpersonal anaphors operates in the same way it does for names and *natural kind terms*. Theoretical terms do not play a special role.

(iii) Wright's Objection of the Impossibility of a Conventional Objectivity Theory

According to the position advanced here, semantic norms are the result of a community's social discursive practice. Crispin Wright has argued that, based on this position, it was impossible to claim the objectivity of these norms. While it was feasible to apply the community's rules to the speech acts of individuals (in this respect, Wright maintains the difference between normative attitudes and normative statuses), there was no similar criterion for the community as such.[505] Hence, any understanding of semantic

---

[503] See Stavropoulos, *Objectivity in Law* (n 389 above) 44.

[504] Stavropoulos is correct in pointing this out, see Stavropoulos, *Objectivity in Law* (n 389 above) 45.

[505] C Wright, *Wittgenstein on the Foundations of Mathematics* (Cambridge MA, 1980) 220.

norms based on the social ratification of normative attitudes would have to abandon the idea of ratification-independent objectivity.[506]

Wright's criticism would defeat an objectivity theory based on two conditions. First, his theory assumes that semantic norms are *without exception* ratification-dependent. Secondly, discursive communities as a whole are unable to err in their use of concepts. These two assumptions do not underlie the objectivity theory defended here. Contrary to the first assumption, I will maintain the difference between deontic attitudes and deontic statuses (a). The possibility of shared mistakes has to be defended against Wright's second assumption (b).

(a) Subjective Attitude and Objective Status

It is the object-relatedness of linguistic meaning which gets in the way of a total ratification-dependency of semantic norms. The inferential normative semantics argued here do accept community practice, yet go beyond it. In addition, it is founded on the idea that assertional speech acts have objective truth conditions. This means that the speakers' attitudes have to answer to objective correctnesses.[507] There is a difference between a speaker's intention of referring to a thing, and his success in doing so—ie between his representational attitude and representational success. It is this difference which makes it possible to use the former to judge the latter as correct or incorrect.[508] Since representational attitudes are a special case of doxastic attitudes,[509] the distinction between status and attitude is valid for attitudes in general.

The deontic statuses of doxastic commitments and attitudes may be instituted in practice, yet—contrary to Wright—their correctness does not extend beyond the actual use of concepts. This crucial specification is based on the fact that distinguishing objective statuses and subjective attitudes is fundamental to the practice of deontic score-keeping. The attributions made by a score-keeper distinguish between their discursive partner's actual deontic status and his deontic attitudes. Otherwise, they would be unable to communicate propositional content.[510] Score-keepers essentially judge the correctness of speech acts based on commitments which they are personally willing to *acknowledge*, ie those which are true according to their background assumptions, and which they correlate with those upheld by the attribution's target person.

---

[506] On Wright's argument and its modification by waiving the anti-realist the premise see Hale, 'Rule-Following, Objectivity and Meaning' (n 276 above) 380–91.
[507] Brandom, *Making It Explicit* (n 1 above) 137.
[508] Brandom, *Making It Explicit* (n 1 above) 41, 63, 78.
[509] See Brandom, *Making It Explicit* (n 1 above) 179.
[510] Brandom, *Making It Explicit* (n 1 above) 197.

This means that the distinction of normative statuses and normative attitudes is relative to the various score-keeping perspectives. From every score-keeping perspective there is a difference between the commitments acknowledged by the score-keeper, and that to which he actually is committed. In this respect, too, semantic norms are social-perspectival in character:

> [O]bjectivity is a structural aspect of the social-perspectival *form* of conceptual contents. The permanent possibility of a distinction between how things *are* and how they are *taken* to be by some interlocutor is built into the social-inferential articulation of concepts.[511]

Depending on the score-keeping perspective, the precise course of the lines between statuses and attitudes differs. The fact that this distinction is made, however, is a necessary element of discursive practice. The distinction is presupposed as an intersubjectively valid form. We can reply to Wright that the objectivity of semantic norms is not a challenge, but rather is a requirement of a meaning theory instituted in social practice. The capacity to judge the object-related truth of claims normatively, and to use terms in an intersubjectively correct way, consists in co-ordinating different score-keeping perspectives. It is only in this assessment—implicit in practice—that the objectivity of semantic norms becomes evident. What is assessed is the relative authority of competing inferential assertions, with no score-keeping perspective singled out from the others. In this significant aspect, the model advanced here does not correspond to the ratification model criticised by Wright, which privileged the community's perspective and was consequently unable to apply any kind of standard to it.

(b)   The Possibility of Communal Errors

We can only speak of an objectivity of semantic norms—both in the sense of intersubjective, generally valid correctness and in the sense of object-related truth—if it is possible for the community as a whole to be mistaken.[512] Otherwise, the objectivity thesis would collapse into conventionalism. Wright's argument that this is the case on the level of the community is a significant objection. This issue is discussed under heading of the possibility of *communal errors* or the *case of the lone dissenter*.[513]

It follows from the above that the objectivity of semantic norms consists not simply in the attitudes of individual speakers or of those of a group (however it may be defined). Rather, it is subject to important restrictions

---

[511] Brandom, *Making It Explicit* (n 1 above) 597.
[512] See the possibility error condition which Raz proposed for objectivity theories, Raz, 'Notes on value and objectivity' (n 425 above) 123.
[513] See Hale, 'Rule-Following, Objectivity and Meaning' (n 276 above) 374. Stavropoulos, *Objectivity in Law* (n 389 above) 117–21.

which result from the object-relatedness of linguistic meaning. Undertaken and attributed doxastic commitments are only judged to be correct if they are determined by objective correctnesses.[514] Hence, even when we look at individual speakers, the correctness of speech acts does not depend on the community alone. Individual speakers are not omniscient about the commitments they enter into by virtue of their use of various expressions. They may be in error as to the anaphoric chains they participate in, just as they are about the individuation of epistemically opaque *de re* ascriptions.[515] In this regard, groups of several speakers or whole communities are no different. Even on the level of the discursive community, the difference between attributed and undertaken claims for truth necessitates the idea of the objectivity of norms. This makes it possible to explain that, no matter how highly justified a claim may be, it may still have to be revised in view of new knowledge, and that a whole community may be mistaken about the correct use of a norm.[516]

Wright's argument, that when following theories of norms grounded in social practice, there could be no correctness of concept use about which a whole community could be in error, disregards the option of combining theories of normativity and objectivity the way it has been done here. In contradistinction to Wright's view, intersubjective objectivity of conceptual norms does exist in that the distinction between normative attitudes and normative statuses is maintained even for the community as a whole.[517] Hence, there is a standard for the community, which can be used to judge normative attitudes to be wrong even when where they are shared by social groups.

(iv) The Objection of Incompatibility

The rejection of Wright's objection is based on the assumption that a combination of a theory of normativity and a theory of objectivity is feasible. The incompatibility objection negates this assumption. While Wright's objection of the impossibility of conventional objectivity is founded on this objection, the latter is systematically autonomous.[518]

The objection of incompatibility accepts that several aspects, taken together, might suffice to explain meaning. However, it maintains that combining them was impossible. Reference was *either* fixed by use *or* by an

---

[514] Brandom, *Making It Explicit* (n 1 above) 137, 497 f
[515] Brandom, *Making It Explicit* (n 1 above) 574, 583.
[516] Brandom, *Making It Explicit* (n 1 above) 594 f.
[517] Brandom, *Making It Explicit* (n 1 above) 54.
[518] Rorty considers Brandom's positions to be incompatible, see RM Rorty, 'Robert Brandom über soziale Praktiken und Repräsentationen' in RM Rorty (ed), *Wahrheit und Fortschritt* (Publisher, Frankfurt am Main, 2000) 196 f.

objective world. Meaning was *either* based on rule-following *or* on objectivity in the sense of *investigation independence*.[519]

According to the view argued here, objectivity is nothing less than a requirement for a use-related theory of meaning. It is a key factor in the theory's coherence. An integrative theory of meaning does not look at the individual aspects of linguistic meaning in isolation. Rather, it focuses on how they complement each other. According to Brandom's analysis, the combination of intersubjectivity and reference is a key element of normative practice.[520] This combination becomes possible because perspectival contents are able to refer to a non-perspectival world without this making the theory incoherent. We have already discussed this aspect.[521]

Independent of Brandom's theory, there are also many reasons in favour of combining correctness and truth, and normativity and reference. During the examination of the concept of normativity, we had already pointed out that the concept of normativity's intrinsic claim for truth results in a necessary connection of truth and normatively-defined linguistic meaning.[522] The empirical properties of the objects to which claims refer are not only relevant for the truth of said claims, but also for their semantic correctness. In assertional practice, it is impossible to apply a term correctly to an object to which it truthfully cannot be applied.[523]

It is assertional practice in particular which involves the extra-linguistic world's truth conditions. Kripke's and Putnam's theory of the meaning of *natural kind terms*—which is widely accepted today—is compatible with Brandom.[524] Once causal theories of reference have abandoned their claim to exclusive validity, extension-determining contexts of reference can be described within the framework of a conventional theory.[525] With Wittgenstein, even the strongest proponent of a theory of meaning grounded in grammatical rules accepts the relevance of object-relatedness: 'If you are not certain of any fact, you cannot be certain of the meaning of your words either'.[526]

---

[519] Wright, 'Rule-following, Objectivity and the Theory of Meaning' (n 4 above) 114. Neuner's position is also grounded in this perspective. He argues in favour of a theory of meaning which 'countering the use-theory of meaning, does sufficient justice to the extra-lingual reference of words', see Neuner, *Die Rechtsfindung contra legem* (n 88 above) 99.

[520] Brandom, *Making It Explicit* (n 1 above) 592–7.

[521] See p 195 above.

[522] See p 101 above.

[523] See Glock, 'Wie kam die Bedeutung zur Regel?' (n 115 above) 439.

[524] See Fricker, 'Analyticity, Linguistic Practice and Philosophical Method' (n 326 above) 232 fn 27. Hence, the same applies to Stavropoulos' justification of linguistic objectivity. To a significant extent, he draws upon semantics following Kripke and Putnam, see Stavropoulos, *Objectivity in Law* (n 389 above) 1–5.

[525] See Glüer, *Sprache und Regeln* (n 6 above) 20 fn 5.

[526] Wittgenstein, *On Certainty* (n 106 above) para 114.

A speaker who observes the implicit norms of a discursive community must have access to objective truths.[527] Contrary to the strict dichotomy between norms and facts maintained by the objection of incompatibility, any full explanation of linguistic meaning has to have recourse to the dual thesis of normativity *and* objectivity argued here. In the face of this complementary relation, there can be no question of eclectic incoherence.

(v) The Objection that There Is No Objective World

Against the objectivity theory, the objection of anti-realism maintains that since there was no reference object, it was impossible to achieve object-relatedness. There simply were no detached objects existing independent of consciousness.[528] At first view, this objection seems to be tremendously effective—after all, it does charge the objectivity theory of meaning with proving the existence of an objective world—but when one looks at it again, it offers very little in the way of success.

The existence of an objective world is one of the key issues of ontology. In the recent history of philosophy, it has become apparent that this problem is precisely and primarily a consequence of language. The examination of the representational intention of propositional content has shown that perspectival concepts refer to objects which are in a strong sense *understood to be* non-perspectival. Hence, we have advanced a hypothesis of the essential requirements of assertional practice that *does not* include ontological existence assumptions. In order to comprehend the concept of objective, truth-based, intersubjectively valid correctness, it is not necessary to maintain the actual existence of non-perspectival facts[529] in terms of naive or external realism, most recently again defended by Searle.[530] It suffices that the distinction between correct claims and correct applications of a concept on the one hand and those which are only held to be correct on the other, was a structural element of every score-keeping perspective.

Whenever we communicate, whenever propositional content is transferred and imparted, the practice of asking for and giving reasons, of attributing and undertaking commitments, assumes the existence of an

---

[527] See J Skorupski, 'Meaning, Use, Verification' in Hale and Wright (eds), *A Companion to the Philosophy of Language* (n 28 above) 50.
[528] Criticism along these lines comes from Rorty, 'Robert Brandom über soziale Praktiken und Repräsentationen' (n 518 above) 192.
[529] Brandom, *Making It Explicit* (n 1 above) 595. See with regard to the project of reconstructing a metaphilosophically safe understanding of representation Brandom, 'Von der Begriffsanalyse zu einer systematischen Metaphysik. Interview von Susanna Schellenberg' (n 129 above) 1014.
[530] See JR Searle, 'Basic Metaphysics. Reality and Truth' in JR Searle (ed), *Mind, Language and Society. Doing Philosophy in the Real World* (London, 1999) 31–3.

objective world.⁵³¹ This *necessary as-if assumption* is enough to explain the objectivity and normativity of meaning. It is not within the scope of this work to look into deeper metaphysical questions.

Davidson has emphasised that propositionally contentful thinking and speaking presupposes a concept of objective truth as well as the assumption of a world of objects separated into shared space and shared time:

> The distinction between a sentence being held true and being in fact true is essential to the existence of an interpersonal system of communication ... The concept of belief thus stands ready to take up the slack between objective truth and the held true, and we come to understand it just in this connection ... Someone cannot have a belief unless he understands the possibility of being mistaken, and this requires grasping the contrast between truth and error—true belief and false belief. But this contrast, I have argued, can emerge only in the context of interpretation, which alone forces us to the idea of an objective, public truth.⁵³²

All propositional thought, whether positive or sceptical, whether of the inner or of the outer, requires possession of the concept of objective truth, and this concept is accessible only to those creatures that are in communication with others.⁵³³

Recently, Davidson also defended the concept of objectivity against Rorty, thus withdrawing from a position they had been sharing since 1981.⁵³⁴

Finally, Habermas has also (dissociating himself from Rorty's contextualism) recently come out in support of realistic intuition. He pointed out the necessity of presupposing an objective world independent of the intersubjectively constituted lived-in world. The particularity of cultural and language-dependent contexts is transcended by the assumption of an objective world to which every speaker refers when making statements about objects in the world. It is this world which gives sense to truth-claiming assertional practice:

> On the one hand, linguistic practice itself must make it possible to refer to language-independent objects about which we assert something. On the other hand, the pragmatic presupposition of an objective world must be but a *formal anticipation* if it is to ensure that any subject whatsoever—rather than just a

---

[531] See in this context Raz' proposal of a 'single reality condition" for objectivity theories, see Raz, 'Notes on value and objectivity' (n 425 above) 125.

[532] D Davidson, 'Thought and Talk' in Davidson (ed), *Inquiries into Truth and Interpretation* (n 84 above) 169 f.

[533] Davidson, 'The Problem of Objectivity' (n 420 above) 220.

[534] Davidson, 'Is Truth a Goal of Inquiry? Discussion with Rorty' (n 414 above) 18. See also M Seel, 'Das Ende einer Affäre' *Die Zeit* 10 February 2000, 64

given community of speakers at a given time—be able to refer to a common system of possible referents and to identify independently existing objects in space and time.[535]

Habermas is thus in agreement with the thesis advanced here. Objectivity is the *formal* structure of assertional practice, creating the connection required between meaning and truth. Taking-true plays the role of an assumption which guides and serves as a guiding point for every argumentative process of justification in which reasons have to be given for the existence of something which is taken to be true.[536]

In conclusion, we may note that it is essential for discursive practice to presuppose the existence of an objective world. It is not necessary, however, for this world to actually exist. The semantic objectivity thesis does not require an ontological objectivity thesis. The issue of metaphysical realism—which is the subject of controversial debate[537]—has been shown to be irrelevant *for the explanation of linguistic meaning*.[538] If we want to explain what we do when we consider a claim to true or false, we can leave unanswered the question of whether an objective world exists independently of language. The objection of the non-existence of an objective world is beside the point.

E. Conclusion on the Objectivity of Linguistic Meaning

The objections against the objectivity theory have been shown to be untenable. The result is a *strong objectivity thesis*: Linguistic meaning is objective, both with regard to reference and intersubjectively. We are able to connect both concepts of objectivity, which have so often been pitted against each other: Linguistic meaning is both 'world-guided' and 'reason-guided'.[539]

Whether a term is used correctly depends on the properties of the objects it refers to. Both individual speakers and whole communities can be in error about the correctness of a given concept in a given situation. An

---

[535] J Habermas, 'Einleitung. Realismus nach der sprachpragmatischen Wende' in Habermas (ed), *Wahrheit und Rechtfertigung. Philosophische Aufsätze* (n 130 above) 44.
[536] See A Gimmler, 'Jürgen Habermas: Wahrheit und Rechtfertigung' (2000) 53 *Philosophischer Literaturanzeiger* 333 at 336.
[537] See Coleman and Leiter, 'Determinacy, Objectivity, and Authority' (n 3 above) 247–52; R Dworkin, 'Objectivity and Truth: You'd Better Believe It' (n 79 above) 96.
[538] See Schellenberg, 'Buchbesprechung Brandom, "Making It Explicit' (n 146 above) 194 f; Wellmer, 'Der Streit um die Wahrheit. Pragmatismus ohne regulative Ideen' (n 477 above) 35. This is overlooked by Neuner, who aims to safeguard reference to an extra-lingual reality through the 'ontological status of intentions', Neuner, *Die Rechtsfindung contra legem* (n 88 above) 99.
[539] Following Postema's terminology. However, he intends this to be a juxtaposition, Postema, 'Objectivity Fit for Law' (n 195 above) 133.

analysis in terms of deontic score-keeping has shown that representational content is the result of social differences—grounded in the different sets of background assumptions—in inferential perspective.

The doxastic gap between speakers can be bridged in assertional practice by using singular terms, interpersonal anaphors, and *de re* ascriptions to clarify what the interlocutors are talking *about* and what their claims are *of*. Epistemic access to what one is talking about presupposes that the speaker has undertaken a non-trivial identity claim which is intersubstitutable with some term used by another speaker.[540] Demonstrative or indexical use of singular terms—which presuppose a particularly close cognitive connection to the object—is only required for the first links of anaphoric chains. Subsequent communication of the representational content can be purely conceptual and interpersonal.[541]

The object-relatedness of propositional and conceptual content means that the practice of score-keeping as such cannot be used as a final measure of correctness. Rather, score-keeping is something that can be done correctly or incorrectly.[542] The speakers' subjective attitudes can be correct or incorrect in determining the objective status of propositional content.

Furthermore, there are three aspects which—in the face of its constitutive foundation in reality—justify speaking of an *intersubjective* validity of linguistic meaning: First, the social-perspectival character of propositional content does not annul references to non-perspectival entities. Secondly, meaning is only possible against a backdrop of intersubjectively shared, basal posits. Thirdly, independently of socially-differentiated contents, objectivity has to be understood as an intersubjectively shared from of meaning. Hence, we are able to speak of strong intersubjectivity, countering Rorty's position—based on doxastic gaps—of the impossibility of inter-conceptional argumentation.[543]

The concepts of objectivity of reference and intersubjectivity are not isolated from each other. Reference is developed as a structure within an intersubjectively shared discursive practice. As can be found in Kant's *Proglegomena*,[544] both concepts of objectivity correlate. Habermas states: 'The objectivity of the world and the intersubjectivity of communication refer to one another'.[545]

---

[540] Brandom, *Making It Explicit* (n 1 above) 549 f.
[541] Brandom, *Making It Explicit* (n 1 above) 568, 572 f.
[542] Brandom, *Making It Explicit* (n 1 above) 184 f.
[543] See Welsch, 'Richard Rorty: Philosophie jenseits von Argumentation und Wahrheit?' (n 61 above) 187.
[544] Kant, *Prolegomena zu einer jeden künftigen Metaphysik, die als Wissenschaft wird auftreten können* (n 427 above) para 18. See n 000 above.
[545] J Habermas, 'Einleitung. Realismus nach der sprachpragmatischen Wende' in Habermas (ed), *Wahrheit und Rechtfertigung. Philosophische Aufsätze* (n 130 above) 25.

Brandom's theory of meaning can thus be considered as proof for Habermas's new concept of truth, which understands truth to be uniformly based on justification and object-relatedness.[546] In this sense, linguistic meaning bridges the gap between practical and theoretical philosophy.

IV. THE RESULTS OF THE SECOND CHAPTER

The key result of the second chapter is the thesis of the *three dimensions of linguistic meaning* (A). With regard to the social-perspectival relativity of linguistic meaning, which is so frequently emphasised, we have to look at the universality challenge (B).[547] Finally, the scope and role of language-analytical discourse have to be emphasised (C).

A. The Three Dimensions of Linguistic Meaning

Linguistic meaning consists of three dimensions: normativity, object-relatedness, and reference. Propositional and conceptual content are characterised by semantic norms which emerge from assertional practice. For the practice of giving and asking for reasons, it is essential that the object-related truth of claims be normatively assessed, and that the use of concepts be intersubjectively correct. The objective world of facts and the social world of norms are interconnected in the three dimensions of linguistic meaning. It is only in combination that objective and normative validity of linguistic norms provide a context-transcending point of reference, which in turn makes possible rationally motivated revision and communication between/across different forms of life.

The reason for the language-philosophical focus of the second chapter was the deconstructive challenge of meaning scepticism which is used to justify the juridical indeterminism thesis.[548] In the third chapter, we will discuss the consequences of the results of the second chapter for legal theory in general and for the specific problem of the limits of the wording. Based on the thesis of the three dimensions of linguistic meaning, it is already possible emphatically to reject meaning scepticism.

---

[546] See Gimmler, 'Jürgen Habermas: Wahrheit und Rechtfertigung' (n 536 above) 336. On the connection between truth and justification see also Wellmer, 'Der Streit um die Wahrheit. Pragmatismus ohne regulative Ideen' (n 477 above) 257–63.
[547] See McKinlay, 'Agreement and Normativity' (n 285 above) 196.
[548] See p 87 above.

208 *Normativity and Objectivity of Linguistic Meaning*

B. The Universality Challenge

The universality challenge concerns the question of how far the analysis of semantic content developed on these pages might claim to have general validity, or whether it is only valid for the game of giving and asking for reasons. Alexy has given the consequences of the latter:

> [T]he basic norms of rational speech would only be significant for those who had decided to participate in the language game of practical reasoning.[549]

Following this, the thesis of the three dimensions would have to be substantially limited. It would only apply to the use of language in the context of rational discourse, and only to meanings expressed in the course of reasonable assertional practice. Irony, sarcasm, exaggeration, lies, and many other language games, would be beyond the scope of analysis.

In the first place, what can be said against this limiting argument is that the requirements connected to speech acts do not depend on the speakers, but on the rules set up by the language community.[550] So what would happen if there were the rule of having a fully ironic discursive practice within a language community? Even in this case, the universality of the analysis developed here cannot be limited. The language games listed above are, after all, parasites of assertional practice. They can only be thought and described against the backdrop of the fundamental language game of assertional practice. Their concept of meaning is derived from the fundamental one accurately described in the thesis of the three dimensions.

It is therefore impossible to imply from the relativity of semantic content—which is the result of the perspectival character of background assumptions—that the thesis of the three dimensions of linguistic meaning was also relative. The latter is universal.

C. Scope and Role of Language-Analytical Discourse

It is only within a normative theory of meaning that the use of concepts by a discursive community can be criticised beyond mere change in the object of reference or discursive topic. It is only in the practice of normative discourse that there is the possibility of linguistic mistakes. The social-perspectival relativity of propositional content means that there is no precisely defined limit to meaning. Yet in our linguistic practice, we assume this limit to be essential, we make it explicit in claims, and thus the subject of specific discourse. Wittgenstein writes:

---

[549] Alexy, *A Theory of Legal Argumentation* (n 5 above) 127.
[550] Alexy, *A Theory of Legal Argumentation* (n 5 above) 127.

> The mythology may change back into a state of flux, the river-bed of thoughts may shift. But I distinguish between the movement of the waters on the river-bed and the shift of the bed itself; though there is not a sharp division of the one from the other.[551]

It is the task of language-analytical discourse to dissolve the tensions existing between the uses of concepts by individual speakers of one discursive community.[552] This discourse can be carried out using Brandomian terminology. The standards implicit in linguistic practice can be made explicit. Formulating as an explicit claim the inferential commitment implicit in semantic content brings it out into the open as being susceptible to challenges and demands for justification.[553] Language-analytical discourses held with expressive reason regulate and improve inferential commitments, and hence the concepts of the discursive community.

---

[551] Wittgenstein, *On Certainty* (n 106 above) para 97.
[552] See Fricker, 'Analyticity, Linguistic Practice and Philosophical Method' (n 326 above) 247 f.
[553] See Brandom, *Making It Explicit* (n 1 above) 127.

Chapter 3

Semantic Normativity in the Law

If it were not possible to communicate general standards of conduct, which multitudes of individuals could understand, without further direction, as requiring from them certain conduct when the occasion arose, nothing that we now recognize as law could exist.[1]

THE THIRD CHAPTER forms a link between the two preceding ones. The legal problem of the limits of the wording (*Wortlautgrenze*) is discussed in the light of the language-philosophical results of the second chapter. This takes place in two steps. First of all, the arguments and issues which were identified in the first chapter as being key[2] are reviewed using the thesis of the three dimensions of linguistic meaning (I). A new theory of the limits of the wording is developed on this basis, and is explained using examples from supreme court precedents (II). The significance of semantic normativity in the law is then summarised (III).

I. ADDRESSING THE THREE CENTRAL ISSUES

The following conclusion was reached in the first chapter: The core problem of the limits of the wording in terms of legal theory is the language-philosophical question of what meaning is and whether it can be recognised, and if so how.[3] A distinction was made between three central issues[4]:

1. Can we distinguish clear and unclear cases of semantic interpretation?
2. Can the meaning of norms be established empirically?
3. Can the meaning of rules be objectified within the juridical interpreters' language game?

These questions can be answered by applying the thesis of three dimensions of linguistic meaning (A) to (C).

---

[1] HLA Hart, *The Concept of Law*, 2nd edn (Oxford, 1994) 124.
[2] See p 81 above.
[3] See p 86 above.
[4] See p 83 above.

A. Clear and Unclear Cases

(i) The Relevance in Legal Theory of the Distinction Between Clear and Unclear Cases

The distinction between clear and unclear cases is a problem which has been discussed passionately in Anglo-American legal theory since Hart's *The Concept of Law*.[5] The debate centres on questions such as the *determinacy of law*, the *objectivity of law* and *judicial discretion*. Secondly, the distinction relates to the possibility of the fourth variant of the juridical indeterminacy thesis. It is put forward by Hart and by analytical legal theory, and considers it to be necessary to *assign* meaning only in semantically-unclear cases.[6] Thirdly, in German legal theory proponents of the limits of the wording invoke the argument of clear cases.[7] This presumes that there are cases in which there is no doubt as to the meaning of legal terms, and that these cases form the overwhelming majority. The argument of necessary failure, by contrast, asserts that the criterion of the limits of the wording is not required in clear cases, whilst in hard cases the meaning is said to be so uncertain that this criterion of necessity fails.[8]

These three groups of problems show that the distinction between easy and hard cases is of great significance in terms of legal theory. The core is based around the third debate, which relates to the application of the distinction to the problem of the limits of the wording.

(ii) The Concept of the Clear Case

(a) Semantic Clarity and Juridical Clarity

The sceptical strategy of the argument of necessary failure has already been compared to the distinction between consensus on the wording and consensus with regard to justice.[9] Accordingly, it is necessary to make an unambiguous distinction between semantically-clear cases and juridically-clear cases. Because of the large number of types of juridical argument, it is not the case that each semantically-clear case is juridically clear; nor is each

---

[5] See B Bix, *Law, Language, and Legal Determinacy* (Oxford, 1995) 63–76; Hart, *The Concept of Law* (n 1 above) 124–54; K Kress, 'Legal Indeterminacy' (1989) 77 *California Law Review* 283 at 296; M Powers, 'Truth, Interpretation, and Judicial Method in Recent Anglo-American Jurisprudence' (1992) 46 *Zeitschrift für philosophische Forschung* 101 at 105.
[6] On the four variants of the legal indeterminacy thesis see p 87 above.
[7] See p 67 above.
[8] See p 69 above.
[9] See p 84 above.

semantically-unclear case juridically unclear.[10] A juridically-unclear case applies particularly if, despite semantic clarity, non-semantic arguments give rise to doubts as to the solution which would be fitting if one were to take a purely semantic view. For this very reason, it is possible to speak of a necessary failure of the limits of the wording.

In connection with the problem of the limits of the wording, the argument of the clear case is to be regarded as a purely *semantic* premise. It asserts the clarity of linguistic meaning for a specific category of case without at the same time making any claim concerning juridical clarity.

(b) Constitutive Clarity and Epistemic Clarity

In accordance with the normativity theory of linguistic meaning put forward here, it is also possible for the community as a whole to be mistaken as to the correct meaning of a concept or of a proposition.[11] For this reason, it is necessary to draw a line between constitutive clarity and epistemic clarity. The clarity of a case does not *lie* in the members of an interpretative community agreeing on the application because of an identical epistemic approach. It is one question whether a case is semantically clear, and another whether and how this is recognised in epistemic terms. For this reason, the very existence of a dispute on the meaning of a concept does not permit one to conclude constitutive unclear meaning.

The distinction between constitutive and epistemic clarity corresponds to the distinction that was introduced in the second chapter between ontological and epistemic meaning scepticism.[12] Epistemic clarity relates to the second of the central issues, namely to the problem of whether and how establishment of linguistic meaning is possible, as is distinct from assignment. This will be followed up at (II). In the context of the first issue, it is necessary to define here what it means in conceptual terms if one states that a case is constitutively clear in semantic terms.[13]

(iii) Semantic Clarity in Accordance with the Model of Deontic Scorekeeping

In accordance with the thesis of the three dimensions, linguistic meaning consists of an inferential structure, the correctness of which has boundaries imposed on it by implicit norms and by virtue of being related to objects,

---

[10] *Cf* Bix, *Law, Language, and Legal Determinacy* (n 5 above) 67.
[11] See pp 106, 150 above.
[12] See p 89 above.
[13] Hence, in the following text 'semantic clarity' means *constitutive* clarity.

and which is hence of general validity in intersubjective terms. The reference dimension is relevant to the second issue, and intersubjectivity to the third issue.

The first dimension is central to the clarification of the first issue. According to this dimension, meaning consists of substantive inferences, the correctness of which is assessed by implicit, socially-instituted norms. It is necessary to study how this fact can be made useable for the concept of semantically-constitutive clarity. The concept of the clear case has not yet been sufficiently clarified in analytical legal theory. Apart from the only very general definition that there is 'no doubt as to the meaning', the classification of unclear cases effects a *negative* delimitation.[14]

The model of deontic scorekeeping facilitates a precise *positive* determination of the concept of the clear case. It is possible to say, very generally, that a case is constitutively clear in semantic terms if the correctness of the substantive inferences has been clarified in normative practice. A case is semantically-constitutively unclear if the correctness of the substantive inferences is not clarified in normative practice. What it means if we say that the inferences are clear can be explained using the inferential structure, which consists in turn of three dimensions.[15] It is possible for clarity or unclear meaning to exist in all three dimensions (a) to (c).

(a) Semantic Clarity in the First Inferential Dimension

Propositional content is explained in the first inferential dimension using the interaction between the two deontic statuses of commitment and entitlement. In accordance with the principle of the two-fold normative significance of the conceptual, each speech act is normatively situated in two ways: It is labelled by correct application conditions and by correct conclusions. A list of four questions arises from the combination[16] of commitment and entitlement on the one hand, and circumstances and consequences on the other. The assertion p of speaker S is semantically clear if all four questions are answered:

1 To which circumstances is S committed by p?
2 Because of which circumstances is S entitled to p?
3 To which circumstances is S committed by p?
4 To which consequences is S entitled by p?

Semantically-unclear meaning arises if there is doubt as to one or more questions. The three types of inferential relations are also covered in the first inferential dimension, namely inheritance of commitment, inheritance

---

[14] See pp 46 ff above.
[15] On the three dimension of the inferential structure see p 129 above.
[16] See p 127 above.

of entitlement and incompatibility. Semantic clarity implies that it has been established for a proposition which commitments and entitlements the proposition inherits, and with which other propositions it is incompatible. Semantically-unclear meaning arises in the three possible cases of doubt: First, if it is doubtful whether a commitment to p of necessity entails a commitment to q; secondly, if it is unclear whether an entitlement to q follows from an entitlement to p; and thirdly, if there are doubts as to whether an entitlement to p excludes an entitlement to q.

(b) Semantic Clarity in the Second Inferential Dimension

The second inferential dimension distinguishes between *intrapersonal* and *interpersonal* consequences of deontic status. Semantic clarity is contingent on it being established to which further commitments and entitlements a commitment or entitlement either entitles or commits the same person or other persons. Unclear meanings can thus occur in *accompanying* or in *communicative* inheritance and incompatibility.

(c) Semantic Clarity in the Third Inferential Dimension

The third inferential dimension relates to the tie between discursive authority and discursive responsibility. An assertion authorises other assertions by causing an entitlement to be inherited. At the same time, the person making the assertion takes on the responsibility, in the shape of a burden of justification, to be able to show his/her entitlement to make the assertion. Semantic clarity in the third inferential dimension is not contingent on the person making the assertion actually being entitled. The actual entitlement is a question of the truth of the assertion. It is sufficient for semantic clarity for it to be clear under what circumstances the person making the assertion *would be* entitled. Only then is the semantic content of the responsibility into which he or she has entered clear. The same applies to the claimed authority. It, too, need not actually exist. Semantic clarity exists if it has been established which authorisation impact an assertion would have if it were true.

(d) Result

The concept of constitutive semantic clarity can be further expanded using the three dimensions of the inferential structure. The status of the commitment, and of the entitlement, is decided on by the deontic attitudes of the participants in a language game who assign and acknowledge this status to one another. The semantic content of an assertional commitment leads to certain changes in the deontic scores which cover various speakers' status configurations. Semantically-unclear meaning exists if there are doubts as to the deontic status. If the deontic status is not clarified in practice, it cannot be said which changes an assertion brings about in the scores. What is more, the conditional and consequential normative significance can also be unclear, so that the inferential relations between the levels of status are not stable.

The consequence of these unclear meanings is that the semantic suitability of a speech act cannot be judged. That the status and the inferences of an assertion are not stable is the same as saying that their meaning is not stable. This is an unclear case in semantically-constitutive terms. If, by contrast, there is clarity with regard to these aspects, then we observe a semantically-constitutive clear case.

All in all, this shows two things. First, the concept of the semantically-constitutive clear case was explained with the thesis of the three dimensions of linguistic meaning. Secondly, it is established that various *degrees of semantic clarity* are possible, depending on how many of the aspects contained in the various inferential dimensions are cumulatively clear. Hence, using the semantic structure developed by Brandom, it is possible to make a terminologically-detailed distinction between clear and unclear cases. It does not follow from this possibility that clear cases also exist in fact. The argument of clear cases, however, contains such an existence thesis in its first sub-assertion. This can also be proven with the aid of the results of the second chapter.

(iv) The Existence of Semantically-Clear Cases

In view of the characteristics of linguistic meaning stated in the thesis of the three semantic dimensions, it is questionable whether the argument of clear cases stands up to the burden of proof for the existence of semantically-clear cases. If it is established that norms exist which can be used to judge the semantic correctness of speech acts, this is a strong indication of the existence of semantically-clear cases.

Regardless of this, the existence of clear cases can be proven on the basis of the results of the second chapter. Three hypotheses are used to achieve this end. All three hypotheses were explained in the second chapter as a precondition of linguistic meaning.

First, the *thesis of the necessary incorporation of fundamental propositions* is presented in the context of the discussion on the reversibility of logical laws.[17] Linguistic understanding is conditional on the communication of propositions which are immune to revision being used as a basis which works as canonical standards. These can be understood to be semantically-constitutive clear cases. If each language has of necessity

---

[17] See p 164 above.

fundamental propositions, and if fundamental propositions are semantically and constitutively clear, then each language has of necessity semantically-constitutive clear propositions. Whilst the thesis of the twofold limitation of semantics also applies to the distinction of easy and hard cases, this is hence chronologically and socially relative insofar as it has not been established *which* cases are acknowledged to be easy. This relativity does not mean, however, that it would be dispensable to take easy cases into a language. Also, *triadic relative OLOL analyticity* speaks—secondly—in favour of the existence of semantically-clear cases.[18]

The central argument against the assumption of clear cases is the statement of ubiquitous reversibility. First, a distinction must be made between *easy* cases and *new* cases. If a previously unclarified application problem occurs, the semantically-unclear meaning initially refers exclusively to how this should be dealt with. It is only necessary to clarify whether a concept is to be expanded in order to extend it to cover the new object. That a semantically-contingent assignment is necessary with regard to this new object does not mean that clear cases of the concept become unclear.[19] If, for instance, the question arises of whether a board attached to a wall without either a bracket or legs falls under the concept of 'chair', and if the available inferences do not clarify this question, an assignment is necessary with regard to this application case. Numerous other clear application cases of the concept of 'chair' nevertheless remain clear.

Secondly, the indication of the reversibility of fundamental propositions is to be compared with the *default-and-challenge structure of entitlement*. This is the third thesis to be used here, which was asserted against Kripke's regress argument. For the assumption of the existence of semantically-constitutive clear cases, it is not necessary for easy cases to be irreversibly categorised as such. Prima facie status suffices. Stavropoulos puts this as follows:

> The doctrine of defeasibility is based on the correct observation that no final formula can be supplied which could govern a concept's application in every possible set of circumstances. However, that is to say that there can be no *unrevisable* formula; not that there can be no defensible, theoretical formula that explains and justifies novel cases' resemblances with the paradigms.[20]

The assumption of ubiquitous reversibility therefore does not shake the assumption of the existence of semantically-constitutive clear cases.

---

[18] See p 179 above. See also E Fricker, 'Analyticity, Linguistic Practice and Philosophical Method' in K Puhl (ed), *Meaning Scepticism* (Berlin, 1991) 234 f.
[19] See *ibid*, 241 f. Stavropoulos argues for a stronger *defeasibility*, see N Stavropoulos, *Objectivity in Law* (Oxford, 1996) 62 f.
[20] Stavropoulos, *Objectivity in Law* (n 19 above) 64.

(v) Limitations in Hard Cases

The argument of necessary failure assumes that the limits of the wording fail precisely where they are supposed to take effect, namely in hard cases. This assumption is countered by the third sub-thesis of the argument of the clear cases, which also asserts semantic restrictions in hard cases. Inferential semantics also favour the argument of clear cases in this question.

In accordance with the model of deontic scorekeeping, a hard case exists if unclear meanings exist in one or more of the three inferential dimensions. This is in particular the case if it is unclear to what an assertion commits [Translator: the speaker] and to what it entitles [him/her]. Such an unclear meaning exists for the seemingly simple concept of a 'chair' with regard to the seat attached to the wall described above. Simple concepts in particular are frequently not sufficiently rich in semantic terms to be able to provide fixed delimitations of new cases. These constitute the internal boundaries of the capacity of linguistic meaning, which make a stipulation necessary. The opposite, however, applies to hard concepts, which are particularly rich in inferential relations. They are thus able to cover more unknown and new cases from the outset.[21] The consequence of the great theoretical wealth of many legal terms is that they show a large number of inferential relations. These offer clear semantic indications of the treatment of hard cases. There is therefore no question that the semantics necessarily have to fail in unclear cases.[22] Linguistically-unclear meaning is not equivalent to semantic triviality.[23]

(vi) Result on the First Issue

The first and third sub-theses of the argument of clear cases were confirmed. There are clear cases in which the meaning of a proposition or of a concept is established in the three inferential dimensions. Over and above this, semantic argumentation is also possible in hard cases. The second sub-thesis, by contrast, remains open, and relates to the number of hard cases in a language. This empirical question is not the subject of this study.

---

[21] *Cf* Fricker, 'Analyticity, Linguistic Practice and Philosophical Method' (n 18 above) 241, 245.

[22] *Cf* Stavropoulos, *Objectivity in Law* (n 19 above) 75.

[23] H-J Koch and H Rüßmann, *Juristische Begründungslehre. Eine Einführung in die Grundprobleme der Rechtswissenschaft* (München, 1982) 191. Hence, Busse's argument against Koch's concept of vagueness is unconvincing, see D Busse, *Juristische Semantik. Grundfragen der juristischen Interpretationstheorie in sprachwissenschaftlicher Sicht* (Berlin, 1993) 129.

Because of the confirmation of the first and third sub-theses of the argument of clear cases, the first issue can be decided in the sense of this argument: It is possible to make a distinction between clear and hard cases of semantic interpretation.

It must also be stated that the legal indeterminacy thesis is defensible only in a very weak form. A distinction was made between three indeterminacy theses.[24] The first indeterminacy thesis states that linguistic meaning can never ensure an application. This indeterminacy is already to be concurred with because it is not possible to conclude legal clarity from semantic clarity.

The third indeterminacy thesis denies the possibility of semantically-clear cases. It is refuted by the existence of clear cases. The fourth indeterminacy thesis restricts the third thesis to hard cases. This thesis is to be concurred with because there is semantic latitude in hard cases—in other words, it is necessary to assign meaning. The extent of this latitude depends on how many and which aspects of the three inferential dimensions are unclear. It is, however, vital that this latitude itself is not unlimited, because hard concepts are typified by a high degree of complexity in the inferential relations which can be made to apply as semantic arguments in the assignment. For this reason, the broad second indeterminacy thesis, according to which linguistic meaning can ensure each application, is to be rejected.

Hence, only a weak legal indeterminacy thesis can be based on language-philosophical arguments.[25] The linguistic meaning of the law is only unclear in hard cases, but is clear in easy cases. Even in hard cases there are semantic borderlines to which an assignment must keep to remain an interpretation.

B. The Epistemic Openness of the Meaning of Norms

The difficulties emanating from an empirical establishment of the meaning of norms have been known for a long time in legal theory.[26] The view put forward here, in accordance with the function of legal theory, intends to defend the theory of the limits of the wording not only against constitutive, but also against epistemic scepticism. The question of the epistemic openness of linguistic meaning constitutes a key challenge to such a view. This is represented by two critical arguments. The *language game argument* refers to the openness and context-dependency of linguistic meaning

---

[24] See p 87 above.
[25] This result is subject to non-semantic reasons for indeterminism, which are not addressed in this book.
[26] See B Mates, 'Zur Verifikation von Feststellungen über die normale Sprache' in G Grewendorf and G Meggle (eds), *Linguistik und Philosophie* (Frankfurt am Main, 1974).

which, it is argued, is to be re-constituted in each speech act.[27] There are two versions of the *argument of the impossibility of the empirical establishment of meaning*. The *complexity argument* refers to the practical difficulties encountered in specialist linguistic research. The *argument of participation* states that an external determination is impossible with regard to the internal relationality of linguistic rules.[28] These critical arguments are opposed by the view of analytical legal theory, which affirms that meaning can be empirically established. This refers partly to the extension-determining function of the intension, and partly to the model of rules for the use of words (*Wortgebrauchsregel*), which can be established.[29]

It can be established with the thesis of the three dimensions of linguistic meaning that both critical arguments contain correct aspects, but that their sceptical conclusions should be rejected (i). The methods of epistemic access that have been developed in analytical legal theory can be linked with the dimensions of normativity and objectivity of linguistic meaning (ii). The argument of epistemic openness of meaning is hence confirmed (iii).

(i) Rejection of the Critical Arguments

The *context-dependency* presumed by the *language game argument* and its sub-arguments can be given a more precise terminological form. It consists of the relativity and perspectivity of linguistic meaning, which follows from the dependence of background commitments. These differ from one scorekeeping perspective to another. It is, however, a mistake to conclude from this that linguistic meaning is re-constituted and re-established with each individual speech act. The *openness* of language games by no means goes so far that no standards are available for the judgement of individual speech acts as correct or suitable. Rather, it is shown by the normativity of meaning which was developed in the second chapter that implicit norms are available for this judgement. With the aid of such norms, it is possible to categorise, analyse and judge correct or incorrect the inferential relations and deontic status.

The *argument of circularity*, put forward both by critical hermeneutic legal theory and by the Müller school, rightly points to the fact of meaning being tied to presuppositions. This is taken into account here by the recognition of the relativity of meaning to background commitments. The assertion derived from the fact of being tied to presuppositions—suggesting that the correct meaning was not found by legal practitioners, but that they

---

[27] See p 70 above.
[28] See p 71 above.
[29] See p 67 above.

established it—entails, regardless of this, a restrictive anchoring to the individual speaker. This isolated view overlooks the social dimension which, according to the connection thesis of semantics and pragmatics, is a major element of linguistic meaning. Propositional and conceptual meaning arise in discursive practice. In accordance with the principle of instituting semantic norms through social practice, meaning is entrenched from the outset in a social context which transcends the individual speaker. The model of deontic scorekeeping can be used to describe the semantic structures which are found by legal practitioners. Also the possibility of semantic error imposes limits on the hermeneutic circular self-norming of meanings by individual speakers.

The *argument of innovation* criticises that conventions are allegedly not suitable as an instrument to impose discipline.[30] Hence, the error of modern normativity criticism which is criticised in the second chapter is repeated, namely to understand normativity exclusively as prescriptivity and to play it off against constitutive normativity. This strategy is brought to a fall by the connection thesis developed in the second chapter, which assigns a two-fold character to linguistic norms, borrowing from von Wright's theory of norms.[31]

The view of the *argument of participation* is confirmed by the results of the second chapter. Normativity of linguistic meaning consists essentially of an internal relation of rules and rule-following. Herbert hence correctly states that an empirical view cannot explain rule-following.[32] The internality of norms of linguistic practice, which Brandom covers with the designation 'implicit', cannot be uncovered with empirical-linguistic methods, but only with hermeneutic ones. This consideration very much places the *complexity argument* in perspective. This is the reason why here, with regard to the second issue, one speaks not of the problem of the possibility of making an empirical establishment, but only of the problem of epistemic openness.

It is, however, questionable whether the sceptical conclusion of the argument of participation is justified. Strictly speaking, it addresses not the epistemic openness of linguistic meaning as such, but only a certain form of access. It will be a matter for further study as to which other means of access may exist which do justice to the condition of internality. Speakers frequently call on their own linguistic competence as *native speakers* in legal theory and in court practice. Its value is, however, disputed,[33] and

---

[30] See p 70 above.
[31] *Cf* the rejection of the argument of incoherence of prescriptivity and constitutivity, p 109 above.
[32] M Herbert, *Rechtstheorie als Sprachkritik. Zum Einfluß Wittgensteins auf die Rechtstheorie* (Baden-Baden, 1995) 90.
[33] See J Neuner, *Die Rechtsfindung contra legem* (München, 1992) 96 fn 51.

faces reservations because of the possibility of semantic errors. The existence of further possibilities is to be examined.

(ii) Confirmation of the Argument of Epistemic Openness

There are two versions of the argument of epistemic openness.[34] According to Alexy, rules for the use of words can be empirically established. According to Koch and Rüßmann, the extension-assigning function of the intension makes it possible to recognise the meaning by taking a look at the objects and their characteristics. The fundamental strategy of this section is to study both versions separately, linking each with different sub-aspects of the thesis of the three dimensions of linguistic meaning. The possibility to establish rules for the use of words is studied using the normativity dimension (a) and the theory of meaning of Koch and Rüßmann using the dimension of object-relatedness (b). The objection of reification (c) speaks against the transfer of the dimension of object-relatedness to the law.

(a) Semantic Normativity and Rules for the Use of Words

According to Alexy, rules for the use of words are rules concerning the meaning of the expressions used in past steps of internal justification. They make it possible to interpret legal norms by formulating a more concrete decision-making norm, which is designated as I_{RW} or R'.[35] Like all other premises used in the internal justification, the rule for the use of words W must be externally justified. In the context of the external justification, the question arises whether, and if so how, rules for the use of words are epistemically open. Alexy explicitly left this question open in his *Theory of Legal Argumentation*.[36]

Alexy's theory as to this question should be supplemented at this point by further structures. The first idea, which is central to this supplement, is that the rules to which Alexy refers as rules for the use of words are a kind of the implicit semantic norm of Brandom's theory. This means that Brandom's extensive analytical terminology can be put to use when seeking to answer the question of the epistemic openness of rules for the use of words, and hence for their external justification. This applies above all to the first dimension of linguistic meaning, namely semantic normativity.

Initially, it can be stated on the basis of the results of the second chapter that a mere empirical establishment of a linguistic consensus of the

---

[34] See p 67 above.
[35] See p 51 above.
[36] Possibilities described by Alexy are for the speaker to rely on his/her own linguistic skills, as well as on empirical surveys, and to refer to the authority of dictionaries.

majority is not possible. This is, however, not—as claimed by the complexity argument—the result of concomitant practical difficulties, such as acquiring extensive specialist linguistic reports in the process. Rather, the cause lies in the possibility of semantic error which also exists for the majority of a linguistic community. Convictions of meaning shared by the majority can be incorrect. Following on from Wittgenstein's considerations on rule-following, it was determined that normativity does not exhaust itself in a mere consensus.[37] The factual agreement of opinions, and the consensual overlapping of idiolects, can have a wide variety of causes.[38] At the same time, a joint form of life is necessary for meaning in accordance with the principle of instituting semantic norms through social practice, but it is not sufficient.[39] Mere empirical counting is hence not a correct epistemic approach.

The second central idea follows Brandom's theory: The epistemic approach to linguistic meaning consists of making explicit the implicit norm—in other words, the rules for the use of words. The latter refer— according to the supplement to be made here—to deontic status and to substantive inferences. The process of making meaning explicit corresponds precisely to what Alexy referred to as *speech analysis discourse*. Brandom's analysis facilitates an extraordinarily rich description of the structures and rules of this discourse.

A first important principle is that it is not sufficient to make explicit the records of individual speakers' scores. There are two decisive reasons for this. First, the perspectivity of the meaning to different social background commitments[40] means that one cannot simply read, in individual scores, which inferences are correct. The determination or non-determination of inferences can be different from each scorekeeping perspective. What is more, individual scorekeepers can be wrong in that they record the inferences incorrectly. The second reason is the rejection of an analytical priority of individualism.[41] The recognition of linguistic meaning is contingent on the observation and explicating coverage of the *entire normative scorekeeping practice*. The openness of holistic structures, which is based on the possibility of an analysis with the aid of the expressive vocabulary, has already been clarified.[42]

In detail, the epistemic approach consists of making the norms, deontic status and substantive inferences explicit. The three types and the three dimensions of the inferential structure play a major role in this process.

---

[37] See p 106 above.
[38] On the reasons for this consensus and its objects see Bix, *Law, Language, and Legal Determinacy* (n 5 above) 63–5.
[39] See p 122 above.
[40] See p 193 above.
[41] See pp 107 ff above.
[42] See p 165 above.

Because semantic content consists in the substantive inferences of suitable consequences from suitable circumstances, epistemic access is possible by virtue of each inference and the norms of their correctness being made explicit.

With regard to the deontic status of commitment and entitlement, it is significant that its making explicit depends in some cases on empirical methods. The status arises in the linguistic community by virtue of the deontic attitudes of the members. These attitudes can be read from the activities of the judgement, which consists of the allocation and recognition of such status. In this regard, knowledge of meaning is contingent on this treating-as of the members inter se being empirically recorded.[43] This, however, does not constitute a reduction of meaning to facts. The normativity condition of anti-reductionist supervenience is held onto in the face of a reductionistic understanding. Meaning is contingent on empirical facts as a basis of supervenience, but does not exhaust itself in them. This is because the empirically-observed sanction of deontic scorekeepers is not external, but internal.[44]

All in all, the speech analysis discourse facilitates a clarification of the specific function of a proposition or of a concept in the network of inferential relations. Hence, the epistemic knowledge of meaning is possible without reducing it to empirically-accessible facts.

(b) Semantic Object-Relatedness and the Theory of Meaning of Koch and of Rüßmann

In their theory of meaning based on a realistic theory of meaning, Koch and Rüßmann put forward the thesis of the extension-determining function of the intension intention.[45] Hence, the subject sphere of an expression is determined by its meaning. Although Koch and Rüßmann refer to problems in this thesis, their concept is that the intension can be determined via the detour of ascertaining an extension. Linguistic meaning is hence epistemically accessible by identifying the articles and their characteristics to which an expression refers.

The thesis of Koch and Rüßmann is criticised by structuring legal theory as constituting a 'features semantics' based on a realistic theory of meaning.[46] This criticism is incomprehensible if only because Koch and Rüßmann at the same time accept the essential conventionality of linguistic meaning.[47] There is hence no question of Koch and Rüßmann representing

---

[43] This is described correctly by Busse, *Juristische Semantik* cf n 23 above
[44] On the difference between internal and external sanctions see p 121 above.
[45] See p 45 above.
[46] See p 56 above.
[47] See pp 45 f above.

dualistic semantics reducing meaning to a reflection of the world.[48] Structuring legal theory does assert that a conventional theory of meaning is incompatible with the statement of the relevance of object-related characteristics.[49] This allegation of incompatibility is, however, refuted by the thesis of the three dimensions of linguistic meaning as an integrative theory of meaning.

Using the results of the second chapter, the thesis of the extension-assigning role of the intension can be confirmed not in its absoluteness, but as a major element of a theory of meaning. The second dimension of meaning, namely semantic object-relatedness, is decisive for this.

Semantic object-relatedness was developed here to provide a link between normativity and truth. This link was reasoned by the claim to truth that is necessary in the practice of giving and demanding reasons. The characteristics of objects which can be empirically established, and to which the linguistic expressions refer, are relevant to the semantic correctness of speech acts.[50] Because of the other two dimensions of linguistic meaning, this relevance, however, does not go so far that meaning could be identified with mere object-relatedness. The thesis of the function of the intension as assigning extension is hence to be understood such that semantic object-relatedness provides a necessary but yet insufficient semantic criterion. If the thesis is understood in this way, the accusation of a 'feature semantics' based on a realistic theory of meaning does not hold water.

The concept mentioned above applies to the epistemic openness of semantic object-relatedness. The openness consists of making the reference explicit. This takes place via the three-fold expressive vocabulary. Singular terms express identity and existence, while attributions *de re* make social differences explicit, which in turn can be bridged by interpersonal anaphora. The scorekeepers thus pursue different referential perspectives on the extension of their linguistic expressions.

Semantic object-relatedness plays a specific role in the speech analysis discourse, in which meaning becomes epistemically open. This discourse contains an empirical-technical, specialist scientific discourse on the characteristics of objects of a world which is understood to be intersubjective and objective. Whether this perspective leads to a reification of the law is subject to dispute.

---

[48] But see Busse, *Juristische Semantik* (n 23 above) 107–11.
[49] Against Busse, *cf* n 23 above.
[50] See pp 101, 183 ff above.

(c) The Objection of the Reification of the Law

The second dimension of linguistic meaning—objectivity in the sense of object-relatedness—was developed in general terms in the second chapter on linguistic meaning. Objections are presented against transferring this general thesis to the law in that it can allegedly only take place at the price of a reification of the law. The dimension of object-relatedness is said to be able to apply to meaning in general terms, but not in the field of law. The objection of the reification of the law is similar to, but goes beyond, the objection of the special role of theoretical concepts.[51]

The objection of the reification of the law is put forward in three different versions.[52] The ontological variant points out that speaking of the object-relatedness of the law is opposed by the fact that there are allegedly no legal entities.[53] The dimension of object-relatedness can allegedly only apply to expressions related to concrete empirical objects, but not to abstract legal expressions such as 'guilt' or 'contract'. The epistemic variant points out that objects of the world can be empirically observed, whilst, because of their theoretical nature, many legal terms are accessible only from the perspective of a participant in a social practice. The variant of awareness (*mind-dependence*), finally, builds on a two-world teaching. Natural objects do not depend on awareness, and because of their externality are valid reference objects of thinking and language. Non-natural objects, such as those of the law, by contrast, are formed by awareness itself. Concepts can hence allegedly not be applied to them correctly or incorrectly.

The objection of the reification of the law is not convincing. First of all, one can establish that many questions also relate to the correct application of concepts to concrete empirical objects in the context of the law. Apart from this, it is true that many legal terms have no direct empirical counterpart. It is, however, not possible to conclude from this that legal language is not object-related. This would only be correct if the concept of object-relatedness were contingent on physical existence. This is incorrectly presumed to be the case by the ontological version of the objection. In rejecting the objection of the non-existence of an objective world, it was determined that the semantic objectivity thesis is not contingent on an ontological objectivity thesis. Language can refer to objects even if they do

---

[51] On the objection of the special role of theoretical concepts see p 197 above.
[52] Cf Stavropoulos, *Objectivity in Law* (n 19 above) 48.
[53] This 'lack of empirical counterparts' is used by HLA Hart for his semantics, see Stavropoulos, *Objectivity in Law* (n 19 above) 52–76.

not physically exist. Stavropoulos proved that it does not make any difference for Hart's semantics whether a concept has empirical *counterparts* or not.[54]

The assumption of the epistemic version of the objection—that the observation of legal meaning is contingent on the internal perspective of participants in a social practice—corresponds exactly to the expressive analysis of deontic scorekeeping pursued here. However, the premise that the meaning of norms could hence not be object-related is incorrect.[55]

The objection of *mind-dependence* is based on a strict subjectivism as to legal terms. This cannot explain the dimension of normativity, and is eliminated with the rejection of the analytical priority of individualism. In conventional practice, the condition of anti-reductionist supervenience can also be met for highly theory-dependent concepts. In assertion practice, *mind-dependent concepts* are of necessity linked to a claim to truth, so that a difference cannot be plausibly reasoned in this sense either. Existence and identity claims regarding non-linguistic objects are relative in social-perspective terms. In other words they are *mind-dependent*. This, however, does not prevent the assumption of the dimension of object-relatedness, since the referential gap between different speakers can be bridged by expressive vocabulary. The dependence of legal terms on social culture and forms of life does not rule out object-relatedness, but indeed includes it. Legal terms are contingent on social practice. They remain epistemically accessible, however, because practice itself can be analysed.

(iii) Result on the Second Issue

Both versions of the argument of the epistemic openness of meaning were linked with a dimension of linguistic meaning. First, the meaning norms, which Alexy refers to as rules for the use of words, can be understood as the implicit norms of assertion practice analysed by Brandom. This dimension of semantic normativity follows the structures analysed in the second chapter. Because of the proof of differentiated inferential relations and the fact of their covering both interpersonal *and* intrapersonal conditions and consequences, deontic scorekeeping facilitates a clear delimitation which is epistemically open to the first person.[56] This shows how the external justification of rules for the use of words is possible. Secondly, it has been possible to show that the thesis of the extension-assigning function of the intension, put forward by Koch and Rüßmann, is to be

[54] See Stavropoulos, *Objectivity in Law* (n 19 above) 68 f.
[55] Stavropoulos has proven that even highly theory-dependent observations can be labelled as being empirical, see *Objectivity in Law* (n 19 above) 77 f.
[56] See p 150 above.

understood in connection with the dimension of semantic object-relatedness. The objection of reification, which defies application of this dimension to the law, was rejected.

The *form* of the establishment of linguistic meaning consists not of counting the consensus of the majority, whatever form it may assume, but of *speech analysis discourse*. Decisive ambivalence leads to a situation in which one speaks of epistemic openness instead of the possibility of an empirical establishment. Because norms are not abstract, but arise in practice, practice must be observed. Because the practice of the majority can be wrong about the inferential relations, such an observation cannot be made by merely counting the majority opinion. What counts is the linguistic community: not the factual consensus in it, but the linguistic norms, which are instituted independently of opinions. Purely empirical activity can, however, also play a role, above all in connection with the discussion of characteristics of reference objects. In this case, an empirical discourse forms part of the speech analysis discourse.

The speech analysis discourse is in turn a discourse regarding the correctness of assertions, namely of assertions regarding meaning. In this sense, the speech analysis discourse is a special case of general-normative discourse. It is distinct from other discourses by virtue of the fact that the type of argument is restricted to specific semantics. It deals with specific semantic structures, which can be analysed in Brandom's terminology. The function of the speech analysis discourse also includes changing and improving the semantic structures of a linguistic community.[57] This future-orientated activity, which can lead to an *assignment* of meaning, is however to be separated from the past- and present-orientated recording of *available* inferential and normative structures in the sense of making explicit. Establishment and assignment remain two clearly-distinguishable types of speech analysis.

The topic of this section was the two structures developed in analytical legal theory which are vital to *establishing speech analysis discourses*. How these means of epistemic access work in detail in speech analysis discourse will be demonstrated at (B). Here, it is sufficient to be assured as a result that both aspects guarantee the epistemic openness of linguistic meaning. Linguistic meaning *is* epistemically accessible. There can hence be no question of 'arbitrariness' and 'free decision', as the establishment of meaning is designated[58] by the structuring legal theory. The second issue is hence also answered in favour of analytical legal theory.

---

[57] See p 208 above.
[58] *Cf* Busse, *Juristische Semantik* (n 23 above) 130; R Christensen, *Was heißt Gesetzesbindung? Eine rechtslinguistische Untersuchung* (Berlin, 1989) 180 f. On the argument of an empirical access to meaning see p 71 above.

C. The Objectivity of the Meaning of Norms

In the third issue, the intersubjective general validity of the meaning of norms is in dispute. The language game argument denies this objectivity, referring to the openness, the context-dependency and the circular innovation of meaning in language games. By contrast, the correction argument, the argument of legal culture and the argument of procedural correctness refer to argumentative standards of the legal interpretative community and the possibility of a review of interpretation assertions in the interpretation discourse.

The only negative argument addressed against objectivity, namely the language game argument, has already been rejected in all its forms. Over and above this, the intersubjective general validity of semantic norms was proven in the second chapter.[59] It is guaranteed by the fact of language referring to objects of a world that is jointly supposed to be objective, as well as by intersubjectively-shared, basic fundamental presumptions and the commonality of a ubiquitous assertion practice. The perspectival relativity of semantic content put forward by the language game argument has proven to be not an obstacle, but a precondition, of the intersubjective application of linguistic norms.

This position confirms the arguments of legal culture, of procedural correctness and of correction possibility only insofar as they do not mean a completely proceduralised correctness concept. In accordance with the view put forward here, the inferential relations, and hence the objectivity of the meaning of norms, exists *ex ante*. They precede the speech analysis discourse. The latter makes *existing* implicit structures explicit. They are not produced en passant in linguistic practice, but are supposed to exist in order to engage in speech analysis discourses *on them*. The concept of proceduralisation, which is linked to that of the speech analysis discourse, relates to the *form* of epistemic access, not to its *subject*. That something is epistemically open to a process does not mean that it is produced in that process. The inferences arise in practice, but they are taken to be the object of knowledge.

D. Result Regarding the Three Central Issues

The three central issues of the problem of the limits of the wording were answered on the basis of the thesis of the three dimensions of linguistic meaning, namely in favour of analytical legal theory. The criticism emanating from structuring legal theory has thus proven not to hold good in the

---

[59] See pp 192 ff above.

three major areas. It is now to be shown how the supplementation relation between analytical legal theory and the thesis of the three semantic dimensions works in detail.

II. THE THEORY OF THE LIMITS OF THE WORDING

The theory of the limits of the wording to be developed here distinguishes between semantically-constitutive clarity (B) and semantically-constitutive unclear meaning (C). Their relationship is to be discussed by way of an introduction (A).

A. The Relationship Between Semantic Clarity and Semantically-Unclear Meaning

The concept of the semantically-clear or unclear *case* refers to concrete speech acts, ie to linguistic expressions in an application situation. No abstract distinction can be created between clear and unclear *concepts*. This means that one may presume *two* different types of case, but only *one* type of linguistic expression, and hence a *single* structure. This structure is a continuum. Linguistic application cases can be more or less clear.[60] The extreme end points of the continuum are marked by the concept of the semantically-clear case, as well as by the classification of semantically-unclear cases.

On the basis of this relationship between semantic clarity and semantically-unclear meaning, one may in principle presume that a *uniform* theory of the limits of the wording can be developed which is applicable to both types of case. The view that it is possible to determine in advance whether a concept is semantically clear or semantically unclear, in order thereupon to apply either method A or method B, is erroneous. The *uniformity thesis* is favoured by the result of the following analysis, which shows a close similarity in the semantic limits in clear and unclear cases. It corresponds to Dworkin's interpretation theory, which states as follows: Hercules does not need one method for hard cases and another for easy ones.[61]

The classification of unclear cases according to ambiguity, vagueness and evaluative openness can hence be understood as an attempt to impose

---

[60] See p 216 above.
[61] R Dworkin, *Law's Empire* (London, 1986) 354. For a unified method, referring to Dworkin, see also N Stavropoulos, *Objectivity in Law* (n 19 above) 140 f; J Waldron, 'Vagueness in Law and Language. Some Philosophical Issues' (1994) *California Law Review* 509 at 521. Dworkin, however, ignores the externality of language to the law: He does not distinguish between semantic and juridical clearness, as can be seen in the following

The Theory of The Limits of The Wording 231

boundaries on the *non-liquet* area of the third form of semantic argument by showing that semantic argumentation is also possible in unclear cases. This means that two approaches can be applied here. First, the different types of semantic limit can be developed using clear cases (B). In the second step, unclear cases are studied (C). There is no need here to develop a second system of these limits. Both categories follow the same semantic norms and structures. Instead, the particularities of unclear cases are to be analysed. It is a matter of emphasising the characteristics shown by unclear cases within the continuum. It should be ascertained whether semantic limits also apply, and semantic arguments are possible, in unclear cases.

B. The Limits of the Wording with Constitutive Semantic Clarity

Semantically-constitutive clear cases of the use of a term constitute the norm both of linguistic assertion practice, and of legal subsumption. Nonetheless, the discussion in legal theory focuses on semantically-unclear cases. This is also because to date there has been no clear concept of the clear case. A more profound explanation of the function of the limits of the wording in clear cases is possible here for the first time because a differentiated concept of the semantically-clear case was developed with the aid of the three inferential dimensions.

The guiding idea above is to be seized upon in order to study the norm of assertion practice for semantic limits. As a result, the rules for the use of words coined by Alexy can be explained using Brandom's normative pragmatics (i). Then semantic limits are shown (ii) to (iv) in all three linguistic dimensions.

(i) The Function of Rules for the Use of Words in the Internal Justification

In accordance with the analysis by Alexy discussed in the first chapter, rules for the use of words are rules relating to the meaning of expressions used in preceding causal steps. The basic structure of the internal justification is as follows[62]:

(1) $(x) (Tx \rightarrow ORx)$ [R]
(2) $(x) (Mx \rightarrow Tx)$ [W]
(3) Ma
(4) ORa (1)–(3)

---

quotation: 'But we cannot locate the unclarity of the text in the ambiguity or vagueness or abstraction of any particular word or phrase in the statutes that provoked these cases'. see Dworkin, *Law's Empire* at 351.

[62] *Cf* R Alexy, *A Theory of Legal Argumentation. The Theory of Rational Discourse as Theory of Legal Justification* (Oxford, 1989) 234, and p 51 above.

In accordance with the guiding concept of the above approach, the rules for the use of words are to be constituted as the norms that are implicitly available in practice, which, according to Brandom, constitute meaning.[63] Two considerations favour this link. First, rules for the use of words make the inferential relations of an expression explicit. They list characteristics which must be met on the basis of the meaning so that the expression can be applied *correctly*. Secondly, in terms of their form, rules for the use of words are themselves inferences. The conclusion follows from the suitable circumstances of the use of the term, which are included in the characteristic catalogue as to the consequence existing in subsumption under T. In deontic scorekeeping, rules for the use of words are licences to draw conclusions, which formulate the correctness of inferential transitions as the content of an assertion on meaning. Brandom himself indicates that inferential content can be expressed in functions.[64] Rules for the use of words and linguistic meaning have the same formal structure.

Rules for the use of words present paradigmatically the link between inferential semantics and normative pragmatics developed by Brandom. Their *validity* can be explained by Brandom's normative pragmatics. They are rules which are implicitly contained in everyday linguistic practice. They are created by the attitudes and evaluations of linguistic participants; in other words, they are instituted through social practice.

As to their *content*, rules for the use of words are constitutive norms. They make meanings of concepts explicit by stating, through the characteristic catalogue M, sufficient conditions for the inferential transition to the use of the term, and hence regulate their semantic correctness.

As to the *possibility to establish* rules for the use of words, reference is to be made to the assertion on epistemic openness.[65] Rules for the use of words are made epistemically accessible by virtue of the fact that they themselves are made explicit. This takes place in the internal justification of legal rulings by explicitly stating the meaning rules used. This facilitates a speech analysis discourse in which the validity of rules for the use of words is clarified. To this end, an analysis must be carried out of the entire normative scorekeeping practice, the structures of which are made explicit using the extensive expressive vocabulary. The analysis of entering into and

---

[63] See p 223 above.

[64] '[O]ne might treat the inferential content expressed by a sentence tokening as a function ... The first element might consist of sets of inferentially sufficient antecedent claims (those from which the claim in question can be inferred) and the second of a set of inferentially necessary consequent claims (those that can be inferred from the claim in question)'. RB Brandom, *Making It Explicit. Reasoning, Representing, and Discursive Commitment* (Cambridge MA, 1994) 482. Brandom admits that he ignores the difference between committive and entitlement-preserving inferences insofar, see *Making It Explicit* at 482 fn 95. By contrast, this difference is acknowledged by the theory developed here, see p 233 below.

[65] See pp 219 ff above.

assignment of deontic status by the members of the linguistic community shows which rules for the use of words are valid.

Rules for the use of words can be analysed using the three dimensions of linguistic meaning. It is possible to establish semantic limits in all three dimensions.

(ii) Semantic Limits in the First Linguistic Dimension

The dimension of normativity is predestined for the search for semantic limits. In it lies the possibility of semantic errors par excellence. This possibility arises in the model of deontic scorekeeping because of the complex structures of inferential relations and normative status. As soon as a scorekeeper incorrectly categorises such relations or incorrectly assigns commitments and entitlements, he or she is in error with regard to deontic status, and hence to the meaning of a linguistic expression. This error regarding inferential relations constitutes the main category of a breach of semantic limits of the normativity dimension (a). Supplements emerge from the circumstance that rules for the use of words are related primarily to subsentential expressions (b).

(a) The Four Limits of Inferential Relations

The limits of inferential relations arise from the concept of semantic clarity, which has been explained using the three inferential dimensions.[66] The *first inferential dimension* emerges as especially fruitful for the question of semantic limits. It relates to the interplay between the deontic status of commitment and entitlement using inferences of suitable circumstances to suitable consequences of a speech act. The four questions[67] that were developed for this purpose correspond to four limits, which are developed in sequence (1) to (4) and are then clarified as to their interrelationship (5).

(1) Conditional Commitment Limit This meaning limit is violated if a speech act links the commitment to circumstances which are incompatible with the actual conditional commitments of the linguistic expressions. The commitments to circumstances entered into from the viewpoint of the speaker counter the actual commitments to circumstances. Semantic errors on the part of individual speakers with regard to the conditional commitments are possible because a singular scorekeeping perspective does not necessarily reflect the actual conditional commitments of a term correctly.

---

[66] See pp 213 ff above.
[67] See p 214 above.

Overstepping the conditional commitment limit is based on a deviation by the individual from the background commitments that are relevant in overall scorekeeping practice.

Conditional commitments are represented in rules for the use of words by the characteristic catalogue M. This catalogue determines the suitable circumstances for the use of the term. The conditional commitment limit is overstepped by speaker S committing him/herself to a specific characteristic catalogue M_2 by using a linguistic expression in a certain situation which is incompatible with characteristic catalogue M_1, which in turn is actually correct for the expression. The rule for the use of words W is incorrectly formulated by S. This is the first type of W error. The inferential relation of the inheritance of commitment is incorrectly presumed for the inference of $M_2 x$ to $T_1 x$.

The conditional commitment may be overstepped in two ways. Depending on the characteristics of the objects to which S applies the linguistic expression, the incorrect wording of W results either in an incorrect M negation or in an erroneous M affirmation. If individual a corresponds to the correct characteristic M_1, but not to M_2, which is erroneously included by the speaker in W, then the speaker erroneously commits him/herself to $\neg M a$. If, by contrast, a fulfils M_2, but not M_1, Ma is erroneously affirmed by S.

These two sub-types of overstepping the conditional commitment limit can be explained using examples. The concept of a criminal 'gang' (*Bande*) in accordance with section 244(1) number 2 of the German Criminal Code (*Strafgesetzbuch* (*StGB*)) was contentious prior to the ruling of the High Senate for Criminal Matters of the Federal Court of Justice dated 3 April 2001. In accordance with the established precedents of the Federal Court of Justice applicable until then, it was sufficient, to fulfil the elements of an offence committed as a member of a gang, that two persons had combined with the serious intent to commit, for a certain period, several independent criminal offences as yet individually undetermined.[68] By contrast, the idea was raised in academic comments for a long time that a gang should not be confirmed until at least three persons were combined.[69] The submitting 4th Criminal Division of the Federal Court of Justice concurred. Both the reference material and the 4th Division, in their

---

[68] *Cf* BGHSt 23, 239 f; 31, 202 (205); 38, 26 (27 f); 39, 216 (217); 42, 255 (257 f); BGH NStZ 1998, 255 f; StV 2000, 259.
[69] *Cf* E Dreher, 'Aus zwei Mitgliedern bestehende Bande. Anmerkung' (1970) *Neue Juristische Wochenschrift* 1803; A Engländer, 'Anmerkung zum Beschluß des BGH v. 14.3.2000—4 StR 284/99' (2000) *Juristenzeitung* 630; R Schmitz, 'Begriff der Bande. Anmerkung' (2000) *Neue Zeitschrift für Strafrecht* 477.

criticism of the precedents to date, invoked the limits of the wording of the term gang. Hence, the 4th Criminal Division found as follows in its submission order:

> The view that it was reconcilable with the word 'gang' to include within this characteristic a criminal association formed of only two persons ... gives rise to considerable reservations ... It is however not incorrectly submitted that this interpretation is incompatible with the limits of the wording; in accordance with the social usage a gang is said rather to be contingent on more than two members.[70]

The central issue between this criticism and the previous precedents of the Federal Court of Justice was the wording of the rule for the use of words W applicable to the concept of a 'gang'. Whilst previous precedents conditionally linked the characteristic M_2 (two persons can be sufficient) with the concept of a gang (T), the criticism presumed the characteristic M_1 (at least three persons).

It is presumed here that the better reasons favour the assumption that the implicit norms of assertion practice correctly record as semantically correct the use of the term 'gang' only when there are at least three persons. For this reason, the previous precedents overstepped the conditional commitment limit by including an incorrect M_2 in W. With respect to an individual *a* (criminal association of two persons), this leads to an erroneous M affirmation, ie to the inclusion of a negative candidate. From the point of view of the previous precedents, by contrast, the criticism includes an incorrect M_1 in the rule for the use of words for the concept of a gang. This semantic error results, for individual *a*, in the exclusion of a positive candidate on the basis of an erroneous M negation. The dispute is hence pursued concerning the conditional commitment limit.[71]

A further example of the violation of the conditional commitment limit is a judgment by a Chamber of the Federal Constitutional Court. It relates to the violation of Article 103(2) of the German Basic Law (*Grundgesetz* (*GG*)) by virtue of an extensive interpretation of section 241(1) of the Criminal Code.[72] This constitutional complaint related to the constitutional limits for the interpretation of the term 'close friend or relative' (*nahestehende Person*) in the element of the offence of threat in accordance with section 241(1) of the Criminal Code. The Local Court and the Regional Court had convicted the complainant, who came from Viet Nam, of insult in concurrence of offences with threat. She had said to a worker at the social welfare office: 'You bad woman, just look out, your children do badly, your children dead'. The complainant did not know at that time that

---

[70] BGH, Order 26. Oktober 2000, 4 StR 284/99.
[71] *Cf* BVerfG NJW 1997, 1910–11; BGHSt 46, 321–8.
[72] BVerfG NJW 1995, 2776–7.

the worker did not have any children. The criminal courts interpreted the concept of 'close friend or relative', against whom the threatened crime must be addressed, such that this person does not need to actually exist. In this sense, it was said to be a matter only of the mental state of the person issuing the threat. The Federal Constitutional Court found that this interpretation overstepped the limits of the wording of the term close friend or relative. The general meaning of the term close friend or relative is said to refer to a person actually existing. The criminal courts based their interpretation on an incorrect rule for the use of words. This conditionally linked an incorrect M_2 (person does not need to actually exist) instead of the correct M_1 (person must actually exist) with the concept of a close friend or relative. With respect to an individual a (the children of the worker existing only in the mind of the complainant), the criminal courts hence reached an erroneous M affirmation.

(2) Conditional Entitlement Limit This limit is violated if the circumstances which justify their use in accordance with the linguistic expressions do not apply on the occasion of a speech act. The actual circumstances of the speech act do not justify the use of the linguistic expression.

In contradistinction to the conditional commitment limit, W was correctly formulated here by the speaker, ie in concurrence with the entire scorekeeping practice. The error lies instead more or less in the subsumption. Two types of error are possible: Either the entitlement to Ma is erroneously presumed and Ta is concluded from it, or the entitlement to ¬Ma is erroneously presumed, and ¬Ta is concluded from that. The first error leads to the linguistic expression being applied to an object to which it does not correctly apply. The second error leads to the linguistic expression not being applied to an object although it does apply to it. The inferential relation of the inheritance of entitlement between Ma and Ta is incorrectly affirmed in the first case, whilst it is incorrectly negated in the second.

The conditional entitlement limit can also be explained using examples. In a ruling from 1999, the Federal Constitutional Court declared unconstitutional the across-the-board exclusion of persons unable to write or speak from testamentary capacity, by sections 2232 and 2233 of the German Civil Code (*Burgerliches Gesetzbuch* (*BGB*)) and section 31 of the German Authentication Act (Beurkundungsgesetz (*BeurkG*)) because of a violation of the guarantee of the right of inheritance of Article 14(1) of the Basic Law, as well as of the general principle of equality of Article 3(1) of the Basic Law, and of the prohibition of discrimination against persons with disabilities in Article 3(3) of the Basic Law. In doing so, the Court also found on the question of whether these norms of civil law could be constitutionally interpreted. The requirement of one's own writing could be broadly interpreted, so that not only writing by hand, but also with the mouth, the foot, with stencils or type-written declarations could be admitted. The forms of expression of pure deaf-and-dumb language or movement symbols could, however, no longer be subsumed among the elements 'written down or on a separate sheet' contained in section 31 of the Authentication Act. According to the Court, this would overstep the limit drawn by the wording of the statute.

Such an overstepping of limits was not based on a W error. A legal practitioner who commits the above error can, rather, correctly observe the semantic characteristics applicable to the element. If he or she subsumes pure movement symbols to the element 'written down or on a separate sheet', he or she instead commits a factual error. He or she erroneously presumes an entitlement to Ma. This erroneous M affirmation leads to negative candidates being included in the subsumption.

An example of overstepping the conditional entitlement limit by erroneous M negation can be derived from a remark of the Federal Constitutional Court. The Federal Constitutional Court had to rule on a constitutional complaint against the seizure of the horror film entitled 'The Evil Dead'.[73] Seizure had been based on the film having violated section 131(1) number 4 of the Criminal Code. This norm is contingent on writings within the meaning of section 11(3) of the Criminal Code depicting cruel or otherwise inhuman acts of violence against human beings. The plot of the film that was seized is about three women and two men who go to a weekend house in a forest, where they are disturbed by inexplicable manifestations. In accordance with a magic formula, they transform all but one, taking on non-humans traits, and hunt one another with destructive intentions. Those who are not yet possessed defend themselves against the attacks, finally killing or destroying those who are. All this is presented in a gruesome manner.

The Federal Constitutional Court found as follows: The prohibition of analogy of Article 103(2) of the Basic Law does not permit the concept of a 'human being' contained in section 131(1) of the Criminal Code to be interpreted such that it also covers human-like beings which are a product of fantasy (so-called zombies). In the interpretation of the term human being, accordingly, the conditional commitment limit is overstepped if the concept of a human being is allocated to an incorrect characteristic M_2, which is intended to be similar to human beings. The Federal Constitutional Court could, however, not prove to the criminal courts that *this* limit had been overstepped. The characters in the horror film 'The Evil Dead' clearly start as human beings and only transform into victims of possession as the plot unfolds. They nonetheless remain human beings from the point of view of the audience and as intended within the film. The criminal

[73] BVerfGE 87, 209.

courts have therefore not presumed an incorrect meaning of the term human being. They subsumed on the basis of the correct characteristic catalogue M_1. This subsumption is not subject to review by the constitutional courts as a non-constitutional-court judgment. The question of whether the victims of violent acts shown in a film are human beings or human-like beings is a factual matter within the remit of the criminal courts, which is not subject to review by the constitutional court.[74]

It must nonetheless be found that such an error of subsumption particularly constitutes an overstepping of the conditional entitlement limit. If we presume that, in another film, it is exclusively human beings who are the victim of violent acts from the outset, the lack of application of section 131(1) of the Criminal Code to this film would constitute a semantically-erroneous M negation based on a factual error regarding the definitions to be applied. The interesting circumstance becomes clear here that the Federal Constitutional Court may not review specific violations of the limits of the wording. This would entail overstepping the conditional entitlement limit in a manner which is always based on subsumption errors pure and simple.

(3) Consequential Commitment Limit   This limit is violated if the commitments to consequences, made with a speech act, are incompatible with the actual consequential commitments of the linguistic expressions. The commitments to consequences entered into from the point of view of the speaker contradict the actual commitments to consequences.

Consequential commitments are represented in rules for the use of words amongst other things by the factual expressions T. These determine a type of suitable consequence of the use of the term. The consequential commitment limit is overstepped by virtue of the fact that the speaker, in using a linguistic expression in a certain situation, has committed him/herself to a specific consequence T_2, which is incompatible with the actual applicable consequence T_1. W is incorrectly formulated by the speaker. This is the second type of W error. The inferential relation of the inheritance of commitment is incorrectly presumed for the inference of M_1x to T_2x.

The consequential entitlement limit can also be overstepped in two ways. Depending on the nature of the objects to which S applies the linguistic expression, either an erroneous T affirmation or an erroneous T negation applies. If individual *a* complies with a correct T_1, but not with the T_2 erroneously included in W by S, T*a* is erroneously negated. If, by contrast, *a* complies with T_2, but not with T_1, T*a* is erroneously affirmed.

It must be asked what it means if we state that an incorrect T is included in W. Characteristics which apply to a legal term T_1 are conditionally

---

[74] BVerfGE 87, 209 (226).

linked by S in W with another legal term, T_2. The consequence of this semantic error is that, because of the characteristic M_1, an individual a is subsumed under T_2 instead of under T_1. Accordingly, another legal term is used for the subsumption. By contrast, the concept which would be correct on the basis of the characteristics is overlooked here.

A ruling of Hanover Finance Court[75] overstepped the consequential commitment limit through an erroneous T negation. The Finance Court had to rule on the income limit of section 32(4) sentence 2 of the German Income Tax Act (*Einkommenssteuergesetz* (*EStG*)), which is detrimental to child benefit entitlement. This norm speaks of 'income and remuneration' of the child which are offset under certain preconditions. The division, however, reached the conclusion that, by means of 'teleological analogy' beyond the wording of the quoted provision, the income limit is to be related to the taxable income within the meaning of section 32a(1) and section 2(5) of the Income Tax Act. The wording of the statutory provision is said to fall far short of the declared statutory purpose with regard to the determination of the income limit.

The division was aware here that it was overstepping the limits of the wording of the term 'income' within the meaning of section 32(4) sentence 2 of the Income Tax Act. The concept of income is legally defined in section 2(2) sentence 2 of the Income Tax Act. The statute hence oversteps a certain M_1 (legal definition in section 2(2) sentence 2 of the Income Tax Act) for legal term T_1 ('income' in section 32(4) sentence 2 of the Income Tax Act). The legal definition makes the concept of income semantically clear. The Finance Court, by contrast, used a second legal term T_2, namely the concept of taxable income within the meaning of section 2(5) of the Income Tax Act. It linked this T_2 with the legal consequence of section 32(4) sentence 2 of the Income Tax Act.

The concept of taxable income covers the total amount of income, minus income-related expenses, operational expenditure, special expenditure and extraordinary expenses. The use of T_2 in place of T_1 therefore leads to a *lower* amount in the concrete case, so that children are *more* likely to be provided for in accordance with section 32(4) sentence 2 of the Income Tax Act. For the taxpayer, an allowance in accordance with section 32(6) of the Income Tax Act is more likely to be recognised. For individual a (the amount of money by which the income of the child exceeds the taxable income in a concrete case), the position of the Finance Court leads accordingly to an erroneous T negation by virtue of the fact of this amount of money not being included in the provision of the income limit which is

---

[75] FG Hannover, 20 July 1999, FR 1999, 1074–6.

detrimental to child benefit entitlement. Hence, the consequential commitment limit is overstepped, in other words creating a further development of the law.

In this sense, the position of the courts cannot be criticised in methodical terms. It is, however, questionable what type of further development of the law this is. For teleological reasons, the Finance Court wanted to see the legal term T_2 (taxable income) behind the expression 'income' in section 32(4) sentence 2 of the Income Tax Act, although this expression, because of the legal definition, stands for the term T_1 (income within the meaning of section 2(5) of the Income Tax Act). In order to achieve this purpose, the Finance Court *constituted* a *new norm* in which the legal consequence of section 32(4) sentence 2 of the Income Tax Act did not apply to T_1, but to T_2. The Finance Court was of the opinion that this was an analogy. The Federal Finance Court concurred in the subsequent ruling on an appeal on points of law (*Revision*).[76] However, because of the legal definition of the term 'income', it negated the existence of a loophole.

What is interesting at this point is not the question of the admissibility of the further development of the law, but the question of whether the application of the law by the Finance Court was correctly referred to as an analogy. Since the concept of taxable income is narrower than that of income, the area of application of the term T_1 is *de facto limited* by the use of the term T_2 for the expression 'income' in section 32(4) sentence 2 of the Income Tax Act. An analogy however expands the area of application of a norm. Hence, this is a teleological reduction of section 32(4) sentence 2 of the Income Tax Act which was incorrectly referred to as an analogy both by the Finance Court, and by the Federal Finance Court.

Particular interest attaches to the fact that overstepping the consequential commitment limit, insofar as it leads to an erroneous T negation, constitutes a further development of the law in the shape of a *teleological reduction*.

An example of overstepping the consequential commitment limit by means of an erroneous T affirmation can be derived from a ruling of the Federal Constitutional Court.[77] The constitutional complaint proceedings related to the question of whether a convict must accept the cost of the proceedings being offset against his pocket money entitlement in accordance with section 109 of the German Prison Act (*Strafvollzugsgesetz (StVollzG)*). The court cashier had applied section 121(5) of the Prison Act analogously. This norm is a provision regarding collection of court costs. The administrative procedure for collection by means of offsetting is governed by the Prison Act, such that the convict's claim to disbursement

---

[76] BFHE 192, 316.
[77] BVerfG NJW 1996, 3146.

of the prisoner's personal money, or house money, (*Hausgeld*) expires by being offset. This makes unnecessary the otherwise customary resort to attachment and transfer. Section 121(5) of the Prison Act permits offsetting explicitly only with regard to a prisoner's personal money account, in accordance with section 47 of the Prison Act. The court cashier had hence analogously applied section 121(5) of the Prison Act to the convict's payment of pocket money (*Taschengeld*) within the meaning of section 46 of the Prison Act. The enforcement courts had approved this analogous application. The convict addressed his constitutional complaint against this.*[78]

The essential problem which emerges in this case is the question of the degree to which a prohibition of analogy is to be presumed under administrative law.[79] The only material matter at this point is that the enforcement courts overstepped the limits of the wording of the term 'house money'—the only term with regard to which the law declares offsetting to be permissible—by also applying the legal consequence of the permissibility of offsetting to the concept of 'pocket money'. Hence, at this point the important realisation is possible that the consequential commitment limit was overstepped by erroneous T affirmation by means of *analogy*.

Finally, the particularities of overstepping the consequential commitment limit are to be re-emphasised. This limit is overstepped if the interpretation amounts to a *textual correction* by legal practitioners. This is not only a restrictive interpretation, but also a teleological reduction (erroneous T negation), or not only an extensive interpretation, but also an analogy (erroneous T affirmation). The wording of the norm is replaced by quasi norm-wording, formulated by the legal practitioner.[80] Such a further development of the law is declared to be an interpretation if it is acted upon as if it were a matter of characteristics for a concept of the statutory elements of the offence, whilst the attribution of these characteristics to this concept fails in reality because of the limits of the wording of this term. In fact, therefore, the legal practitioner inserts a second elementary term in the norm, thus amending it.[81]

---

[78] * Translator's note: The official (Federal Ministry of Justice) translation of s 47 of the German Prison Act reads as follows: 'The prisoner shall be permitted to spend three-sevenths per month of his earnings regulated in this Act (house money) and of the pocket money (s 46) on purchases (s 22(1)) or to use it for other purposes'.
[79] See O Konzak, 'Analogie im Verwaltungsrecht. Entscheidungsbesprechung' (1997) *Neue Zeitschrift für Verwaltungsrecht* 872 f.
[80] See M-E Geis, 'Die "Eilversammlung" als Bewährungsprobe verfassungskonformer Auslegung. Verfassungsrechtsprechung im Dilemma zwischen Auslegung und Rechtsschöpfung' (1992) *Neue Zeitschrift für Verwaltungsrecht* 1025 at 1027.
[81] M Seebode, 'Wortlautgrenze und Strafbedürfnis. Die Bedeutung des Wortlauts der Strafgesetze am Beispiel eigennütziger Strafvereitelung' (1998) *Juristenzeitung* 781 at 782.

This amendment of the norm is disguised if one pretends that it is a matter of the definition of the term of the norm. The major characteristic of overstepping the consequential commitment limit is this: The rule for the use of words which is used for the subsumption is incorrectly formulated insofar as it is not the concept T_1 which is selected by the statutory norm, but another concept T_2. The inclusion of additional elements in the norm can lead to a restriction or expansion of its area of application. In the first case it is a teleological reduction. Here, the inclusion of an incorrect T results in an erroneous T negation. The second case is an analogy. In that case, the inclusion of an incorrect T results in an erroneous T affirmation.

(4) Consequential Entitlement Limit This limit is violated if a speech act requires an entitlement to consequences which are incompatible with the actual consequence entitlement of the linguistic expressions. The entitlement to consequences claimed within a speech act contradicts the actual entitlement to consequences.

As with the conditional entitlement limit, W is correctly formulated by S. S is, however, in error as to the subsumption. Here too—mirroring the conditional entitlement limit—there are two types of error. The speaker either erroneously presumes the entitlement to T*a*, or erroneously negates this entitlement.

The first error (erroneous T affirmation) leads to the linguistic expression being applied to an object to which it does not correctly apply. The second error (erroneous T negation) leads to the linguistic expression not being applied to an object although it does apply to it. The semantic error of overstepping the consequential entitlement limit is not based on a mis-assessment of the inheritance of entitlement from M*x* to T*x*. Instead, it arises out of an exclusively T-centred perspective.

It is to be asked at this point what it *means* in terms of content to erroneously negate or erroneously affirm T. The score of the speaker's commitments contains three elements: The correctly-formulated W, the correct subsumption under M*a* (in other words the correct commitment to M*a* or ¬M*a*), and the semantically-erroneous subsumption under T*x* (in other words the commitment to T*a* or ¬T*a*). The set of these three elements is incoherent. The erroneous T affirmation or negation must be based on non-semantic reasons because there is no other way of explaining why, despite a correct W and the correct subsequence subsumption, the speaker reaches the erroneous T affirmation or negation. Such reasons are gained from the other legal forms of argument. They lead the speaker to introduce exceptional reasons or to carry out further development of the law by analogy or teleological reduction *in order to* be able to make a commitment T*a* or ¬T*a*.

This shows what it means to claim semantically-erroneous consequence entitlements from a T-centred perspective. For the speaker it is ascertained for non-linguistic reasons that T is to be affirmed or negated, although in semantic terms this means overstepping the consequential entitlement limit.

(5) The System and Function of the Inferential Limits   The system and function of the inferential limits are explained by seven supplementary remarks.

First, all inferential limits refer to *linguistic expressions* in general terms. This covers both propositions and subsentential expressions. Primarily, inferential relations exist between propositions. The reason for this is the analytical priority of the propositional meaning.[82] Also the limits of the wording are hence primarily to be reconstructed at propositional level. The rules for the use of words refer as a rule to individual concepts. Such subsentential expressions take on *indirect* inferential significance, which will be directly analysed in (b).

A further common feature of all inferential limits lies, *secondly,* in the fact that they are based on the *concept of incompatibility*.[83] This emerges as a major guiding concept for the limits of the wording. Incompatibility exists in all cases between the actual deontic status of linguistic expressions and those which a speaker enters into with a speech act. This establishment lends much greater precision to the limits of the wording. That incompatibility is required and mere deviation or non-concurrence are insufficient is understandable in view of the social perspectivity of conceptual content. Latitude exists for mere deviations in that the individual background commitments never entirely cover themselves. It is only with incompatibility that one may speak of overstepping the semantic limit.

The linguistic community can react in different manners to overstepping. If incompatibility is insisted on, the entitlement of the speaker to the contested speech act ceases to apply. This makes it clear that overstepping the limit in scorekeeping practice is categorised as such, ie the doxastic commitment is not accepted for semantic reasons. The linguistic community then deals with speaker S as if he or she had not spoken. In particular, other scorekeepers do not add the incompatible commitment to the scores held by them for S. This establishes that a semantic limit has been overstepped.

If, by contrast, the deontic scorekeepers wish to accept a conditional commitment of a speaker going beyond the conditional commitment limit in accordance with the implicit norms of the *previous* practice, they can

---

[82] See p 122 above.
[83] In contradistinction to the other limits, this is not directly comprehensible in the conditional entitlement limit because it does not contain the concept of incompatibility in the above formulation. On the merits, here too this is also an incompatibility which exists between the justifying circumstances entered into with a speech act and the actual circumstances which do not show this entitlement.

add the new commitment to their scores. At the same time, all commitments which are incompatible with it are deleted because the entitlement to them in the inferential network can no longer be proven because of incompatibility. The decisive point is that such a *change to the scores* can be so described. It is then an accepted *assignment* of meaning. It can also be said in very general terms that changes in the deontic scores can be described as such. This is the central argument in favour of the thesis that a distinction can be made between establishment and assignment of linguistic meaning.

Thirdly, the concept of incompatibility in conjunction with W permits a precise analysis of the system of the inferential limits. Reference has already been made to some contexts. Here, one may now presume that only two types of limit initially exist using the rule for the use of words W, which can be referred to as *positive and negative limits of the wording*. A speech act p oversteps the positive limits of the wording if it marginalises a positive candidate. This corresponds to non-adherence to the first form of semantic argument in the categorisation given by Alexy.[84] Here, there is incompatibility with W because two commitments are entered into by virtue of speech act p, which cannot be maintained at the same time as W (p: Ma $\wedge \neg$Ta). A speech act q oversteps the negative limits of the wording if it includes a negative candidate. This corresponds to non-adherence to the second form of the semantic argument in the categorisation given by Alexy. Here too there is incompatibility with W because two commitments are entered into with the speech act, which cannot be simultaneously maintained with W (q: $\neg$Ma $\wedge$Ta). These two types are to be referred to as the two *main types of general semantic limit*.

The four inferential limits constitute *sub-types*. They can be assigned to the two main types. This assignment is possible because incompatibilities in the two main types of limit of the wording can each be based on four different errors, which can be depicted with the four inferential limits. The errors each refer either to the subsequens, to the consequens or to the conditional of W, ie the link of subsequens and consequens in a rule for the use of words.

The *incompatibility of the positive limits of the wording* arises, first, if the first sub-type of the conditional commitment limit is overstepped. Here, the error lies in the conditional. W is incorrectly formulated because an incorrect M is included, in other words M_2 in place of M_1. The speaker fails to recognise from his perspective that Ma has been complied with, and hence erroneously commits him/herself to $\neg$Ma and concludes $\neg$Ta. Secondly, the incompatibility of the positive limits of the wording comes about if the first sub-type of the conditional entitlement limit is overstepped.

---

[84] See p 52 above.

Here, speaker W has formulated correctly in his/her background commitments. He or she is, however, factually in error as to the subsequens by virtue of erroneously negating M*a*, in other words concluding ¬T*a*, although the entitlement to M*a* is given. Thirdly, incompatibility lies in the positive limits of the wording if the first sub-type of the consequential commitment limit is overstepped. Here the error lies in the conditional. W is wrongly formulated because an incorrect T is selected, in other words instead of T_1 for instance T_2. The speaker does not recognise from his or her perspective that T_1 has been complied with, and hence erroneously commits him/herself to ¬T*a*. The fourth case is the overstepping of the first sub-type of the consequential entitlement limit. Here, speaker W formulates correctly, but erroneously presumes the entitlement to ¬T*a*. This error hence relates to the actual subsumption with regard to the consequens in W.

The *incompatibility of the negative limit of the wording* also arises in four cases: First, when the second sub-type of conditional commitment limit is overstepped. The speaker formulates W incorrectly by linking an incorrect M_2 as subsequens with T. The consequence of this is that the speaker fails to recognise from his or her perspective that the correct M_1 has not been complied with. He or she hence insists on $M_2 a$ and concludes T*a* although $M_1 a$ in fact does not apply. Incompatibility arises, secondly, when the second sub-type of conditional entitlement limit is overstepped. Here, the speaker formulates W correctly, but is factually in error as to the subsequens. He or she erroneously presumes the entitlement to M*a* and concludes the entitlement to T*a* although the entitlement to M*a* is not given.

Thirdly, incompatibility with the negative limit of the wording arises when the second sub-type of consequential commitment limit is overstepped. The error of S lies in the conditional. W is wrongly formulated because an incorrect T_2 is presumed instead of the correct T_1. The speaker does not recognise from his/her perspective that T_1 has not been complied with, and hence erroneously commits him/herself to T*a*. On the basis of the commitment $M_1 a$, he or she subsumes under an incorrect T_2. The fourth case is the overstepping of the second sub-type of consequential entitlement limit. The speaker formulates W correctly, but is factually in error when it comes to the consequens by wrongly presuming the entitlement to T*a*.

Fourthly, it should be emphasised that this inferential system is entrenched in the practice of deontic scorekeeping. The correctness of the inferences cannot be judged solely using the inferential relations, but emerges from norms implicit in practice. Only the interplay between inferential semantics and *normative pragmatics* makes it possible to establish whether limits have been violated, and if so which.

Fifthly, the semantic limits which have been portrayed can be explained using the *second inferential dimension.*[85] A distinction is made in the second inferential dimension between intrapersonal and interpersonal consequences of deontic status. The inheritance of commitments and entitlements can be viewed for the same person or for other persons. In law, the communicative inheritance impact is important above all. The semantic interpretation of laws relates to *interpersonal inheritance* of semantic commitments and entitlements of the legislature on legal practitioners. Legal interpretation views the complex inferential structures of a community. These interpersonal structures of semantic content are already represented by the four limits of the first inferential dimension. All four limits are based on a contradiction between the individual use of linguistic expressions by individual speakers and the correct usage, which emerges from a community's view of the interpersonal inheritance structures.

At intrapersonal level, semantic limits which are of general validity for the scorekeeping practice cannot be drawn. No consequences for the semantic correctness of speech acts emerge from a purely internal view of the individual scorekeeping perspective. The view of the intrapersonal structure, however, is necessary in order to cover the different sets of background commitments and individual inheritance relations. Only on this basis is it possible to determine the precise course of the interpersonal, supraperspective inferential limits, as well as whether they are overstepped by individual speech acts. Although the intrapersonal impact of deontic status is not sufficient to explain meaning and its limits, intrapersonal contents are nonetheless a necessary part of such an explanation. The intrapersonal dimension is significant as a preliminary step towards the inferential limits. The clarification of the interpersonal inheritance impact is contingent on clarity existing concerning what individual speakers are entitled to according to their own scorekeeping perspective, which further commitments they have entered into on the basis of inheritance of commitment, etc.

Sixthly, the semantic limits are to be explained using the *third inferential dimension.* The third inferential dimension takes into account the link between authority and responsibility in the discourse. In the universal assertion practice, which consists of giving and demanding reasons, the authority of commitments entered into and allotted consists of basing further commitments on inferential reasons. It reaches only as far as the speaker can meet his or her discursive responsibility, ie the reasoning responsibility entered into with speech acts by giving rise, in turn, to an assertion used as a reason.

---

[85] On the three inferential dimensions see p 129 above.

The semantic authority of a proposition is limited. It is not possible to conclude from one commitment other unrelated commitments. Inheritance of commitment is, rather, specifically determined within the inferential network on the basis of implicit norms. This circumstance can be described as a *limit of discursive authority*. A speech act oversteps this limit if it does not consider the actual inheritance impact of a doxastic commitment.

The limit of discursive authority asks which inheritance impact emerges from a proposition. It relates to the inferential *consequences*, and hence constitutes a *type of description* of the consequential commitment limit and the consequential entitlement limit. Overstepping these two latter limits signifies non-adherence to the discursive authority of a proposition.

Corresponding with this, a *limit of the discursive responsibility* can be presumed. It relates to the inferential *circumstances* of a proposition and asks whether correct reasons can be stated for this proposition. This examination of the entitlement constitutes a semantic limit because arbitrary reasons cannot be stated in order to prove the entitlement to a proposition. The limit of the discursive responsibility is a type of description of the conditional commitment limit and of the conditional entitlement limit.

The entitlement to a proposition can be demonstrated in a variety of ways.[86] The statement of reasons takes place in the structure of the internal justification of a legal ruling by means of rules for the use of words for the various steps being used.[87] This is the case if the existence of M on the one hand is reasoned with a rule for the use of words W', which in its turn contains as subsequens a characteristic catalogue M', which in turn is justified with a rule for the use of words W", etc. This *structure of M steps* reflects the inferential network of the meanings of the linguistic expressions used, which is opened by making the internal structure explicit. The formal justice rules formulated by Alexy, which require as far-reaching an explication as possible, apply to this opening of the limit of the discursive responsibility.[88]

The default-and-challenge structure of the discursive entitlement also holds considerable significance in this context.[89] Fundamental propositions and basal fundamental presumptions of a language enjoy a status of entitlement prima facie. This can be shaken by the secondary speech acts expressing the distancing or the challenge only if these doubts in turn are justified. The consequence of this is that unjustified or wrongly-founded doubt with regard to such propositions constitutes a particularly grievous breach of the limit of discursive responsibility.

---

[86] See p 130 above.
[87] Cf Alexy, *A Theory of Legal Argumentation* (n 62 above) 224–8.
[88] Alexy, *A Theory of Legal Argumentation* (n 62 above) 227 f.
[89] On the default and challenge structure of entitlement see p 149 above.

Seventhly, there is a need to study the *relationship between the inferential limits*. The analysis put forward here is very delicate. The inferential limits are highly interdependent in content terms. It is hence only a terminological question as to whether they are understood as separable, different types of limit, or as different descriptions of the fact that the inferential role of a linguistic expression is wrongly understood, whether as four different limits, or as four types of expression of a single limit.

One objection which suggests itself is that this analysis is allegedly too delicate. Such an objection could be reasoned with the consideration that the inferential consequences belong with the circumstances, ie with the characteristic catalogue M. A speaker S is said to determine by the speech act 'That is a window' the consequence 'I can open it' *because* windows are allegedly defined by the *characteristic* of being able to be opened. The separation of circumstances and consequences carried out here is thus said to have undue analytical depth.

It should be said against this that consequences indeed also belong with M. There is, however, nothing against emphasising the specific consequence Ta as a special inferential consequence. This is the only way to correctly include the specific function of W in the internal justification. A speaker determines that a specific opening in a building wall is a window because he or she enters into a specific consequence commitment. The focus lies particularly on the idea that the opening is subsumed under 'window'. He or she determines the consequence without looking at the characteristic catalogue M at all. This point of view is clearly distinct from an M-centred perspective.

The difference lies not in the fact, but in the detail of the analysis. All four inferential limits have in common that the inferential role of a speech act is incorrectly understood in the network of the assertions. The benefit of the structural analysis entered into here consists of the fact that it makes explicit the different types of semantic error by showing in precisely what area the overstepping of meaning limits can lie. These are ultimately different views of the same thing, namely the inferential structures of deontic status.

(b) The Inferential Limits at Subsentential Level

The simplified version of the internal justification quoted above may not mislead one into overlooking the fact that word usage rules state the characteristic catalogue M usually for individual concepts in T. They do not refer to T *en bloc*, but to subsentential expressions which are contained in T. This means in particular that they are to be analysed using the theory of the meaning of subsentential expressions developed by Brandom.

It was explained in the second chapter that linguistic meaning is primarily propositional. Subsentential expressions themselves cannot occur as premises and conclusions in inferences of assertion practice. They can, however, occur in propositions which comply with this function. In this sense, subsentential expressions have a derived, indirect inferential meaning. The fundamental definition of the theory of subsentential meaning is that of *substitution*. The method of substitution can be applied at two levels. First, propositions can be exchanged for others in assertion inferences. Secondly, subsentential expressions can be replaced in propositions with other expressions. The interlinking of the two levels led to the following *principle*[90]:

> The meaning of a subsentential expression is determined by the volume of the words with which it can be substituted whilst the content of the propositions in which it occurs remains the same.

The entire internal justification of legal rulings is based on the principle of the substitution of subsentential expressions. In this structure, rules for the use of words take on the function of substitution licences. They facilitate the inferential transition of abstract norms R to more concrete norms R' by their justification of the substitution of Tx by characteristic catalogues Mx. At *propositional level*, rules for the use of words license the substitution inferences within the internal justification.

At *definitional level*, W itself can be included as a substitution inference. Rules for the use of words fall within the category of simple substantive substitution-inferential commitments (SMSICs[91]). In line with Brandom, it is possible to distinguish between two types of SMSICs. In (stronger) symmetrical identity assertions, singular terms are substituted, whilst predicates are substituted in (weaker) asymmetric families of predicates. The logical form of W shows clearly that rules for the use of words are the second type of SMSICs. The predicate T is substituted by the predicate M, while because of the conditional the inference Mx →Tx is only valid in one direction, and hence is asymmetric. Through substitution of the predicate, rules for the use of words define *variant propositional frameworks* which are equivalent in meaning to the statutory proposition framework T. The logical form of W illustrates the guiding principle just quoted for the meaning of subsentential expressions.

No new types of semantic limit can be discerned at subsentential level. Rather, the four inferential limits from the propositional level are broken down at definitional level. The inferential limits indirectly continue at subsentential level via the mechanism by means of which subsentential meaning depends on propositional meaning. Non-adherence to W, on which all inferential limits are based, can hence be understood such that the SMSICs of a term are not adhered to.

---

[90] See pp 135 f above.
[91] On the category of SMSICs see p 138 above.

(iii) Semantic Limits in the Second Linguistic Dimension

The second linguistic dimension takes into account that language relates to objects of an objective world which is presumed to be intersubjective. The reference of language to non-linguistic matters was developed here as a necessary condition of semantic correctness.[92] Accordingly, semantic limits are derived from the object-relatedness of linguistic expressions.

In particular the expressive means of the singular terms and the attributions are available *de re* in the representational dimension. Their use in legal argumentation is manifold. The rules for the use of words W relate, by the individual variable, to non-linguistic objects. In the subsumption, attributions are used *de re* and singular terms are used in connection with apodictic assertions, as the following example sentences show.

> The court alleges *of the prison cell* that it is not a dwelling.
>
> The court alleges *of the accused Schmidt* that he is not guilty.

The concept of the truth is intrinsically linked to semantic correctness.[93] Understanding and semantically-correct language use are hence not purely linguistic skills, but are contingent on empirical knowledge. This knowledge can be revised in relation to the background commitments of linguistic communities and speakers and, being temporary, can always be revised. The impact of revisions consists of changed rules for the use of words, in which a characteristic catalogue M_1, which had been presumed until now, is replaced by a new catalogue M_n. Such revisions, however, change nothing as to the fundamental finding that a certain rule for the use of words always applies and that its re-constitution can be recognised as a change in the meaning.

The definition of death can be used as a legal example of the thesis of the second dimension that empirical knowledge is a precondition for the semantically-correct usage of concepts. It plays a major role in many legal fields, including in inheritance law and criminal law. The second linguistic dimension means here that it is not a purely linguistic matter whether a human being is to be designated as dead. The semantically-correct usage of the definition of death is contingent on medical, physiological and anthropological knowledge. At the same time, this example shows the transitional nature of this knowledge. The definition of death has changed in line with advances in medicine. Whilst, previously, the definition was the complete cessation of circulation and breathing, today brain-death is generally regarded as being decisive.[94] However, this state of knowledge is also not

---

[92] See pp 183 f above.
[93] See pp 184 ff above.
[94] Section 16(1) no 1 of the Transplantation Act (*TransPlG*) refers in this sense to the competence of the Federal Medical Association. See Bundesärztekammer, 'Richtlinien zur

necessarily definitive, as new knowledge shows.[95] The decisive element is that, depending on which definition of death is empirically correct, the expression 'death' has a variety of non-inferential circumstances of the correct application, and hence also different inferential contents.

This demonstrates two things. First, it is clear how a semantic limiting of object-relatedness can result. The semantic error lies in the error on conditional circumstances—in other words non-inferential starting conditions of the usage of the term—which are integrated as *language entry moves* in inferential semantics.[96] It is important that meaning and truth are not merely identified so that the difference between incorrect usage and usage with another meaning, in other words the condition of semantic error, is retained. The characteristic catalogue states the conditions for the truth of an assertion. These conditions are, in turn, a condition for semantic correctness. If a speech act does not comply with the conditions, the assertion is empirically wrong. If, by contrast, a speech act deviates from the catalogue of conditions, the assertion is semantically not correct. Hence, here, one should speak of a semantic *limit of truth conditions*.

The above-mentioned order of the Federal Constitutional Court—which relates to the violation of Article 103(2) of the Basic Law by extensive interpretations of the term 'close friend or relative' in accordance with section 241(1) of the Criminal Code—can be used as an example of a violation of the limit of truth conditions.[97] The complainant had been convicted because of a threat against non-existent persons, whereby the criminal courts overstepped the conditional commitment limit. At the same time, the criminal courts acknowledged in this case, by their speech act 'the accused threatened a close friend or relative', that they did not include the characteristic of the actual existence of the prospective victims in the list of the truth conditions of the term 'close friends or relatives'. Because of the implicit rule for the use of words applicable in assertion practice, the speech act is nevertheless only true, however, if the envisaged victims really exist. The criminal courts have hence also overstepped the limit of truth conditions by their use of the term 'close friend or relative'.

As this example shows, the limit of truth conditions obtained from the second linguistic dimension can only be breached together with an inferential limit of the first linguistic dimension. At the same time, the overstepping of an inferential limit violates the limit of truth conditions if there are

---

Feststellung des Hirntodes. Dritte Fortschreibung 1997 mit Ergänzungen gemäß Transplantationsgesetz' (1998) 95 *Deutsches Ärzteblatt* B 1509: 'In natural science and medical terms, the death of a human being is determined by brain death'.

[95] N Siegmund-Schultze, 'Und er bewegt sich doch. Reflexe bei Gehirntoten irritieren Transplantationsteams. Verfassungsrecht soll Vorschriften verschärfen', *Süddeutsche Zeitung* (20 February 2001) V2/11.
[96] See pp 184 f above.
[97] BVerfG NJW 1995, 2776–7.

also truth conditions among those inferential relations, which a speech act incompatibly includes in its commitments.

Secondly, it is found that the accusation of 'features semantics'[98] arising in the legal theory against rules for the use of words is obsolete. The second linguistic dimension means that semantics must of necessity be based on the characteristics and particularities of objects. A theory is only erroneous if it identifies meaning purely with object characteristics. Apart from such an extreme reference theory of meaning, the relevance of object characteristics is confirmed by the second linguistic dimension. Analytical legal theory is correctly based on object characteristics which are amenable to empirical science, which are covered by characteristic catalogues and which set the conditions for the semantically-correct usage of the concepts.

(iv) Semantic Limits in the Third Linguistic Dimension

The thesis of the third linguistic dimension supposes the general intersubjective validity of semantic norms. On the basis of the doxastic gap, conceptual content is perspectival. Hence, the objectivity of semantic norms was constructed here as relative or discursive objectivity.[99] Three points of view were decisive to this process in order to give rise to a strong objectivity thesis despite the paradoxon of relative objectivity. Each of these three aspects acts as a semantic limit.

It is not possible to conclude from the relativity of the background presumptions the relativity of the reference objects of linguistic expressions. Definitional content is perspectival, but relates to a world which is not perspectival. This reference aspect is already contained in the second linguistic dimension. If a speech act does not take account of this, therefore, the limits of the second and the third linguistic dimensions are overstepped at the same time.

Secondly, with the *thesis of the necessary incorporation of fundamental propositions*, trivial propositions and basal fundamental presumptions of a language were shown to be of necessity intersubjectively valid.[100] If a speech act is incompatible with fundamental propositions of a language, a semantic limit is overstepped insofar as the entitlement to deviate or revise is not proven. This semantic limit is to be referred to as a *limit of the fundamental propositions*. This was also already investigated by it being determined that, because of their prima facie entitlement, the overstepping of fundamental propositions is regarded as constituting a particularly grievous breach of semantic limits.[101] The limit of the fundamental

---

[98] See Busse, *Juristische Semantik* (n 23 above) 107–11.
[99] See p 193 above.
[100] See pp 165, 193 f above.
[101] See p 248 above.

propositions is violated by speech acts which are based on a complete re-definition of the fundamental concepts of a language.

These fundamental concepts include the propositions of logic.[102] Logically contradictory speech acts thus violate the limit of the fundamental propositions. An example of this is the 'cypress hedge order' of the Federal Constitutional Court.[103] The civil courts had sentenced the complainant in a neighbourhood dispute to move back a cypress hedge because it was too close to the plot boundary. In accordance with section 39(1) number 3 of the Hesse Act Governing the Law between Neighbours (*HessNRG*), a distance of 0.25 m is to be kept with 'hedges up to 1.2 m in height'. The complainant's hedge was 1.2 m high in accordance with the expert report. In contradiction to its own factual finding, the Local Court sentenced the complainant, in application of section 39(1) number 1 of the Hesse Act Governing the Law between Neighbours, to remove the hedge back to a distance of *0.75 m*.

The Federal Constitutional Court considered the prohibition of arbitrariness of Article 3(1) of the Basic Law to have been violated by means of this application of section 39(1) number 3 of the Hesse Act Governing the Law between Neighbours. The court stated as follows:

> The impugned rulings are based... not only on a manifestly erroneous application of non-constitutional law; over and above this, they are simply factually unjustifiable, and hence arbitrary in objective terms... The ruling of the Local Court is *not comprehensible*; it is hence arbitrary in objective terms... The ... grounds of the appellate court are bereft ... of *logic*. The judgment is simply *incomprehensible* in this sense, and in the result clearly counter to the facts of the case.[104] (emphasis added)

In the terminology used here, this means that the civil courts had overstepped the limit of the fundamental propositions by means of their logically-contradictory rulings as to the wording of section 39(1) of the Hesse Act Governing the Law between Neighbours.

Over and above the fundamental propositions, conceptual content is relative in social-perspective terms. In intersubjective terms, a division is, however, made, thirdly, in terms of the form and structure of linguistic usage. The practice of deontic scorekeeping is universal.[105] The semantic limit of this third aspect is overstepped by deliberately meaningless speech. Speech acts which completely ignore semantic norms and inferential relations by denying them as structural characteristics of their linguistic practice are outside sensible assertion practice. They deny the context of rational discourse. This is the semantic *limit of intersubjective readiness to*

---

[102] See pp 158 ff above.
[103] BVerfGE 70, 13.
[104] BVerfGE 70, 13 (97 f).
[105] See p 195 above.

understand. The limit of intersubjective readiness to understand is violated by speech acts which are semantically arbitrary, and which do not even claim to constitute semantically-understandable, intersubjectively-comprehensible usage of language.[106]

(v) The System of Semantic Limits

It was possible for the various types of semantic error to be demonstrated in observation of the normal case of linguistic assertion practice. On the basis of the concept of semantically-constitutive clarity, semantic limits were proven in all three linguistic dimensions.

Four limits exist in the normativity dimension which link to the system of inferential relations between deontic statuses. Each of these limits can be specifically linked to the implicit norms designated by Alexy as rules for the use of words. They can be furthermore assigned to both main types of general semantic limit. Special semantic limits were described in addition, which emerge from the second and third inferential dimensions, as well as from both objectivity dimensions of linguistic meaning.

The following overview shows this system of semantic limits:

A. General semantic limits
   I. Positive semantic limits ($Ma \land \neg Ta$)
      1. Conditional commitment limit (erroneous M negation because of W error)
      2. Conditional entitlement limit (erroneous M negation because of subsumption error)
      3. Consequential commitment limit (erroneous T negation because of W error)
      4. Consequential entitlement limit (erroneous T negation because of subsumption error)
   II. Negative semantic limits ($\neg Ma \land Ta$)
      1. Conditional commitment limit (erroneous M affirmation because of W error)
      2. Conditional entitlement limit (erroneous M affirmation because of subsumption error)
      3. Consequential commitment limit (erroneous T affirmation because of W error)

---

[106] Federal Constitutional Court NJW 1998, 1135–6. The Federal Constitutional Court finds on a constitutional complaint challenging the extensive interpretation of the element of obtaining items by devious means in accordance with section 265a(1) of the Criminal Code: 'A conviction also constitutes a contradiction of the fundamental concept contained in Art 103(2) of the Basic Law which is based on an objectively-untenable and hence arbitrary interpretation of substantive criminal law'. Hence, the Federal Constitutional Court refers not only to semantic arbitrariness. The latter is however a sub-case of the arbitrary interpretation.

4. Consequential entitlement limit (erroneous T affirmation because of subsumption error)
B. Special semantic limits
   I. Limit of discursive authority
   II. Limit of discursive responsibility
   III. Limit of truth conditions
   IV. Limit of fundamental propositions
   V. Limit of intersubjective readiness to understand

Also the thesis of the three dimensions of linguistic meaning does not show where the semantic limit is drawn in each individual case. The theory pursued here is not a realistic conceptual one. On the contrary, it stresses the relativity of linguistic meaning to the background presumptions of individual speakers and to basal assumptions and fundamental propositions of the linguistic communities, as well as to their conceptions of the world presumed to be objective.

The theory developed here facilitates a precise description of the limits of the wording. It shows precisely where the semantic error lies, ie the overstepping of a meaning limit. At the same time, it was possible to show that rules for the use of words can be analysed in concepts of deontic scorekeeping. Such an analysis enlightens their function and system.

This set of terminological tools is a major advantage for the rationality of the speech analysis discourse. It shows that the dispute as to the limits of the wording is a dispute concerning what a speaker is committed to, to what he or she is entitled, and which inferential relations of the deontic status lend its concepts meaning. Brandom's theory, accordingly, has a two-fold benefit for the problem of the limits of the wording. First, it is possible to show that the limits of the wording actually exist in the sub-types shown. And secondly, the semantic dispute in an individual case can be engaged in using the terminology developed here more precisely than was possible to date.

C. The Limits of the Wording with Constitutive Semantically-Unclear Meaning

This section consists of two parts. First of all, the *concepts* of semantically-unclear meaning are clarified, followed by the corresponding semantic *limits*. The first chapter touched upon the classification of semantically-unclear cases developed in the analytical legal theory. This is taken up here and linked to inferential semantics (i). The semantically-unclear cases are surveyed one after the other for semantic limits (ii) to (v), using the thesis of the three dimensions of linguistic meaning. Here, it can be presumed, in accordance with the relationship[107] between semantic clarity and semantically-unclear meaning developed above, that the system of semantic limits developed for semantic clarity in principle also applies to semantically-unclear cases. It is to be examined how far this application reaches and what modifications and particularities are to be presumed on the basis of the respective unclear meaning categories.

(i) The Classification of Semantically-Unclear Cases in Inferential Semantics

Semantically-unclear meaning is sub-divided in analytical legal theory into vagueness, ambiguity, inconsistency and evaluative openness.[108] At this point, this classification is harmonised with the theory of meaning put forward here. The concepts of the categories are to be portrayed on the basis of the concept of semantic clarity developed above in Brandom's inferential semantics (a) to (d).

Combinations of the various categories are possible.[109] This is the case, for instance, if a multiple-meaning expression is vague or evaluatively open in individual contexts. Such combinations do not cause any additional difficulties. The following analysis therefore focuses on the basic structures of the classification.

(a) The Concept of Vagueness

The concept of semantic vagueness has for some considerable time formed the core of surveys on the semantic indeterminacy thesis.[110] It is the focus of study because it is particularly problematic in contradistinction to the other categories of semantically-unclear meaning. It is possible to say in very general terms that linguistic expressions are vague if they are neither true nor false in borderline cases.

---

[107] See p 230 above.
[108] See p 46 above.
[109] See M Herberger and H-J Koch, 'Zur Einführung: Juristische Methodenlehre und Sprachphilosophie' (1978) *Juristische Schulung* 810 at 814 fn 55; Waldron, 'Vagueness in Law and Language. Some Philosophical Issues' (n 61 above) 514 and fn 10.

[110] According to Alexy, vagueness is the practically most important case of a semantic leeway, see R Alexy, 'Die logische Analyse juristischer Entscheidungen' (1980) NF 14 *Archiv für Rechts- und Sozialphilosophie: Beiheft* 24. Cf D Lewis, 'Scorekeeping in a Language Game' in D Lewis (ed), *Philosophical Papers. vol I* (Oxford, 1983) 244–6; Waldron, 'Vagueness in Law and Language. Some Philosophical Issues' (n 61 above) 512. See generally R Keefe and P Smith, *Vagueness. A Reader* (Cambridge MA, 1997); TAO Endicott (ed), 'Law Is Necessarily Vague' (2001) 7 *Legal Theory* 379; T Williamson (ed), Issue on Vagueness 81(2) *The Monist* 1998, and T Horgan (ed), Vagueness, 33 *Southern Journal of Philosophy Suppl.* 1994. For an economic perspective see GK Hadfield, 'Weighing the Value of Vagueness. An Economic Perspective on Precision in the Law' (1994) *California Law Review* 541. From the viewpoint of forensic linguistics see L Solan, *The Language of Judges* (Chicago, 1993).

The problem of vagueness is relevant in two contexts.[111] The classical area relates to so-called *Sorites vagueness*. These are paradoxes, which can be traced back to Zenon.[112] They are based on the principle that a recognised conceptual classification is confronted with a continuum, and hence is made impossible. So-called *family similarities vagueness* was formulated by Wittgenstein.[113] It consists of the meaning of complex predicates not being stated using a catalogue of necessary and sufficient characteristics, but only being stated in the shape of similarities with other complex predicates.

Various theories are put forward to explain semantic vagueness. The *epistemic vagueness theory* presumes that vague concepts can also be defined in terms of classifications.[114] Its potential for uncertainty is explained with a lack of knowledge of the classifications and definitions. This theory also makes it possible to retain the bivalent logic in borderline cases. The latter is renounced by the *ontological vagueness theory*. According to this theory, the vagueness of propositions arises by virtue of the fact that the reference objects of language itself do not have a defined truth-value.[115] The spatial-chronological limits of an object can be just as unclear as the question of the identity of two objects or of the characteristics of objects. Non-definite propositions can be based on these unclear meanings.

Both theories have advantages; they can be useful in particular in the area of the second and third linguistic dimensions. Apart from this, the finding, however, remains that the semantic limits of some concepts are clarified neither through characteristics of the objective world, nor by explicit or implicit norms. The epistemic and the ontological theories can hence at best be used to provide supplementary explanations. They cannot fully explain the problem of vagueness. The difficulty of the condition of doing justice to anti-reductionist supervenience also speaks against the epistemic theory.[116]

---

[111] Waldron, 'Vagueness in Law and Language. Some Philosophical Issues' (n 61 above) 517. See Endicott (ed), 'Law Is Necessarily Vague' (n 109 above) 379; J Raz, 'Sorensen: Vagueness Has No Function in Law' (2001) 7 *Legal Theory* 417; R Sorensen, 'Vagueness Has No Function in Law' (2001) 7 *Legal Theory* 387.
[112] Aristoteles, *Physik. Vorlesung über Natur. 2. Halbband: Bücher V-VIII* (Hamburg, 1988) ch 5, 250a, line 19 f ; M Sainsbury, *Paradoxes*, 2nd edn (Cambridge 1995) 23–51.
[113] L Wittgenstein, *Philosophical Investigations*, 2nd edn (Oxford 1963) para 67.
[114] C Wright, 'The Epistemic Conception of Vagueness' (1994) 33 *Southern Journal of Philosophy* 133. See also M Sainsbury and T Williamson, 'Sorites' in B Hale and C Wright (eds), *A Companion to the Philosophy of Language* (Oxford, 1997) 481.
[115] But see G Evans, 'Can There Be Vague Objects?' in Keefe and Smith (eds), *Vagueness. A Reader* (n 109 above) 317. M Sainsbury, 'Why the World Cannot Be Vague' (1994) 33 *Southern Journal of Philosophy* 63 at 78 f.
[116] This is explicitly acknowledged by Sainsbury and Williamson, 'Sorites' (n 113 above) 480 f.

Here, therefore, the view is to be further followed that vagueness is a specifically semantic problem, which requires a *semantic theory*.[117] Semantic vagueness theories differ from epistemic ones by virtue of the thesis that a linguistic expression has no definitive truth-value because of vagueness in borderline cases. Semantic theories differ from ontological ones by virtue of the fact that they regard the language, and not the reference objects, to be the cause of the vagueness.

The thesis that a definite truth-value does not exist in borderline cases can be implemented in different ways in technical terms. It is either presumed that a truth-value is simply lacking, which is the same as renouncing the bivalent logic, or that the concept of the truth-value is modified. The latter can take place by virtue of the bivalent logic being expanded to include a new category of 'neutral', thus becoming trivalent, or by the dichotomy of true and false being replaced by a continuum of degrees of truth.[118] To explain vagueness, it is sufficient to carry out such modifications for the object level. A bivalent meta-language is introduced in order to describe a non-bivalent object language. The bivalent logic is accordingly maintained at a higher level. In accordance with these theories, vagueness can be described in classical logical attributions and models.[119]

Such a strategy is also pursued by the semantic theory of the *three-candidate model*. It shares with the modification theories the fundamental problem of *higher-order vagueness*.[120] The attribution to the three categories 'positive', 'negative' and 'neutral', or to degrees of truth, can in turn be understood as vague. This applies to all higher-grade meta-languages, so that semantic vagueness theories are problematic because they treat the meta-language for a vague object language as if it were precise. In fact—according to the objection to the three-candidate model—the categorisation of concepts of the language L_1 could be repeated for concepts of the meta-language L_2. There are therefore positive-positive candidates, neutral-positive candidates and negative-positive candidates, etc. This repetition can be continued endlessly for higher-grade languages L_3 to L_n, so that the attempt to classify the spectrum fails.[121] Therefore a continuum thesis and a categories thesis face one another in the dispute regarding the

---

[117] Against semantic theories of vagueness D Hyde, 'Vagueness, Ontology and Supervenience' (1998) 81 *The Monist* 297.

[118] See T Williamson, 'Vagueness' in PV Lamarque and RE Asher (eds), *Concise Encyclopedia of Philosophy of Language* (Oxford, 1997) 205. D Edgington, 'Vagueness by Degrees' in Keefe and Smith (eds), *Vagueness. A Reader* (n 109 above) 294.

[119] Sainsbury and Williamson, 'Sorites' (n 113 above) 471.

[120] On higher-order-vagueness see TAO Endicott, *Vagueness in Law* (Oxford, 2000) 82–4.

[121] This strategy of refuting the three-candidates-model is mentioned by Raz, see J Raz, 'Legal Reasons, Sources, and Gaps' in J Raz (ed), *The Authority of Law. Essays on Law and Morality* (Oxford, 1979) 74 fn 18. It is visualised by Endicott, *Vagueness in Law* (n 119 above) 86 f. Also in favour of the continuum thesis, rejecting the three-candidates-model are Bix, *Law, Language, and Legal Determinacy* (n 5 above) 32; M Sainsbury, 'Is There

three-candidate model. It is exactly this problem which leads in legal theory to the dispute about the three-candidate model. Critical authors such as Neumann[122] or Herbert[123] put forward the continuum thesis, whilst analysts such as Alexy or Koch and Rüßmann are proponents of the categories thesis.

From the point of view of analytical legal theory, the problem of *higher-order vagueness* is not virulent. The three-candidate model keeps to bivalence insofar as a proposition has either a definite or an indefinite meaning. Questions of doubt are consistently attributed to the neutral area.[124] This view is, however, subject to new objections. Burns criticises that such a clarity model describes not the philosophically dangerous, but only a harmless form of vagueness.[125] One could only speak of real vagueness if there were uncertainty as to the attribution to the categories. Busse objects to the expansion of the area of the neutral candidates. If slight doubt prevented the assignment to the positive or negative area, these areas are said to be almost empty.[126]

The problem of higher-order vagueness can be clarified using the *thesis of the three dimensions of linguistic meaning*, and the difficulties asserted by critics of the three-candidate model can be avoided. One should ask how the concept of vagueness is to be portrayed in the theory of meaning put forward here, and how this deals with the problem of higher-order vagueness. It should be clarified here what it means in inferential semantics to be a positive, negative or neutral candidate. It should then be examined whether an inferentially-understood three-candidate model can solve the problem of higher-order vagueness.

Inferential semantics have two possibilities for the portrayal of the concept of vagueness. The fundamental concept of both possibilities is that

---

Higher-Order Vagueness?' (1991) 41 *Philosophical Quarterly* 167 f. See also Waldron, 'Vagueness in Law and Language. Some Philosophical Issues' (n 61 above) 521.

[122] U Neumann, *Rechtsontologie und juristische Argumentation. Zu den ontologischen Implikationen juristischen Argumentierens* (Heidelberg, 1979) 72–7.

[123] Herbert, *Rechtstheorie als Sprachkritik* (n 32 above) 252. See also P Schiffauer, *Wortbedeutung und Rechtserkenntnis. Entwickelt an Hand einer Studie zum Verhältnis von verfassungskonformer Auslegung und Analogie* (Berlin 1979) 164.

[124] 'After all, someone who is in any shadow of a doubt is in doubt'. Endicott, *Vagueness in Law* (n 119 above) 82. See also the definition of clear cases by C Wright, 'Further Reflections on the Sorites Paradox' (1987) 15 *Philosophical Topics* 227 at 245. Against Sainsbury, 'Is There Higher-Order Vagueness?' (n 120 above) 177.

[125] 'Where there is a clearly delimited class of cases to which the term applies, another to which it does not apply, and a third sharply delimited class of neutral instances there seems to be no real uncertainty anywhere'. LC Burns, *Vagueness. An Investigation Into Natural Languages and the Sorites Paradox* (Dordrecht, 1991) 25. Against also Endicott, *Vagueness in Law* (n 119 above) 82 f and Waldron, 'Vagueness in Law and Language. Some Philosophical Issues' (n 61 above) 521.

[126] Busse, *Juristische Semantik* (n 23 above) 128.

the inferential relations, which by definition determine the meaning of a linguistic expression, determine the category in which a candidate is to be placed.

The first possibility treats equally all inferential relations of a term which *in their totality* make up its meaning. A positive candidate is hence one with regard to which all inferences of a term are correct. A negative candidate is defined by all inferences of a term not relating to him or her. With neutral candidates, some inferences agree, whilst others do not. This model is similar to the semantic vagueness theory, which is used by Dummett and is referred to as *supervaluation*.[127] It is based on the method that vague expressions can be described by various sets of more precise expressions, so-called *sharpenings*. Truth is understood as truth according to all sharpenings.

That all inferences of a term are met with a candidate and that all inferences are not met takes place relatively seldom. The first model therefore leads to a relatively large neutral area. Busse's criticism is indeed correct with regard to this model. Extremely demanding requirements are made for attribution to the positive and negative areas, and these are rarely met.

This does not apply without restriction to the second model, which distinguishes between two classes of inferential relations. Some inferences are necessary conditions of the linguistic expression. They constitute the concept, and they form the first class, which is to be referred to here as the *class of constituting inferences*. The second class covers those which apply as a rule, but by no means of necessity or only coincidentally. This class is referred to here as the *class of the peripheral inferences*. Only the inferences of the first class are used for a depiction of the three-candidate model.

However, the question of whether the second model of an inferential reconstruction of the three-candidate model is correct does present problems. Brandom himself was against the idea that it would be possible to subdivide the inferences into necessary and contingent. As a main difficulty, he correctly infers the problem of naming criteria for the privileging of some inferences.[128] He therefore proposes to renounce the idea of the possession of a conceptual core-content common to all speakers. The only thing (he said) which was shared by all speakers was the joint practice of deontic scorekeeping.[129]

---

[127] M Dummett, 'Wang's Paradox' in M Dummett (ed), *Truth and Other Enigmas* (Cambridge MA, 1978) 250. On the pros and cons of this theory *cf* Sainsbury and Williamson, 'Sorites' (n 113 above) 471–5.

[128] Brandom, *Making It Explicit* (n 64 above) 483 f.

[129] Brandom, *Making It Explicit* (n 64 above) 485. See also *Making It Explicit* at 485 fn 99: 'Concrete scorekeeping practices do the duty of abstract intension-functions'. Brandom gives two reasons for his position, *ibid*, 633–5.

These considerations by Brandom appear at first sight to refute an inferentially-based three-candidate model. If one takes a closer look, however, it is revealed that they already bear the core of an argument leading to its confirmation.[130] This core is the indication of joint practice. This corresponds to what was referred to here as a third linguistic dimension. In contradistinction to Brandom, it is presumed here that the difference in status asserted between the two classes of inference can be explained in concepts of discursive scorekeeping practice. That speakers share a practice, but not also a core-content of concepts, is barely plausible.[131] The intersubjectivity dimension is primarily, but not exclusively, to be based on the shared form of the discourse.[132] If the inferential considerations made here are supplemented by the dimension of linguistic normativity, there is much in favour of fundamental propositions also being shared in a linguistic community; propositions which express the fundamental basal presumptions, and which are even treated as stable when they are counterfactual.[133] The thesis of the necessary incorporation of propositions that are immune to revision can also be listed here.[134] Finally, one should refer to the triadic relative OLOL analyticity, which guarantees a sufficient degree of constancy and stability of certain inferential relations within concrete language games.[135]

The criterion aspired to for the privileging of some inferences as definition-constituting is therefore to be found by linking inferential semantics with normative pragmatics.[136] Inferences which can be traced back to fundamental or OLOL-analytical propositions of a language are definition-constituting inferences. They are shared by all speakers jointly. The background relativity of conceptual content affects only the second class of inferential relations, in which the peripheral commitments are covered. The problem of vagueness may be a real challenge in artificial languages for the attempt at well-ordered definitions. There are good reasons in natural languages for the speaker encountering a continuum with classifying concepts and categories.

---

[130] Brandom himself insinuates such a possibility by referring to Sellars' suggestion of treating contrafactual robust inferences as constitutive, see Brandom, *Making It Explicit* (n 64 above) 484 with fn 97. *Cf ibid*, 636.

[131] Brandom acknowledges that ‚there is an undeniable intuitive basis' for distinguishing two inferential categories, see Brandom, *Making It Explicit* (n 64 above) 634.

[132] See pp 193 ff above.

[133] Brandom himself insinuates that the differentiation of two inferential categories might be pragmatically reasonable in spite of Quine's *Two Dogmas*. *Cf* Brandom, *Making It Explicit* (n 64 above) 634.

[134] On the thesis of necessary incorporation of immune sentences see p 164 above.

[135] On OLOL-analyticity see p 179 above.

[136] *Cf* also Endicott's *paradox of trivalence*, see Endicott, *Vagueness in Law* (n 119 above) 88–91.

If inferential semantics are viewed in the context of the normativity dimension, it is shown that the two core arguments which are advanced against the three-candidate model are untenable. First, the infinity spiral of *higher-order vagueness* can be discontinued by the normativity of linguistic meaning. Certain inferential attributions are shared jointly by the speakers. Secondly, it is by no means the case that any arbitrary doubt leads to attribution to the category of neutral candidates. In accordance with the default-and-challenge structure of entitlement,[137] this only applies to sufficiently-justified doubt. Already for this reason there can, contrary to Busse's assumption, be no question of the fields of positive and negative candidates being virtually empty.

This, hence, shows that the three types of candidate can be distinguished in inferential semantics. What it *means* in inferential semantics to be a positive, negative or neutral candidate can be shown using the distinction between propositional level and definitional level. At the *definitional level*, the substitution of Ta by Ma is licensed by a positive candidate, whilst the substitution of ¬Ta by ¬Ma is licensed by a negative candidate, and the licensing of substitutions with neutral candidates is unclear. At *propositional level*, positive candidates license the substitution of R by the more concrete decision-making norm I_{RWPos}; negative candidates license the substitution of R by I_{RWNeg}; while for neutral candidates the substitution impact is unclear.

The three-candidate model can be correctly portrayed in inferential semantics, a distinction being made between definition-constituting and peripheral inferences.

(b) The Concept of Ambiguity

The concept of ambiguity is much easier to clarify using inferential semantics and the concept of semantic clarity than the concept of vagueness. The general definition is that a concept is ambiguous if it has different meanings in different contexts.[138]

In contradistinction to the general concept of semantic clarity, it is therefore necessary to distinguish in the case of ambiguity between various contexts. *Within* these contexts, it is, however, possible to presume *in each*

---

[137] On the default and challenge structure of entitlement see p 149 above.

[138] See p 47 above. A similar definition is used by Waldron, 'Vagueness in Law and Language. Some Philosophical Issues' (n 61 above) 512. On the problem of constructing the phenomenon of ambiguity in a truth-conditional semantics, see JL Cohen, 'A Problem About Ambiguity in Truth-Theoretical Semantics' (1985) 45 *Analysis* 129 at 130 f; BS Gillon, 'Truth Theoretical Semantics and Ambiguity' (1990) 50 *Analysis* 178 at 181. The relation of ambiguity and vagueness is controversial, see R Sorensen, 'Ambiguity, Discretion, and the Sorites' (1998) 81 *The Monist* 215.

case the inferentially-characterised concept of semantic clarity. There are no particularities in this respect. The difficulty consists of identifying the various contexts.

(c) The Concept of Inconsistency

A linguistic expression is inconsistent if it is used by various speakers in the same contexts with various meanings.[139] This definition is first of all simply a description of actual linguistic usage by various speakers. In contrast to the other categories, it does not use linguistic expression. This can be evaluated as an indication that a different level is tackled here than with the other categories.

This finding is confirmed if the concept of inconsistency is described with the theory of meaning put forward here. Accordingly, inconsistency means that the speakers handle the assignment and undertaking of commitments differently. Deontic status and inferential relations of an inconsistent expression are not stable within the speaker community. This is caused by a particularly high degree of social-perspectival relativity, which in turn exists under two conditions. First, the meaning of the expression must depend to a considerable degree on background commitments. Secondly, these background commitments differ widely from one speaker to another. These characteristics correspond to the concept of the unclear case, which was developed in the first section.[140]

The concept of inconsistency describes semantically-unclear meaning, but—in contradistinction to the other categories—names no causes for these. Inconsistency can be based on ambiguity, vagueness or evaluative openness. It constitutes an obstacle to epistemic access to conceptual contents and to the explicit-making of deontic status, but is not a separate cause of semantically-unclear meaning. It is hence misleading of Koch and Rüßmann to include inconsistency as a separate category in the classification of unclear cases.[141] It will not be considered below.

(d) The Concept of Evaluative Openness

The dispute mentioned in the first chapter concerning whether evaluative openness constitutes a separate category of semantically-unclear meaning is to be decided on at this point. Koch and Rüßmann negate this question, whilst Alexy affirms it. In general terms, it can be said that Alexy lists the

---

[139] See p 47 above.
[140] On the concept of unclear cases see p 215 above.
[141] According to Alexy and Waldron, inconsistency is not a separate category, see Alexy, 'Die logische Analyse juristischer Entscheidungen' (n 109 above) *Beiheft* 24; Waldron, 'Vagueness in Law and Language. Some Philosophical Issues' (n 61 above) 512 f.

more convincing reasons for not restricting the potential to constitute commitments of evaluatively-open concepts only to the descriptive meaning component. This favours the independence of the category.[142]

These reasons can be seen in the theory of meaning put forward here. The meaning of evaluatively-open concepts depends heavily on a specific type of background commitment, namely on normative convictions. Speakers enter into a special kind of commitment with the internal claim to evaluative correctness. They are commitments to *evaluative* circumstances and consequences, with which the speaker takes on a special kind of discursive responsibility. The reactions of the other scorekeepers, their entitlement assignments and applying of sanctions where there is no entitlement show this speciality also. Evaluative commitments have a special scorekeeping significance which differs from the significance of mere ambiguity or vagueness. It hence makes sense to treat evaluatively-open concepts as a separate category.

The evaluatively-open expressions referred to according to Gallie as *essentially contested concepts* are also recognised as a separate category in Anglo-American legal theory. Waldron proves that they fulfill important functions in legal language over and above the mere indeterminacy of ambiguity and vagueness.[143]

(e) Result on the Classification of Unclear Cases

Vagueness was emphasised as being central to the classification of unclear cases. It was shown in the case of ambiguity that it does not lead to any difficulties over and above the particularity of various contexts. Inconsistency was rejected as a category in its own right, whilst evaluative openness was confirmed in the same respect. One must hence presume the three categories of vagueness, ambiguity and evaluative openness. It was shown how these categories are to be depicted in the theory of meaning proposed here. In particular, it is to be established that inferential semantics are able to confirm the three-candidate model in the event of vagueness.

---

[142] Alexy, 'Die logische Analyse juristischer Entscheidungen' (n 109 above) *Beiheft* 24 and fn 42.

[143] Waldron, 'Vagueness in Law and Language. Some Philosophical Issues' (n 61 above) 533. *Cf* J Gray, 'On Liberty, Liberalism and Essential Contestability' (1978) 8 *British Journal of Political Science* 385 at 388; AC MacIntyre, 'The Essential Contestability of Some Social Concepts' (1973) 84 *Ethics* 1 at 7. On the merits of vagueness generally see Williamson, 'Vagueness' (n 117 above) 204. On Gallie's theory see also Bix, *Law, Language, and Legal Determinacy* (n 5 above) 56–8.

(ii) Semantic Limits in the Case of Vagueness

The concept of vagueness is also explicable in inferential semantics using the three-candidate model. For the question of semantic limits, the implicit norms which are referred to by Alexy as rules for the use of words, and which regulate the correctness of inferential relations of deontic status, have proven to be fruitful. A connection suggests itself in order to answer the question of which semantic limits apply in the case of vagueness between the three-candidate model and the model of rules for the use of words. Such a connection integrates the various approaches in analytical legal theory (a). On this basis, it would be necessary to examine the degree to which the system of semantic limits can be applied to vague expressions (b).

(a) Connection Between the Three-Candidate Model and the Model of Rules for the Use of Words

The theories of Koch/Rüßmann and Alexy are to be combined in a model here.[144] To this end, six preliminary considerations are needed (1). On this basis, two model structures are developed (2) and (3) and finally summarised (4).

(1) Preliminary Considerations   First of all, it is necessary to formalise the three-candidate model. The three-candidate model can be described in rules K_1 to K_3[145]:

K_1:   If x is a positive candidate, then it is necessary to subsume x.
K_2:   If x is a negative candidate, then it is prohibited to subsume x.
K_3:   If x is a neutral candidate, it is neither necessary nor prohibited to subsume x.

Formalised, this reads[146]:

K_1:   (x) (Posx → OSubx)
K_2:   (x) (Negx → FSubx)
K_3:   (x) (Neutrx → ¬OSubx ∧ ¬FSubx)

Only K_1 and K_2 are significant to the reconstruction of the limits of the wording, since they mark both border-lines.[147]

Secondly, since there are two border-lines, two different schemes need to be developed, one for the positive and one for the negative border-line.

---
[144] On this combination *cf* H-J Koch, 'Ansätze einer juristischen Argumentationstheorie?' (1977) 36 *Archiv für Rechts- und Sozialphilosophie* 364 fn 10.
[145] These rules are meta-rules on the application of legal norms.
[146] This formalisation is elliptical, since the predicates are triple-digit.
[147] See p 244 above.

Thirdly, the universe of discourse[148] additionally be restricted to interpretation in the narrower sense of the word. The schemes only say something about the positive and negative border-lines of interpretation in the narrower sense. They say nothing about the permissibility of further development of the law.

Fourthly, the substantial reason for the link between the two models lies in the rule for the use of words W determining whether a positive or a negative candidate is available. According to Alexy, it has the general form $(x) (Mx \rightarrow Tx)$. For the purpose pursued here, a distinction is to be made between a positive and a negative rule for the use of words. The positive rule for the use of words is identical to the general form according to Alexy. It reads as follows: If x complies with specific characteristics, then x complies with the element. Formalised this reads: W_{pos}: $(x) (Mx \rightarrow Tx)$. The positive rule for the use of words states, with Mx, a sufficient condition for fulfilling the element. The negative rule for the use of words reads as follows: If x does not comply with specific characteristics, then x does not comply with the element. Formalised this reads: W_{neg}: $(x) (\neg Mx \rightarrow \neg Tx)$. This negative rule for the use of words is equivalent to $(x) (Tx \rightarrow Mx)$. Mx is a necessary condition in W_{neg}; quite the contrary to in W_{pos}. Here we encounter a significant asymmetry between positive and negative rules for the use of words, which is reflected in the dichotomy of the 'sufficient' and 'necessary' conditions. The positive rule for the use of words gives sufficient conditions with Mx for the existence of a positive candidate. The negative rule for the use of words, by contrast, formulates as a sufficient condition for the existence of a negative candidate that a necessary condition for the existence of a positive candidate is missing: $(x) (\neg Mx \rightarrow \neg Tx)$. The negation of the characteristic Mx (necessary for the existence of a positive candidate) is a sufficient condition for x not being T. This asymmetry can be explained using the example of the 'window ruling' of the Federal Court of Justice. The positive rule for the use of words reads as follows here: If x lets air through, then x is a window. The negative rule for the use of words reads: If x does not let light through, then x is not a window, thus: If x is a window, then it lets air through. Permeability to air is a sufficient condition in the positive rule for the use of words, but by contrast in the negative rule for the use of words it is a necessary condition.

Fifthly, a similar distinction is also necessary for the general norm scheme R. According to Alexy, this norm scheme is as follows: $(x) (Tx \rightarrow ORx)$. R says something about when the legal consequence for x is necessary. This is sufficient for the purpose of determining the positive border-line. The negative border-line must, however, state a prohibition of

---

[148] *Cf* WVO Quine, *Grundzüge der Logik*, 10th edn (Frankfurt am Main, 1998) 127, 134 ff.

The Theory of The Limits of The Wording 267

the legal consequence. Hence, a negative norm scheme R_{neg} is to be formulated: If x does not comply with the element, then the legal consequence for x is certainly not necessary in accordance with R.[149] Formalised this reads: (x) ($\neg$Tx $\to$ $\neg OR_R$x).[150] The general norm scheme R, by contrast, is to be designated R_{pos} for our present purpose.

Lastly, in order to bring the individual rules into a corresponding form, some of them must be re-constituted. These re-constitutions are different for each of the schemes to be developed.

(2) The Scheme of the Positive Limits of the Wording Re-constitution rule U_1 applies to the re-constitution of K_1.[151] If it is necessary to subsume x, then x complies with the element, and vice versa. Formalised this reads: (x) (OSubx $\Leftrightarrow$ Tx). From K_1 and U_1 follows K_1': If x is a positive candidate, then x complies with the element, and vice versa. Formalised this reads: (x) (Posx $\Leftrightarrow$ Tx).[152] The re-constitution of K_1 has the following deductive structure:

(1)   (x) (Posx $\to$ OSubx)   [K_1]
(2)   (x) (OSubx $\Leftrightarrow$ Tx)   [U_1]
(3   x) (Posx $\Leftrightarrow$ Tx) (1), (2)   [K_1']

---

[149] Here too, it is necessary to point out that the *universe of discourse* is restricted to the interpretation in the narrow sense. Whether therefore for reasons of the further development of the law the legal consequence for x is nonetheless to apply is not for discussion here. Over and above this, R_{neg} can only determine that the legal consequence according to rule R is not necessary; it can nonetheless be necessary in accordance with other norms. To put it differently: T*a* is a sufficient condition for the application of the legal consequence, $\neg$T*a* is however not a sufficient condition for the non-application of the legal consequence, but only for the non-application of the legal consequence in accordance with R.

[150] Index R shows that the legal consequence is only not necessary according to rule R, *cf* n 149 above.

[151] That the re-constitution of K_1 is necessary emerges from the following consideration: Both the first and the second premises of the following deduction link the object and meta-level. The meta-level must however be eliminated if K_1 is to be linked to W_{pos}, since W_{pos} contains no expression of the meta-level.

[152] It could be objected against the biconditional that the formula it contains (x) (Tx $\to$ Posx) is factually not correct. This states that Posx is a necessary condition for Tx. However, the objection continues, a case is also conceivable in which x is a neutral candidate. Also a neutral candidate can however be a T, namely if it is attributed to the group of positive candidates. Posx is thus not a necessary condition for Tx. This objection is not tenable because of the restriction of the *universe of discourse* which is carried out. This restriction presumes that only positive and negative candidates are available. The neutral candidates are ruled out here from the outset since a determination of both border lines is only possible in the positive and negative areas. It is a matter of drawing a boundary by reference to *established* rules for the use of words. In the area of neutral candidates, however, an *assignment* is always necessary. The formula (x) (Tx $\to$ Posx) is hence factually correct because it applies to established rules for the use of words and in the case of the non liquet *after* the assignment of such a rule.

The rule for the use of words W_{pos} is to be re-constituted by K_1'[153]:

(1)   (x) (Mx → Tx)   [W_{pos}]
(2)   (x) (Posx ⇔ Tx)   [K_1']
(3)   (x) (Mx → Posx)   [W_{pos}'] (2), (3)

It is now possible to state the structure of the positive limits of the wording:

(1)   (x) (Tx → ORx)   [R]
(2)   (x) (Posx ⇔ Tx)   [K_1']
(3)   (x) (Mx → Posx)   [W_{pos}']
(4)   (x) (Mx → ORx)   (1) – (3) [I_{RWpos}]
(5)   Ma
(6)   ORa   (4), (5)

The decisive linking of a three-candidate model and rule for the use of words W_{pos} is found in premise 3. The positive rule for the use of words states which characteristics x must comply with for x to be a positive candidate. If *a* complies with these characteristics, then the legal consequence is necessary in accordance with I_{RWpos}. Therefore, *a* cannot be ruled out of the subsumption without overstepping the positive border-line of the interpretation.

(3) The Scheme of the Negative Limits of the Wording   Re-constitution rule U_2 applies to the re-constitution of K_2[154]. If x is not a T, then it is prohibited to subsume x, and vice versa. Formalised this reads: (x) (FSubx ⇔ ¬Tx). K_2 and U_2 lead to K_2': If x is a negative candidate, then x is not a T, and vice versa. Formalised this reads: (x) (Negx ⇔ ¬Tx).[155] The deduction of K_2' has the following structure[156]:

(1)   (x) (Negx → FSubx)   [K_2]
(2)   (x) (FSubx ⇔ ¬Tx)   [U_2]
(3)   (x) (Negx ⇔ ¬Tx)   (1), (2) [K_2']

---

[153] This re-constitution is necessary so that the expression Posx occurs in W. Only by these means is a link with K_1' possible.

[154] The same consideration applies to the necessity of re-constituting K_2 as to the re-constitution of K_1, cf n 151 above.

[155] Here too an objection against the biconditional is conceivable. It does not apply however for the reasons stated in n 152 above.

[156] Proposition categories are used with varying status in this deduction. The first premise concludes from the object level (x is a negative candidate) to the meta-level (it is prohibited to subsume x). The second premise links the object level (x is not a T) and the meta-level (it is prohibited to subsume x) with the biconditional. The meta level is eliminated in the conclusion: It links two assertions of the object level with the biconditional, and hence establishes a linguistic rule on what it means that x is a negative candidate and that x is not T.

The Theory of The Limits of The Wording 269

The rule for the use of words W_{neg} is to be re-constituted using K_2'.[157]

(1)   (x) (¬Mx → ¬Tx)   [W_{neg}]
(2)   (x) (¬Tx ⇔ Negx)   [K_2']
(3)   (x) (¬Mx → Negx)   [W_{neg}'] (1), (2)

It is now possible to state the structure of the negative border-line:

(1)   (x) (¬Tx → ¬OR$_R$x)   [R_{neg}]
(2)   (x) (Negx → ¬Tx)   [K_2']
(3)   (x) (¬Mx → Negx)   [W_{neg}']
(4)   (x) (¬Mx → ¬OR$_R$x)   (1) – (3) [I_{Rwneg}]
(5)   ¬M*a*
(6)   ¬OR$_R$*a*   (4), (5)

In turn, the decisive linking of the three-candidate model and the rule for the use of words can be taken from premise 3. Negative rule for the use of words W_{neg} states that x is a negative candidate if x does not comply with specific characteristics. If *a* does not comply with the characteristics, the legal consequence in accordance with I_{RWneg} for *a* is not necessary in accordance with R. Therefore, *a* can certainly not be included in the subsumption on the basis of R without overstepping the negative border-line of the interpretation.[158]

(4) Summary It has been shown that the three-candidate model can be adjusted in the structure of the internal justification according to Alexy. It is possible to formulate two structural schemes which clarify the functioning of the three-candidate model and the rules for the use of words W_{pos} and W_{neg} within the structure of the internal justification. The decisive content connection is that the rules for the use of words define when a positive or negative candidate exists. An interesting asymmetry was found to exist between positive and negative rules for the use of words, in that Mx is a sufficient condition in the positive rule for the use of words, while in the negative rule for the use of words, on the contrary, it is a necessary condition for Tx. By contrast, the models say nothing for the area of neutral candidates. In this area, it is not possible to establish a rule for the use of words making possible an attribution of an object in the positive or in the negative area of a term. Here, the *assignment* of a rule for the use of words is necessary which meets this attribution as a stipulation on the basis of non-semantic arguments.

---

[157] This re-constitution is necessary so that the expression Negx occurs in W. Only by these means is *a* by these means with K_2' possible.
[158] The structural scheme deducts from a negation (Premise 1). This approach is not without its problems. With regard to the negation of principle norms and in general terms on the counterconclusion problem *Cf* E Ratschow, *Rechtswissenschaft und formale Logik* (Baden-Baden, 1998) 135–40.

270 *Semantic Normativity in the Law*

(b) The System of Semantic Limits with Vagueness

In view of the result just formulated, the way in which the system of semantic limits can be transferred to vagueness is evident. The two types of rules for the use of words, W_{pos} and W_{neg}, correspond exactly to the two types of general semantic limits. These therefore also apply with their corresponding sub-types to the positive and negative areas of vague expressions. In the neutral area, semantic limits cannot apply for a lack of stability of the implicit norms, apart from two exceptions. Only the limit of the fundamental propositions and the limit of intersubjective willingness to understand can exert a binding impact in the neutral area. This by no means signifies that legal practitioners were without any semantic indications for the assignment of meaning necessary in this respect. There are many inferential relations available which, however, are not common, but relative to the perspective of the respective speaker. Vagueness arises when the scorekeeping of the individual speakers is too far apart. They, however, remain accessible semantic criteria in the assignment of meaning.[159]

(iii) Semantic Limits with Ambiguity

Herberger and Koch propose to also apply the three-candidate model to determine semantic limits with ambiguous expressions.[160] It would only be necessary to redefine the three areas. A positive candidate of an ambiguous expression is said to be an article to which the expression applies according to all variants of meaning. A candidate is said to be negative to which the expression did not apply according to any of the variants. Candidates falling under the concept according to at least one, but not all, variants are said to be attributed to the neutral area.

As Herberger and Koch readily admit, this transfer of the vagueness model only works if joint positive candidates of all meaning variants are available. However, there is said to be a second type of ambiguity in which this precondition is allegedly not met. What is more, joint negative candidates can also be lacking, so that a third type of ambiguity emerges.[161] In accordance with this *transfer model*, one of the two border-lines of the limits of the wording is missing in the latter type of ambiguity. In the first case (lack of joint positive candidates), the limits of the wording cannot work such that specific candidates may not be

---

[159] On limits even in hard cases see also p 218 above.
[160] Herberger and Koch, 'Zur Einführung: Juristische Methodenlehre und Sprachphilosophie' (n 108 above) 814.
[161] Herberger and Koch only mention the type of ambiguity with consists in the lack of common positive candidates.

The Theory of The Limits of The Wording 271

removed from the application. In the second case (lack of joint negative candidates), its impact cannot be that specific candidates may not be included in the application.

Border-lines may be defined with this transfer of the three-candidate model for ambiguous concepts. The disadvantage that this makes extremely exacting demands on the existence of positive or negative candidates can, however, not be ignored. Already the concept of a 'castle' as an example from colloquial language makes it clear that there are no individuals who fall under it according to all variants of meaning of this term. This result is obligatory in accordance with the transfer model, but it is highly implausible. Application of the three-candidate model with ambiguity is hence to be rejected.

It is more promising to argue with the distinction of establishment and assignment of rules for the use of words. A decision is taken in the context of determined rules for the use of words if one of the determined variants of meaning is selected as decisive.[162] If, by contrast, a meaning variant is selected which is not among those determined, there is already an overstepping of a semantic limit for this reason. This is to be designated here as a *limit of established variants*.

The Federal Administrative Court also proposes the conception of the limit of the determined variant put forward here. In an order which can be related to the problem of ambiguity, it found:

> It is clarified in supreme court precedents that the limit of interpretation is marked by the possible meaning of the word... and not by one specific interpretation of the wording out of several.[163]

This is a specific semantic limit which only applies in the case of ambiguity. The model based on the limit of the determined variants leaves the interpreter reduced latitude when compared with the transfer model. This is additionally minimised by the fact that the normal semantic limits apply within the selected variant of meaning.

The question of the criteria by which the relevant meaning variant is to be selected hence emerges as a core problem of ambiguity. In particular, one should decide whether only purely semantic or indeed non-linguistic reasons may be used for this selection. This question has not yet been clarified. Only Koch and Rüßmann refer as a permissible reason to 'for instance [the] accommodation of the legislative ideas of purpose'.[164]

---

[162] This model of semantic limits in case of ambiguity is insinuated by Waldron, 'Vagueness in Law and Language. Some Philosophical Issues' (n 61 above) 515; Koch and Rüßmann, *Juristische Begründungslehre* (n 23 above) 194.
[163] BVerwG v 6 September 1999, Az 11 B 40/99.
[164] H-J Koch and H Rüßmann, *Juristische Begründungslehre* (n 23 above) 194.

The fact that the semantic interpretation is hence generally subordinated to other arguments speaks against the accommodation of non-linguistic arguments. The semantic limits can hence only have an indirect impact. This is unfortunate because the limits of the wording are to provide a limit for non-linguistic interpretation reasons. On the other hand, it should not be overlooked that ambiguity is one of the semantically-unclear cases. The semantic interpretation leads to a *non liquet*, so that with a purely semantic view it is unclear which context is to be chosen. In the case of ambiguity, there is a semantic argument of the third form.[165]

Accordingly, therefore, non-linguistic reasons absolutely must be included before the semantic limits can take effect within the selected context. The accommodation of the non-linguistic arguments is relatively limited when it comes to the selection of the relevant meaning variant. The difficulties in the selection should not be exaggerated, moreover. The selection is made easier the more different are the contexts between which the selection is to be made. The contexts are highly divergent in most cases of ambiguity.[166]

(iv) Semantic Limits with Evaluatively-Open Concepts

The system of semantic limits that has already been developed can be transferred largely unmodified to evaluatively-open concepts. Because of the descriptive meaning component, the *limit of truth conditions*, gained from the second linguistic dimension, namely object-relatedness, applies.[167] The normal inferential limits apply to the normative meaning component. These emerge from the normative commitments—linked to the use of an evaluatively-open expression—to consequences and circumstances, as well as from the entitlements to such commitments. In this sense, the limits of the discursive authority and of the discursive responsibility also depend on specific evaluative commitments. The special quality of the commitments changes nothing with regard to the system of semantic limits. This is indifferent as to the nature of the commitments, and is thus of general validity.

---

[165] On the three forms of semantic arguments see R Alexy, *A Theory of Legal Argumentation* (n 62 above) 235 and p 52 above.

[166] See Waldron, 'Vagueness in Law and Language. Some Philosophical Issues' (n 61 above) 515.

[167] Waldron, 'Vagueness in Law and Language. Some Philosophical Issues' (n 61 above) 528.

D. Result on the Theory of the Limits of the Wording

The theory of the limits of the wording developed here focuses on the normal case of linguistic communication and the application of the law, ie the case of semantic clarity. A system of semantic limits was developed using the thesis of the three dimensions of linguistic meaning. The general semantic limits form the focus of this system. They are based on the first linguistic dimension, ie the inferential relations, and to be more precise on the first inferential relation.

The analysis has revealed in this respect that semantic limits can be overstepped in two cases. In the first case, the rule for the use of words for a legal term is wrongly formulated. In the second case, the rule for the use of words is correctly formulated, but the speaker is wrong about the subsumption under the concepts contained in the rule for the use of words. In both cases, the semantic error can relate either to the semantic characteristic catalogue M or to the legal term T. The semantic errors result in each case either in erroneous affirmation or erroneous negation of the legal term. The combination of these possibilities leads to a system totalling eight general semantic limits. Depending on whether the semantic errors result in erroneous affirmation or negation of the legal term, the general semantic limits can be summarised under the umbrella terms of the positive general semantic limit and the negative general semantic limit.

The special semantic limits emerge from the second and third inferential dimensions, as well as from the second and third linguistic dimensions. The special semantic limits cannot be independently violated. They are always violated together with a general semantic limit. In content terms, they include various aspects of the use of language in the system of semantic limits: The discursive authority, the discursive responsibility, the truth conditions of a speech act, the fundamental propositions of a language, as well as the intersubjective readiness of the speaker to understand.

The system of semantic limits was explained—where possible—using examples from legal precedents (case law). The analysis led in this respect to a certain focus on the commitment limits. These are based in each case on a W error. By contrast, far fewer or no examples at all are found in the precedents for the entitlement limits, which are based on errors in the factual, so-called subsumption errors (S errors). This may be a result of the fact that the Federal Constitutional Court does not review a violation of mere S errors. It is not a super-revision instance. The interesting result should be noted that the Federal Constitutional Court does not review a specific type of violation of semantic limits, namely the overstepping of the entitlement limit.

Particular significance is attached, finally, to the fact that the distinction recognised in legal theory between teleological reduction and analogy can be depicted using the system of semantic limits that has been developed here. Both types of further development of the law are to be attributed to the consequential commitment limit. They are based not on legal practitioners using semantic characteristics for a legal term T_1, but on the applicable norm being changed by linking its legal consequence with another legal term T_2. If this change results in an erroneous T negation—related to the correct legal term T_1—there is a teleological reduction. If, by contrast, this change results in an erroneous T affirmation, it is an analogy.

The system that was developed was then transferred to cases of semantically-unclear meaning.

III. THE RESULT OF THE THIRD CHAPTER

A. Results

The core problem, in legal theory, of the limits of the wording is the language-philosophical question of the structure of and possibility of recognising meaning. In the first part of the third chapter, the three central issues between analytical legal theory and structuring legal theory were decided in favour of the former. This means on the one hand that only a very weak legal indeterminacy thesis can be based on language-philosophical arguments. The linguistic meaning of the law is only undetermined in hard cases, whilst in easy cases it is clear. Even in hard cases it is possible to argue based on the semantics. Secondly, it was confirmed that linguistic meaning is epistemologically accessible. The form for the establishment of linguistic meaning is the speech analysis discourse. This is sub-divided into two quite distinct types, namely the establishment and the assignment of meaning. Finally, it was possible using the third linguistic dimension to confirm the thesis that the norms of the meaning are generally valid intersubjectively.

It was then shown how the results, to date, of analytical legal theory can be linked with the thesis of the three semantic dimensions to form a new theory of the limits of the wording. This theory focuses on the concept of semantic clarity. A system of semantic limits was developed using the central thesis that linguistic meaning exists within the total of the inferential relations. The classification of semantically-unclear cases could be depicted in inferential semantics. It was shown here that the semantic limits in principle also work with unclear semantic meaning, albeit that some particularities need to be considered. Using an analysis of Supreme Court case law, it was possible to obtain further important knowledge on the theoretical structure of semantic limits and their functioning in practice.

The rules for the use of words that are accessible in the speech analysis discourse make it possible to distinguish between interpretation and further development of the law. If a decision is taken in the context of the rules for the use of words that have been established, an interpretation has been effected. In the context of the established rule for the use of words, first, a decision is taken in the case of direct understanding: Here, only the establishment bears the decision, in other words exclusively the semantic argument in forms one or two.[168] Over and above this, interpretation may also exist with indirect understanding. With indirect understanding, doubts arise which make it necessary to assign a rule for the use of words. These doubts may be purely semantic in nature, or may be based on other, in particular systematic and teleological considerations. The former applies to the third form of argument of the semantic argument. It cannot be definitively ascertained here solely by empirical means whether W_1 or W_2 applies. The guidelines put forward apply to these semantically-unclear cases.

Also the theory of the limits of the wording developed here does not show where the semantic limits of a term or of a proposition are in each individual case. In this sense, no generally-valid assertions on individual concepts can be made because linguistic meaning is relative to background commitments of individual speakers and of entire linguistic communities. The need to engage in speech analysis discourse remains. The essential form of argument pursued in this discourse is the reference to rules for the use of words.

The benefit of the theory developed here is two-fold. First, it proves the existence of semantic limits. Secondly, it can be used to make a distinction for the first time between various types of semantic limit. With the terminology developed here, the speech analysis discourse about the application of rules for the use of words and the structure of the meaning of legal terms can be undertaken in a more differentiated and precise manner. Brandom describes this major advantage as follows:

> Formulating as an explicit claim the inferential commitment implicit in the content brings it out into the open as liable to challenges and demands for justification, just as with any assertion. In this way explicit expression plays an elucidating role, functioning to groom and improve our inferential commitments and so our conceptual contents.[169]

The project is the rectification of concepts: clarifying them by explicitating their contents. It is *saying* what their inferential role is: what follows from the applicability of each concept and what its applicability follows from.[170]

---

[168] On the three forms of semantic arguments see Alexy, *A Theory of Legal Argumentation* (n 62 above) 235.
[169] Brandom, *Making It Explicit* (n 64 above) 127.
[170] Brandom, *Making It Explicit* (n 64 above) 109.

> [T]he payoff from expressing explicitly (in the form of judgements) the content-constitutive commitments that were implicit in prior inferential practice is the clarification and rectification of those conceptual contents.[171]

All in all, this led to the development of a theory which is suited to the prominent legal and constitutional significance of the limits of the wording, thus countering the deconstructivist tendencies in linguistic philosophy and in legal theory.

B. The Rehabilitation of Semantic Argumentation in the Law

In the face of the vehement criticism of theoretical attempts to analyse the continuum of linguistic meaning by categories and structures, as well as with regard to the difficulties that have been recognised in cases of semantically-unclear meaning, the semantic argumentation of legal theory has increasingly been viewed with unease, if not with contempt. The extreme position is characterised by the thesis that semantic argumentation is alleged not to have any status of its own, but rather that the meaning of the law *exclusively* emerged from other forms of legal argument. Schefer should be quoted as paradigmatic for these positions: 'Therefore, linguistic argumentation remains referred to reasoning based on other types of constitutional argumentation'.[172]

This brings us to the relationship between semantic argumentation and the other forms of legal argument. Two positions are put forward to this end in legal theory, which can be referred to as the linking thesis and the separation thesis. Authors of structuring legal theory presume that the speech analysis discourse is of necessity incorporated in a teleological one and that it is intrinsically linked with it. This is opposed by the position of analytical legal theory, which with the separation thesis conserves the independence of the speech analysis discourse.

The thesis of the three dimensions of linguistic meaning confirms the separation thesis. Brandom writes:

> [T]he meanings of linguistic expressions ... should be understood ... in terms of playing a distinctive kind of role in reasoning.[173]

> Claiming, being able to justify one's claims, and using one's claims to justify other claims and actions are not just one among other sets of things one can do

---

[171] Brandom, *Making It Explicit* (n 64 above) 110.
[172] MC Schefer, *Konkretisierung von Grundrechten durch den U.S.-Supreme Court. Zur sprachlichen, historischen und demokratischen Argumentation im Verfassungsrecht* (Berlin, 1997) 154. On the usefulness of semantic arguments see also M Van Hoecke, *Norm, Kontext und Entscheidung. Die Interpretationsfreiheit des Richters* (Leuven, 1988) 108–11.
[173] RB Brandom, *Articulating Reasons. An Introduction to Inferentialism* (Cambridge MA, 2000) 1.

with language. They are not on a par with other 'games' one can play. They are what in the first place make possible talking, and therefore thinking: sapience in general.[174]

The use of language is by its structure a discourse of assertions. This makes the implicit normativity, which is immanent to linguistic assertion practice, a structural characteristic of this practice, which precedes all contents. Only the separation thesis does justice to this special function of linguistic meaning for the possibility of discourses.

The interpretation of statutes on the whole has the character of a discourse. Interpretations are assertions regarding the meaning of a term used by the law.[175] These assertions are given by legal practitioners, claiming correctness and stating reasons. Semantic normativity is independent within the class of these reasons. It is therefore possible to speak of the *externality of language for the law*. Semantic normativity is brought into a distinct speech analysis discourse in the legal argumentation, to be separated from the other forms of argument. The fact that the application of the law is embedded in a specific legal interpretation practice and is relative to its background commitments changes nothing in this respect.

The externality of language for the law means that the number and nature of the arguments in the speech analysis discourse are restricted. Only semantic reasons are permitted. In accordance with the basic idea pursued here, the discourse, which according to Brandom is facilitated by the expressive role of the logical vocabulary, is identical to the speech analysis discourse à l'Alexy. The speech analysis discourse has the function of determining meaning by making existing norms explicit. It is a discourse on the entitlement of individual speakers to commitments, on the deontic status of individual speech acts and on the inferential relations of propositional and subsentential meaning. The theory of meaning presented here makes available an established terminological system, which supplements the previous speech analysis models of legal theory.

The structures of semantics developed here can be understood as the cornerstone of a new theory of semantic interpretation. All in all, one may hence speak of a *rehabilitation of the semantic interpretation for the law*. This is also significant to the dispute about the sequence of the interpretation criteria. On the basis of the theory of meaning developed here, this rehabilitation is possible because semantics are freed of the burden of documenting a meaning which is established without a temporal dimension. This was the false dilemma of the dispute about the goal of interpretation. Here, semantics were linked instead to normative pragmatics. Linguistic practice is not to be understood within the meaning of a

---

[174] *Ibid*, 14 f.
[175] See p 50 above.

non-binding *façon de parler* characterised by boundless linguistic arbitrariness, as is presumed by deconstructivistic positions. Rather, implicit norms are available in practice, the structure of which can be analysed and reconstructed with the terminology presented here. In this manner, the structures by means of which conceptual content forms a linguistic community become accessible.

C. The Objectivity of Legal Rulings

At the same time as the question of the possibility of the limits of the wording, the question emerges as to the objectivity of legal rulings.[176] This question is fundamental to legal theory.[177] That the wording of the norm is able to determine the content of the norm, and hence its application, constitutes a major condition for the legal objectivity thesis. The function attributed to the wording of the norm, namely to be a general and generally-understandable determination of the norm content, can be complied with only under the precondition that linguistic meaning is on the whole objective.

In his *theory of legal argumentation*, Alexy developed the thesis that legal rulings can be described as objective under certain preconditions. The thesis of the three linguistic dimensions developed here confirms essential basic rules of the theory of legal argumentation. Hence, fundamental rule 1.4 of the general practical discourse is contingent on the possibility of joint linguistic usage. Alexy determines that there is contention as to how these commonalities can be ensured. He rightly stresses that there is much in favour of initially presuming the colloquial meaning, and only determining the usage when unclear meanings and misunderstandings occur. Such a determination was said to be contingent on the analysis of the expressions used.[178]

These considerations are underpinned in two ways by the thesis of the three linguistic dimensions. First, its three elements—namely normativity, object-relatedness and the intersubjectivity of linguistic meaning—confirm the thesis of the possibility of joint linguistic usage. Secondly, the inferential semantics presented here can be used as a tool for the analysis of linguistic expressions called for by Alexy. This was meant when it was determined that the theories of meaning presented here can be understood as the cornerstone for a new theory of semantic interpretation in the law.

---

[176] Stavropoulos, *Objectivity in Law* (n 19 above) 127 f.
[177] The relevance of this question is denied by CR Sunstein, *Legal Reasoning and Political Conflict* (Oxford, 1996) 3–12. Sunstein's position is, however, correctly confuted by DO Brink, 'Legal Interpretation, Objectivity and Morality' in B Leiter (ed), *Objectivity in Law and Morals* (Cambridge, 1997) 50–54.
[178] Alexy, *A Theory of Legal Argumentation* (n 62 above) 188–91.

Also, the theory of meaning developed here is in paradigmatic agreement with the common-sense rule of the practical discourse, designated by Alexy as the general reasoning rule. The general reasoning rule demands that each speaker justify his or her own assertions on request, unless he or she can state reasons justifying refusal to provide reasoning.[179] With this rule, Alexy places the speech act of the allegation in the centre of his theory of practical discourse. According to the theories of meaning put forward here, the speech act of the allegation constitutes the basis for any linguistic usage.

Finally, the structure of the semantic arguments analysed by Alexy is confirmed by the distinction based on rules for the use of words between establishment and assignment of meaning.[180] All in all, three major elements of Alexy's theory were confirmed thereby as being tenable on the basis of a normative theory of meaning. This favours the thesis that linguistic meaning, contrary to many criticisms, can comply with the basic responsibility for the objectivity of legal rulings which is imposed on it.

In Anglo-American legal theory, arguments regarding functions and characteristics of linguistic meaning play a prominent role in the discussion of questions such as *determinacy* and the *objectivity of law*, as well as the possibility of a theory of rationality in law.[181] This debate is a part of the general discussion on the objectivity of assertions in the area of ethics.[182] The thesis that legal interpretation and argumentation are allegedly objective has received prominent support from Dworkin.[183] Legal rulings are, accordingly, objective in the sense that objectively-correct answers exist to legal problems.[184]

---

[179] Alexy, *A Theory of Legal Argumentation* (n 62 above) 192.
[180] Alexy, *A Theory of Legal Argumentation* (n 62 above) 235 f.
[181] Bix, *Law, Language, and Legal Determinacy* (n 5 above); W Lucy, *Understanding and Explaining Adjudication* (Oxford 1999) 372–386; Stavropoulos, *Objectivity in Law* (n 19 above). A *modest objectivity thesis* is defended based on semantic arguments by JL Coleman and B Leiter, 'Determinacy, Objectivity, and Authority' in A Marmor (ed), *Law and Interpretation. Essays in Legal Philosophy* (Oxford, 1995) 236. The authors deem their position to be compatible with Dworkin's, see 'Determinacy, Objectivity, and Authority' at 274. Against A Marmor, 'Four Questions About the Objectivity of Law' in A Marmor (ed), *Positive Law and Objective Values* (Oxford, 2001) 139–41. *Cf* OM Fiss, 'Objectivity and Interpretation' (1982) 34 *Stanford Law Review* 762; T Nagel, *The Last Word* (, Oxford, 1997) chs 2 and 4. Against J Raz, 'Explaining Normativity. On Rationality and the Justification of Reason' in J Raz (ed), *Engaging Reason. On the Theory of Value and Action* (Oxford, 1999) 78–80.
[182] *Cf* B Leiter, *Objectivity in Law and Morals* (Cambridge, 2001); A Miller, 'Objectivity' in E Craig (ed), *Routledge Encyclopedia of Philosophy*, vol 7 (London, 1998) 57 f.
[183] R Dworkin, 'Can Rights Be Controversial?' in R Dworkin (ed), *Taking Rights Seriously* (Cambridge MA, 1980); R Dworkin, 'Is There Really No Right Answer in Hard Cases?' and 'On Interpretation and Objectivity' in R Dworkin (ed), *A Matter of Principle* (Oxford 1986); Dworkin, *Law's Empire* (n 61 above) 78–86; R Dworkin, 'Objectivity and Truth: You'd Better Believe It' (1996) 25 *Philosophy & Public Affairs* 87.
[184] See B Leiter, 'Objectivity, Morality, and Adjudication' in B Leiter (ed), *Objectivity in Law and Morals* (Cambridge, 1997) 66.

Dworkin's theory is the object of vehement criticism. Raz objected to Dworkin that his thesis of the ubiquity of the interpretation allegedly led to radical indeterminacy.[185] Fish objects with his anti-formalist and strongly pragmatically-orientated view of the interpretative community that there are allegedly no correct interpretations, but only ones accepted by the interpretative community. *Approval by the relevant interpretive community* hence becomes the sole criterion of the correctness of an interpretation.[186] The objectivity thesis is vehemently disputed over and above this by MacKinnon[187] and the *Critical Legal Studies*.[188]

Dworkin's theory depends decisively on it being possible to distinguish between interpretation and further development of the law.[189] The dispute relating to the objectivity of legal rulings hence leads directly to the problem of the limits of the wording. Ultimately, this highly fundamental debate about the dispute between legal positivism and common sense relates to the concept of the law.[190] That is not the subject-matter of this work. Against the backdrop of this debate, however, we can ask what the objectivity of linguistic meaning put forward here means for the objectivity of legal rulings.

In accordance with the results of this document, scepticism of the objectivity of legal rulings can only be reasoned if one demands from the wording of the norm a causal determination of the ruling of legal practitioners, and objectively declares all other links between the wording of the norm and the ruling not to be objective. Such a position makes excessive demands of the objectivity thesis.[191] Stavropoulos was able to prove that, in particular, the indeterminacy objection put forward by Raz against Dworkin is based on a false dilemma.

There are not only the two options, either to be able to submit an evident and undoubted interpretation of a law or to have to consider

---

[185] J Raz, 'Dworkin: A New Link in the Chain' (1986) 74 *California Law Review* 1103 at 1111 f.

[186] See R Dworkin, 'My Reply to Stanley Fish (and Walter Benn Michaels): Please Don't Talk About Objectivity Any More' in WJT Mitchell (ed), *The Politics of Interpretation* (Chicago, 1983) 287; S Fish, 'Working on the Chain Gang. Interpretation in Law and Literature' (1982) 60 *Texas Law Review* 551; S Fish, 'Wrong Again' (1983) 62 *Texas Law Review* 299; Stavropoulos, *Objectivity in Law* (n 19 above) 165; M Brint and W Weaver, *Pragmatism in Law and Society* (Boulder, CO 1991); S Fish, 'Still Wrong after All These Years' (1987) 6 *Law and Philosophy* 401.

[187] C MacKinnon, *Toward a Feminist Theory of the State* (Cambridge MA, 1989) 106 f, 116, 121 f.

[188] Kress, 'Legal Indeterminacy' (n 5 above) 283; J Singer, 'The Player and the Cards. Nihilism and Legal Theory' (1984) 94 *Yale Law Review* 1.

[189] See Stavropoulos, *Objectivity in Law* (n 19 above) 128.

[190] See JL Coleman, *The Practice of Principle. In Defence of a Pragmatist Approach to Legal Theory* (Oxford, 2001) 156; A Marmor, 'The Separation Thesis and the Limits of Interpretation' in A Marmor (ed), *Positive Law and Objective Values* (Oxford, 2001) 72.

[191] See Coleman and Leiter, 'Determinacy, Objectivity, and Authority' (n 180 above) 240 f.

everything to be interpretable in an arbitrary fashion. Stavropoulos rightly objects that this dilemma overlooks the fact that practice can be restrictive in a manner which supports the thesis of the objectivity of the interpretation. The theory of meaning put forward here, which presumes intersubjectively-valid implicit normativity of linguistic meaning, can be understood as an *objective conception of practice*, as Stavropoulos rightly asserts against Raz as a third option.[192]

The second linguistic dimension, namely *object-relatedness*, is significant to the legal interpretation. Concepts of the law relate to objects of the world. Brink rightly states:

> Insofar as legal interpretation is concerned with the meaning and extension of the language in which legal provisions are expressed, it must make and defend substantive commitments about the nature and extension of the kinds and categories that legal terms refer to, and cannot simply appeal to conventional beliefs about the extension of those terms.[193]

Also when it comes to the third linguistic dimension, namely *intersubjectivity*, the same problems arise for linguistic meaning and legal rulings. In the same way as the participants of an assertion practice, legal practitioners also place their assertions in the context of an objectivity which is presumed to be generally valid as intersubjective. Even if this presumption were not to apply to individual cases, the presumption of objectivity can work as a regulative idea in both contexts within the meaning of Kant.[194]

The key support however goes to the legal objectivity thesis in the shape of the first linguistic dimension, namely by the thesis of semantic *normativity*. In accordance with the pragmatic establishment of linguistic normativity put forward here, Fish correctly recognises that the reactions of other participants in language games are essential for the formation of meaning. He is, however, wrong to presume that meaning is exhausted in mere concurrence, and hence in the consensus of an interpretative community. By contrast, a theory was put forward here which includes the sanctions of other scorekeepers, but which places the focus on the implicit normative structures arising thereby.

Since the inferential commitments implicitly contained in the concept can be made explicit as assertions within the theory presented here, they are made amenable to objections and demands for justification. This explicit-making of the implicit structures of conceptual content in a speech

---

[192] Stavropoulos, *Objectivity in Law* (n 19 above) 159.
[193] Brink, 'Legal Interpretation, Objectivity and Morality' (n 176 above) 25. See also MS Moore, 'The Semantics of Judging' (1981) 54 *Southern California Law Review* 151; MS Moore, 'A Natural Law Theory of Interpretation' (1985) 58 *Southern California Law Review* 277.
[194] See Brink, 'Legal Interpretation, Objectivity and Morality' (n 176 above) 48 f.

analysis discourse, and in the stating of W in the internal justification, constitutes progress in the rationality and objectivity of legal rulings.

What is more, only in a normative theory of meaning is it possible to explain the difference between *substantial disagreement* and *conceptual disagreement*.[195] The first linguistic dimension ensures that there can be rational discourses on linguistic problems and objective rulings on legal problems at all. Positions that are sceptical of meaning must presume that each *substantial disagreement* is absorbed in a *conceptual disagreement*. Such an assumption is implausible. The semantic thesis of the three dimensions of linguistic meaning constitutes a tenable foundation for the legal-theory thesis of the possibility of objective legal rulings.

---

[195] See Bix, *Law, Language, and Legal Determinacy* (n 5 above) 57 f; Stavropoulos, *Objectivity in Law* (n 19 above) 125–7.

Bibliography

ADORNO, TW, 'Taubstummenanstalt' in Adorno, TW (ed), *Minima moralia. Reflexionen aus dem beschädigten Leben* (Frankfurt am Main, 1969) 179–80

ALBERT, H, *Kritik der reinen Hermeneutik. Der Antirealismus und das Problem des Verstehens* (Tübingen, 1994)

ALEXY, R, *Theorie der juristischen Argumentation. Die Theorie des rationalen Diskurses als Theorie der juristischen Begründung* (Frankfurt am Main, 1978)

—— 'Die logische Analyse juristischer Entscheidungen' (1980) NF 14 *Archiv für Rechts- und Sozialphilosophie: Beiheft* 181

—— *A Theory of Legal Argumentation. The Theory of Rational Discourse as Theory of Legal Justification* (Oxford, 1989)

—— 'Juristische Interpretation' in Alexy, R (ed), *Recht, Vernunft, Diskurs. Studien zur Rechtsphilosophie* (Frankfurt am Main, 1995) 71–92

—— *Theorie der Grundrechte*, 3rd edn (Frankfurt am Main, 1996)

—— 'Law and Correctness' in Freeman, MDA (ed), *Current Legal Problems* (Oxford, 1998) 205–21

ALSTON, WP, 'Meaning' in Edwards, P (ed), *The Encyclopedia of Philosophy* (New York, 1967) 233–41

ANWEILER, J, *Die Auslegungsmethoden des Gerichtshofs der Europäischen Gemeinschaften* (Frankfurt am Main, 1997)

AOUN, J, *A Grammar of Anaphora* (Cambridge MA, 1985)

ARDEN, TR, 'The Interpretation of UK Domestic Legislation in the Light of European Convention on Human Rights Jurisprudence' (2004) 25 *Statute Law Review* 165

ARISTOTELES, *Physik. Vorlesung über Natur. 2. Halbband: Bücher V–VIII* (Hamburg, 1988)

ARMSTRONG, DM, *Universals and Scientific Realism* (Cambridge, 1978)

AYER, AJ, *Language, Truth and Logic* (London, 1936)

—— *Philosophy in the Twentieth Century* (London, 1984)

BAKER, GP and HACKER, PMS, *Wittgenstein: Rules, Grammar and Necessity. An Analytical Commentary on the Philosophical Investigations, vol 2* (Oxford, 1985)

BEALER, G, 'Analyticity' in Craig, E (ed), *Routledge encyclopedia of philosophy. vol 1* (London, 1998) 234–9

BENGOETXEA, J, *The Legal Reasoning of the European Court of Justice. Towards a European Jurisprudence* (Oxford, 1993)

BENNION, F, 'What Interpretation Is "Possible" Under Section 3(1) of the Human Rights Act 1998?' (2000) *Public Law* 77

BILGRAMI, A, 'Meaning, Holism and Use' in LePore, E (ed), *Truth and Interpretation. Perspectives on the Philosophy of Donald Davidson* (Oxford, 1986) 101–22

—— A, 'Norms and Meaning' in Stoecker, R (ed), *Reflecting Davidson. Donald Davidson Responding to an International Forum of Philosophers* (Berlin, 1993) 121–44

BIX, B, *Law, Language, and Legal Determinacy* (Oxford, 1995)
BLACKBURN, S, 'The Individual Strikes Back' (1984) 58 *Synthese* 281
—— 'Theory, Observation and Drama' (1992) 7 *Mind and Language* 187
—— 'Supervenience' in Craig, E (ed), *Routledge Encyclopedia of Philosophy. vol 9* (London, 1998) 235–8
BÖCKENFÖRDE, E-W, 'Die Methoden der Verfassungsinterpretation – Bestandsaufnahme und Kritik' (1976) 29 *Neue Juristische Wochenschrift* 2089
BOGHOSSIAN, PA, 'The Rule-Following Considerations' (1989) 98 *Mind* 507
—— 'Analyticity' in Hale, B and Wright, C (eds), *A Companion to the Philosophy of Language* (Oxford, 1997) 331–68
BONJOUR, L, *The Structure of Empirical Knowledge* (Cambridge MA, 1985)
—— *In Defense of Pure Reason. A Rationalist Account of A Priori Justification* (Cambridge, 1998)
BORCHARDT, K-D, 'Richterrecht durch den Gerichtshof der Europäischen Gemeinschaften' in Randelzhofer, A, Scholz, R and Wilke, D (eds), *Gedächtnisschrift für Eberhard Grabitz* (München, 1995) 29–43
BRADDON-MITCHELL, D and JACKSON, F, *The Philosophy of Mind and Cognition* (Oxford, 1996)
BRANDOM, RB, *Making It Explicit. Reasoning, Representing, and Discursive Commitment* (Cambridge MA, 1994)
—— 'Von der Begriffsanalyse zu einer systematischen Metaphysik. Interview von Susanna Schellenberg' (1999) 6 *Deutsche Zeitschrift für Philosophie* 1005
—— *Articulating Reasons. An Introduction to Inferentialism* (Cambridge, MA 2000)
—— 'Facts, Norms, and Normative Facts. A Reply to Habermas' (2000) 8 *European Journal of Philosophy* 356
BRINK, DO, 'Legal Interpretation, Objectivity and Morality' in Leiter, B (ed), *Objectivity in Law and Morals* (Cambridge, 1997) 12–65
BRINT, M and WEAVER, W, *Pragmatism in Law and Society* (Boulder, CO 1991)
BUNDESÄRZTEKAMMER, 'Richtlinien zur Feststellung des Hirntodes. Dritte Fortschreibung 1997 mit Ergänzungen gemäß Transplantationsgesetz' (1998) 95 *Deutsches Ärzteblatt* B 1509
BURNS, LC, *Vagueness. An Investigation Into Natural Languages and the Sorites Paradox* (Dordrecht, 1991)
BUSSE, D, 'Zum Regel-Charakter von Normtextbedeutungen und Rechtsnormen' (1988) *Rechtstheorie* 305
—— 'Was ist die Bedeutung eines Gesetzestextes? Sprachwissenschaftliche Argumente im Methodenstreit der juristischen Auslegungslehre—linguistisch gesehen' in Müller, F (ed), *Untersuchungen zur Rechtslinguistik. Interdisziplinäre Studien zur praktischen Semantik und Strukturierender Rechtslehre in Grundfragen der juristischen Methodik* (Berlin, 1989) 93–148
—— *Juristische Semantik. Grundfragen der juristischen Interpretationstheorie in sprachwissenschaftlicher Sicht* (Berlin, 1993)
BYDLINSKI, F, *Juristische Methodenlehre und Rechtsbegriff*, 2nd edn (Wien, 1991)
CANARIS, C-W, *Die Feststellung von Lücken im Gesetz. Eine methodologische Studie über Voraussetzungen und Grenzen der richterlichen Rechtsfortbildung praeter legem* (Berlin, 1964)

CARNAP, R, 'Meaning Postulates' in Carnap, R (ed), *Meaning and Necessity. A Study in Semantics and Modal Logic* (Chicago, 1956) 222–9
—— *Der logische Aufbau der Welt* (Hamburg, 1998)
CARRUTHERS, P, 'Baker and Hacker's Wittgenstein' (1984) 58 *Synthese* 451
CASSAM, Q, 'Rationalism, Empiricism, and the A Priori' in Boghossian, PA and Peacocke, C (eds), *New Essays on the A priori* (Oxford, 2000) 43–64
CAVELL, S, 'Must We Mean What We Say?' in Cavell, S (ed), *Must We Mean What We Say? A Book of Essays* (Cambridge, 1976) 1–43
CHASTAIN, C, 'Reference and Context' in Gunderson, K (ed), *Language, Mind, and Knowledge* (Minneapolis, 1975) 194–269
CHRISTENSEN, R, 'Gesetzesbindung oder Bindung an das Gesetzbuch der praktischen Vernunft. Eine skeptische Widerrede zur Vorstellung des sprechenden Textes' in Mellinghoff, R and Trute, H-H (eds), *Die Leistungsfähigkeit des Rechts: Methodik, Gentechnologie, internationales Verwaltungsrecht* (Heidelberg, 1988) 95–126
—— 'Der Richter als Mund des sprechenden Textes. Zur Kritik des gesetzespositivistischen Textmodells' in Müller, F (ed), *Untersuchungen zur Rechtslinguistik. Interdisziplinäre Studien zu praktischer Semantik und Strukturierender Rechtslehre in Grundfragen der juristischen Methodik* (Berlin, 1989) 47–91
—— *Was heißt Gesetzesbindung? Eine rechtslinguistische Untersuchung* (Berlin, 1989)
CLAYTON, R, 'The Limits of "What's Possible": Statutory Construction under the Human Rights Act' (2002) *European Human Rights Law Review* 559
COATES, P, 'Kripke's Sceptical Paradox: Normativeness and Meaning ' (1986) 95 *Mind* 77
COHEN, JL, 'A Problem About Ambiguity in Truth-Theoretical Semantics' (1985) 45 *Analysis* 129
COLEMAN, JL, *The Practice of Principle. In Defence of a Pragmatist Approach to Legal Theory* (Oxford, 2001)
COLEMAN, JL and LEITER, B, 'Determinacy, Objectivity, and Authority' in Marmor, A (ed), *Law and Interpretation. Essays in Legal Philosophy* (Oxford, 1995) 203–78
CONSTANTINESCO, L-J, *Das Recht der Europäischen Gemeinschaften* (Baden-Baden, 1977)
CRIMMINS, M, 'Language, Philosophy of' in Craig, E (ed), *Routledge Encyclopedia of Philosophy. vol 5* (London, 1998) 408–11
DÄNZER-VANOTTI, W, 'Unzulässige Rechtsfortbildung des Europäischen Gerichtshofs' (1992) *Recht der Internationalen Wirtschaft* 733
DAVIDSON, D, 'Communication and Convention ' in Davidson, D (ed), *Inquiries into Truth and Interpretation* (Oxford, 1984) 265–80
—— 'The Inscrutability of Reference' in Davidson, D (ed), *Inquiries into Truth and Interpretation* (Oxford, 1984) 227–41
—— 'The Method of Truth in Metaphysics' in Davidson, D (ed), *Inquiries into Truth and Interpretation* (Oxford, 1984) 199–214
—— 'Radical Interpretation' in Davidson, D (ed), *Inquiries into Truth and Interpretation* (Oxford, 1984) 125–39
—— 'Thought and Talk' in Davidson, D (ed), *Inquiries into Truth and Interpretation* (Oxford, 1984) 155–70

—— 'The Myth of the Subjective' in Krausz, M (ed), *Relativism. Interpretation and Confrontation* (Notre Dame IN, 1989) 159–72

—— 'The Social Aspect of Language' in McGuiness, B and Olivieri, G (eds), *The Philosophy of Michael Dummett* (Dordrecht, 1994) 1–16

—— 'The Problem of Objectivity' (1995) *Tijdschrift voor filosofie* 203

—— 'Is Truth a Goal of Inquiry? Discussion with Rorty' in Zeglen, UM (ed), *Donald Davidson: Truth, Meaning and Knowledge* (London 1999) 17–19

—— 'Mental Events' in Davidson, D (ed), *Essays on Actions and Events* (Oxford, 2001) 207–27

DE MOOR, A, 'Nothing Else to Think? On Meaning, Truth and Objectivity in Law' (1998) 18 *Oxford Journal of Legal Studies* 345

DEMMERLING, C, 'Bedeutung' in Sandkühler, HJ (ed), *Enzyklopädie Philosophie. Band 1* (Hamburg, 1999) 111–14

DEPENHEUER, O, *Der Wortlaut als Grenze. Thesen zu einem Topos der Verfassungsinterpretation* (Heidelberg, 1988)

DEVLIN, P, 'Judges and Lawmakers' (1976) 39 *Modern Law Review* 1

DREHER, E, 'Aus zwei Mitgliedern bestehende Bande. Anmerkung' (1970) *Neue Juristische Wochenschrift* 1802

DREIER, R, 'Zur Problematik und Situation der Verfassungsinterpretation' in Dreier, R (ed), *Recht, Moral, Ideologie. Studien zur Rechtstheorie* (Frankfurt am Main, 1981) 106–45

DREIER, R and SCHWEGMANN, F (eds), *Probleme der Verfassungsinterpretation. Dokumentation einer Kontroverse* (Baden-Baden, 1976)

DRIEDGER, EA, *Driedger on the Construction of Statutes*, 3rd edn (Toronto, 1994)

DUHEM, P, *Ziel und Struktur der physikalischen Theorien (1908)* (Hamburg, 1978)

DUMMETT, M, *Frege. Philosophy of Language* (London, 1973)

—— 'Is Logic Empirical?' in Dummett, M (ed), *Truth and Other Enigmas* (Cambridge MA, 1978) 269–89

—— 'The Justification of Deduction' in Dummett, M (ed), *Truth and Other Enigmas* (Cambridge MA, 1978) 290–318

—— 'Realism' in Dummett, M (ed), *Truth and Other Enigmas* (Cambridge MA, 1978) 145–65

—— 'The Social Character of Meaning' in Dummett, M (ed), *Truth and Other Enigmas* (Cambridge MA, 1978) 420–30

—— (ed), *Truth and Other Enigmas* (Cambridge MA, 1978)

—— 'Wang's Paradox' in Dummett, M (ed), *Truth and Other Enigmas* (Cambridge MA, 1978) 248–68

—— 'A nice derangement of epitaphs. Some comments on Davidson and Hacking' in LePore, E (ed), *Truth and Interpretation. Perspectives on the Philosophy of Donald Davidson* (Oxford, 1986) 459–76

—— 'Introduction' in Dummett, M (ed), *The Logical Basis of Metaphysics* (London, 1991) 1–19

—— 'Meaning, Knowledge, and Understanding' in Dummett, M (ed), *The Logical Basis of Metaphysics* (London, 1991) 83–106

—— 'Realism and Anti-Realism' in Dummett, M (ed), *The Seas of Language* (Oxford, 1993) 462–78

—— 'What Do I Know When I Know a Language?' in Dummett, M (ed), *The Seas of Language* (Oxford, 1993) 94–105

—— 'What Does the Appeal to Use Do for the Theory of Meaning?' in Dummett, M (ed), *The Seas of Language* (Oxford, 1993) 106–16
—— 'What Is a Theory of Meaning? (II)' in Dummett, M (ed), *The Seas of Language* (Oxford, 1993) 34–93
—— 'Reply to Davidson' in McGuiness, B and Olivieri, G (eds), *The Philosophy of Michael Dummett* (Dordrecht, 1994) 257–67
DWORKIN, R, 'Can Rights Be Controversial?' in Dworkin, R (ed), *Taking Rights Seriously* (Cambridge MA, 1980) 279–90
—— 'Law as Interpretation' (1982) 60 *Texas Law Review* 527
—— 'My Reply to Stanley Fish (and Walter Benn Michaels): Please Don't Talk About Objectivity Any More' in Mitchell, WJT (ed), *The Politics of Interpretation* (Chicago, 1983) 287–313
—— 'Is There Really No Right Answer in Hard Cases?' in Dworkin, R (ed), *A Matter of Principle* (Oxford, 1986) 119–45
—— *Law's Empire* (London, 1986)
—— *A Matter of Principle* (Oxford, 1986)
—— 'On Interpretation and Objectivity' in Dworkin, R (ed), *A Matter of Principle* (Oxford, 1986) 167–77
—— 'Pragmatism, Right Answers and True Banality' in Brint, M and Weaver, W (eds), *Pragmatism in Law and Society* (Boulder CO, 1991) 359–88
—— 'Law, Philosophy and Interpretation' (1994) 80 *Archiv für Rechts- und Sozialphilosophie* 463
—— 'Objectivity and Truth: You'd Better Believe It' (1996) 25 *Philosophy & Public Affairs* 87
EBBS, G, *Rule-Following and Realism* (Cambridge, MA 1997)
EDGINGTON, D, 'Vagueness by Degrees' in Keefe, R and Smith, P (eds), *Vagueness. A Reader* (Cambridge MA, 1997) 294–316
EGGINTON, W and SANDBOTHE, M, *The Pragmatic Turn in Philosophy. Contemporary Engagements between Analytic and Continental Thought* (Albany, 2004)
ENDICOTT, TAO, *Vagueness in Law* (Oxford, 2000)
—— 'Law Is Necessarily Vague' (2001) 7 *Legal Theory* 379
ENGISCH, K, *Die Idee der Konkretisierung in Recht und Rechtswissenschaft unserer Zeit*, 2nd edn, (Heidelberg, 1968)
ENGISCH, K and WÜRTENBERGER, T, *Einführung in das juristische Denken*, 9th edn (Stuttgart, 1997)
ENGLÄNDER, A, 'Anmerkung zum Beschluß des BGH v. 14.3.2000—4 StR 284/99' (2000) *Juristenzeitung* 630
ESFELD, M, 'Semantischer Holismus' in Bertram, GW and Liptow, J (eds), *Holismus in der Philosophie. Ein zentrales Motiv der Gegenwartsphilosophie* (Weilerswist, 2002) 41–58
ESKRIDGE, WN, *Dynamic Statutory Interpretation* (Cambridge MA, 1994)
ESSER, J, *Grundsatz und Norm in der richterlichen Fortbildung des Privatrechts* (Tübingen, 1956)
—— *Vorverständnis und Methodenwahl in der Rechtsfindung. Rationalitätsgrundlagen richterlicher Entscheidungspraxis*, 2nd edn (Frankfurt am Main, 1972)
EVANS, G, 'Identity and Predication' (1975) 72 *Journal of Philosophy* 343

—— 'Can There Be Vague Objects?' in Keefe, R and Smith, P (eds), *Vagueness. A Reader* (Cambridge MA, 1997) 317

EVERLING, U, 'Richterliche Rechtsfortbildung in der Europäischen Gemeinschaft' (2000) *Juristenzeitung* 217

FERRAND, F, *Cassation française et révision allemande. Essai sur le contrôle exercé en matière civile par la Cour de cassation française et par la Cour fédérale de Justice de la République Fédérale d'Allemagne* (Paris, 1993)

FIKENTSCHER, W, *Methoden des Rechts in vergleichender Darstellung. Band I: Frühe und religiöse Rechte, Romanischer Rechtskreis* (Tübingen, 1975)

—— *Methoden des Rechts in vergleichender Darstellung. Band III: Mitteleuropäischer Rechtskreis* (Tübingen, 1976)

—— *Methoden des Rechts in vergleichender Darstellung. Band IV: Dogmatischer Teil. Anhang* (Tübingen, 1977)

FISH, S, 'Working on the Chain Gang. Interpretation in Law and Literature' (1982) 60 *Texas Law Review* 551

—— 'Wrong Again' (1983) 62 *Texas Law Review* 299

—— 'Still Wrong after All These Years' (1987) 6 *Law and Philosophy* 401

—— 'Almost Pragmatism. The Jurisprudence of Richard Posner, Richard Rorty and Ronald Dworkin' in Brint, M and Weaver, W (eds), *Pragmatism in Law and Society* (Boulder CO, 1991) 47–81

FISS, OM, 'Objectivity and Interpretation' (1982) 34 *Stanford Law Review* 739

FODOR, J and LEPORE, E, *Holism. A Shopper's Guide* (Oxford, 1993)

FREGE, G, 'Booles rechnende Logik und die Begriffsschrift' in Frege, G (ed), *Nachgelassene Schriften* (Hamburg, 1969) 9–59

—— *Begriffsschrift und andere Aufsätze. Nachdruck Halle 1879*, 3rd edn (Darmstadt, 1977)

—— *Die Grundlagen der Arithmetik. Eine logisch mathematische Untersuchung über den Begriff der Zahl* (Stuttgart, 1987)

—— 'Über Sinn und Bedeutung' in Frege, G (ed), *Funktion, Begriff, Bedeutung. Fünf logische Studien* (Göttingen, 1994) 40–65

FRICKER, E, 'Analyticity, Linguistic Practice and Philosophical Method' in Puhl, K (ed), *Meaning Scepticism* (Berlin, 1991) 218–50

FROMMEL, M, *Die Rezeption der Hermeneutik bei Karl Larenz und Josef Esser* (Ebelsbach, 1981)

FULLER, LL, 'Positivism and Fidelity to Law. A Reply to Professor Hart' (1958) 71 *Harvard Law Review* 630

GADAMER, HG, *Wahrheit und Methode. Grundzüge einer philosophischen Hermeneutik*, 6th edn (Tübingen, 1990)

GADAMER, HG, *Truth and Method*, 2nd edn (London, 2004)

GAMPEL, EH, 'The Normativity of Meaning' (1997) 86 *Philosophical Studies* 221

GAST, W, 'Rezension' (1991) 77 *Archiv für Rechts- und Sozialphilosophie* 556

GEIS, M-E, 'Die Eilversammlung als Bewährungsprobe verfassungskonformer Auslegung. Verfassungsrechtsprechung im Dilemma zwischen Auslegung und Rechtsschöpfung' (1992) *Neue Zeitschrift für Verwaltungsrecht* 1025

GENY, F, *Méthode d'interprétation et sources en droit privé positif. Essai critique*, 2nd edn (Paris, 1919)

GIBBARD, A, 'Meaning and Normativity' (1994) 5 *Philosophical Issues* 95

GIBBARD, A, 'Thought, Norms, and Discursive Practice. Commentary on Robert Brandom, Making It Explicit' (1996) 56 *Philosophy and Phenomenological Research* 699

GIBSON, RF, *The Philosophy of W.V. Quine* (Gainesville FL, 1982)

GILLON, BS, 'Truth Theoretical Semantics and Ambiguity' (1990) 50 *Analysis* 178

GIMMLER, A, 'Jürgen Habermas: Wahrheit und Rechtfertigung' (2000) 53 *Philosophischer Literaturanzeiger* 333

GLOCK, H-J, 'Wittgenstein vs Quine on Logical Necessity' in Teghrarian, S (ed), *Wittgenstein and Contemporary Philosophy* (Bristol, 1994) 185–222

—— 'Wie kam die Bedeutung zur Regel?' (2000) *Deutsche Zeitschrift für Philosophie* 429

GLÜER, K, 'Sense and Prescriptivity' (1999) 14 *Acta Analytica* 111

—— *Sprache und Regeln. Zur Normativität von Bedeutung* (Berlin, 1999)

GLÜER, K and PAGIN, P, 'Rules of Meaning and Practical Reasoning' (1999) 118 *Synthese* 207

GOLDFARB, W, 'Kripke on Wittgenstein on Rules' (1985) 82 *Journal of Philosophy* 471

GRAHAM, PJ, 'Brandom on Singular Terms' (1999) 93 *Philosophical Studies* 247

GRAY, J, 'On Liberty, Liberalism and Essential Contestability' (1978) 8 *British Journal of Political Science* 385

GREENAWALT, K, 'Constitutional and Statutory interpretation' in Coleman, JL, Shapiro, S and Himma, KE (eds), *The Oxford Handbook of Jurisprudence and Philosophy of Law* (Oxford, 2002) 268–310

GRICE, HP, *Studies in the Way of Words* (Cambridge MA, 1989)

GRICE, HP and STRAWSON, PF, 'In Defense of a Dogma' (1956) 65 *The Philosophical Review* 141

GRICE, P, 'Meaning' (1957) 66 *The Philosophical Review* 377

GRIMES, TR, 'The Myth of Supervenience' (1988) 69 *Pacific Philosophical Quarterly* 152

GRIMM, J and GRIMM, W, *Deutsches Wörterbuch. Band 7* (Leipzig, 1889)

GRUNDMANN, S and RIESENHUBER, K, 'Die Auslegung des Europäischen Privat- und Schuldvertragsrechts' (2001) *Juristische Schulung* 529

GUMMOW, WMC, *Change and Continuity. Statute, Equity, and Federalism* (Oxford, 1999)

GUMPERZ, JJ and LEVINSON, SC, *Rethinking Linguistic Relativity* (Cambridge, 1996)

GUNSON, D, *Michael Dummett and the Theory of Meaning* (Aldershot, 1998)

HABERMAS, J, 'Richtigkeit vs. Wahrheit. Zum Sinn der Sollgeltung moralischer Urteile und Normen' (1998) 46 *Deutsche Zeitschrift für Philosophie* 179

—— 'Einleitung. Realismus nach der sprachpragmatischen Wende' in Habermas, J (ed), *Wahrheit und Rechtfertigung. Philosophische Aufsätze* (Frankfurt am Main, 1999) 7–64

—— 'Von Kant zu Hegel. Zu R. Brandoms Sprachpragmatik' in Habermas, J (ed), *Wahrheit und Rechtfertigung. Philosophische Aufsätze* (Frankfurt am Main, 1999) 138–85

HADFIELD, GK, 'Weighing the Value of Vagueness. An Economic Perspective on Precision in the Law' (1994) *California Law Review* 541

HALE, B, 'Realism and its Oppositions' in Hale, B and Wright, C (eds), *A Companion to the Philosophy of Language* (Oxford, 1997) 271–309

—— 'Rule-Following, Objectivity and Meaning' in Hale, B and Wright, C (eds), *A Companion to the Philosophy of Language* (Oxford, 1997) 369–96

HARE, RM, *The Language of Morals* (Oxford, 1972)

HARENBURG, J, *Die Rechtsdogmatik zwischen Wissenschaft und Praxis. Ein Beitrag zur Theorie der Rechtsdogmatik* (Stuttgart, 1986)

HARMAN, G, 'Quine on Meaning and Existence I' (1968) 21 *Review of Metaphysics* 124

HART, HLA, 'Jhering's Heaven of Concepts and Modern Analytical Jurisprudence' in Hart, HLA (ed), *Essays in Juriprudence and Philosophy* (Oxford, 1983) 265–77

—— *The Concept of Law*, 2nd edn (Oxford, 1994)

HART, HM and SACKS, AM, *The Legal Process. Basic Problems in the Making and Application of Law* (Westbury NY, 1994)

HASSEMER, W, *Tatbestand und Typus. Untersuchungen zur strafrechtlichen Hermeneutik* (Köln, 1967)

—— 'Juristische Hermeneutik' (1986) 72 *Archiv für Rechts- und Sozialphilosophie* 195

HASSOLD, G, 'Strukturen der Gesetzesauslegung' in Canaris, C-W and Diederichsen, U (eds), *Festschrift für Karl Larenz zum 80. Geburtstag* (München, 1983) 211–40

HEGENBARTH, R, *Juristische Hermeneutik und linguistische Pragmatik. Dargestellt am Beispiel der Lehre vom Wortlaut als Grenze der Auslegung* (Königstein/Ts, 1982)

HERBERGER, M, 'Eine Frage des Prinzips. Auslegung, Rechtsfortbildung und die Wirksamkeit nicht umgesetzter Richtlinien' in Forstmoser, P (ed), *Rechtsanwendung in Theorie und Praxis. Symposion zum 70. Geburtstag von Arthur Meyer-Hayoz* (Basel, 1993) 35–43

HERBERGER, M and KOCH, H-J, 'Zur Einführung: Juristische Methodenlehre und Sprachphilosophie' (1978) *Juristische Schulung* 810

HERBERT, M, 'Buchbesprechung' (1993) 24 *Rechtstheorie* 533

—— *Rechtstheorie als Sprachkritik. Zum Einfluß Wittgensteins auf die Rechtstheorie* (Baden-Baden, 1995)

—— 'Buchbesprechung "Bruha/Seeler, Die Europäische Union und ihre Sprachen' (2001) *Der Staat* 635

HEßBRÜGGEN-WALTER, S, 'Objektivität' in Sandkühler, HJ (ed), *Enzyklopädie Philosophie. Band 2* (Hamburg, 1999) 975–8

HEUN, W, 'Original intent und Wille des historischen Verfassungsgebers. Zur Problematik einer Maxime im amerikanischen und deutschen Verfassungsrecht' (1991) 116 *Archiv des öffentlichen Rechts* 185

HINTIKKA, J and KULAS, J (eds), *Anaphora and Definite Descriptions. Two Applications of Game-Theoretical Semantics* (Dordrecht, 1985)

HOFFMANN, LH, 'The Intolerable Wrestling with Words and Meanings' (1997) 114 *South African Law Journal* 656

HOPKINS, ER, 'The Literal Canon and the Golden Rule' (1937) 15 *Canadian Bar Review* 689

HORWICH, P, 'Wittgenstein and Kripke on the Nature of Meaning' (1990) 5 *Mind and Language* 105
—— 'What It Is Like to Be a Deflationary Theory of Meaning?' (1994) 5 *Philosophical Issues* 133
—— 'Meaning, Use and Truth' (1995) 104 *Mind* 355
—— 'Stipulation, Meaning, and Apriority' in Boghossian, PA and Peacocke, C (eds), *New Essays on the A priori* (Oxford, 2000) 150–69
HRUSCHKA, J, *Das Verstehen von Rechtstexten. Zur hermeneutischen Transpositivität des positiven Rechts* (München, 1972)
HURLEY, SL, *Natural Reasons. Personality and Polity* (New York, 1989)
HYDE, D, 'Vagueness, Ontology and Supervenience' (1998) 81 *The Monist* 297
IGLESIAS VILA, M, *Facing Judicial Discretion. Legal Knowledge and Right Answers Revisited* (Dordrecht, 2001)
JANSSEN, TMV, 'Meaning Postulate' in Lamarque, PV and Asher, RE (eds), *Concise Encyclopedia of Philosophy of Language* (Oxford, 1997) 150–51
JEAN D'HEUR, B, 'Bedeutungstheorie in Sprachwissenschaft und Rechtswissenschaft. Der Kruzifix-Beschluß aus rechtslinguistischer Sicht.' in Brugger, W and Huster, S (eds), *Der Streit um das Kreuz in der Schule. Zur religiösweltanschaulichen Neutralität des Staates* (Baden-Baden, 1998) 155–64
JELLINEK, G, *Allgemeine Staatslehre*, 3rd edn (Berlin, 1921)
JELLINEK, W, *Gesetz, Gesetzesanwendung und Zweckmäßigkeitserwägung* (Tübingen, 1913)
KAMBARTEL, F, 'Analytisch' in Mittelstraß, J (ed), *Enzyklopädie Philosophie und Wissenschaftstheorie. Band 1* (Stuttgart, 1995) 105–6
KANT, I, *Prolegomena zu einer jeden künftigen Metaphysik, die als Wissenschaft wird auftreten können*, 6th edn (Hamburg, 1976)
—— *Kritik der praktischen Vernunft*, 10th edn (Hamburg, 1990)
KANT, I, *Kritik der reinen Vernunft*, 3rd edn (Hamburg, 1990)
KAUFMANN, A, *Analogie und 'Natur der Sache'. Zugleich ein Beitrag zur Lehre vom Typus*, 2nd edn (Heidelberg, 1982)
—— *Rechtsphilosophie*, 2nd edn (München, 1997)
KAUFMANN, M, *Rechtsphilosophie* (Freiburg, 1996)
KAVANAGH, A, 'The Elusive Divide between Interpretation and Legislation under the Human Rights Act 1998' (2004) 24 *Oxford Journal of Legal Studies* 259
KEEFE, R and SMITH, P, *Vagueness. A Reader* (Cambridge MA, 1997)
KENNEDY, D, 'Strategizing Strategic Behaviour in Legal Interpretation' (1996) *Utah Law Review* 785
KERSTING, W, 'Baseball ist unser Leben' *Frankfurter Allgemeine Zeitung* (7 August 2000) 49
KIM, J, 'Concepts of Supervenience' (1984) 45 *Philosophy and Phenomenological Research* 153
KLATT, M, *Theorie der Wortlautgrenze. Semantische Normativität in der juristischen Argumentation* (Baden-Baden, 2004)
—— 'Taking Rights Less Seriously. A Structural Analysis of Judicial Discretion' (2007) 20 *Ratio Juris* 506
KNELL, S, 'Die normativistische Wende der analytischen Philosophie. Zu Robert Brandoms Theorie begrifflichen Gehalts und diskursiver Praxis' (2000) *Allgemeine Zeitschrift für Philosophie* 225

KOCH, H-J, 'Das Postulat der Gesetzesbindung im Lichte sprachphilosophischer Überlegungen' (1975) 61 *Archiv für Rechts- und Sozialphilosophie* 37
—— 'Ansätze einer juristischen Argumentationstheorie?' (1977) 36 *Archiv für Rechts- und Sozialphilosophie* 355
—— (ed), *Die juristische Methode im Staatsrecht. Über Grenzen von Verfassungs- und Gesetzesbindung* (Frankfurt am Main, 1997)
KOCH, H-J and RÜSSMANN, H, *Juristische Begründungslehre. Eine Einführung in die Grundprobleme der Rechtswissenschaft* (München, 1982)
KOHLER, J, 'Über die Interpretation von Gesetzen' (1886) 13 *Zeitschrift für das Privat- und Öffentliche Recht der Gegenwart* 1
KOMMERS, DP, *The Constitutional Jurisprudence of the Federal Republic of Germany* 2nd edn (Durham NC, 1997)
KONZAK, O, 'Analogie im Verwaltungsrecht. Entscheidungsbesprechung' (1997) *Neue Zeitschrift für Verwaltungsrecht* 872
KRESS, K, 'Legal Indeterminacy' (1989) 77 *California Law Review* 243
KRIELE, M, *Theorie der Rechtsgewinnung. Entwickelt am Problem der Verfassungsinterpretation* (Berlin, 1967)
KRIPKE, SA, *Naming and Necessity* (Oxford, 1980)
—— *Wittgenstein on Rules and Private Language. An Elementary Exposition* (Oxford, 1982)
—— 'A Priori Knowledge, Necessity, and Contingency' in Moser, PK (ed), *A priori Knowledge* (Oxford, 1987) 145–60
KÜNNE, W, *Abstrakte Gegenstände. Semantik und Ontologie* (Frankfurt am Main, 1983)
KUTSCHER, H, 'Thesen zu den Methoden der Auslegung des Gemeinschaftsrechts aus der Sicht eines Richters' in Gerichtshof der Europäischen Gemeinschaften (ed), *Begegnung von Justiz und Hochschule am 27. und 28. September 1976. Berichte* (Luxemburg, 1976) I/3–56
LANCE, MN and HAWTHORNE, J, *The Grammar of Meaning. Normativy and Semantic Discourse* (Cambridge, 1997)
LANGENBUCHER, K, 'Vorüberlegungen zu einer europarechtlichen Methodenlehre' in Ackermann, T and Arnold, A (eds), *Jahrbuch junger Zivilrechtswissenschaftler 1999. Tradition und Fortschritt im Recht* (Stuttgart, 2000) 65–83
LARENZ, K, 'Entwicklungstendenzen der heutigen Zivilrechtsdogmatik ' (1962) *Juristenzeitung* 105
—— 'Über das Verhältnis von Interpretation und richterlicher Rechtsfortbildung' in Lejman, F (ed), *Festskrift tillägnad Professor, Juris Doktor Karl Olivecrona* (Stockholm, 1964) 384–404
—— 'Die Bindung des Richters an das Gesetz als hermeneutisches Problem' in Forsthoff, E, Weber, W and Wieacker, F (eds), *Festschrift für Ernst Rudolf Huber* (Göttingen, 1973) 291–309
—— *Methodenlehre der Rechtswissenschaft* 6th edn (Berlin, 1991)
LARENZ, K and CANARIS, C-W, *Methodenlehre der Rechtswissenschaft*, 3rd edn (Berlin, 1995)
LAUDENKLOS, F, 'Rechtsarbeit ist Textarbeit. Einige Bemerkungen zur Arbeitsweise der Strukturierenden Rechtslehre' (1997) *Kritische Justiz* 142

LEGE, J, *Pragmatismus und Jurisprudenz. Über die Philosophie des Charles Sanders Peirce und über das Verhältnis von Logik, Wertung und Kreativität im Recht* (Tübingen, 1999)
LEGRAND, P, 'European Legal Systems Are Not Converging' (1996) 45 *International & Comparative Law Quarterly* 52
LEIBNIZ, GW, 'Non inelegans specimen demonstrandi in abstractis' in Leibniz, GW (ed), *Opera Philosophica Omnia* (Aalen, 1959) 94–7
LEITER, B, 'Objectivity, Morality, and Adjudication' in Leiter, B (ed), *Objectivity in Law and Morals* (Cambridge, 1997) 66–98
—— *Objectivity in Law and Morals* (Cambridge, 2001)
LESTER, A, 'English Judges as Law Makers' (1993) *Public Law* 269
LEWIS, D, *Convention. A Philosophical Study* (Cambridge MA, 1969)
—— 'Languages and Language' in Gunderson, K (ed), *Language, Mind, and Knowledge* (Minneapolis, 1975) 3–35
—— 'Scorekeeping in a Language Game' in Lewis, D (ed), *Philosophical Papers. vol I* (Oxford, 1983) 233–49
LIMBACH, J, 'The Concept of the Supremacy of the Constitution' (2001) 64 *Modern Law Review* 1
LOCKE, J, *Essay Concerning Human Understanding (1690)* (London, 1997)
LOEWER, B, 'A Guide to Naturalizing Semantics' in Hale, B and Wright, C (eds), *A Companion to the Philosophy of Language* (Oxford, 1997) 108–26
LOWE, EJ, 'A Priori' in Lamarque, PV and Asher, RE (eds), *Concise Encyclopedia of Philosophy of Language* (Oxford, 1997) 11–12
LÜCKE, HK, 'Statutory Interpretation: New Comparative Dimensions' (2005) 54 *International & Comparative Law Quarterly* 1023
LUCY, JA, *Language Diversity and Thought. A Reformulation of the Linguistic Relativity Hypothesis* (Cambridge, 1992)
LUCY, W, *Understanding and Explaining Adjudication* (Oxford, 1999)
—— 'Adjudication' in Coleman, JL, Shapiro, S and Himma, KE (eds), *The Oxford Handbook of Jurisprudence and Philosophy of Law* (Oxford, 2002) 206–67
LYONS, J, 'Bedeutungstheorien' in Stechow, Av and Wunderlich, D (eds), *Semantik. Ein internationales Handbuch der zeitgenössischen Forschung* (Berlin, 1991) 1–24
MACCORMICK, N, *Legal Reasoning and Legal Theory* (Oxford, 1978)
—— 'Arguing About Interpretation' in MacCormick, N (ed), *Rhetoric and the Rule of Law. A Theory of Legal Reasoning* (Oxford, 2005) 121–42
MACDONALD, C and MACDONALD, G, *Philosophy of Psychology* (Oxford, 1995)
MACINTYRE, AC, 'The Essential Contestability of Some Social Concepts' (1973) 84 *Ethics* 1
—— *Dependent Rational Animals. Why Human Beings Need the Virtues* (London, 1999)
MACKINNON, C, *Toward a Feminist Theory of the State* (Cambridge MA, 1989)
MARMOR, A, 'Four Questions About the Objectivity of Law' in Marmor, A (ed), *Positive Law and Objective Values* (Oxford, 2001) 131–59
—— 'The Separation Thesis and the Limits of Interpretation' in Marmor, A (ed), *Positive Law and Objective Values* (Oxford, 2001) 71–88
—— *Interpretation and Legal Theory*, 2nd edn (Oxford, 2005)
MATAR, A, *From Dummett's Philosophical Perspective* (Berlin, 1997)

MATES, B, 'Zur Verifikation von Feststellungen über die normale Sprache' in Grewendorf, G and Meggle, G (eds), *Linguistik und Philosophie* (Frankfurt am Main, 1974) 154–67

MAUS, I, 'Zur Problematik des Rationalitäts- und Rechtsstaatspostulats in der gegenwärtigen juristischen Methodik am Beispiel Friedrich Müllers' in Deiseroth, D (ed), *Ordnungsmacht. Über das Verhältnis von Legalität, Konsens und Herrschaft* (Frankfurt am Main, 1981) 153–79

MAYER, V, 'Regeln, Normen, Gebräuche. Reflexionen über Ludwig Wittgensteins "Über Gewißheit' (2000) *Deutsche Zeitschrift für Philosophie* 409

MCDOWELL, J, 'Wittgenstein on Following a Rule' (1984) 58 *Synthese* 325

—— 'Intentionality and Interiority in Wittgenstein' in Puhl, K (ed), *Meaning Scepticism* (Berlin, 1991) 148–69

—— *Mind and World* (Cambridge MA, 1994)

—— 'Brandom on Representation and Inference' (1997) 57 *Philosophy and Phenomenological Research* 157

MCGINN, C, *Wittgenstein on Meaning* (Oxford, 1984)

—— *Mental Content* (Oxford, 1989)

—— *The Problem of Consciousness* (Oxford, 1991)

MCKINLAY, A, 'Agreement and Normativity' in Puhl, K (ed), *Meaning Scepticism* (Berlin, 1991) 189–200

MEGGLE, G and SIEGWART, G, 'Der Streit um die Bedeutungstheorien' in Dascal, M, Gerhardus, D, Lorenz, K and Meggle, G (eds), *Sprachphilosophie. 2. Halbband* (Berlin, 1995) 964–89

MILLAR, A, 'Analyticity' in Lamarque, PV and Asher, RE (eds), *Concise Encyclopedia of Philosophy of Language* (Oxford, 1997) 93–5

—— 'Objectivity' in Craig, E (ed), *Routledge Encyclopedia of Philosophy. vol 7* (London, 1998) 73–6

MILLETT, T, 'Rules of Interpretation of E.E.C. Legislation' (1989) *Statute Law Review* 163

MILLIKAN, RG, *Language, Thought, and Other Biological Categories. New Foundations for Realism* (Cambridge MA, 1984)

—— 'Truth Rules, Hoverflies, and the Kripke-Wittgenstein Paradox' (1990) 99 *Philosophical Review* 323

MOORE, MS, 'The Semantics of Judging' (1981) 54 *Southern California Law Review* 151

—— 'A Natural Law Theory of Interpretation' (1985) 58 *Southern California Law Review* 277

MOSER, PK, 'A Priori' in Craig, E (ed), *Routledge Encyclopedia of Philosophy. vol 1* (London, 1998) 3–6

MÜLLER, F, *Strukturierende Rechtslehre*, 2nd edn (Berlin, 1994)

—— *Juristische Methodik*, 7th edn (Berlin, 1997)

—— 'Observations on the Role of Precedent in Modern Continental European Law from the Perspective of "Structuring Legal Theory"' (2000) 11 *Stellenbosch Law Review* 426

NAGEL, T, *The Last Word* (Oxford, 1997)

NEUMANN, U, 'Der mögliche Wortsinn als Auslegungsgrenze in der Rechtsprechung der Strafsenate des BGH' in Savigny, Ev (ed), *Juristische Dogmatik und Wissenschaftstheorie* (München, 1976) 42–59

—— *Rechtsontologie und juristische Argumentation. Zu den ontologischen Implikationen juristischen Argumentierens* (Heidelberg, 1979)
—— *Juristische Argumentationslehre* (Darmstadt, 1986)
NEUNER, J, *Die Rechtsfindung contra legem* (München, 1992)
NEURATH, O, 'Soziologie im Physikalismus' (1931) 2 *Erkenntnis* 393
OGDEN, CK and RICHARDS, IA, *The Meaning of Meaning. A Study of the Influence of Language upon Thought and of the Science of Symbolism*, 5th edn (London, 1938)
OKASHA, S, 'Holism About Meaning and About Evidence. In Defence of W.V. Quine' (2000) 52 *Erkenntnis* 39
ORENSTEIN, A, 'Quine, Willard Van Orman' in Craig, E (ed), *Routledge Encyclopedia of Philosophy. vol 8* (London, 1998) 3–14
PAGIN, P, 'Rules' in Lamarque, PV and Asher, RE (eds), *Concise Encyclopedia of Philosophy of Language* (Oxford, 1997) 170–77
PAPINEAU, D, *Philosophical Naturalism* (Oxford, 1993)
PAWLOWSKI, H-M, *Methodenlehre für Juristen. Theorie der Norm und des Gesetzes*, 3rd edn (Heidelberg, 1999)
PEACOCKE, C, 'Holism' in Hale, B and Wright, C (eds), *A Companion to the Philosophy of Language* (Oxford, 1997) 227–47
PENNER, JE, 'Nicos Stavropoulos: Objectivity in Law' (1997) 60 *Modern Law Review* 747
PERREAU, ÉEH, *Technique de la jurisprudence en droit privé* (Paris, 1923)
PLATON, *Theätet* 6th edn (Hamburg, 1955)
POSTEMA, GJ, 'Objectivity Fit for Law' in Leiter, B (ed), *Objectivity in Law and Morals* (Cambridge, 1997) 99–143
POWERS, M, 'Truth, Interpretation, and Judicial Method in Recent Anglo-American Jurisprudence' (1992) 46 *Zeitschrift für philosophische Forschung* 101
PUFENDORF, S, *De jure naturae et gentium (Liber primus—Liber quartus)* (Berlin, 1998)
PUHL, K, 'Introduction' in Puhl, K (ed), *Meaning Scepticism* (Berlin, 1991) 1–11
PUTNAM, H, 'The Analytic and the Synthetic (1962)' in Putnam, H (ed), *Mind, Language, and Reality. Philosophical Papers. vol 2* (Cambridge, 1975) 33–69
—— (ed), *Mind, Language and Reality. Philosophical Papers vol 2* (Cambridge, 1975)
—— *Reason, Truth and History* (Cambridge, 1981)
—— 'Analyticity and Apriority. Beyond Wittgenstein and Quine' in Moser, PK (ed), *A Priori Knowledge* (Oxford, 1987) 85–111
PUTNAM, H and CONANT, J, *Realism with a Human Face* (Cambridge MA, 1990)
QUINE, WVO, *Word and Object* (Cambridge MA, 1960)
—— 'Ontological Relativity' (1968) 65 *The Journal of Philosophy* 185
—— 'Carnap and Logical Truth' in Quine, WVO (ed), *The Ways of Paradox and Other Essays* (Cambridge MA, 1976) 107–32
—— 'Truth by Convention' in Quine, WVO (ed), *The Ways of Paradox and Other Essays* (Cambridge MA, 1976) 77–106
—— 'Use and Its Place in Meaning' in Quine, WVO (ed), *Theories and Things* (Cambridge MA, 1981) 43–54
—— *Pursuit of Truth* (Cambridge MA, 1990)
—— *Grundzüge der Logik*, 10th edn (Frankfurt am Main, 1998)

—— 'Logic and the Reification of Universals' in Quine, WVO (ed), *From a Logical Point of View. Nine Logico-Philosophical Essays* (Cambridge MA, 1999) 102–29
—— 'On What There Is' in Quine, WVO (ed), *From a Logical Point of View. Nine Logico-Philosophical Essays* (Cambridge MA, 1999) 1–19
—— 'Two Dogmas of Empiricism' in Quine, WVO (ed), *From a Logical Point of View. Nine Logico-Philosophical Essays* (Cambridge MA, 1999) 20–46
RABAULT, H, *L'interprétation des normes. L'objectivité de la méthode herméneutique* (Paris, 1997)
RADBRUCH, G, 'Klassenbegriffe und Ordnungsbegriffe im Rechtsdenken' in Radbruch, G (ed), *Rechtsphilosophie III* (Heidelberg, 1990) 60–70
RAILTON, P, 'A Priori Rules. Wittgenstein on the Normativity of Logic' in Boghossian, PA and Peacocke, C (eds), *New Essays on the A priori* (Oxford, 2000) 170–96
RATSCHOW, E, *Rechtswissenschaft und formale Logik* (Baden-Baden, 1998)
RAWLS, J, 'Two Concepts of Rules' (1955) 64 *The Philosophical Review* 3
RAZ, J, *The Authority of Law. Essays on Law and Morality* (Oxford, 1979)
—— 'Legal Reasons, Sources, and Gaps' in Raz, J (ed), *The Authority of Law. Essays on Law and Morality* (Oxford, 1979) 53–77
—— 'Dworkin: A New Link in the Chain' (1986) 74 *California Law Review* 1103
—— 'Interpretation without Retrieval' in Marmor, A (ed), *Law and Interpretation. Essays in Legal Philosophy* (Oxford, 1995) 155–75
—— 'Explaining Normativity. On Rationality and the Justification of Reason' in Raz, J (ed), *Engaging Reason. On the Theory of Value and Action* (Oxford, 1999) 67–89
—— 'Notes on value and objectivity' in Raz, J (ed), *Engaging Reason. On the Theory of Value and Action* (Oxford, 1999) 118–60
—— *Practical Reason and Norms* (Oxford, 1999)
—— 'Sorensen: Vagueness Has No Function in Law' (2001) 7 *Legal Theory* 417
RICKETTS, TG, 'Rationality, Translation, and Epistemology Naturalized' (1982) 79 *Journal of Philosophy* 117
RÖHL, KF, *Allgemeine Rechtslehre. Ein Lehrbuch* (Köln, 1995)
ROHS, P, 'Die transzendentale Deduktion als Lösung von Invarianzproblemen' in Philosophie, Ff (ed), *Kants transzendentale Deduktion und die Möglichkeit von Transzendentalphilosophie* (Frankfurt am Main, 1988) 135–92
RORTY, RM, 'Robert Brandom über soziale Praktiken und Repräsentationen' in Rorty, RM (ed), *Wahrheit und Fortschritt* (Frankfurt am Main, 2000) 179–200
ROSEN, G, 'Who Makes the Rules Around Here?' (1997) 57 *Philosophy and Phenomenological Research* 163
ROTTLEUTHNER, H, 'Hermeneutik und Jurisprudenz' in Koch, H-J (ed), *Juristische Methodenlehre und analytische Philosophie* (Kronberg/Ts, 1976) 7–30
RUSSELL, B, 'The Philosophy of Logical Atomism' in Russell, B (ed), *Logic and Knowledge. Essays 1901–1950* (London, 1956) 177–281
RÜßMANN, H, 'Sprache und Recht. Sprachtheoretische Überlegungen zum Gesetztesbindungspostulat' in Zimmermann, J (ed), *Sprache und Welterfahrung* (München, 1978) 208–33

RÜTHERS, B, 'Richterrecht—rechtswidrig oder notwendig?' (1988) 112 *Archiv des öffentlichen Rechts* 268
—— *Rechtstheorie. Begriff, Geltung und Anwendung des Rechts* (München, 1999)
RYLE, G, *The Concept of Mind* (London, 2000)
SAINSBURY, M, 'Is There Higher-Order Vagueness?' (1991) 41 *Philosophical Quarterly* 167
—— 'Why the World Cannot Be Vague' (1994) 33 *The Southern Journal of Philosophy* 63
—— *Paradoxes*, 2nd edn (Cambridge 1995)
—— 'Concepts without Boundaries' in Keefe, R and Smith, P (eds), *Vagueness. A Reader* (1997) 251–64
SAINSBURY, M and WILLIAMSON, T, 'Sorites' in Hale, B and Wright, C (eds), *A Companion to the Philosophy of Language* (Oxford, 1997) 458–84
SCALIA, A, *A Matter of Interpretation. Federal Courts and the Law. An Essay* (Princeton NJ, 1997)
SCHAUER, F, *Playing by the Rules. A Philosophical Examination of Rule-Based Decision-Making in Law and in Life* (Oxford, 1991)
—— 'Judicial Supremacy and the Modest Constitution' (2004) 92 *California Law Review* 1045
SCHEFER, MC, *Konkretisierung von Grundrechten durch den U.S.-Supreme Court. Zur sprachlichen, historischen und demokratischen Argumentation im Verfassungsrecht* (Berlin, 1997)
SCHELLENBERG, S, 'Buchbesprechung Brandom, Making It Explicit' (1999) *Philosophischer Literaturanzeiger* 187
SCHIFFAUER, P, *Wortbedeutung und Rechtserkenntnis. Entwickelt an Hand einer Studie zum Verhältnis von verfassungskonformer Auslegung und Analogie* (Berlin, 1979)
SCHLINK, B, 'Juristische Methodik zwischen Verfassungstheorie und Wissenschaftstheorie' (1975) 6 *Rechtstheorie* 94
—— 'Bemerkungen zum Stand der Methodendiskussion in der Verfassungsrechtswissenschaft' (1980) 19 *Der Staat* 73
SCHMITZ, R, 'Begriff der Bande. Anmerkung' (2000) *Neue Zeitschrift für Strafrecht* 477
SCHÜNEMANN, B, 'Die Gesetzesinterpretation im Schnittfeld von Sprachphilosophie, Staatsverfassung und juristischer Methodenlehre' in Kohlmann, G (ed), *Festschrift für Ulrich Klug. Band 1* (Köln, 1983) 169–86
SCHWEMMER, O, 'Intersubjektivität' in Mittelstraß, J (ed), *Enzyklopädie Philosophie und Wissenschaftstheorie. Band 2* (Mannheim, 1984) 282–4
SEARLE, JR, *Speech Acts. An Essay in the Philosophy of Language* (Cambridge, 1969)
—— 'Basic Metaphysics. Reality and Truth' in Searle, JR (ed), *Mind, Language and Society. Doing Philosophy in the Real World* (London, 1999) 1–37
—— *Mind, Language and Society. Philosophy in the Real World* (London, 2000)
SEEBODE, M, 'Wortlautgrenze und Strafbedürfnis. Die Bedeutung des Wortlauts der Strafgesetze am Beispiel eigennütziger Strafvereitelung' (1998) *Juristenzeitung* 781
SEEL, M, 'Das Ende einer Affäre' *Die Zeit* (10 February 2000) 64
SELLARS, W, 'Inference and Meaning' (1953) 62 *Mind* 313

SHAPIRO, S, 'The Status of Logic' in Boghossian, PA and Peacocke, C (eds), *New Essays on the A Priori* (Oxford, 2000) 333–66

SHIEH, S, 'Some Senses of Holism. An Anti-Realist's Guide to Quine' in Heck, R (ed), *Language, Thought and Logic. Essays in Honour of Michael Dummett* (Oxford, 1997) 71–103

SIEGMUND-SCHULTZE, N, 'Und er bewegt sich doch. Reflexe bei Gehirntoten irritieren Transplantationsteams. Verfassungsrecht soll Vorschriften verschärfen' *Süddeutsche Zeitung* (20 February 2001) V2/11

SINGER, J, 'The Player and the Cards. Nihilism and Legal Theory' (1984) 94 *Yale Law Review* 1

SKINNER, BF, *Verbal Behavior* (London, 1957)

SKORUPSKI, J, 'Meaning, Use, Verification' in Hale, B and Wright, C (eds), *A Companion to the Philosophy of Language* (Oxford, 1997) 29–59

SMITH, BC, 'Meaning and Rule-Following' in Craig, E (ed), *Routledge Encyclopedia of Philosophy. vol 6* (London, 1998) 214–19

SOLAN, L, *The Language of Judges* (Chicago, 1993)

SORENSEN, R, 'Ambiguity, Discretion, and the Sorites' (1998) 81 *The Monist* 215

—— 'Vagueness Has No Function in Law' (2001) 7 *Legal Theory* 387

STARCK, C, '§ 164: Die Verfassungsauslegung' in Isensee, J and Kirchhof, P (eds), *Handbuch des Staatsrechts der Bundesrepublik Deutschland. Band VII* (1992) 189–228

STAVROPOULOS, N, *Objectivity in Law* (Oxford, 1996)

STEGMÜLLER, W, 'Rudolf Carnap: Induktive Wahrscheinlichkeit' in Speck, J (ed), *Grundprobleme der großen Philosophen. Philosophie der Gegenwart I* (Göttingen, 1985) 47–99

STERELNY, K, 'Reference. Philosophical Issues ' in Lamarque, PV and Asher, RE (eds), *Concise Encyclopedia of Philosophy of Language* (Oxford, 1997) 234–43

STEYN, J, 'Does Legal Formalism Hold Sway in England?' (1996) 49 *Current Legal Problems* 43

STOLJAR, N, 'Survey Article: Interpretation, Indeterminacy and Authority. Some Recent Controversies in the Philosophy of Law' (2003) 11 *Journal of Political Philosophy* 470

STONE, M, 'Focusing the Law: What Legal Interpretation Is Not' in Marmor, A (ed), *Law and Interpretation. Essays in Legal Philosophy* (Oxford, 1995) 31–96

STRAWSON, PF, 'Propositions, Concepts and Logical Truths' in Strawson, PF (ed), *Logico-Linguistic Papers* (London, 1971) 116–29

SUNSTEIN, CR, 'Interpreting Statutes in the Regulatory State' (1989) 103 *Harvard Law Review* 405

—— *Legal Reasoning and Political Conflict* (Oxford, 1996)

TEUBNER, G, 'Generalklauseln als sozionormative Modelle' in Hassemer, W, Hoffmann-Riem, W and Weiß, M (eds), *Generalklauseln als Gegenstand der Sozialwissenschaften* (Baden-Baden, 1978) 13–35

THIEL, C, 'Objektiv/Objektivität' in Mittelstraß, J (ed), *Enzyklopädie Philosophie und Wissenschaftstheorie. Band 2* (Mannheim, 1984) 1052–4

UKROW, J, *Richterliche Rechtsfortbildung durch den EuGH. Dargestellt am Beispiel der Erweiterung des Rechtsschutzes des Marktbürgers im Bereich des vorläufigen Rechtsschutzes und der Staatshaftung* (Baden-Baden, 1995)

VOCKE, M, *Verfassungsinterpretation und Normbegründung. Grundlegung zu einer prozeduralen Theorie der Verfassungsgerichtsbarkeit* (Frankfurt am Main, 1995)

VOGENAUER, S, *Die Auslegung von Gesetzen in England und auf dem Kontinent. Eine vergleichende Untersuchung der Rechtsprechung und ihrer historischen Grundlagen* (Tübingen, 2001)

VON BOGDANDY, A, 'Beobachtungen zur Wissenschaft vom Europarecht. Strukturen, Debatten und Entwicklungsperspektiven der Grundlagenforschung zum Recht der Europäischen Union' (2001) *Der Staat* 3

VON HOECKE, M, *Norm, Kontext und Entscheidung. Die Interpretationsfreiheit des Richters* (Publisher, Leuven, 1988)

VON SAVIGNY, E, *Grundkurs im wissenschaftlichen Definieren. Übungen zum Selbststudium* (Publisher, München, 1970)

VON SAVIGNY, FK, *System des heutigen römischen Rechts. Band 1* (Berlin, 1840)

VON WRIGHT, GH, *Norm and Action. A Logical Enquiry* (New York, 1963)

—— *Erklären und Verstehen*, 3rd edn (Frankfurt am Main, 1991)

VOSSENKUHL, W, 'Artikel "normativ/deskriptiv" in Ritter, J, Bien, G and Eisler, R (eds), *Historisches Wörterbuch der Philosophie, Band 6* (1984) 931–2

WALDRON, J, 'Vagueness in Law and Language. Some Philosophical Issues' (1994) *California Law Review* 509

WANK, R, *Die juristische Begriffsbildung* (München, 1985)

WEBER, M, 'Die "Objektivität sozialwissenschaftlicher und sozialpolitischer Erkenntnis' (1904) 19 *Archiv für Sozialwissenschaft und Sozialpolitik* 22

WEIR, R, 'Holism' in Lamarque, PV and Asher, RE (eds), *Concise Encyclopedia of Philosophy of Language* (Oxford, 1997) 117–19

WELLMER, A, 'Der Streit um die Wahrheit. Pragmatismus ohne regulative Ideen' in Sandbothe, M (ed), *Die Renaissance des Pragmatismus. Aktuelle Verflechtungen zwischen analytischer und kontinentaler Philosophie* (Weilerswist, 2000) 253–69

WELSCH, W, 'Richard Rorty: Philosophie jenseits von Argumentation und Wahrheit?' in Sandbothe, M (ed), *Die Renaissance des Pragmatismus. Aktuelle Verflechtungen zwischen analytischer und kontinentaler Philosophie* (Weilerswist, 2000) 167–92

WIKFORSS, AM, 'Semantic Normativity' (2001) 102 *Philosophical Studies* 203

WILLIAMS, SG, 'Meaning and Truth' in Craig, E (ed), *Routledge Encyclopedia of Philosophy. vol 6* (London 1998) 219–26

WILLIAMSON, T, 'Vagueness' in Lamarque, PV and Asher, RE (eds), *Concise Encyclopedia of Philosophy of Language* (Oxford, 1997) 204–5

WITTGENSTEIN, L, *Philosophical Investigations*, 2nd edn (Oxford, 1963)

—— *On Certainty* (Oxford, 1974)

—— *Philosophical Grammar* (Oxford, 1974)

—— *Philosophical Remarks* (Oxford, 1975)

—— *Tractatus logico-philosophicus. Werkausgabe Band 1* (Frankfurt am Main, 1997)

WOLFF, HJ, 'Typen im Recht und in der Rechtswissenschaft' (1952) 5 *Studium Generale* 195
WOLTERS, G, 'Analytizitätspostulat' in Mittelstraß, J (ed), *Enzyklopädie Philosophie und Wissenschaftstheorie. Band 1* (Stuttgart, 1995) 106–7
WRIGHT, C, *Wittgenstein on the Foundations of Mathematics* (Cambridge MA, 1980)
—— 'Rule-following, Objectivity and the Theory of Meaning' in Holtzman, SH and Leich, CM (eds), *Wittgenstein: To follow a Rule* (London, 1981) 99–117
—— 'Kripke's Account of the Argument Against Private Language' (1984) 81 *Journal of Philosophy* 759
—— 'Rule-following, Meaning and Constructivism' in Travis, C (ed), *Meaning and Interpretation* (Oxford, 1986) 271–97
—— 'Further Reflections on the Sorites Paradox' (1987) 15 *Philosophical Topics* 227
—— 'The Epistemic Conception of Vagueness' (1994) 33 *Southern Journal of Philosophy* 133
ZANDER, M, *The Law-Making Process*, 6th edn (Cambridge, 2004)
ZIMMERMANN, R, 'Statuta Sunt Stricte Interpretanda? Statutes and the Common Law: A Continental Perspective' (1997) 56 *Cambridge Law Journal* 315
ZIPPELIUS, R, *Juristische Methodenlehre. Eine Einführung*, 7th edn (München, 1999)

Index

ambiguity, 9, 47, 66, 230, 262, 270 ff
analogy, 10 f, 18, 42, 237–241
analyticity, 167–179
  OLOL analyticity, 179 f, 261
anaphor, 139 ff, 191 ff, 201, 235
antirealism, 93, 203
aprioricity, 168 f
argument,
  of analogicity, 42 ff, 66
  of circularity, 70, 75 ff, 220
  of clear cases, 67, 83, 212, 216–219
  of context dependency, 70
  of empirical discernibility of meaning, 67
  of excessive commitment, 71
  of features semantics, 71, 73, 224, 252
  of innovation, 70, 221
  of lacking normative necessity, 69
  of legal culture, 68, 82 f, 229
  of necessary failure, 69, 83, 212 f, 218
  of objectivism, 71
  of ontological hermeneutics, 65, 72
  of openness, 70
  of possible corrections, 68, 83
  of practical ineffectiveness, 69, 82
  of procedural correctness, 66, 68, 78, 83 ff, 229
  of reversal, 70
  of the impossibility of the empirical determination of meaning, 71
  of the indefiniteness of the legal text, 68, 76
argumentation, semantic, 218, 231, 276
attitudes, normative, 119 ff, 134, 138, 149, 160, 193 ff
authority, discursive, 130, 159, 177, 215, 247, 255, 272 f

circle, hermeneutic, 36 f, 41–44, 56, 65 f, 70, 75 f
clarity,
  constitutive, 213 f, 254
  epistemic, 213
  legal, 219
  semantic, 212 ff, 231 ff, 256, 262, 273 f
commitment, 22, 127 ff, 166 ff, 197 ff, 220 ff, 275 ff

entitlement, 127 ff, 150, 214 ff, 233 ff, 274 ff
  default and challenge structure of, 22, 149 f, 180, 217, 247, 262
error,
  communal, 200 f
  semantic, 220 ff, 233 ff, 254 f, 273

features semantics, 71, 73, 224, 252
further development of the law, 5 f, 38 f, 62, 84 f, 240 f, 266, 274 f, 280

hermeneutics, ontological, 33 ff, 64 f, 78
holism,
  epistemological, 151 f
  global, 152, 167
  moderate, 154, 165 ff, 180, 197
  ontological, 151
  semantic, 151 ff, 166, 180
Human Rights Act 1998, 3, 13

inconsistency, 47, 66, 263 f
indeterminism, legal, 2, 20
individualism, 107, 223
inference, material, 123 ff, 140
intentionality, 101, 118, 183
internality, condition of, 99 f, 114, 180, 221
interpretation, discursive character of, 50 f

interpretation, radical, 108 f, 165
investigation-independence, 182, 202

justification,
  external, 20, 51 ff, 222, 227
  internal, 51 ff, 231 ff, 248 f, 269, 282

law-applying, 9 ff
law-making, 1, 3, 9 ff
limit,
  conditional commitment, 233 ff, 243 f, 251, 254
  conditional entitlement, 236 ff, 242, 244, 247, 254
  consequential commitment, 238 ff, 254, 274
  consequential entitlement, 242 ff, 254 f
  in the first linguistic dimension, 233 ff
  in the second linguistic dimension, 250 ff
  in the third linguistic dimension, 252 ff
  inferential, 243 ff, 272
  of discursive authority, 247, 255
  of discursive responsibility, 247, 255
  of fundamental propositions, 255
  of intersubjective readiness to understand, 253 ff, 270
  of truth conditions, 251, 255, 272
  system of semantic limits, 254 ff, 270 ff

meaning,
  assigning of, 45, 53, 57, 66
  establishing of, 45, 53, 66, 86
  objectivity of, 30, 194
  propositional, 122 ff, 133 ff, 166 f, 243
  subsentential, 135 ff, 249, 277
  three dimension of, 207, 216 ff, 259, 273, 276, 282
meaning skepticism, 87 f, 142 ff, 156 ff, 207
mind-independence, 182

modality, 168 f

naturalism, 29, 92, 147 ff, 157
normativity,
  and internal relation, 103 f
  and rationality, 104 f
  and regularity, 106
  and truth, 101, 187, 225
  implicit, 117 ff, 277, 281
  semantic, 96 ff, 180, 277, 281
norm-concretization, 28, 55, 63, 73 ff

objectivity,
  as intersubjectivity, 192 ff
  as reference, 183 ff
  concept of, 181 ff, 204
  relative, 193 ff, 252
openness, evaluative, 66, 230, 256, 263 ff

pragmatics, normative, 3, 25, 116 ff, 180, 231 ff, 245, 261, 277
pre-judgement, 35 ff, 65, 76
principle of charity, 166

Quine-Duhem-Thesis, 156

realism, 25, 93 ff
reduction, teleological, 5, 241 f, 273 f
reductionism, 95, 98, 147 f, 153
regress, 118, 143 ff, 217
regularism, 118 f
relativity, triadic, 175 ff

score-keeping, deontic, 131 ff, 218 ff, 245 ff, 261 ff
semantics, inferential, 122 ff, 180, 185, 218, 232, 256 ff, 274
speech acts, secondary, 247
status, deontic, 127 ff, 199, 214 ff, 233, 243 ff, 264 ff, 277
Structuring Theory of Law, 23, 30, 54 ff, 72 ff, 224 f, 274, 276
substitution, 135 ff, 186 ff, 249, 262

supervenience, 98, 106, 148, 224, 257

translation, radical, 171 ff
typology, 40 ff, 65

vagueness, 1 f, 19 ff, 48 ff, 256 ff, 270
  higher-order, 21, 258 ff

word usage rule, 44, 51 ff, 64 ff, 77, 85, 248